THE
PEOPLE'S
THEOLOGIAN

THE PEOPLE'S THEOLOGIAN

Writings in Honour of **Donald Macleod**

Edited by **Iain D. Campbell**
& Malcolm Maclean

ⰃENTOR

Published and printed in 2011
in the
Mentor Imprint
by
Christian Focus Publications Ltd.,
Geanies House, Fearn,
Tain, Ross-shire, IV20 1TW, Scotland.

www.christianfocus.com

Cover design by www.moose77.com

Printed and bound by
Bell & Bain, Glasgow

Mixed Sources
Product group from well-managed
forests and other controlled sources
www.fsc.org Cert no. TT-COC-002769
© 1996 Forest Stewardship Council

Contents

Theology and the Church

Appreciations

Introduction

Alex J. MacDonald

I think I first came across Donald Macleod in April 1973 when he spoke at the Free Church Youth Conference in St Ninian's, Crieff. That was an eventful week for me. I was a divinity student in my final year at the Free Church College, and on the Wednesday I had been summoned to appear before the august Training of the Ministry Committee for the offence of wearing an army jacket to the Dingwall Prayer Meeting (I know, it's difficult to believe now). It was one of many run-ins I had with some of the more conservative brethren in the Church. Little did I think then that the speaker at the Conference that weekend would in later years defend me publicly from some of these attacks, particularly in *The Monthly Record*. But that is typical of the man. At that time he was perhaps more conservative in some ways than now, but he obviously felt that the attacks were unfair and said so. If there is one thing that has remained constant with him over the years, it is his sympathy for the underdog, the mistreated or the oppressed.

We instinctively feel that some people are complex and others are more straightforward. In Biblical terms it is undoubtedly the case that every human being is complex. We are all made in the image of God. Those who appear simple souls on the surface have hidden depths, perhaps undetected by others. However, as a useful rule of thumb, people are either of the what-you-see-is-what-you-get variety or the what-you-get-is-not-necessarily-what-you-see variety.

Donald Macleod is most emphatically in the latter category. He is not predictable. Over the years people have been constantly taken aback, surprised, shocked and even outraged by the positions he has taken up and the views he has expressed – from his rejection of the Received Text (on which the AV is based) in the early days to his more recent disagreement with the Free Church's position on worship. Some would charge him with inconsistency for changing his views on various issues. I am sure he would retort that only perfect people don't need to change their views and, this side of glory, none is perfect.

Donald's guiding star has been and remains 'What says the Scripture?' And if something does not agree with the word of God, so much the worse for it! There is no tradition or practice that cannot be re-examined in the light of Scripture. He has constantly reminded us of the great Reformation principle – our authority is 'Scripture Alone'.

Another emphasis is the rediscovery of Scottish Theology. While the church at large drank deeply at the well of continental theology, and while Donald is widely read in that area, he has helped a new generation to rediscover William Cunningham, Thomas Chalmers, Hugh Martin, Andrew Melville and John Knox. That being said, he neglects no source that may shed light on the meaning of Scripture, from whatever background, whether it be Barth, Bonhoeffer or Moltmann.

This highlights what has been a growing development in his thinking – the ecumenical. It would be difficult to think of a theologian who has such a wide appeal and recognition as Donald Macleod. He regularly speaks in various church contexts from the solidly Reformed to the broadly evangelical to the decidedly liberal. He has been honoured both by an honorary doctorate from Westminster Seminary and a visiting professorship from the University of Glasgow.

However, what I am sure is more important to him than these honours is that, like his Master, the common people hear him gladly. Donald Macleod makes little concession in his lecturing or preaching to ignorance of Biblical or theological truth, and he makes no apology for Biblical and theological language. Nevertheless, because he makes doctrine come alive, people are drawn in, people of all different backgrounds.

Donald breaks all the rules in preaching (as in other ways). He has no eye contact with his audience, he gazes into the far distance.

His voice is low and hesitant as he begins, but by the time he reaches his peroration it approaches the decibel level of an electric guitar! His preaching ceases to follow the natural cadences of human speech, and rises to some esoteric Celtic torrent of its own. And yet... and yet, if you yield to the Spirit speaking through this man, you feel his eyes are seeing far-off things which he is helping you to glimpse, you are drawn into a new world of exciting vistas of undreamed-of theological truth, you are raised by high oratory to a new level of understanding of your God and Saviour.

I never benefited from studying under Professor Macleod (too old, you see), but I have benefited from his ministry on numerous occasions through his sermons and lectures and of course through his books. What always strikes me is his focus on Christ. Evangelical preachers all hold that they preach Christ and him crucified. Often that is more in theory than in practice. As they preach through Scripture, they find it difficult to make the big connections to Christ. Not so with Donald Macleod. Christ is always at the centre.

Donald of course has been through great personal struggles. He was at the centre of the controversy that threatened to put an end to the Free Church of Scotland in the 1990s. These events are well documented and I will not recap them here. However, it ought to be remembered that during those years, Donald Macleod was under attacks and pressures that would have destroyed many of us. It is a testimony to the grace of God that he survived and during those years wrote some of his greatest theological works.

It was, of course, his journalistic skills combined with his theological insight that brought him to national attention when he edited *The Monthly Record* and wrote for the *West Highland Free Press* and numerous other newspapers. While not everyone agreed with what he wrote, everyone avidly read (and continues to read) what he had to say, and he communicated in a strong, forthright and lucid style. His editorials and articles in *The Monthly Record* kept many of us going from month to month (particularly those of us in the ministry). Our spiritual commitment was revived, our vision renewed, and we felt indeed we could do all things through Christ who strengthens us.

Undoubtedly one of his greatest contributions to the Free Church of Scotland was securing the validation of the Free Church College course. Few know the huge amount of work that he put into that enterprise. But it is a legacy from which the church, and not just the

Free Church, in Scotland and beyond will benefit from in years and perhaps generations to come.

How would we sum up Donald Macleod? To attempt that I return to the words I penned as an endorsement (as if any were needed) for one of his books. 'Donald Macleod is the people's theologian – or at least would be in a sane world. He combines a profound grasp of the language of Scripture and the history of Christian doctrine with a penetrating understanding of the dilemmas of life at the beginning of the third millennium. Through it all shines his adoration of Jesus Christ and his deep sympathy with people. He never loses sight for a moment that he is addressing people – people who are hurting, or confused or ill-informed or tempted. This is theology straight from the heart of a great preacher of the gospel.'

Alex J. MacDonald,
Buccleuch and Greyfriars Free Church of Scotland,
Edinburgh

Contributors

Martin Cameron is Librarian in the Highland Theological College in Dingwall, Scotland.

Iain D. Campbell is minister of Point Free Church of Scotland on the Island of Lewis in the Scottish Hebrides. He is also Adjunct Professor of Church History at Westminster Theological Seminary, Philadelphia. For several years he was editor of the monthly magazine of the Free Church of Scotland. He has written several books, both at the academic and popular levels.

Mary Ferguson is Librarian at Western Isles Library in Stornoway, Scotland. She lives near Stornoway and has co-ordinated the delivery of the part-time course of the Free Church College in Lewis.

Richard B. Gaffin, Jr. is Professor of Biblical and Systematic Theology, Emeritus, at Westminster Theological Seminary, Philadelphia, where he has taught since 1965. He has written several books, including *Perspectives on Pentecost, Calvin and the Sabbath, By Faith, Not By Sight and Paul and the Order of Salvation.*

David George is minister of Mount Pleasant Evangelical Baptist Church in Maesycwmmer in Wales.

Contributors

Michael W. Honeycutt is Associate Professor of Historical and Practical Theology at Covenant Theological Seminary, St Louis, Missouri, USA. Previously he was Senior Pastor of Southwood Presbyterian Church, Huntsville, Alabama, USA.

Fergus MacDonald is Chairman of the Scottish Evangelical Theological Society. Now retired from the ministry of the Free Church of Scotland, he was for several years the General Secretary of the Scottish Bible Society.

Alex J. MacDonald is minister of Buccleuch and Greyfriars Free Church of Scotland in Edinburgh, Scotland.

Donald M. MacDonald served for 15 years as a medical missionary in India with the Free Church of Scotland. On his return to Scotland he completed his theological training and became minister of Bishopbriggs Free Church. From 1997 to 2009, Donald held the chair of Apologetics and Practical Theology in the Free Church College.

Malcolm Maclean is minister of Greyfriars Free Church of Scotland in Inverness in the Scottish Highlands. Previously he was Managing Editor of Christian Focus Publications and still looks after their Mentor range of titles. He has authored a book entitled *The Lord's Supper*.

Alasdair I. Macleod studied at Aberdeen University, the Free Church of Scotland College, and Westminster Theological Seminary in Philadelphia. He has pastored three congregations of the Free Church of Scotland (Muir of Ord in the Scottish Highlands, Leith in Edinburgh, and presently in St. Andrews), and for several years taught Practical Theology in the Free Church of Scotland College in Edinburgh.

Donna Macleod is a native of Point on the Isle of Lewis. She worked in the offices of the Stornoway Gazette and is involved in many aspects of local church life.

John Macleod, born in Lochaber in 1966, is an author and journalist and Dr Macleod's eldest son. He worships in the Stornoway congregation of the Free Presbyterian Church.

David Meredith is minister at Smithton-Culloden Free Church, Inverness, Scotland, where he has been for 26 years. He is currently (2010–2011) Moderator of the General Assembly of the Free Church of Scotland. A former student of Donald Macleod, he is well-known as a conference speaker on both sides of the Atlantic. He is known for his passion for contemporary Calvinism although says he is too old to be young, restless and reformed. He loves travel, reading and motorcycling.

Contributors

Guy Richard is minister of First Presbyterian Church in Gulfport, Mississippi. He studied at Reformed Theological Seminary in Jackson, Mississippi, and at New College in Edinburgh. Dr. Richard has published a book on the theology of Samuel Rutherford, entitled *The Supremacy of God in the Theology of Samuel Rutherford* (2008).

Changwon Shu is senior pastor of Samyang Presbyterian Church in Seoul, South Korea. Following studies at the Free Church College, Pastor Shu served churches in Seoul and taught Puritan theology and Presbyterian church history at Chongshin Theological Seminary. He is a prolific author and preacher.

Derek W. H. Thomas is Associate Minister of First Presbyterian Church, Columbia, South Carolina, and Adjunct Professor of Systematic Theology at Reformed Theological Seminary in Atlanta, Georgia. Until recently, he was the John E. Richards Professor of Systematic and Practical Theology at Reformed Theological Seminary in Jackson, Mississippi. Before moving to America in 1996, he pastored a church in Belfast, Northern Ireland, for seventeen years. In addition to his work at the seminary, he serves as the Minister of Teaching at First Presbyterian Church in Jackson. He is the author of numerous books at both academic and popular levels.

Carl R. Trueman is Professor of Historical Theology and Church History at Westminster Theological Seminary, Philadelphia, USA. Previously he was Senior Lecturer in Church History at the University of Aberdeen, Scotland. He was Editor of *Themelios* from 1998 to 2007. He is the author of several books.

Rowland S. Ward is a graduate of the Free Church of Scotland College and holds a doctorate from the Australian College of Theology. He was ordained in 1976 by the Presbyterian Church of Eastern Australia and has ministered in his home town of Melbourne since 1981. He is an authority on Presbyterianism in Australia, and publishes widely on historical and theological subjects.

Brian Wilson was founding editor of the *West Highland Free Press*. Between 1987 and 2005, he was Labour MP for Cunninghame North and held five Ministerial posts under Tony Blair. The family home is now in his wife's native village of Mangersta, Uig, Lewis.

1

Logic on fire:
the life and career of Donald Macleod

John Macleod

Through four decades the memory is vivid, burnished. My father is carrying me, strong, laughing; and he is young, still only in his twenties. The arm about me is lithe and muscled, and the sun burns in his hair, which is brown, with a redness where the light fires it. Most of the time, though – in these years of the late 1960s, in that distant summer of love, as he forges his trade in his first pastorate – he is busy, or occupied, or absent. Once, on the glebe outside his study – the vestry of the old Free Church at Corpach, long since demolished – an ominous bee lands on my chest, and my mother, not knowing quite what to do, calls for him. My father emerges, slender, beaming; he is in full black canonicals, the minister's collar white about his throat. He has a wooden ruler and onto this he lures the menace and flicks it away into the Lochaber sky, as I peer apprehensively down my chin.

Over forty years on, my father and I, these days, prop up middle-age from either end. Though past his seventieth birthday, he seems at eerie levels rather younger than I am. He is, as my mother has always maintained, yet better looking than any of his sons. The suits he favours – double-breasted, of sober pinstripe, charcoal or soft navy – hang beautifully from the broad shoulders he built half a century ago in summer farm-labouring, and has never lost. He still works prodigiously hard, seldom putting in less than a twelve-hour day. In odd – and atypical – progression – he is more flexible, more radical, more of the political Left than the earnest and very young minister he once was – that distant, doughty defender of the head-covering in public worship, or of capital punishment; the man who went forth on polling-day, as he once wryly observed, to vote for Churchill and the Empire – 'both of whom had been dead for a long time.'

He has a young mind, young eyes, a young body – some months ago, after tea, he and I went for a brisk walk up a nearby hill, where I struggled to keep up with him, and watched him vault a fence or two with cautious ease – but an old head of white hair, like a senatorial halo. He has, after all, been a professing Christian for half a century: a minister of the Free Church of Scotland for forty-six years.

Donald Macleod, my father, was born at 3 Habost, Ness, Isle of Lewis, on 24th November 1940. He was the first son of Donald MacLeod, *Domhnall Cheic*, a wiry 30-year old joiner from the nearby township of Cross, and of his formidable and pretty wife, Alice Thomson, *Alis Sheumais*, born herself at 3 Habost in 1912. He was a great grandson of Murdo Macleod, *Am Piobair*, from Gress, who headed the last family to live on North Rona and had finally settled at 28 Cross. She was a direct descendant of James Thomson, an eighteenth-century schoolmaster from the mainland who had set up shop in Ness shortly before the 1745 Rising, and who is the progenitor of all the Thomsons in rural Lewis. My grandparents, though born not two miles apart, had only come to know one another in Glasgow, and married there in April 1938, making their home at Greenfield Street, Govan. But my grandfather – like so many young Lewismen of his generation – had joined the Royal Naval Reserve and was mobilised just before the launch of the Second World War. Soon afterwards his wife returned to Lewis with their little girl, Annie Murray, to stay with her twice-widowed father, Angus Thomson. In May 1940, on a beautiful summer's day and within a few horrifying hours, her daughter had sickened and died of meningitis, a tragedy that haunted my grandmother for the rest of her very long life.

It was in these circumstances, amidst national crisis besides, that my father came into the world – early in the morning, in an 'improved' black house built by his formidable Thomson great-grandfather, with drystone walls and a thatched roof, a gable-end with fireplace and a loft-bedroom. No photograph survives – it was replaced by a standard 'Board' bungalow in 1953 – though some of the flooring stones can still be seen. Early in 1941, my grandparents took brief sub-let of a council house at Bennadrove on the outskirts of Stornoway and, later that year, lodgings at Point Street in the town centre. By war's end my grandfather, already in troubled health, was shore-based at Stornoway; and among my father's earliest memories is the night his father carried him shoulder-high round the harbour among enthusing crowds and sounding ships' whistles, the night of victory in Europe. By 1947 the resourceful joiner had acquired a 'lot' from the Stornoway Trust in Newmarket, on the Barvas road, and a redundant RAF hut which, borne to the site in sections and, encased in block and extended and improved over the years, became the Macleod home. Little Angus had joined them in 1942, and Annie Mary two years after that; eleven years later, in 1955 (his survival was, for some days, touch and go) Murdo Iain's birth delighted everyone.

Lewis is the largest of the Outer Hebrides and, indeed, the largest of all the United Kingdom's offshore islands. Though still broadly (and, in 1940, overwhelmingly) Gaelic-speaking, it was moulded strongly by Norse occupation in the centuries bracketing the first millennium. The tools, the customs and the vocabulary of the Vikings survive on the island to this day; the people of Lewis still speak (in Gaelic and English) with an accent unique in the Hebrides ('an intelligent, curious, obstinate voice,' writes Roger Hutchinson, 'fully aware of and wholly indifferent to its insistent inflection'). Besides, even in an age of rampant secularism and increasingly shameless assault on its Christian values, Lewis is still profoundly coloured by the advent of Reformed, evangelical religion in the 1820s – replenished into the 1980s by repeated revival – and, especially, the Free Church of Scotland, to which in 1940 some 80% of the people of Lewis adhered, including my grandparents.

Coming to a personal knowledge of Christ in her mid-teens, as far as can be ascertained, my grandmother was a professing Christian by her marriage. It seems, too, that the Lord also dealt with my grandfather as a relatively young man; but he was in his late forties before making a public profession of faith. (In his absence, in 1941, and in the awkward circumstances of separation from her Glasgow congregation, my grandmother arranged my father's baptism on her own profession and at the Point Street flat by the minister of Ness, Rev. John Morrison – whose obituary would appear in the July/August number of the Free Church's *Monthly Record* in 1977, the first under my father's editorship.)

This household, then, was a believing home, a home where family worship was kept morning and night; each Sabbath, they walked into town, in all weathers, to worship in the vast Free Church congregation, under the ministry of the redoubtable Rev. Kenneth A. MacRae. But it was also, until the mid-1950s, a household of laughter, serenity and happiness.

My father has written winsomely of his childhood, in all its wonders and terrors. By broader measure, these years in Lewis between the end of the Second World War and, say, the early 1970s seem in retrospect something of a golden age. There was full employment. New medical advances removed much of the terror from daily life. By then, too, mains water and electricity had transformed domestic comfort. (My father still remembers, even in Newmarket in the late 1940s, the constant chore of fetching water from the well.) Housing rapidly improved; the welfare state underpinned society as a safety-net. And, until the advent of television, it was a vibrant Gaelic culture, one of fellowship and humour and close-knit community.

It was a world of sports: my father and his contemporaries played exuberant football and even constructed a serviceable cricket-pitch on the moor downhill from the street. (He has never lost those interests: in one of the very few betrayals of his blue-collar origins, he always reads the back page of a newspaper first.) It was a world of song; the Laxdale School had a noted Gaelic choir, and its visit to the Mod at Edinburgh in 1950 (where it won a trophy or two) afforded my father his very first trip off the island. (Again, he has never lost this; to this day and when particularly in all's-well-with-the-world trim, he is apt to burst into Gaelic strains in some far corner of the home, the anthemic *Balaich an Iasgaich* being particularly favoured in the bathroom.) He joined the Air Force Cadets and, as a lad of seventeen, enjoyed a jaunt to distant Folkestone and still holds a certificate in gliding. He also grew close to his grandfather, Angus Thomson of Habost, a frequent visitor to Newmarket (where they often shared a bed) and of very similar build and character. Told, in 1961, of young Donald's recognition as a student for the ministry, the erect old man had but one word of counsel – 'Make yourself heard!' When he died, early in 1971 at the age of ninety – buried beside the wife he had outlived by fifty-five years and the last interment in the old Swainbost cemetery - my father's inability – on mean Free Church pay and so soon after a costly flitting from Lochaber – to go home for his funeral was an undoubted sorrow. He took genuine pleasure, many years later, in erecting a dignified gravestone.

There were shadows nevertheless. My father does not care to discuss his schooldays and in our own day was extraordinarily averse to meeting our teachers or setting foot on school premises. Yet he endured, applied himself, and in 1952 passed the '11-plus' exam then essential for admission to grammar school, Stornoway's notable Nicolson Institute. (As a signal reward for winning the 'qually', my grandmother – who kept the tightest rein generally on the thin domestic budget – bought the family their first wireless.) In 1956, though, crisis struck on several fronts. My grandfather was struck down by severe asthma; at almost the same time my grandmother was diagnosed with tuberculosis, and consigned to hospital for months for painful, immobilising treatment. Both would fully recover. But for the duration, still only fifteen, my father all but ran the household – nursing the baby, preparing meals, laundering clothes. It was a painful permanent end to his youth. It was in this period, too, that his brother Angus – whom the overwhelmed elder sibling was in little position to control – fell into evil company. By his twentieth birthday, he had a serious alcohol problem, an increasingly unstable presence in the house.

Yet – emphatically – this was a world of faith, a faith that coloured the entire community, that came to the fore on occasions of birth or marriage or bereavement, and was part of the weave of everyday life.

'I must say first of all,' my father recalled, pushed to give something of his experience at a Free Church gathering in 1987, 'that from my earliest childhood I was surrounded by Christian people. I was brought up in a Christian home and that home was always full of visitors who were, for the most part, believing Christians. I am profoundly thankful to God for that experience because my early years are linked in my memory with many hours of what I can only call the most edifying entertainment. Many of the men who came to the house had been on active war service. They were, from every point of view, men's men: men of courage, men of experience and men of integrity. They were also men who were endlessly kind to children; men possessed of a keen sense of humour; men of enormous intelligence and wit; above all, men who loved to argue about and to discuss the truth of God. It was my privilege to sit, sometimes for hours, as these men (and women) described the way God had led them... From my earliest years I wanted to make these people my people.'

Securing admission to the University of Glasgow, he headed south by MacBrayne mailboat and train in October 1958, enrolling in first-year Arts classes, with a view to finally securing an Honours degree and, perhaps, making a career in teaching. The 'Ordinary' degree, unique to Scotland, reflected its esteem of a broad education and had to include a language and a science. He opted for French and Geology, taking classes besides in English Language, English Literature, Modern History and Moral Philosophy.

Certainly he fell effortlessly into the warm social base of Partick Highland Free Church and the Lewis diaspora of that corner of the city. Here dozens of his parents' friends still lived, and worshipped, and Partick Highland was now the pastoral charge of a highly respected Nessman, Rev. Malcolm Morrison. Though already in his sixties, Morrison – a serene, assured veteran of the Great War – had been ordained late in life (holding charges first at Coigeach, then Scalpay) and only after long and sacrificial service as a 'home-missionary', or resident lay-preacher, in a variety of difficult situations. He was a first-class pastor and, in my father's judgement, was never really recognised for his gifts as a preacher, especially in Christ-centred appeal to the unconverted.

Photographs show a very thin, diffident, smartly dressed youth in the very conservative student fashions of the time. Excited letters home break such shocking new experiences as spending all of £1 on a classy fountain-pen. Within months, though, the lad was in profound spiritual crisis – in the form of awful, tormenting atheistic temptation. 'It was an experience of radical doubt,' he told that 1987 gathering, 'an experience in which I lost, or seemed to lose, all my faith in God. The questions were posed to me at a radical and personal level – does God exist? Is the Bible God's Word? Is Jesus Christ really still alive and still the Lord of all?... It was not due to any particular argument... It was simply, as far as I understand it today, something that came directly from Hell itself.... It was the sowing of a seed of doubt and in a single moment all the lights in my world went out: no faith in God, no faith in the Bible, no faith in Christ.'

I have heard him remark of this time that 'I envied the lamp-posts.' It was a 'thoroughly miserable experience,' he has related; and he has no comprehension of happy atheism. 'For me it was desolation. It was darkness. It was a world without hope, a world without joy, a world without meaning, and a world without purpose.' Dominating his memories of this nightmare, half a century ago, is the frightful smog of 1950s Glasgow– 'virtually impenetrable darkness, even during the day; and that in many ways matched my condition in that state of doubt.' He went one night to hear an eminent Church of Scotland divine – 'a Professor and a Doctor of Divinity, with endless letters after his name... I went with a longing soul but the man told stories and I got nothing to meet my need.'

It is unclear how long this condition lasted; certainly, many months: indeed, he has described it as 'years', which suggests the anguish stalked his heels even after he had been brought to public profession of faith. What is striking, too, is that it sounds far more like the awful trial of one already – and long – regenerate than the conversion-throes of a careless young man. They were 'years during which I prayed; years during which I stuck with God's people...' And, above all – driven to find answers – they were years when he read, devouring yards and yards of hardback theology like a starving soul. 'I seemed to have the whole of Glasgow University's theological library to myself: thousands and thousands of books in which I searched for answers to the questions troubling my soul. Theology was not then (as it may be now) something which one does detachedly and dispassionately. It was something I did for survival because I had to find answers. At last, after waiting and waiting, studying and praying, God took me out of that pit and placed my feet on the Rock.

'I went to John Calvin. I found him explaining Paul's teaching. I found Calvin saying to me that there is a sense of deity in every heart. I heard Calvin saying that God has sown the knowledge of Himself in every heart. I heard Calvin saying that the seed of religion is in every heart. I heard Calvin saying that there is no man so brutalised but that his conscience, at least now and again, summons him before God's tribunal. And I knew that all Paul said, and all that Calvin said, was true of me. I know that even in those days when atheism seemed to be engulfing me, I prayed, I stayed with the people of God and with the Word of God because there was this sense of deity and this seed of religion, this inescapable awareness of God...

'If I couldn't worship Jesus Christ I would worship the man who created Him. I remember constantly the great words of William Guthrie of Fenwick: when faith looks at Christ it says, "Less would not satisfy and more is not desired." For me the search for truth ends with Christ. Less would not satisfy me: more is not desired. If this light went out, all the lights would go out. Many of you have never known my kind of struggle. I am not sure that I envy you. But I do marvel at many of you. It seemed to me, it seems to me still, impossible to believe that Jesus is Lord without bowing the knee. And yet many people in our churches do just that. How I envied all those adherents who had no doubts! How I wondered that their knees were not bowed! The moment I saw the truth I had to bow the knee.'

No one can understand Donald Macleod without grasping the defining importance of this period. It left him in permanent habits of all-consuming study; of a startling capacity for concentration and industry. It left him with a tenderness for men and women under the preached Word – lending a profoundly pastoral note to all his pulpit labours, the intimacy to sermons preached as much to himself at to others. And it begot the tension and energy of the preacher truly called, that earnestness Martyn Lloyd-Jones has aptly described as 'logic on fire.'

It was not then the done thing to move swiftly, lightly to the Communion table after winning the liberty of the gospel. My father waited at least a year, and seems to have professed faith at Partick Highland Free Church in April 1960. In fact, at this time in the Free Church of the West Highlands and especially on Lewis there were very, very few young Christians. And they were viewed suspiciously, scrutinised constantly, on occasion baited to their face. As was perhaps inevitable in this milieu, the believers of this generation became quickly and in every respect of sober, even middle-aged habit.

There remains some doubt as to how he was directed to apply for recognition as a student for the Free Church ministry. It was by no means a step lightly taken. For one – and the phrase is much less cynical than it sounds – he lacked 'patronage'; the close sponsorship and interest of a powerful Free Church minister, which helped parachute others of lesser gifts into fine situations. There were in fact no near relations of any professional standing. Such a glass ceiling must have been intimidating. Besides, his parents – even by village standards – were poor, with my grandfather's health rapidly deteriorating as a consequence of hard war service. There was a strong temptation to seek some easy career and help support them in their later years.

Mr Morrison, the Partick Highland minister, would many years later suggest that my father first approached him. In fact, he sought young Donald out, and pressed him urgently to consider very seriously the desperate need for gifted, godly young men of upright character in the pastoral ministry. My father had already such thoughts himself, but could barely see over the encircling mountains of difficulty and long odds. His minister's intervention, in Providence, was startling encouragement. 'But what of your Honours, Donald?' asked Morrison. 'A waste of time,' said my father. The College session already looming, he was – most unusually – recognised by the Free Presbytery of Glasgow before formal examination by his own Kirk Session. He duly graduated, in July 1961, and began classes at the Free Church College in Edinburgh that October. He had already taken his first service – in emergency, at Stornoway Free Church one evening, seized at the door after Rev. Kenneth MacRae took ill. It might be thought that my grandmother would be overjoyed to see her firstborn son turn to the ministry. In fact, her immediate reaction was horror. 'You'll spend your life in people's mouths,' she said, darkly and indeed prophetically.

The Free Church of Scotland was a much larger body in the early 1960s than it is today. Probably around 30,000 Scots then reckoned themselves her adherents and in great tracts of the Highlands she was effectively the established, parish church, with most adherents and the best buildings. The ministry, too, was then a most respected profession and the country was not then nearly so far down the road of militant godlessness as she has since come. The Church of Scotland had reached its historic peak only in the mid-1950s; and its great personalities – the likes of William Barclay, James Stewart, Murdo Ewen MacDonald and Leonard Small – were better known to the public then than Cabinet Secretaries of the Scottish Government are now; the doings of the General Assemblies won pages of newspaper coverage, and practically all state schools held daily, if most formal, Christian worship.

After the crisis of 1900, the minority Free Church had shaped herself as a tolerant, courteous coalition, predominately Highland and very conservative but with some surviving, indigenous Lowland charges – from towns like Leith and Coatbridge to mining villages in Fife. Yet she was still using the Authorised Version universally, standing to pray and sitting to sing almost everywhere, and would cling exclusively to the 1650 Scottish Psalter until the mid-1990s. Practically every minister wore a clerical collar – all the time – and generally donned frock-coats or even Geneva gowns for such high days as a Communion Sabbath. The Free Church in fact remains quiet, sensible, and generally united, full of upright people who go about doing good, her publications too often giving the impression of a much sillier body than is in fact the case.

Even in the 1980s – by which time my father was a permanent fixture himself – the Free Church College, its apartments carved out of an elegant eighteenth-century tenement on The Mound, had a timebound feel. In 1961, the faculty must have seemed almost as venerable as the premises. Principal Peter W Millar had been ordained to Campbeltown, Argyll, as long before as 1915: his youngest colleague, Professor W J Cameron (Greek and New Testament), was already fifty-three. Among the others was Professor Roderick Finlayson, ordained to Urray in 1922, son of Lochcarron, veteran of the Great War, of shy and scathing wit, cordially loathed by certain colleagues and the Free Presbyterians. He presided over Systematic Theology, taught on highly conservative lines and with a taste for sarcasm. 'Careful now, Mr MacLean,' he carolled as an uncle of mine tried desperately to tell the class the difference between a sinner's 'state' and his 'condition', 'don't go too deep for us!'

These were men who would don academic gowns for a class of two or three students, who trooped as one to high funerals in frock-coats and top hats. They marked essays by fountain-pen – in flowing copperplate, viewed books published since the mid-nineteenth century with profound suspicion, and presided at 'High Table' in the College dining-room – men of Victorian rectitude and Edwardian habits.

But these were happy years. My father enjoyed flat-life with other Lewis students, most five years to a decade his senior – Murdo Alick MacLeod, and two men who would become his brothers-in-law, Malcolm MacLean and Alastair Montgomery. The Free Church Students Association organised earnest debates and lectures. In St Columba's Free Church, atop the Royal Mile, a packed congregation – largely Highlanders – enjoyed the rich ministry of Rev. G. N. M. Collins, a gifted and urbane figure. It was there my father first met Mary MacLean, from Shawbost, dark and poised and petite, younger sister of his fellow-student Malcolm and a new and bright Christian. They started increasingly to enjoy one another's company.

These days we are apt to make far too much fuss of divinity students. In the early Sixties, and especially in a Highland context, they were a low form of life, hard-pressed at College, burdened not merely with pulpit-supply duties but additional academic chores by their Presbyteries during vacation, not generally allowed in the West

Highlands at this period even to conduct public worship from the pulpit, but consigned to the precentor's desk. Even during term-time the preaching burden was considerable and to this day there are no College classes on Mondays, reflecting a more conscientious era when Christians avoided unnecessary travel on the Lord's Day. The first year of the standard three-year course (for University graduates; many, against the backdrop of war-time conscription and later National Service, were admitted on lenient non-graduate terms for a four-year 'Modified Course') centred on the study of Greek and Hebrew; only after these were grasped could students in Second Year and subsequently brave Professor Finlayson and Systematic Theology.

My father recalls with particular affection a summer placement at Stoer, in 1962. He was lodged at Balcladdich, where the Reverend Alexander MacLeod – an important figure at the dawn of Lewis Evangelicalism in the 1820s – had been born, and where a great-aunt from Cross had made her married life decades previously; there were still cousins about in the early 1960s, and the flash of Trumpan Head lighthouse could be seen across the Minch. Assynt was then a very warm, vibrant Gaelic community – today it seems a sea of holiday-cottages and English settlers – with a rich, thoughtful culture; until the 1980s, too, there were two Free Church congregations – Stoer and Drumbeg; and Lochinver and Elphin. Even by Highland standards, though, Assynt fellowship had more than a dose of the old Separatist rigour. In 1962, between three denominations, there was only one male communicant in the entire parish. There were still excellent congregations, with the Sabbath kept as strictly as in Lewis, but a great reluctance publicly to commit. Someone grimly reminded my father of Principal John MacLeod's wry verdict on the district – that the folk of Assynt did not come to hear the gospel, but to hear if you had it. I have heard my father fret that, in Stoer and district that long-ago summer, he delivered the best sermons of his life.

In the spring of 1964, he negotiated the last rapids of examination and was in May duly 'licensed to preach the gospel' by the Free Presbytery of Glasgow. Home in Lewis, practically his first duty – in the full canonicals then *de rigeur* even for an unordained probationer, including Homburg and dog-collar – was his own minister's funeral, Kenneth MacRae having passed away a few days before. My uncle Murdo Iain, not nine years old, still remembers the shock of the clerical apparition who came to collect him from school.

In 1963, Collins had been promoted to the Church History chair in succession to Professor Renwick, and St Columba's duly called the Reverend Donald Lamont – a diffident, gracious Skyeman, ordained only in 1956 – in his stead. That left a vacancy in Lochaber, the charge of Kilmallie and Arisaig, and by the summer of 1964 they were taking keen interest in Donald Macleod. The match was egged on by Robert Park, a genial fellow from Scalpay who had been settled in Fort William only the previous year; a letter survives gaily assuring my father of the most lenient 'ordination trials', usually some *viva voce* grilling in Greek and production of a 'controversial essay.' On 5th November 1964, in the old Free Church at Corpach – 'Guy Fawkes Day', he would record in *Who's Who In Scotland* – my father was ordained to the ministry of the gospel, and admitted to the pastoral charge of Kilmallie and Arisaig in the Free Presbytery of Abertarff. As remains Free Church custom, he was 'preached in' the following Sabbath morning by Rev. John Angus Gillies, the Skye-born minister of Glenurquart.

For weeks thereafter my father came to grips with his job and found occasion to write a great many excited letters to Edinburgh. My parents' wedding, in St Columba's on 7th January 1965 – with Murdo Alick MacLeod as best man – ended the need for such correspondence. My mother and father are in many ways of different personalities and interests and emphases, and have come through many things; but – of keen intelligence, steely resolve and immense practicality – she has for nigh on half a century been the wind beneath his wings. After the distressing loss of one unborn infant, I was safely delivered in April 1966; Murdo followed in June 1967. With Angus's arrival, in March 1970, the family was complete.

The parish of Kilmallie – the land some ten miles north of Fort William and twenty-four miles south-west of Fort Augustus, bordered to the south by Loch Eil and Loch Leven and, until its 1974 abolition, in the county of Inverness-shire – is the biggest in Scotland, covering 219.5 square miles, overwhelmingly moor and mountain and loch, with three tiny offshore islands. This is wild country and until after the Rising of 1745 it knew little of the rule of law or any meaningful gospel. It was almost the nineteenth century before Presbyterianism took firm root on what had hitherto been hostile ground, and the ministry of Donald MacGillivray – presented in 1772 – was the first to know Evangelical blessing, though Lochaber was first gripped by revival under his successor, Thomas Davidson, settled in 1829.

Practically everyone 'went out' at the Disruption of 1843, casting in their lot with the new Free Church, but the laird – the latest Cameron of Lochiel – was a bigoted Episcopalian, and for years Davidson and his flock were brutally harassed. When Lochiel finally granted a site in Corpach for church and manse, it was in a bog so notorious that it had been used of old to trap wild horses. (The building was never stable and in 1976 was demolished, though the pulpit and latron found new premises in Callanish Free Church.)

The parish was generally fortunate in its ministers, though there were protracted vacancies after 1900, despite derisory United Free Church support. At length the formidable Rev. Jonathan Campbell was settled in 1932. A confident Skyeman, Campbell had a flair for local politics – he sat for many years on the County Council – and, in the late 1950s, shrewdly planned a new church in the burgeoning housing-estate of Caol, across the Caledonian Canal from Corpach; he secured a prime site, too, at the centre of the sea-front, though he had retired by the building's completion in 1961. To fund the development, though, he shut down and sold the Free Church in Arisaig over the heads of furious adherents, a despotism recalled bitterly to this day, and thus forfeited the sole Evangelical witness in a district dominated by Roman Catholicism.

After the brief ministry of Rev. Alexander MacLeod, Rev. Donald Lamont gave six years of service, also held the County Council seat, and sold the historic manse, building a new modern villa beside it and within feet of the church door – though he had gone to Edinburgh before it was complete. With bright picture windows, parquet flooring and a kitchen with every electric convenience, the house – finally sold early this century, before the 2004 settlement of Rev. Christopher MacRae – had every appearance of Sixties modernity, though it could be inordinately cold.

So my father began, amidst the inordinate rain of his first winter, to master his trade. It might carelessly be thought that Kilmallie Free Church was the rough country cousin of the Fort William charge. In fact, Kilmallie was the tweedier and more prosperous of the two, a congregation of tradesmen and shopkeepers and professionals. The morning service was held at Corpach and of a Sabbath evening at Caol. In addition, my father was the last minister to keep a regular Gaelic service, on Sabbath afternoons and with a bare carload in attendance. ('I would preach for two people,' he recalls of the final, withering months, 'but not for one.')

But there were duties in farflung districts too. The young minister visited in Arisaig, encountering understandable hostility – he recalls one uncomfortable encounter with an old lady who, of the understandable impression that her pastor must *ex officio* be a councillor, complained bitterly he had not yet secured her a house. Preparing to marry a young girl in the congregation, he travelled up Glen Arkaig, in the wilds of the Cameron estate, to visit her parents in a remote shepherd's cottage – bashful people who, as quickly became evident, scarcely left that dale and seldom saw any stranger. He kept regular services besides at assorted hamlets round the sea-loch – at Kinlochiel, on the road to Mallaig; at Blaich in Ardgour, and at Trislaig, across Loch Linnhe from Fort William itself – all this in an ecclesiastical landscape of unusual breadth for the Highlands. Lochaber supported four Presbyterian denominations, including Free Presbyterians and the United Free Church. The parish minister of Kilmallie was a genial, kilt-wearing Moderate. The Roman Catholic tradition was indigenous and respected; and there were besides Episcopalians. (My father, giving a lady in his congregation a lift, asked her casually how she had enjoyed a High Anglican wedding days earlier in Fort William. 'Wedding!' she exclaimed. 'I was up an' doon like a coo at the calving.')

It was 1966 before he passed his driving test and for his first year in ministry he walked as much as he could, between his principal churches and around his parishioners in Corpach, Caol, Banavie and Tomonie and Mucomir and Lochyside. Office-bearers and adherents frequently played chauffeur and he developed great affection for the kindly local priest, Fr. John Angus Morrison, a native of South Uist who had made his name as 'Father Rockets' after doughtily opposing a contentious range there – and delighted in giving the Free Church minister a lift. Eventually my father became the proud owner of his first car, a blue two-door Morris Minor, of uncertain handling but robust build: driving the following winter to a sad little funeral in Lochcarron, and finding a bridge at Glen Shiel had just been swept away by spate, he boldly revved up his car, left the road and simply forded the foaming stream. Another time – driving a sister-in-law through wild conditions in Glencoe – they were stuck in drifting snow; he extricated the vehicle by sacrificing his University scarf, wedging it under a tyre for traction.

My father's first pastorate coincided with great change. Lochaber had long been energised by the aluminium industry; and been a hub of secret, often lethal military training during the Second World War.

Work now proceeded apace on an enormous pulp mill at Corpach, typical of the monumental schemes of the era for Highland regeneration, and which finally opened in April 1966. My earliest memories are dominated by a village reduced to a building site, acres of housing going up in every direction, constant works everywhere. Kilmallie boomed, and so did the Free Church congregation. The considerable distance from markets and an obsolete pulping process – using highly corrosive chemicals – troubled no one. 'Bungalow Hill' mushroomed to the west of Corpach; over all hung the rubbery smell of stewing wood-chip.

To this day, there are several completing claims for the first couple he married and the first baby he sprinkled: Donald Macleod himself cannot remember or is too tactful to say. There were Presbyterial duties too. When he declined to serve as Moderator of Presbytery, he found himself instead gleefully landed with the clerkship. He still believes he made his worst pastoral mistake in Kilmallie. In his absence, office-bearers had quite improperly authorised the use of the Caol building for a rally of the Faith Mission, an evangelistic movement with which the Free Church had doctrinal differences. My father, on his return, was furious, and after the close of sermon delivered a sharp public rebuke. Tension hung in the air for weeks; it was an error he never repeated.

There was wider family life. With two baby boys born in quick succession, my mother welcomed the support of the MacPhees next door – an exuberant family from Acharacle – and other kindly parishioners, such as Morag and Donald Bruce of Caol. Her brother Malcolm was ordained to Lochcarron in 1965; in 1967 Rev. Alastair Montgomery, now minister of Scalpay, married her eldest sister, Chrissie. Joan had in 1959 wed Rev. Angus Smith, Govan-reared minister of Snizort in Skye. With such a profusion of collars in the rising generation, some-one joked decades later at a family wedding, my new Shawbost grandfather should have hung a 'KMO' sign at the door – 'Keep Ministers Out!'

It was a time in my father's career, especially as his confidence grew in Gaelic preaching, when he was greatly in demand as a junior minister at Communion seasons around the Free Church. It was at almost his first engagement, at St Columba's in Edinburgh, that he met Rev. Professor John Murray of Westminster Theological Seminary, Pennsylvania. Born in Badbea, Sutherland, in 1898, Murray had trained for the Free Presbyterian ministry after Great War service, but parted company almost on the eve of his licensing as he took additional classes at Princeton University in the USA: the Free Presbyterian Synod had adopted a strong new stance on the use of public transport on the Lord's Day – forbidding it on pain of church discipline – which he could not in conscience endorse. Increasingly close to J. Gresham Machen and other staunchly Reformed clergy under increasing persecution in the Presbyterian Church of North America, Murray cast his lot in with them after they were disgracefully expelled, and supported the formation of what became the Orthodox Presbyterian Church, in which he was duly ordained. After many years' service at the new Seminary, he had now retired to Scotland and uncomfortable exile – still *persona non grata* with the Free Presbyterians, but quietly refusing to join the Free Church. He nevertheless took many Free Church services and, on this occasion, found fast rapport with the young Lewisman.

My father remembers Professor Murray for his intellect, but still more for his quiet, palpable holiness. They began to correspond, my father first inquiring as to Murray's views on the 'Establishment principle,' the historic Presbyterian belief that that the 'civil magistrate' or State and the Church are in mutually supportive relationship. In July 1966, Professor Murray came to Corpach to perform my own baptism, endorsing the back of my birth certificate to record the fact. He was most taken with my Laxdale grandfather – their very quiet, serene spirituality was a shared attraction – and, in later years, Professor Murray and my father continued on occasion to meet; but the theologian's subsequent marriage – followed by the still more sensational begetting, in his eighth decade, of two children – anchored him in new domestic responsibilities.

It was largely by Murray's aegis that my father became involved with the Banner of Truth Trust, a recently founded charity to promote Reformed doctrine and re-publish significant Reformed literature. The young minister began to attend the annual Leicester Conference, striking up friendship with other thoughtful rising stars – John J. Murray, John R. de Witt, Geoffrey Thomas, Erroll Hulse, and especially that eminent London minister, D. Martyn Lloyd-Jones, the austere but eloquent Welshman who was by any measure the greatest preacher of the twentieth century. My father, too, began frequently to contribute to the Trust's monthly magazine and, by 1968 – still only

twenty-seven years old – was one of six 'associate editors', under Iain
H. Murray and John J. Murray (neither of whom, be it noted, was
related either to each other or the eminent Professor).

The conservatism of this early writing is striking, and still more
so an already mature and most clear prose. Typical contributions in
1968 and 1969 were tight essays on 'Misunderstandings of Calvinism',
'The Christian Experience of Suffering', 'The Lord's Supper as a Means
of Grace', 'Qualifications for Communion', 'The Real Presence', 'The
Doctrine of Election', 'The Christian Doctrine of Providence' and two
on 'The Divine Messiah'. The young minister wrote besides on 'The
Human Nature of Christ' (March 1970); 'The Second Coming of
Christ' (July/August 1970), 'The Incarnation' (December 1970); 'The
Bible and Textual Criticism' (June 1972) – one of his early outings in
controversy; it was assailed by the Trinitarian Bible Society and joyously
dissected by Rev. Donald MacLean in the *Free Presbyterian Magazine*;
'The Doctrine of the Church' (February 1973); 'Reconciliation' (July/
August 1973); 'Federal Theology – An Oppressive Legalism?' (February
1974); 'Christian Assurance' (November 1974); 'The Covenant' (April
1975) and 'Ambassadors for Christ' (May 1977). Vividly recalled
besides are two articles on the role of woman, with tightly argued
advocacy of the 'head-covering' in public worship.

Donald Macleod's Presbytery role necessitated a firm grasp of Free
Church procedure – and a cool head – at higher bodies of the Free
Church besides. It was largely by his efforts at the Synod of Moray
and Ross – the intermediate 'court of review' – that a gifted Ross-
shire pastor survived in the ministry after a humiliating drink-driving
conviction. The rules my father drafted in the late 1960s for building-
finance in new church-extension charges – that the congregation are
granted a third of the funds, borrow a third of the funds, and must raise
a third of the funds – operate to this day. On a lighter note, after reorganisation – when local charges were absorbed into a new court, the
Free Presbytery of Lochaber and Lorne – the Clerk had the draining
task of drawing up papers for the ordination of the Reverend David
Fraser to the pastorate of Mull – or, as it was majestically described, the
charge of 'Tobermory and Torloisk, Toronsay, Ross and Brolas'; it had
to be typed out many, many times.

Inevitably my father's rising profile began to attract interest. Few
now recall that as early as May 1965 he was nominated as a candidate
for the Chair of Systematic Theology, only months after his ordination

and on the retirement of Professor Finlayson. It was enthusiastically
moved by his Glenurquhart colleague, Rev. John Angus Gillies, but
never had serious prospect of success. Late in 1966, too – in what
he still recalls as one of his most difficult positions – the minister of
Kilmallie had, after agonised and prayerful reflection, to decline a call
to his ancestral Cross – he still has that document and the 'minute of
adherents', signed by over a thousand people including his own uncles
and aunts and even his 85-year old grandfather. The charge was later
filled by his brother-in-law, Rev. Angus Smith, who retired in 1997
and is now in the Free Presbyterian Church of Scotland.

Wise Presbyterian heads have always been aware of the perils in
remaining too long in the situation of a rural parish, where one can
in time run in ruts, grow stale. One wonders too what impact had the
sudden death of my uncle Angus, late in January 1970 (small as I was,
I can still recall the nightmarish journey home for the awful Lewis
funeral) on my father's sense of settlement: his brother, troubled and
brittle, had been a frequent visitor to Corpach. Early that same year,
Rev. Malcolm Morrison had – following his seventy-fifth birthday –
demitted his Glasgow charge: in October 1970, Donald Macleod was
inducted as minister of Partick Highland Free Church. Determined not
in the least to cause any difficulty for his eventual successor, he kept for
years thereafter a near-absolute distance from Kilmallie: in June 1986,
though, he preached at the anniversary service of the church at Caol,
and in November 2004, soon after the settlement of 'Kiki' MacRae –
the fourth minister since 1970 – Kilmallie Free Church hosted us all
in celebration of my father's forty years in the ministry. Though the
'adherent' body of the congregation had in a much more careless age
greatly declined, four decades on the number of committed believers
in this sturdy charge was practically identical.

Partick Highland Free Church was a surprisingly new congregation,
born of a mission during the Great War to Gaelic-speaking island
girls engaged in domestic service in Glasgow's West End. It became a
'sanctioned charge' in 1924 and by 1927 had its first minister (Rev. Peter
M. Chishom) and its own building – a handsome pre-fabricated 'zinc
church' of the type then still widespread in the Highlands, in a prime site
on Highburgh Road. By 1934, when Rev. Murdo Campbell – another
Lewisman – was inducted – it was too small; in 1937, the former
Dowanvale United Free Church building on Dowanhill Street, surplus
to Kirk requirements after the 1929 Union, was bought on easy terms.

Little modification was required, save for the removal of a pipe-organ.

The pastorates of Campbell and Morrison had seen signal blessing and the consolidation of a Gaelic witness in what by the Second World War was a remarkably Gaelic community, with practically every stair in the tenements of Partick and Partickhill holding at least one Gaelic-speaking family. Partick Highland fitted in, of course, with wider Highland ethnicities in the city: as recently as 1970, five Free Church congregations still held regular Gaelic services, and at Communion seasons a thousand-strong gathering was still possible. (I myself can remember Partick Highland full, even the galleries overflowing, for the Gaelic Sabbath evening service of a Communion some forty years ago.)

My father's flock were at his induction still largely in Partick itself; almost all in tenement flats and most within walking distance of the church. Partick Highland men worked largely on or from the Clyde itself – the docks and river-ferries and lighters and steamers; but some too in the Albion bus factory, the Springburn railworks, the Meadowside Granaries and so on. Many had come before the war and duly married girls who had moved south to serve as maids and cooks in the big houses of Hillhead or Kelvinside. They had raised families – Gaelic-speaking, Glasgow-reared children who seemed effortlessly to move between two worlds and even two different English accents. By 1970, though, many new arrivals were University students, or launching vocations in nursing and teaching.

There was much to be done, and initially from some domestic discomfort. The manse at Jordanhill, though imposing without and with much garden-ground, was dated, neglected and dirty. There was regular flooding by the backdoor, a dubious solid-fuel range, gloriously antiquated bathroom fittings. It took some years to accomplish basic improvements and for my father to subdue the jungle of a garden, though it took his successor to win central heating: I succumbed routinely each winter to bronchitis, waking often to ice – in the hard winters of the late 1970s – on the inside of the windows of the chill room I shared, into my teens, with my brothers.

As a young minister against strong, established personalities, inclined to shoot down even the most modest talk of reform or adaptation less by logic than by force, it took time and patience for my father to win round the Partick Highland courts and address evident and urgent problems. A priority was to throttle irregularities in Kirk

Session order that had snuck in during the vacancy: my father insisted, from the start and thereafter, that the Session do its business by the book, following in all points the *Manual of Free Church Practice and Procedure*. He had also to confront an established problem in the Free Church culture of Lewis: extraordinary laxity in baptism. At the first relevant meeting of Session, there were eleven applicants – most of them young fathers seldom or never seen at sermon. The new minister sustained only two, and had little difficulty on that front thereafter.

There were also immediate concerns about Partick Highland finances, with curious anomalies and unconvincing records. My father – who has a keen head for numbers and is no mean manager of budgets – fast smelled a rat and quietly forced the issue, calling for auditors. In short order there were dramatic consequences: a flight, a confession, painful church discipline and aghast office-bearers, as it dawned on them that over the years thousands and thousands of pounds had been stolen. But their new pastor had won priceless political capital, and he chose deliberately not to prolong the woe with criminal proceedings. He established elementary reforms: for instance, that at least two men at all times collated and counted the Sabbath collection.

It was in the aftermath of this sad episode that the most urgent question could be addressed: more English services. As Dr John Kennedy observed long ago in his biography of Rev. John MacDonald, the 'Apostle of the North' – whose first pastorate was the Edinburgh Gaelic Chapel, in early nineteenth-century Edinburgh – this inevitably becomes an issue in any Highland-émigré congregation. It had already wrought real damage to the Free Church in North America. In 1970, my father was alarmed how few of the Glasgow-reared young people in the congregation came to church at all and only one, in fact, professed faith.

For the first year or so he went along with the arrangements he had inherited: Gaelic at eleven on Sabbath morning, Gaelic again at three in the afternoon, English at night, the prayer meeting – entirely in Gaelic – on Thursday evening; and the Communion services, twice-yearly and from Thursday to Monday, early in April and October, almost entirely in Gaelic.

Finally he secured Session assent to holding the morning service in English. He compensated by adding an extra evening service – Gaelic, immediately after the English one – and even, incredibly, offered to maintain the afternoon service besides (though he was not taken up on it.) Even so, there was considerable sensation and some very bitter attacks, from elsewhere in the Free Presbytery of Glasgow and even from Lewis.

In short order, parallel Communion services were agreed to – in English, held in the hall downstairs – and by 1976 he had an additional English prayer meeting, on Wednesday evening, to say nothing of a winter Bible Class for his eager young people, held on Friday nights. He instituted besides a Youth Fellowship – which met frequently, though not invariably, in the manse. From April 1977, aware that assorted youth-organisations were quietly stealing away Free Church children to the mainstream churches, my father had initiated a Junior Club, which met on Friday evenings and had a wonderful range of outings and activities; later a 'Junior Fellowship' was instituted on Sabbath evening, downstairs in the church for children whose parents supported the late-evening Gaelic service. My mother gamely led the activities of the Women's Foreign Missionary Association, though after the three of us were in 1975 gruesomely sick from the vast quantity of sweets bestowed on us during the annual manse-hosted 'bring and buy' fundraiser – and perhaps especially after my parents overheard us plotting, next year, to sit at the foot of the stairs with our piggybanks – my father and us were thereafter banished from the premises for its duration, wandering the city streets as the forlorn and unmanned.

Partick Highland unexpectedly benefitted besides from the steady decline of the 'Free Presbyterian Relief Congregation', following the death of Rev. Roderick MacKenzie in 1972: two men, Finlay MacInnes and Colin MacKay, became highly esteemed elders. 1974 saw extensive renovations to the church building and, by 1976, the manse was almost cosy and everywhere elegant. That was the first year, too, that the spring Communion was moved back to the first Sabbath in March, both Partick Highland sacramental seasons having hitherto clashed with those at Back on Lewis. There was quiet, but extremely rapid, social change too, the Gaelic attendance already in steady decline and more and more families moving out to Glasgow's suburbs, motoring into sermon each Sabbath. The congregation, too, gained an international flavour, with English and American and Australian accents now heard on the pavement after the benediction – and Partick itself was fast regenerating, the worst slums demolished and startled tenements emerging, in pink or honey, as a century of soot was, street by street, blasted away. Yet things endured that, today, might startle some. Throughout his Glasgow ministry my father always wore his clerical collar, donning his 'Prince Albert' frock-coat for the Sabbath morning Communion service. It was made plain that any woman who professed faith wore a head-covering in public worship. As long as my father was the settled minister, we sat conspicuously with my mother in the 'manse pew', the rear cross-pew to the left of the pulpit and the cynosure of all eyes – an early, intimidating training for small boys. To this day, I never have the least trouble in feigning rapt attention at a public event: we learned to sing like banshees (or risk severe consequences afterwards), to find the relevant chapter in the Pauline epistles before most of the office-bearers, to retire after the second singing to Sabbath School with the winsome smiles of minor royalty. It must in these first years have been a signal trial for my mother.

These were exciting developments on the back of deftly directed adjustment to changing times and new circumstances. But only a young pastor could have borne such gruelling arrangements: for much of the year, Donald Macleod effectively preached six times a week. Though the nature of his charge largely spared him the conduct of actual funeral services – almost all the Partick Highland deceased were buried on Lewis – he had besides frequent 'wakes', taking formal mid-evening worship after bereavement. There were a lot of weddings, especially in the summer. As a Highland minister in Glasgow besides, he was constantly telephoned – usually from Lewis – with demands to go and visit such-and-such in hospital (the one part of a minister's job which he is not really good at; he detests infirmaries) and for much of this pastorate, too, he had a tutorial role at Jordanhill College of Education (the Free Church having secured ongoing access to these establishments in the settlement of the 1900 dispute). For a time, too, he was interim-Moderator of the Drumchapel congregation. He seemed to be in even more demand on the Communion circuit and he was now being invited on the Reformed trail overseas, his first trip – to Pennsylvania – being his adventure in June 1974. There would be two more American jaunts before decade's end; a first outing to Australia in September 1976. He declined a call to the Free Church congregation in Aberdeen; earlier, he had also refused a curious offer from Dr Lloyd-Jones in London, to become Principal of his new Theological College in the capital.

That winter following, a certain unease seemed to linger in things and on Friday 4th February 1977 the congregation was devastated by the tragic death of a very young deacon, Donald MacDonald – *Dollan Late*, from Garrabost in Point, who could not be revived after what should have been a simple exploratory operation. He had married not eighteen months earlier. It was the first time I had seen either of my parents cry. All weekend, the manse seemed to seethe with the stunned and grieving; that Sabbath morning, expounding as best he could the Twenty-Third Psalm, my father repeatedly broke down in the pulpit. In hindsight, it seems almost a tipping-point, as if a bright morning had ended and only unease and upheaval could lie ahead.

With Principal W. J. Cameron retiring that summer, my father was under real pressure to accept nomination for the vacated Chair of Greek and New Testament. At the last moment he firmly withdrew – Rev. Archibald Boyd, minister of Oban, was appointed instead – but, on a tied vote and by decision of the Moderator (Rev. Kenneth J Nicolson, Barvas) my father was elected editor of the Free Church organ, the *Monthly Record*. It would considerably increase his workload (and his profile), but also gave him cover to break a connection he now found embarrassing: he shortly quit his role as an Associate Editor of the Banner of Truth Trust. The increasing cult of flattery and veneration about the ageing Lloyd-Jones irritated him – as it troubled the tough old fellow himself, though he was too diffident to do anything about it. My father was besides unhappy about curious new views 'The Doctor' now expounded on the call to the ministry, with more than a hint of a second 'Spirit baptism'; and my father thought his demand that Reformed ministers in 'theologically mixed' denominations secede into ill-defined, united evangelical fellowship both naive and overbearing. But no one had ever before walked away from the Trust; Macleod's departure was not counted to him for righteousness.

In 1978, though, the clamour to succeed Rev. Professor James Mackintosh in the Systematics department proved insurmountable. My father's anguish that spring cannot be understated. There is no joy as great in preaching and ministering to the same flock, year upon year, in mutually enriching relationship. We had all put down firm Glasgow roots. But a Free Church College appointment is in itself a pastoral charge in canon-law terms, to which one is inducted, and when a previous pastoral tie must be automatically severed. The pressure this time was irresistible, both within the family and within the great and the good of the Free Church, some most important people making plain that, if necessary, the General Assembly had it in its power to draft my father to the position by absolute and episcopal authority. In the face of such threats, he acceded and in May 1978 was decisively elected to the Chair of Systematic Theology by the General Assembly. The induction, delayed until the very eve of the College session as the retiring Mackintosh eked out every last possible hour of service, was on the Monday of our October Communion, and neither my mother nor ourselves could attend: my father scurried off in his car in the early evening, with the air of one helping the police with their inquiries.

My father genuinely believed he could successfully combine full-time pastoral ministry with Free Church College duties and for eighteen dreadful months did his best to do so, even as an interim-Moderator was appointed for Partick Highland, we fled the manse pew and the congregation bravely tried to call him back. Of this time, and its all-pervading unhappiness, the less said the better: in March 1980, we at last flitted to Edinburgh, downsizing wretchedly into an upstairs flat, my father forced to leave behind some of his most cherished things. In January 1982, a much more suitable townhouse was acquired in Morningside, and we made the best of the Scottish capital. By then, Rev. John Angus Gillies had been settled in Partick Highland: in the new century, and restored to its original name – Dowanvale Free Church – it has again witnessed growth and blessing.

The 1980s were a time of great encouragement for the Free Church of Scotland – new congregations, many new ministers, even growth in membership. But they were singularly unsettling years for my father. Rather late in life, he had to cope with such novelties as a mortgage and utility bills – and, with Britain in recession, unwonted new worries. As if to signal new beginnings, he discarded for ever his clerical collar: it had its last ever outing in July 1981, when he married his brother Murdo Iain in Stornoway. He had to adapt to life as a worshipper in the pews, after years in the pastoral ministry; and a considerable burden of 'supply' preaching, which went with his new job. Fortunately he was on excellent terms with Rev. Donald Lamont, his predecessor at Kilmallie and still minister of St Columba's, in a difficult pastoral situation and with not a few discouragements. Like most men in their forties, too, Donald Macleod had the typical strains of midlife – financial burdens; adolescent offspring who start to push determinedly at boundaries (though he maintains kindly we gave him very little trouble); elderly and increasingly vulnerable parents. The 1980s, too, were a decade of considerable travel, with several protracted jaunts to Australia, a genuinely shocking visit (in 1982) to apartheid South Africa; what remains his only trip to New Zealand; other North American trips and, in 1990, a memorable tour of post-revolutionary Romania.

These years are perhaps most vividly remembered for his editorship of the *Monthly Record*. One cannot recall these days without remembering all the morning mail – he received practically every denominational magazine in the English-speaking world, to say nothing of books for review and letters (frequently incandescent) for publication – or the long evenings at the dining-table, with great galley-proofs spread in all directions and the awful, giddying reek of Cow Gum, with which he slathered copy to the page. We eventually converted him to Pritt, but the actual assembly of the magazine – once proofs had been corrected and photographs chosen – was of majestic simplicity; he simply took an old copy of the *Monthly Record* and, with mighty scissors and his Cow Gum, stuck all the new material onto its pages in desired arrangement. This sticky offering was then delivered to the splendid printers, Lindsay & Co. of Dalry in Edinburgh; they would even accept hand-written copy, though reasonably asked that Gaelic content be typed. It is a sobering point, thirty years later and with all the technological wonders of today, that the lead-time was then far shorter – a few days, rather than weeks; misprints were rare in the extreme; and the magazine of, say, 1980, looked at now, is remarkably fresh and undated in appearance, its comment fearless, topical, and relevant.

It took him several years, though, to settle finally on a 'look' for the product, though one early reform – junked quickly by his successor – was to adopt an uncluttered two-column layout. He fast discarded the very dated and fussy cover, complete with a crawling thistle, the burning-bush logo and a verse of Scripture – though some vocally deplored the death of what they were pleased to call the 'Free Church motto and badge.' But he was never entirely happy with the result – especially the cover photograph 'bled off' at the bottom – and in 1982 adopted a striking new design, experimenting a little with colour before settling on a bold red cover-font in 1983.

He knew his constituency and, while determined to craft a product pitched essentially to the educated layman, cleverly kept those features appealing to little old ladies – the monthly 'league table' of congregational givings on the back cover, the General Treasurer's acknowledgement of private donations, and the monthly timetable of Communion seasons. My father determinedly reflected all strains of thought in the Free Church, regularly soliciting its most conservative ministers – Revs. Hugh Cartwright, Angus Smith and so on – to contribute articles. Nor was he afraid to publish stuff from beyond the denomination (Winnie Ewing, for instance, delivered a stimulating piece on Israel) and indeed from beyond the country. He refused to publish anonymous letters, but took sly pleasure in carrying the most ferocious attacks on himself, without feeling the need to append acres of defensive post-script: there was a reliable 'tidal effect', with plenty writing in the next month in doughty defence of the editor.

He quickly fashioned two distinct pulpits. The opening editorial – which he wrote himself, yielding only for the July/August issue to the Moderator's Address – was a lengthy, uncompromising essay on some great theme, usually theological, sometimes moral. The magazine had featured a cluttered section of topical discussion, called 'Notes and Comments', for as long as anyone could remember: this was now re-dubbed 'Focus', put right in the centre-spread of the magazine – where it could quickly be found by journalists – and was robust, hard-hitting and at times very funny; especially his lighter asides on, for instance, the hazards of Lothian buses, laden with '...forty human beings and a professor of theology'; the sad decline of Scottish football, with some stars 'sporting beer-bellies a darts player would be proud of'; and the thrawn behaviour of certain precentors, whose weakness for the *basso profundo*, he sighed, threatened to give him a double-chin.

He launched his reign in the July/August 1977 number with what remains a splendid (and still relevant) analysis of the Free Church and her witness, 'Peculiar People.' He quickly got used to the ways of the press, recovering from an early atrocity when a carefully crafted 2,000-word editorial on the Christian education of children – with one brief aside on the vulgarity creeping into their TV programmes – was headlined by *The Scotsman* as 'Free Church slams Basil Brush.' (He sent a pained note to the mortified editor, and a copy of the original article: the reporter was ordered in person to the Free Church College to apologise.)

Space does not unfortunately afford much coverage of these thirteen years. For most of his editorship – until overseas engagements and mounting frustration put him off it – he reported General Assembly proceedings himself, reclining on a cross-pew by the Clerk's table and taking reams of notes. In 1979 he was aghast when – with journalists hanging out of the gallery – the Assembly imprudently debated, at length and with some singularly ill-judged speeches, the propriety of women wearing trousers. Anticipating the imminent public-relations disaster, he actually appealed to the "house" – unsuccessfully – that the Moderator be overruled by majority vote and the discussion not proceed. 'I was never forgiven for it,' he recalled publicly in December 2010, 'but it was my right.' In 1980 he was not afraid publicly to deplore a personal attack on a Bishopbriggs minister by one Hebridean padre, who denounced the young pastor (who had slightly long hair and a neatly trimmed beard) as a 'caveman'; it was not so much the jibe itself (the clergyman in question being a notorious boor) as the disgraceful failure of the Moderator to intervene. The arrangements for the General Assembly itself – comprised of 'commissioners', usually only a quarter of all members of Presbytery, and with an established nomenclatura of ruling eminences returned year after year as 'assessors' for obscure corners of the Dominions – offended his sense of democracy: that, too, was voiced.

But the unabashed political comment, especially in the early years of the Thatcher government, caused the widest sensation. The real problem was, of course – for thousands of readers who had hitherto assumed Christian profession entailed lifelong support of the Conservative Party – was that he seemed to espouse the wrong politics. In fact, my father was not nearly as left-wing as many thought, or as he himself likes to believe. Until 1983 – when he cast his ballot for the SDP/Liberal Alliance – he had always voted Tory; when (in my view, imprudently) he publicly endorsed a Labour candidate in the Western Isles in 1992, he had never voted Labour in his life. Like the mass of Lewismen, marked by the appalling conditions of pre-war Scotland and their long hangover, he believed in strong welfare provision: but he also supported robust national defence, NATO membership and a British nuclear deterrent. He is besides a lifelong European, unhesitatingly voting for the Common Market in the 1975 referendum and refusing to have any truck with talk of withdrawal. He has besides been always a Unionist, with an intense and visceral dislike of the Scottish National Party.

In fact, his early collisions with the Free Presbytery of Lewis – a constant bugbear, at least till reorganisation and a new name in 2000 – both centred on politics. The Free Church on Lewis had close ties with the SNP and its Westminster leader, local MP Donald Stewart, and bewailed the *Record*'s call for a 'No' vote in the 1979 devolution referendum. More seriously, when massive military additions were proposed to Stornoway Airport – an extended runway and a large, permanent, manned presence – my father refused to have any truck with the 'Keep Nato Out Campaign', an unprecedented alliance of the local Labour Party, the SNP, the *West Highland Free Press* and the Free Church. He pointed out reasonably that one must either be against all defence installations in principle, which was sheer pacifism; or only support them as long as they were somewhere else, which was sheer selfishness. The Presbytery responded with ringing denunciations.

Almost more blistering was a flap in July 1983, shortly after the return of the Conservative government with an enormous Commons majority, when Parliament considered the restoration of capital punishment. As recently as 1979, my father had editorialised – with evident reluctance – in favour. By 1983, and especially on the terms proposed that summer, he was against. Even so, it would have attracted little attention had he not been scheduled to preach in Stornoway Free Church the Sabbath before the vote in Parliament and on a day when the Convener of the Free Church Public Questions Committee had issued – for all the world as if it were a Papal encyclical – a statement to be read from every pulpit in the land, ordering the faithful to lobby their MPs and bring back hanging. Donald Macleod flatly refused to read this proclamation, as did at least one other preacher that day, and they were amply within their rights to do so; but the press got hold of it, and there was much Free Church controversy.

There is no doubt that throughout this period my father's politics on many matters and in general party-identification shifted sharply. In some respects this was the knee-jerk reaction of many other Scotsmen of his time, as Malcolm Rifkind would ruefully observe, who were positively repelled by Thatcher and her style of government: 'Mrs Thatcher was a woman, an English woman and a bossy English woman; the Scots might have been able to cope with one of those traits, but not all three'. But there was also genuine alarm at what was being done to the country, new doctrinaire policies – and unforeseen fiscal consequences of the surge of North Sea oil – triggering a long and bitter recession that fell particularly hard on Scotland, overly reliant on ageing heavy industries that employed working-class men by the tens of thousands. In later years he has also paid tribute to the working men – members and adherents – of Partick Highland, who often spoke quietly to him of the real pastoral service they found from their shop-stewards and union officials (they even asserted that the Communists were most conscientious of all) and how they distrusted a Church that still regarded all industrial action as self-evidently wicked and generally reflected the politics of the *Daily Telegraph.*

Theirs was evidently a slow influence. My father had initially hailed the Conservative victory of 1979 with mild but obvious pleasure, bouncing into our bedroom to declare 'Maggie's in!' But he retained remarkable regard for her Tory predecessor, Edward Heath; and the final closure of the Wiggins Teape pulp-mill at Corpach in 1980 – it had been in evident difficulty for two years – hit him very personally. The Lochaber economy was, for years, all but eviscerated. Hundreds of men lost their jobs – many of whom he knew. One Kilmallie Free Church stalwart was forced to go to sea, away from his family for months at a time, to keep a roof over their heads. The cynicism of Wiggins Teape – handsomely funded for many years out of taxpayer funds in this enterprise – enraged him further: these sort of businessmen, perfectly happy with 'socialism for the rich', were, to him, Thatcher's people.

There were other tussles for Macleod as editor. One was the bleeding sore of Northern Ireland: though yielding to none in his contempt for the atrocities of the Provisional IRA, he did not hesitate to question the non-negotiable verities of Ulster Unionism and could not hide his disdain for the cod-Presbyterian pretensions of the Reverend Ian Paisley (who, genuinely stung, responded robustly). Much more remembered is the Macleod *Record* on apartheid South Africa: in the autumn of 1982, aghast at what he had seen there, he wrote a hard-hitting analysis, shocked at the fatuity of local believers who refused to support the liberal opposition party because of its stance on 'moral issues' and continued Free Church indifference. The Afrikaner is 'good to his dogs,' he observed, 'he cannot see that they are not dogs.'

The Free Church maintained an extensive mission field in what she persisted in calling 'Southern Africa', though hardly anyone else in the international community went along with Pretoria's fiction that the 'homelands' of Transkei, Ciskei and so on were autonomous countries. It seems, today, morally incredible that anyone could have disputed my father's verdict on a wicked system. But, though the Free Presbyterian Synod had unequivocally condemned apartheid as early as 1962, the Free Church had never done so. Many elders of that generation, not least on Lewis, spoke innocently but unashamedly of 'darkies'. In my own hearing, in 1977, one Free Church missionary in the veldt assured Partick Highland people that 'all blacks are thieves and liars.' The *Monthly Record* soon received – and published – letters from irate others in the field, accusing my father of meddling in matters he knew nothing about and speaking of South Africa's black majority in profoundly disturbing terms. It would be 1988 – by which time opinion everywhere, even in the Conservative Party, had turned decisively against the South African regime – before the General Assembly could bring itself even mildly to deplore this racist social order.

There was, besides, mounting tension with the Banner of Truth Trust. In March 1981, Dr Lloyd-Jones died. It was immediate cue for acres of lionising tribute in the evangelical press, much of it in self-serving 'I knew him well' vein; soon, the cult was blasphemous, with the *Evangelical Times* advertising Lloyd-Jones tapes and literature under the banner, 'APOSTLE AND PROPHET OF THE TWENTIETH CENTURY', complete with a Lloyd-Jones graphic that seemed even to include a halo. My father was in a difficult position when Iain H. Murray's wholly uncritical two-volume biography duly appeared. Again, the courteously phrased Macleod misgivings seem, a quarter-century on, unremarkable; but they aroused extraordinary fury.

My father also editorialised in 1982 against the bid to remove Norman Shepherd from faculty at Westminster Theological Seminary, ostensibly on the grounds of dubious doctrine, but directed not by the Church but powerful lay-trustees of the organisation. (In the event, and despite exoneration from heresy – though he had perhaps expressed himself unwisely – Shepherd was removed anyway and on the most dubious pretexts, finally assuming a pastorate.) Trust eminences were besides involved in still other unedifying campaigns, which also on occasion attracted fearless and trenchant comment from the *Monthly Record*.

These were but little local difficulties. The fact was that on a wider scale, in its freshness and topicality and – in terms of prevalent Free Church stereotype – unexpected perspective, the *Monthly Record* had won new status as a must-read publication, my father himself winning new confidence in dealing with journalists and becoming a frequent guest on radio and television. Not all welcomed such evidence of a broader Free Church world-view. In hindsight, the tide probably turned at the May 1986 General Assembly, when there was a most unfortunate opening Address from the new Moderator and an authoritarian resolution to consider denying membership to Freemasons. (The Free Church has always deplored the Craft, in no uncertain language; but alteration of the terms of communion is no light matter and the issue subsequently died a death.)

But the 1987 General Assembly was even worse, with a colourful account of the 'London Presbyterian Conference' in the March issue of the *Free Presbyterian Magazine* attributing sensational stances both to my father and to the London Free Church minister, Rev. John Nicholls, and new hysterics from the Free Presbytery of Lewis, who duly had an overture tabled at the Assembly demanding new and absolute homologation of 'purity of worship.' My father was already deeply worried about an emerging, neo-conservative Highland backlash – he saw it, rightly, as an ill-informed and witch-hunting variant of 'North Country Separatism', and gave very serious thought that year to quitting as editor of the *Monthly Record*. In the event, he served on until May 1990: it has always been his view not to occupy such a position too long, where judgement and perspective must finally falter. The magazine, in a landscape admittedly still more ungodly and where even the national Church of Scotland now struggles for coverage, has never recovered the stature or circulation of the 1980s.

My father has now served as Professor of Systematic Theology at the Free Church College for over three decades. The broad pattern of his working life has not greatly changed from his first session of classes between 1978 and 1979. As some competence in the Biblical languages is required for the two-year theology course, he has no first-year students. Classes are held in the mornings from Tuesday till Friday. He does not allow questions or interruption during a lecture, but provides ample opportunity for query and discussion at the end of a stipulated unit. He declined from the start to wear an academic gown – save for formal College events and the annual 'football-team' photograph of students and faculty – and has always, often to the disarray of his timetable and our occasional dismay as a family, kept an 'open door' policy for students or indeed anyone else who needs his help. Indeed, it is a chief reason for what remains his typical 12-hour day on the premises; only in the evening can he be sure of the time and peace to have written work done.

In 1978 – only two years after a massive refurbishment of the building's physical fabric – the College still had a quaint, dated air. Extraordinary little artefacts crammed drawers and cupboards in my father's office, amassed – it would seem – by every predecessor since 1900: a box of Victorian dissection knives, a packet of Waverley pen-nibs, fusty sermon notes and ancient lecture outlines. His office now boasts a majestic grandfather clock left to the Free Church by Principal MacCulloch; the Senate Room – one of the building's loveliest apartments – retains the couch where Principal John Kennedy Cameron in 1946 collapsed and expired. There is still in his office an open fire with a 'register' grate – though it is never lit; on the back of a closet door hangs a box with built-in mirror – this is where he is meant to store his wig, and powder it through the course of the day. Mighty oak desks – complete with inkwell, tip-up lid and stark plank seat – were the student furnishing in his classroom until 1987 – indeed, when they were finally removed, in December 1986, he characteristically insisted on helping to ferry them downstairs, tripped on a riser and painfully broke a couple of ribs. Much else has featured, over the years, that were scarcely in the job-description. The joiner's son still regularly takes in his tool-box to complete some quick repair job, practically anywhere in the building – a bent hinge, a dripping tap, a jamming cupboard – and, indeed, often in a student flat. He has been, as occasion demanded, a press liaison officer, a marriage-guidance counsellor, the source of medical advice, a canon-lawyer, a *pastor pastorum*, a children's entertainer, a special constable, a stretcher-bearer, a computer consultant and Bob the Builder. He has besides, since 1982, served as College Librarian, another opportunity to make the most of his eye for organisation. Much of this fell on Macleod because, in the early years, he was not only the most practical of the professors but significantly the youngest. In 1978, he had broken bread and shared Senate counsel with the wry and engaging Principal Clement Graham (Apologetics and Pastoral Theology), the regal Collins – who finally retired in his eighty-second year, Professor of Church History and Church Principles; the waspish Professor James Fraser (Hebrew and Old Testament) who retired months before his death in 1983; and the gentle Professor 'Archie' Boyd (Greek and New Testament). Boyd's death in 2008, shortly after the passing of the inimitable Graham, left my father the wistful and sole survivor of that College generation.

He has been at it so long that he has trained all but three Free

Church ministers currently serving. He has adapted readily to new expectations – computer provision, private study space, vast quantities of printed hand-outs to supplement scrawled lecture notes. He has faced new pressures – the perils of student plagiarism, for instance, in the age of the Internet; is pleased by some improvements – the standard of written work is far better than it was in the 1980s, as Scottish schools have moved back to more traditional teaching methods – and troubled by other, much more witless winds of change.

One constant problem has been a sustained hostility to the College by elements within the Free Church herself, though it has yet to become an overwhelming threat and, at its last high tide at the 2005 General Assembly, the threat of yet another 'review' at the direction of an office-bearer who himself sat on the board of a competing Scottish institution was neutralised by deft politics. My father's boyhood minister, Kenneth MacRae, must take some blame; in his 1950s tussles with Professors A. M. Renwick and R. A. Finlayson over the Billy Graham crusade and other issues, he sowed the abiding impression on Lewis that the College was a nest of innovation, sedition and potential heresy. Many ministers of a past generation bore continued resentment after arduous College training. More recently, local empire-building has become a factor – an ill-judged scheme to restructure Free Church finances, to the disadvantage of small and especially rural congregations; or the fad for full-time workers and assistant ministers. And there are always the pietists, who maintain the building is both hugely valuable and most costly to run: that it should all be sold off, that the proceedings be presumably given to the poor, and the whole enterprise no doubt relocated in a bunch of Portakabins in Invergordon. (That the Free Church would thereby squander a priceless chunk of its own history, lose an asset against which important funds are secured, and forsake a most visible presence in the Scottish capital seems to elude them.)

Now my father is simply not one of nature's politicians. He has never had a faction, or consciously cultivated a policy, and has posi-tively discouraged any following by students: he does not, for instance, attend ordinations and inductions (though he always sends a message). My brothers and I occasionally joke he has no friends. In fact he has a very few and trusted people with whom he keeps in close if very quiet touch: the point is that he has no cronies, and the ministers he was closest to – Rev. J. Douglas MacMillan and Rev. Murdo Alick MacLeod – are both dead, as is the nearest he ever had to a mentor

in the Free Church, Rev. Angus Finlayson of North Tolsta, who often
and ferociously stuck up for him. He also learned, long ago, that very,
very few people are worthy of trust.

The College has survived because of the increasing respect it has
won beyond the Free Church, especially when even the Church of
Scotland now struggles to identify credible arrangements for training
her ministers as faculties of divinity wither from modernism into
irrelevance; and because of the marked improvement in the standard
of preaching in recent decades, not least after the belated abolition of
the unduly lenient 'modified course.' It is the last in Britain to have
compulsory training in Hebrew for would-be ministers and one of
the very few still teaching elementary Greek. For many years, too, my
father has fought to open it up to Free Church people and encourage
close engagement by the wider church. It was at his instigation that
grand College occasions – the opening and closing of sessions –
became intimated, public events. It was also his idea – now widespread
– that the licensing of students by Presbytery be done publicly. He has
also fought to reduce the burden on Free Church funds, arguing from
1982 that four Professors were all the institution needed, rather than
five. He himself quietly took on the burden of the Church History
course after the departure of Rev. Professor Hugh Cartwright in
1998 and, though Rev. John McIntosh was eventually appointed to
revive that chair in 2006, the department of Apologetics and Practical
Theology has now in turn been suspended and my father has assumed
the teaching of Homiletics.

In 1999, he was decisively elected Principal by the General
Assembly. There had been yet another review and restructuring and
he was in fact the first Principal simply to be appointed, not inducted.
Yet the post was more onerous than ever, with many more duties and
new responsibilities, though with no significant augmentation in pay,
no new office, and not even his own secretary. (There is a College
Secretary to serve the whole institution, but the secretary throughout
my father's years as Principal was frequently absent through ill-health.)
The new Principal Macleod not only chaired the Senate and reported
to the College Board, but opened mail and stuffed envelopes. The new,
remorseless facility of email only increased his toils.

He has also, in a decade at the top, worked hard to win overseas
students; battled fatuous new Government bureaucracy (especially the
daft 'validation' scheme imposed, at great cost on private educational

institutions, by the London government) – and his most important achievement was to win degree-validated status with the University of Glasgow, after a similar deal with the University of Edinburgh was torpedoed at the eleventh hour. He had already, in 1999, been appointed a Visiting Professor at his *alma mater*, though the honour that meant most to him (and still more to us as a family) was the Doctorate of Divinity conferred on him by Westminster Theological Seminary in 2008, the first such award from a credible institution to a Free Church minister in over half a century. 'Town and gown' endeavours with the wider Free Church continued and expanded, most notably with a part-time theology course for laity, taught roughly on Open University lines with the monthly use of video-link from Saturday diets at the College to centres like Stornoway and Inverness. (His new colleague, Rev. Professor John Angus MacLeod, who took up the Greek and New Testament tuition in 1999, has been a vital asset: MacLeod is relaxed and expert in the necessary technology.)

My father may have left the pastoral ministry thirty years ago. And he retired as College Principal in May 2010, while remaining in harness as Professor of Systematic Theology. But that work has not ceased: his students apart, he has been involved in helping a variety of people, some in particularly trying situations and in one or two cases over many years. There have also been a surprising number of calls to resume a pastoral charge, the approaches including St Vincent Street, Glasgow (1983), Greyfriars in Inverness (1984), St Columba's (1988) and Buccleuch (1992, while he was serving as interim-Moderator after Douglas MacMillan's early death in August the previous year). He left it to the General Assembly in 1983 to dismiss a call to the St George's (Sydney) congregation of the Presbyterian Church of Eastern Australia, and never felt able to accede to Bon Accord Free Church in Aberdeen, who tried three times to secure his ministry in over twenty years. Probably most painful of all was the bid of the Partick Highland people to win him back in 1980, though it is most unlikely he would have been allowed to accept it. He discouraged an optimistic attempt from one Church of Scotland charge late in 1996; the last approach of all, when he was already sixty-one, was informal and from the Barvas congregation in rural Lewis, in 2002.

A conscientiously assumed work-load, frequent preaching duties and continued murderous hours have entailed much sacrifice. Fortunately my father has the constitution of an ox: he has only twice, in my entire recollection, ever been forced to bed by an illness, the last occasion in 1992. But it is hard not to feel he could have written a great deal more from the less overwhelming circumstances of a parish ministry. Most of his scholarly writing has been in learned journals and it was almost the present century before he produced a major, original book – *The Person of Christ*, in 1998. Practically everything else has been compiled from earlier duties: *From Glory to Golgotha*, for instance (2002) was a collection of theological editorials from the *Monthly Record*; and the popular *A Faith to Live By* (1999) – a most lucid and accessible volume of systematic theology, pitched to lay-people – was born as long series of eagerly anticipated lectures at two Free Church congregations. The first edition of *The Trinity and the Fellowship of God's People*, over twenty years ago, included (with his less than enthusiastic approval) some remarkable cartoons ('Nicaea Welcomes Wise Bishops'!) and had one humourless evangelical publication in hysterics. Being spared and well, the years to come will afford much more time for authorship. Meanwhile, since 1993, he has enjoyed a weekly column in the *West Highland Free Press*, and contributes occasionally to national newspapers

Within the family, we perhaps most regret how little time he has enjoyed over many years for private recreation. He used wistfully to cite as his hobbies under a *Who's Who in Scotland* entry, 'Dreaming of cricket, fishing and gardening.' He is rarely able to spend more than a fortnight a year on Lewis, almost invariably the cue for the death and unavoidable funeral of a relative or prominent ecclesiastical personality, and seldom without an unexpected preaching engagement. Even in my Glasgow childhood, family holidays were twice unexpectedly cut short by word of a pastoral emergency back home: cue, deaf to protests and enraged small boys, for the car to be loaded and booked on the ferry. Today I quietly fixed a light-fitting downstairs in my parents' Edinburgh home: it had been broken for months, unnoticed, though he would have dropped everything to go and mend a sink in a student's flat. Last summer I could not find his electric hedge-trimmer; it had been left at Livingston Free Church. He is constantly lending out books to people who never return them; on occasion, he has kindly donated even some of my own. My father is not the only minister who vaunts the 'servant mentality'; he is almost the last of the generation who actually practised it.

My father plans, the Lord willing, to serve out his time as Professor of Systematic Theology, which will take him to May 2011, followed by a last bolstering year with the senior class. Writing up the day's doings during an Edinburgh visit in November 2002, I noted that he "returned shortly before eight o'clock this evening, after a day's duties as an external examiner at the Highland Theological College – leaving at 7am this morning to drive to Dingwall and back. Last week, he conducted Communion services at Buccleuch Free Church; a week ago, he spent a long evening at New College, and the previous Friday – another day-trip – he gave an evening lecture at Inverness. These commitments, executed flawlessly and with his usual indefatigable energy, were on top of all his normal duties and, like all his speaking or preaching engagements (College lectures apart, I am told) were delivered without notes. He will be out of the house tomorrow, as usual, by 8.30 in the morning, weeks into his seventieth year".

He has already outlived many of his contemporaries, from Laxdale school-fellows to ordinands of the 1960s to students – like the late Rev. Callum Matheson – he himself trained. He has lived through a world war, decades of unprecedented social change, and from a time of booming churches and highly respected parish ministers to a new, devolved Scottish order, increasingly, aggressively anti-Christian. Within the Free Church – where his point of view is too often discounted and where a restless new generation occasionally give the impression they can scarcely wait till he goes – he sometimes muses, in rueful humour, that he managed to go from dangerous young upstart to ageing has-been without ever consciously enjoying an unchallenged prime. He regrets the passing of the ministers of a former day, the old war-veterans and deeply exercised Highlanders – they had 'class', he says – and also the continued decline of a robust and intelligent eldership. Certain trends emerging in the Free Church, in the continued imbalance since the 2000 secession, trouble him greatly: the primacy of preaching is increasingly discounted, the American business-influenced model of local church management is too frequently extolled, and there is a casual lawlessness – an antinomianism – taking hold among the professing of all churches.

We cannot afford, he mused publicly in July 2009, leaders who think they are part-time; members who think it is more important to be cool than to be godly. But then Donald Macleod will shake his head, and remember his own grandfather, and his inveterate pessimism, and chuckle. We cannot tempt Providence. It may be that my father's best years on earth lie ahead of him. He himself, reviewing all, would have but one sombre thought: '...we are unprofitable servants: we have done that which was our duty to do.'

Bibliographical

2

Footnotes Columnist in
The West Highland Free Press

Brian Wilson

The first-ever issue of the *West Highland Free Press* contained an article entitled 'The Birth of a Newspaper' by Tom Hopkinson, editor of the war-time *Picture Post* and one of the great men of British journalism. By then, Tom ran the postgraduate journalism course at University College, Cardiff, which I attended.

Drawing on the example of Berrow's *Worcester Journal*, first published in 1690, Tom attributed the life prospects of a newspaper to the tolerance of its readers. 'Above all,' he wrote, 'they did not expect to agree with every word they read. They looked for honesty of expression rather than tame conformity, showing a certain largeness of mind in allowing the newspaper, and other readers, to differ from themselves.'

That is the basis on which the *West Highland Free Press* has always proceeded and is indeed why it has survived. Better to be disagreed with than to have no opinion and fortunately our readers have exercised the generosity of spirit required to take the same view. According to exactly the same principle, the *Free Press* has always encouraged diversity of opinion within our columns and only those who have never read it could maintain otherwise.

It was against this background that we recruited the distinguished Professor Donald Macleod to the ranks of our columnists in 1991. The title of the column did not take long to devise, given the great man's universally acknowledged nickname. Equally, there was no remit. We did not ask him to write about religion or not to write about religion, though it would have been pretty odd to expect the latter. Neither did we suggest to him that there was some particular political line to follow, either in general or on any particular subject. And for almost twenty years, he has followed that lack of direction to the letter!

The idea of inviting him to become a columnist arose, of course, from his previous incarnation as Editor of the *Free Church Monthly Record* which had become required reading in the newsrooms of Scotland for the trenchant and sometimes counter-intuitive pronouncements contained in its editorial column. For most of us, this was the first introduction to Donald Macleod as a journalist and the pattern was clearly set. Whatever the subject he wrote on, temporal or theological, challenging views and intellectual stimulation were guaranteed. And his economical, evocative use of the English language was superb.

It would be disingenuous to pretend that, by 1991, Donald's espousal of the Labour cause at recent General Elections did not encourage the decision to invite him to write for the *Free Press*. However, it would be equally wrong to over-state this consideration since it was all along clear that he was also capable of being highly critical when the occasion demanded. And so it has transpired. His regular readers have shared in the highs and lows of optimism and dissent as he has dissected, with unfailing intellectual rigour if not always entirely consistent conclusions from week to week, the politics of these past two decades. But then, as he wrote himself: 'My late teacher, Professor R.A. Finlayson, often took refuge in the dictum: "Consistency is a virtue of small minds".'

What was in it for Donald Macleod to maintain this prodigious output in the columns of the *West Highland Free Press*? I am sure that some of his co-religionists would have disapproved of the setting, even if they had never read the paper. But Donald was never troubled by that for he had read the paper and understood the point about diversity of opinion – which embraced unfailing respect for the beliefs of others. I think that it was precisely because of the paper's role as a literate forum for public debate, tinged with a radical agenda of its own, that he felt at home in it. And for someone with his abilities as a writer, it would have been remiss not to share those talents with a wider audience than the one that his own principal vocation offered.

The other strength of the *Free Press* as a platform for Donald was that it provided him with a Hebridean, largely Gaelic, audience. For although he has lived for many years in Edinburgh, one of Donald Macleod's great strengths as a writer is that he has never lost touch with his roots and feels a deep need to continually cultivate them. Many of his finest columns in the Free Press have not been opinionated to any significant extent; rather, they have drawn on his knowledge and love of the place and the culture that made him what he is.

Columnists who deal only in polemic invariably turn into bores and they also run out of easy subjects on which to opinionate. One of the great strengths of Donald Macleod's writing is that he constantly informs and educates as well as provoking thought and fresh analysis. Whether he is writing about Scotland's religious heritage, the great issue of the day or the social and cultural forces that helped to forge the present-day Hebridean communities, he always manages to bring new insights and erudition to subjects that might not otherwise be of interest to the reader.

I spent a day in Stornoway Library going through some of his old columns and found myself spoilt for choice in what to quote here, in order to illustrate the qualities that I describe. But try this extract from a column about the death of Princess Diana in 1997; a subject on which billions of pointless words were expended. But few succeeded, in the space of a few short sentences, in saying more about the circumstances of her death and the hypocrisies that surrounded it:

> The nation will bury her on Saturday and the occasion will doubtless be cathartic. Let's not forget however that we are present only by courtesy of the Spencers. They must have been sorely tempted to keep her to themselves. Her former husband has no right to her; he divorced. The Queen-in-Parliament has no right to her: it stripped her of her title. The Establishment has no right to her; it loathed her. The public have no right to her; our tabloid voyeurism destroyed her.

Many tried, but nobody said the same thing better in a hundred times more words! At a more local level, something similar could be said of how he summarised the debate about poaching (which, for the benefit of younger readers, was still a very big issue on Lewis of the 1990s):

> Until I have a lobotomy, I will never be persuaded that poaching is a crime or even a sin... Nature decreed that the advantage of living in

London was that you could make money and the advantage of living in Balallan was that you could eat venison. The British Establishment has over-ruled nature. London shall have both the money and the venison; Balallan is to have neither.

Or how about this reflection on the state of Gaelic? I have often tried to make the point that the fate of the language is irredeemably connected to the state of the economy and the impact that has on the demographics of the Gaelic heartlands. But compare that clumsy piece of phrase-making with Donald's version, written in 1994:

> Why is there no Gaelic on Scarp? Is it because there are no Gaelic-medium schools? Or because it cannot receive 'Machair'? Or because the church services are in English? No! It is because there are no people there. The community has been destroyed. And the same tale can be told a thousand times.... The culture can be saved only by saving the economy.

Donald often brings knowledge to bear on religious affairs, both current and historical, which are only vaguely known about by the lay reader and indeed by many who might have a more direct interest. For example, I have often heard about the Lewis Revival of the 1950s but awareness of its existence was about the extent of my knowledge. In 2004, Donald MacLeod devoted a column to the separation of facts and fictions. A few paragraphs brought the whole episode to life and revealed a scepticism which must undoubtedly have existed at the time but had become lost in more prosaic accounts. Writing of Duncan Campbell, a Faith Mission figure who was central to the Revival, Donald wrote:

> What Campbell brought was a new religion; preaching that majored on sin and judgement; late-night cottage meetings that began at 10 p.m. and sometimes went on till six in the morning; lorry-loads and bus-loads of groupies who followed the preacher everywhere; people swooning and groaning and going rigid and falling into trances and singing on the shore in the dead of night; a constant eye to statistics regularly reporting to Headquarters the number of conversions and professions; and a whole new language as unknown to the Bible as it is to the Highland pulpit.

Thus, in a single, brilliant paragraph, Donald Macleod summoned up extraordinary images of a period which some of his readers must have lived through and taken an active part in. A distant episode in local church history is brought to life and all sorts of questions raised. How widely was such scepticism shared? Do those who still speak in hushed tones of a Lewis Revival acknowledge the problematic aspects of the last one? There is a movie in this; not just a column. And the great thing about having a writer of Donald Macleod's calibre delving into the past, without sentiment or indeed any desire to avoid controversy, is that knowledge can be shared, curiosity stimulated and myths debunked or indeed defended.

It has long surprised me that no larger circulation newspaper in Scotland has tried to secure Donald Macleod's services on a regular basis. He is, after all, by far the most literate and stimulating columnist writing in the Scottish press. The only other newspaper that gives him regular space is *The Observer* which sets him and a few other philosophers some great moral issue of the hour to confront. It is a sad comment on standards of debate within Scotland that no such outlets, either in the printed or broadcast media, seem to exist within our parochial borders.

Of course, it is not all one way traffic having Donald as a columnist. I am sure many people only buy the *Free Press* because he is there. There are also some who do not buy it for the same reason! Of such are the schisms of Scottish Presbyterianism. There was also the case of a recently-arrived Catholic priest in the islands who took offence at an article Donald wrote about the views of the Pope on some matter or other. The offended cleric urged his flock to abstain from buying the *Free Press* and was lobbying for a wider boycott unless Footnotes was dropped. Wiser counsels prevailed but of course the best response would be for someone to start writing as literately, as cogently and as regularly from another perspective, rather than trying to suppress the one that is already there. There just aren't many of them about.

My somewhat reverential view of Donald Macleod and his writings in the Free Press have been built up over two decades but it is always good to check perceptions against current reality. So I looked at his most recent column at time of writing. And it stands up to the test; a defence of fish farming in Broad Bay, but a lot more than that. Evocative memories of childhood; hard-hitting reflection on the irony of Lewis's talent for bemoaning unemployment but turning away economic opportunities; and a quote from Henry Cockburn about things not getting done because it was right or abolished because it was wrong. 'Things get done and things get abolished only when there is a clamour.'

I hope that Donald Macleod will continue to share his insights and erudition for many years to come. Journalism will always be a secondary calling but it is one which he has graced with substance and style. *The West Highland Free Press* and its readers have been the fortunate beneficiaries.

3

Editor of *The Monthly Record*

Iain D. Campbell

Donald Macleod's tenure as editor of the monthly magazine of his denomination, a post which he held from 1977 until 1990, earned him a place among the leading social and religious commentators and columnists of the turbulent 1980s; yet it almost never happened. Two names were proposed to the General Assembly of 1977 to fill the vacancy of Editor of *The Monthly Record of the Free Church of Scotland*, and the Assembly's vote was evenly divided between the two men. It was the acting Moderator who cast his deciding vote in favour of Donald Macleod, a remarkable instance of God's fixed will establishing the contingency of second causes!

From the outset, Donald's pen was used in two distinctive ways in the magazine, as he both spoke *to* the church and *for* the church. On the one hand there were the editorials, ranging from subjects as diverse as anti-intellectualism to apartheid, textual criticism to Spirit baptism, the nature of Christ to the nature of the ministry. Many of us cherished the theological articles as textbooks second to none while theological students in Donald's classroom, and have been delighted to see some of the editorials re-published in books such as *From Glory to Golgotha* and *A Faith To Live By*.

On the other hand there was 'Focus', the column – usually spread over two pages – in which the church and the world came in for incisive, and not always constructive, criticism. This was the forum for the expression of Donald's political views in the 1980s, in the era of Thatcher, unemployment, Northern Ireland and strikes. One did not always agree with Donald's conclusions, but one always admired the breadth of knowledge and the grasp of world affairs which enabled him to see more deeply than many, and one always came away wishing one could write with such an expressive command of the English language.

The first editorial, in the July/August 1977 edition of *The Monthly Record*, was entitled 'Peculiar People', and was, in effect, a statement on the distinctives of the Free Church – a church, Donald argued, with a peculiar theology, a peculiar form of worship and a peculiar form of discipline. Such peculiarities, in his view, determined our relations with other churches, but also required critical self-evaluation from within. The gauntlet was laid down from the outset: an appreciation of the church's tradition, and a readiness to critique her in the light of the tradition were to be stock in trade under Donald's editorship. Arguably no-one has done either so thoroughly or so painstakingly. I doubt that Donald could write the same article thirty years on – but that is no bad thing for a radical theologian in the best sense.

In the same edition, 'Focus' alluded to the call of R.T. Kendall to Westminster Chapel, the opening of London Theological Seminary, the Biblical Creation Society, the training of Roman Catholic teachers and Bothans (a Gaelic word, pronounced 'bo-hans', meaning illegal drinking dens, for which the Isle of Lewis was once notorious). The comments were well thought out and the conclusions incontrovertible, but the polemical edge was beginning to show itself.

Donald's expertise and wide-ranging familiarity with the field of theology was evident in early editorials of *The Monthly Record*. Critiques appeared of John Hick's *The Myth of God Incarnate* (October 1977) and James Barr's *Fundamentalism* (December 1977) – as might have been expected. But the unexpected came with a critique of Lloyd-Jones' views on the sealing of the Spirit (January 1979) – an article which provoked a variety of responses, as the 'Letters to the Editor' in March of that year demonstrated.

But Donald had his heroes too. One was John Murray of Westminster Theological Seminary. I have never forgotten, and have cited often, the closing sentence of his editorial review of the publication of Volume 3 of Murray's *Collected Writings* (March 1983). Donald had spoken with quiet majesty on the testimony of Murray's life to the grace of God, and concluded with the words, 'In its combination of humility and grandeur it had an almost revelatory quality, so that when doubt insinuates itself – Can it all be true? – one can still hear a voice that says, If not, how then do you account for John Murray?' (March 1983, p. 53). It was the touch of the consummate writer, reminding us that we are all standing on the shoulders of the giants of the past.

Yet often, for Donald, that was the question he longed to hear his own church ask. Who are the heroes? The question was raised, and well answered, in an editorial on 'Our Fathers, where are they?' Noting that the centenary of John Kennedy (Dingwall)'s death had recently passed, Donald pressed the point that the tradition of Highland evangelical spirituality could not stop at Kennedy – it had to go much further back than that: 'if we want to know what "the Fathers" taught, it is not enough to consult John Kennedy and Lachlan Mackenzie, great men of God though they undoubtedly were. We have to listen also to Tertullian, Athanasius, Augustine, Luther, Calvin and many others' (May 1984, p. 100). It was possible, of course, to revere the past – at that level no-one has been more traditional than Donald Macleod – but, in his own words, 'this praising of times past is essentially a ministry of discouragement. Its real interest is not so much to praise God for former days as to denigrate the present' (p. 101). At that level, no-one more than Donald has been more concerned to develop the tradition and make it relevant for the present, effectively critiquing it from within.

That, however, was never an easy thing to do. By his own admission[1] one of the loneliest stands he took was questioning the ethical and scriptural basis for capital punishment. 'So much reasonable doubt now attaches to our judicial system as a whole,' he wrote in 'Focus' in September 1983, 'that the certainty necessary to launch a soul into eternity is unattainable. Our major premise, "It is right to hang murderers", stands at best on only one text. Our minor premise, "This man is a murderer", rests on the eloquence of counsel and the diets of juries.... Hanging is now a dead issue. We hope it will stay dead' (p. 193).

The following editions carried strong letters, from Scotland, England, Ireland, and Canada against these views. That Donald

---

[1] Speaking on a Gaelic documentary programme about his life and work ('Freumhan', Corran Media and MG Alba, broadcast October 2009).

was willing to publish hostile correspondence without comment is a credit to his magnanimity as editor; but the strength of the opposition was not insignificant. The fact that he was perceived as an iconoclast, destroying long-cherished views, led to an increasing marginalisation of the editor by some sections of his denomination. It one thing to preach winsomely and persuasively in the pulpit, as he had done, and continued to do; it was another entirely – and too much for some – to commit to print perspectives that ran counter to the received wisdom.

The maturity and strength of Donald's standing as a theologian was demonstrated in the responses from men of stature, such as Professor Torrance, who was clearly ruffled by Donald's insistence in October 1983 that the Kirk should define the substance of the faith (without such a definition, Donald had written, 'the people of the Church of Scotland have no protection from irresponsible theological whizz-kids', p. 217). Torrance responded with a letter birthed in apoplexy: 'my position is that the Kirk adheres to and must adhere to the Declaratory Articles where the Reformed and Protestant character of the Kirk is safeguarded' (December 1983, p. 273). Of course, Torrance never did answer Donald's question – what *is* the substance of the faith?

The cleavage between Scotland's premier theologians also came to a head over one of Donald's editorials – in my mind, the best thing he ever wrote – on 'Did Christ have a fallen human nature?' (March 1984). Arguing that 'fallenness' and 'sinfulness' are co-relative, and that fallenness is no part of the definition of humanness, Donald argued that 'to say that Adam had a fallen nature is to say that Adam was fallen. The same logic must apply to Christ. If He had a nature that was fallen, then He Himself was fallen' (p. 53). Torrance, in turn, in a letter in May 1984, accused Donald of missing the important elements of the Christological tradition, of raising a man of straw, and of domesticating Roman Catholic dogma within the Free Church! This was, however, no mere academic debate, and bore witness both to the fact that Donald's views attracted comment at the highest levels of academic theology, and also to the fact that few could equal him at the level of intuitive Calvinism.

But there were other issues. The teachers' strike in 1985 brought scathing criticism from the editor – 'when schools close through industrial action we can do nothing. We can only try, by the grace of God, to control the mounting fury generated by the crime committed against our children' (March 1985, p. 61). Mounting fury was also evident when attempts were made to outlaw Freemasonry with overtures to the Assembly which would make it impossible for freemasons to be church members. Donald's response was devastating: 'blithely, and without the least sense of crisis, we are changing the terms of communion ... what other amendments will our poor Constitution have to suffer as we pass detailed legislation to ensure that we've covered everything people disapprove of, from "outsiders" to clerical collars and NIVs?' (November 1986, p. 248).

The same criticism was applied to Dutch Reformed support for apartheid, with lessons drawn from Scotland's own past: 'Apartheid is a disgrace to Calvinism, and the rest of us have no right to feed Christianity to the Bantu as an opiate to keep them content. If the Scottish Highlands had risen in rebellion against the Clearances they would have been fully justified' (January 1987, p. 13). Donald's comments on the situation in Ulster was also bound to provoke deep feelings of resentment. His stated wish that 'the clergy would get out of politics' (December 1987, p. 268) was more than a dig at Iain Paisley – it was a recognition that although Ireland's problems had a religious dimension, it was not clear, then or now, 'to what extent the Irish conflict is a religious one'.

These opinions were not always welcome; they were, however, always informed, always germane and never ignored. Donald's was a voice from within the Free Church which demonstrated that Calvinism was not only a theology but a worldview. As such, there was no area beyond the reach of theology, and no theology beyond the critique of the Bible.

One of Donald's last editorials was entitled 'Scotland's Greatest Theologian', an excursus into the life and legacy of William Cunningham. Second to none, in Donald's view, as a systematiser of biblical truth, Cunningham never recovered from the College Controversy. Cunningham's view that the Free Church should have only one theological college lost out to Candlish's policy of theological colleges in each of Scotland's major cities. Cunningham felt rejected and isolated, but, Donald wrote, he was wrong; 'not wrong about the issues, but wrong about the Church's attitude to him' (March 1990, p. 52). It could almost have been a self-description; in later years, when Donald felt most isolated, many within the Church would have described *him* as Scotland's greatest theologian. Certainly, within Scotland's galaxy of theological minds, I have no doubt that Donald most resembled Cunningham, even as he drew some of his greatest inspiration from him.

And who can forget his final editorial in June 1990 on 'Heaven', with its great description of the place where we shall live *with* Christ and shall live *in* Christ: 'here the participation is partial, limited by the weakness of our own faith. But ultimately it will be carried to the highest conceivable (and even inconceivable) level of perfection ... Every need is met. Every longing is fulfilled. Every goal is achieved. Every sense is satisfied. We see him. We are with him. He holds us and hugs us and whispers "This is for ever"' (pp. 123, 125). And with wit to match the sublimity of these thoughts, he bowed out with the lines, 'For ourself, the last thirteen years have been an adventure we would not have missed. For some sections of the Church, however, they have been a sore trial and these good people deserve a rest. To Mr Christie [his successor], then, Welcome. From we, Goodbye' (p. 133).

In October 1983, Focus carried a witty piece on why the editor referred to himself in the first person plural. Prompted by a letter in the issue, Donald wrote: 'Curiously, not all agree with us ... We are a humanist. We engage in political comment. We use irony. But these are as nothing compared with the most damaging accusation of all. We call ourself *we*. Why?' (p. 216).

Donald's answer to the question is superb: 'The *we* is a symbol of the fact that all editorship is pretentiousness; and that this editor knows it. Inside the man who writes Focus is another man who thinks the editor is ridiculous. *We* is an invitation to smile at a man who attempts to put the universe right in 2000 words per month' (p. 217). He continued: 'But not only at that man. A church which produces an endless succession of oracular reports, recommendations, findings and pronouncements must always call itself *we*: because before God we are always not only sinful but ridiculous.'

This was penmanship and literary artistry at its best: a critical eye cast on others, but always first at himself. Perhaps Donald's thousands of words didn't quite put the universe right, but it made a generation of Christian readers think twice about why they believed what they believed. I doubt that Donald would have wished for anything else.

4

Writings of Donald Macleod

Martin Cameron

Books

Hold Fast Your Confession: Studies in Church Principles [Editor] (Edinburgh: Knox Press, 1978).

The Spirit of Promise (Tain: Christian Focus Publications, 1986).

Shared Life: the Trinity and the Fellowship of God's People (London: Scripture Union, 1987; Fearn: Christian Focus, 1994; Jackson: Reformed Academic Press).

Rome and Canterbury: a view from Geneva (Fearn: Christian Focus Publications, 1989).

Behold Your God (Fearn: Christian Focus, 1990. Revised edition, 1995).

The Humiliated and Exalted Lord: a study of Philippians 2 and Christology (Jackson: Reformed Academic Press, 1993).

A Faith to Live By: understanding Christian Doctrine (Fearn: Mentor, 1998; expanded edition, 2002, 2010).

The Person of Christ (Leicester: InterVarsity Press, 1998).

Jesus is Lord: Christology Yesterday and Today (Fearn: Mentor, 2000).

From Glory to Golgotha: controversial issues in the life of Christ (Fearn: Christian Focus, 2002).

Priorities for the Church: rediscovering leadership and vision in the church (Fearn: Christian Focus, 2003).

The Living Past (Stornoway: Acair, 2006).

Calvinism, Literature and the Imagination (Stornoway: Islands Book Trust, 2009).

Contributions to other books

'Luther and Calvin on the place of Law' in *Living the Christian Life*, Westminster Conference, 1974.

'The thorn in the flesh' in *So We Preach* (ed. William D. Graham, Edinburgh: Knox Press, 1976).

'Preaching and Systematic Theology' in *Preaching: the Preacher and Preaching in the Twentieth Century* (ed. S. T. Logan, Welwyn: Evangelical Press, 1986).

'Testimony' in *He Found Me*: ten Christians tell how they met the Lord Jesus (Fearn: Christian Focus, 1991).

'Thomas Chalmers and Pauperism in Scotland in the Age of Disruption' (eds. Stewart J Brown and Michael Fry, Edinburgh: Edinburgh University Press, 1993).

In *Dictionary of Scottish Church History & Theology* (Organizing Editor, Nigel Cameron), Edinburgh, T & T Clark, 1993: articles on the Atonement, Christology, Covenant Theology, William Cunningham, Justification, and Systematic Theology.

'Hugh Miller, the Disruption and the Free Church of Scotland' in *Hugh Miller and the Controversies of Victorian Science* (ed. Michael Shortland, Oxford: Oxford University Press, 1996).

'Free Church College 1900-1970' in *Disruption to Diversity: Edinburgh Divinity 1846-1996* (eds. David F Wright, Gary D Badcock, Edinburgh: T&T Clark, 1996).

'The Highland Churches Today' in *The Church in the Highlands* (ed. James Kirk, Edinburgh: Scottish Church History Society, 1998).

'Calvin into Hippolytus' in *To Glorify God: essays on modern Reformed theology* (eds. B. Spinks and I. Torrance, Grand Rapids: Eerdmans, 1999).

'The Christology of Chalcedon' in *The Only Hope: Jesus, Yesterday, Today, Forever* (eds. Mark Elliott and John L. McPake, Fearn: Christian Focus Publications, 2001).

'Jesus and Scripture' in *The Trustworthiness of God* (eds. P. Helm and C. Trueman, Leicester: Apollos, 2002).

'Confessing the Faith Today' in *Reformed Theology in Contemporary Perspective* (ed. Lynn Quigley, Edinburgh: Rutherford House, 2006).

'The Holy Spirit in the Life of Jesus' in *Spirit of Truth and Power: studies in Christian Doctrine and Experience* (ed. David. F. Wright, Edinburgh: Rutherford House, 2007).

'The Doctrine of God and Pastoral Care' in *Engaging the Doctrine of God: contemporary Protestant perspectives* (ed. Bruce L. McCormack, Edinburgh: Rutherford House, 2008).

' "Church" Dogmatics: Karl Barth as Ecclesial Theologian' in *Engaging with Barth* (eds. David Gibson and Daniel Strange, Nottingham: Apollos, 2008).

'The Basis of Christian Unity' in *Ecumenism Today* (eds. F. A. Murphy and C. Asprey, Aldershot: Ashgate Publications, 2008).

'Celtic Spirituality' in *Worship and Liturgy in Context* (eds. Forrester and Gay, London: SCM, 2009).

'Word and Sacraments in Reformed Theologies of Worship: a Free Church Perspective' (Ibid.).

'The New Perspective: Paul, Luther and Judaism' in *The Westminster Confession into the 21st Century: Essays in Remembrance of the Westminster Assembly*, Vol. 3, (General Editor, J. Ligon Duncan III, Fearn: Mentor, 2009).

Journal and Magazine Articles

'Neglected Aspects of the Cross' (Banner of Truth 1967, Issue 48).

'Misunderstandings of Calvinism' (Banner of Truth 1967, Issue 51).

'Misunderstandings of Calvinism' (Banner of Truth 1968, Issue 53).

The Christian Experience of Suffering (Banner of Truth 1968, Issue 56).

The Lord's Supper as a Means of Grace (Banner of Truth, 1969, Issue 64).

The Lord's Supper as a Means of Grace (Banner of Truth, 1969, Issue 65).

The Lord's Supper as a Means of Grace (Banner of Truth, 1969, Issue 66).

The Doctrine of Election (Banner of Truth, 1969, Issue 67).

Christian Doctrine of Providence (Banner of Truth, 1969, Issue 70).

Divine Messiah: Deity of Christ (Banner of Truth, 1969, Issue 74).

Divine Messiah: Deity of Christ (Banner of Truth, 1969, Issue 75).

The Human Nature of Christ (Banner of Truth, 1970, Issue 78).

The Place of Women in the Church (Banner of Truth, 1970, Issue 81).

The Second Coming of Christ (Banner of Truth, 1970, Issue 82).

Has the Charismatic Age Ceased? (Banner of Truth, 1970, Issue 85).

Women's Headgear (Banner of Truth, 1970, Issue 85).

The Incarnation (Banner of Truth, 1970, Issue 87).

Paul's Use of the Term 'The Old Man' (Banner of Truth, 1971, Issue 92).

Liberty of Conscience (Banner of Truth, 1971, Issue 94).

Tradition (Banner of Truth, 1971, Issue 98).

Westminster Confession Today (Banner of Truth, 1972, Issue 101).

The Bible and Textual Criticism (Banner of Truth, 1972, Issue 105).

The Doctrine of Sanctification (Banner of Truth, 1972, Issue 109).

The Bible and Textual Criticism – Reply to Terence H. Brown (Banner of Truth, 1972, Issue 111).

The Doctrine of the Church (Banner of Truth, 1973, Issue 113).

The Lord's Day (Banner of Truth, 1973, Issue 115).

The Lord's Day (Banner of Truth, 1973, Issue 116).

Reconciliation (Banner of Truth, 1973, Issue 118).

God's Image in Man (Banner of Truth, 1973, Issue 122).

Federal Theology: an Oppressive Legalism (Banner of Truth, 1974, Issue 125).

Christian Assurance (Banner of Truth, 1974, Issue 133).

Christian Assurance (Banner of Truth, 1974, Issue 134).

Covenant (Banner of Truth, 1975, Issue 139).

Covenant (Banner of Truth, 1975, Issue 141).

Ambassadors for Christ (Banner of Truth, 1977, Issue 164).

The Doctrine of the Trinity (Scottish Bulletin of Evangelical Theology, Spring 1985, Vol. 3, No. 1).

Unity in Truth (Churchman, Vol. 101, No. 3, 1987).

The crisis facing the Church of England (Churchman, Vol. 102, No.1, 1988).

The way ahead for Anglican Evangelicals (Churchman, Vol. 102, No. 4, 1988).

The Atonement of the Death of Christ: In Faith, Revelation and History (Scottish Journal of Theology, Vol. 41, No. 4, 1988).

Writings of Donald Macleod

The Doctrine of the Incarnation in Scottish Theology: Edward Irving (Scottish Bulletin of Evangelical Theology, Spring 1991, Vol. 9, No 1).

The Political Theology of the Disruption Theologians (Evangelical Quarterly, Vol. 66, January 1994).

Is Evangelicalism Christian? [Response to Robert Letham's article] (Evangelical Quarterly, Vol. 67, January 1995).

Deacons and Elders (Scottish Bulletin of Evangelical Theology, Vol. 13, Spring 1995).

God or god?: Arianism, Ancient and Modern (Evangelical Quarterly, Vol. 68, April 1996).

The Christology of Jurgen Moltman (Themelios, Vol. 24, February 1999).

Dr. T. F. Torrance and Scottish Theology: A Review Article (Evangelical Quarterly, Vol. 72, No.1, January 2000).

The Christology of Wolfhart Pannenberg (Themelios, Vol. 25, No. 2, 2000).

Scottish Calvinism: A Dark Repressive Force? (Scottish Bulletin of Evangelical Theology, Autumn 2001, Vol. 19, No 2).

By what authority? (Title on contents page) By what standard? (Title at head of article), Theology in Scotland, Vol. IX No 2, Autumn 2002.

The New Perspective: Paul, Luther and Judaism (*Scottish Bulletin of Evangelical Theology*, Spring 2004, Vol. 22, No 1).

How right are the justified? Or, What is a Dikaios? (*Scottish Bulletin of Evangelical Theology*, Autumn 2004, Vol. 22, No 2).

Bavinck's Prolegomena: Fresh light on Amsterdam, Old Princeton, and Cornelius Van Til (*Westminster Theological Journal*, 2006, Vol. 68, No 2).

Be a Ground Breaker (*Free Magazine*, August/September 2006).

The Feill: The Lord's Supper as Feast (*Theology in Scotland*, Volume XV, No 2 Autumn 2008).

Amyraldus redivivus: a review article (*Evangelical Quarterly*, 2009, Vol. LXXXI No 3).

The influence of Calvinism on politics (*Theology in Scotland*, Vol. XVI, No 2 Autumn 2009).

The X-factor of its Day?: The place of reformed theology in Scotland (*Life and Work*, December 2009).

71

Historical Theology

5

Robert Bruce and the Lord's Supper

Malcolm Maclean

The contributors to this volume who had the privilege of studying under Donald Macleod have their own preferences concerning which classes meant most to them. Personally, the class I enjoyed the most was a set of lectures that were available only for a few years when he took students through the history of Protestant theology in Scotland and introduced us to several theologians and the best of their writings. One of the earliest of these theologians was Robert Bruce (1554–1631) and his classic work entitled *The Mystery of the Lord's Supper*.

By any assessment Robert Bruce was a remarkable man. He possessed gifts of statesmanship – a combination of family privilege, suitable education and personal character – as was evident when he was chosen by the king, James VI, to supervise the government of Scotland during his absence in Denmark in 1589.[1] Bruce's calling by the General Assembly to become minister of St. Giles in Edinburgh at a time of difficulty for the Scottish church reveals the confidence his ecclesiastical colleagues had in his abilities. His fame as a preacher was recognised by his contemporaries. Today, Bruce's experience of uncommon encounters with God has made him a person of interest to theologians of the charismatic movement.[2] This exploration is encouraged by the

---

[1] See D. C. McNicol (1907), *Master Robert Bruce*, Oliphant, Anderson and Ferrier, 78ff. for biographical details.

[2] Jack Deere (1996), *Surprised by the Voice of God*, Kingsway, 75-76.

knowledge that even George Gillespie regarded it as likely that Bruce was a prophet raised up by God to deliver his Word in a crucial moment of church history.[3] Bruce's teachings about the person and work of Christ led T.F. Torrance to ask whether or not Bruce anticipated much of the incarnational theology championed by Torrance.[4] Yet the prominent reason for his ongoing fame today is none of these reasons – instead it is his small book of sermons called *The Mystery of the Lord's Supper.*

The sermons were preached in February and March of 1589, and published in the following year. They were taken down by a hearer and published without any re-writing or improving by Bruce, although the publication was supervised by him. In his preface, addressed to James VI, Bruce indicated that the collection of sermons on the Lord's Supper was his first venture into publishing and that the book appeared at the insistence of his Kirk and Session. The first editions were in Scots, but in 1614 the sermons on the Lord's Supper were published in English under the title, *The Mystery of the Lord's Supper.* Three years later, a new English edition also contained other sermons that had been published in Scots, this new publication having a rather pointless title, *The Way to True Peace and Rest* (a title that had no connection to the contents, and which was not chosen by Bruce). Those two English editions indicate that there was an interest in Bruce's sermons in England as well as Scotland.

Subsequent editions of Bruce's sermons appeared in 1843, 1901 and 1958. The 1843 edition was edited by William Cunningham of New College, Edinburgh, and the sermons were the Scots version (this edition also contained a life of Bruce by Wodrow). The 1901 edition was edited by John Laidlaw, also of New College, and contained only a new English translation of the sermons on the Lord's Supper and a biography of Bruce by the editor. In 1958, Thomas F. Torrance, again of New College, published another new translation of the sermons on the Lord's Supper in which he re-arranged some of the sentences in order to clarify Bruce's meaning – Torrance also changed the Bible version from the Geneva Bible of Bruce to either the Authorised or the Revised Versions.[5] The involvement of three prominent Scottish

---

[3] George Gillespie (1649), 'A Treatise of Miscellany Questions,' in *The Works of George Gillespie*, Still Water Revival Books (1991 rpt), Vol. 2, 29.

[4] Thomas F. Torrance (1996), *Scottish Theology*, T. and T. Clark, 55-58.

[5] Robert Bruce (1958), *The Mystery of the Lord's Supper* (translated and edited by Thomas F. Torrance), James Clarke & Co. Quotations in this chapter are taken from this Torrance edition. It is currently published by Christian Focus Publications in a different format.

theologians in re-publishing Bruce's work at different times indicates the importance of Bruce's work as a contribution to Scottish theology.

Inevitably Bruce's treatment of the Lord's Supper was made within his contemporary ecclesiastical situation. The Scottish Reformation had been established for about three decades when Bruce delivered his sermons. This state of affairs meant that Roman Catholicism was still a matter of public concern and as far as the Lord's Supper was concerned Bruce had to give space to deal with transubstantiation, the view of the Roman church regarding the Lord's Supper, and his criticisms duplicate those common among the previous generation of Reformers. Bruce also considered the role of the pastor during the Lord's Supper and also the importance of self-examination before participating in the Supper, and in both these areas his thought merits careful consideration. In this chapter I want to focus on his teaching concerning what occurs at the Lord's Supper, as participants listen to a sermon, watch what happens to the elements of bread and wine, and then eat and drink them.

The rites of the Supper

What is the connection between listening to a sermon and participating in the Lord's Supper? In a service that includes the Lord's Supper Bruce regarded the Supper as a seal of the covenant of grace and mercy. It was a seal because it served the same purpose as a common seal did; such a seal confirmed what was written in the sealed document. The Lord's Supper sealed the contents of the Covenant. Bruce regarded it as a holy seal because its elements were changed from a common to a holy use. Yet, just as an ordinary seal had to be attached to a document, so the Supper had to be attached to the preached Word. Just as a document did not need a seal in order to be true, so the preached Word does not need the Sacrament in order to be effective. But just as a seal without a document did not confirm anything, so the Sacrament without the preached Word did not achieve any benefits.

This suggestion had implications for both preacher and participant. It was important for a preacher to be audible, simple and biblical in the sermon that preceded the Supper, otherwise the participant would not receive any benefit from the Supper. A biblical explanation will include making known 'what is the people's part, what is his own part, declaring how he ought to deliver and distribute the bread and wine, and how the people ought to receive the bread and wine at his hands.'

He is to inform their faith 'as to how they are to receive the Body and Blood of Christ signified by the bread and wine'. In addition, he will teach them to approach the Table with 'great reverence' and 'communicate with the precious Body and Blood of Christ'.[6]

Obviously there is a connection between what happens at an ordinary meal and at the Lord's Supper in that the latter is also a meal, so it is helpful to observe the connection even if all that is intended is that an ordinary meal helps to illustrate the meaning of the Supper as a means of spiritual nourishment. Such an illustration helps us appreciate why Bruce regarded it as of great importance for believers to maintain in their thinking the distinction between the substance (Christ) and the fruits (such as growth in faith), even although the substance and the fruits cannot be separated. He argued from what occurs in physical absorption of food. A person has to eat food in order to experience the benefits of nourishment: eating the food is a picture of feeding on Christ the substance, and the benefits of nourishment (such as physical strength) illustrate the spiritual fruits that a believer receives from Christ. It would be absurd to expect a person to have nourishment without eating; so a believer cannot have the fruits without feeding on Christ. 'Think of how impossible it is to be fed with food that never comes into your mouth, or to regain your health by medicine that is never applied or procured out of the apothecary's shop. It is just as impossible for you to be fed by the Body of Christ, or to get your health from the Blood of Christ, unless first of all you eat His Body and drink His Blood.'[7]

Why do the elements of the bread and the wine have this power? Bruce's answer is that they have it because of the institution of Christ.[8] Nevertheless, although given by Christ, the power is temporary, lasting only as long as the Supper lasts. The repetition of the words that Christ used by the officiating minister are the beginning of the period when the elements have this special power.

During the Supper, various rites are required and Bruce mentions three more in addition to the words of institution. First, the breaking of the bread is essential because it depicts not the breaking of the physical

[6] Torrance, 113. Note the words of the Scots Confession: 'Moreover, if the sacraments are to be rightly used it is essential that the end and purpose of their institution should be understood, not only by the minister but also by the recipients. For if the recipient does not understand what is being done, the sacrament is not being rightly used, as is seen in the case of the Old Testament sacrifices.'

[7] Torrance, 75.

body of Jesus but the fact that 'it was broken in pain, in anguish and distress of heart, under the weight of the indignation and wrath of God, which He sustained in bearing our sins.' Second, the pouring out of the wine is essential because it signifies 'that His Blood was severed from His flesh' and it 'tells you that He died for you, that His Blood was shed for you.' Third, the giving and the taking of the elements are essential rites at the Supper.

These rites are necessary for the spiritual benefit of believers. They have to be *observed* by those participating and applied personally. For Bruce, 'every sign and ceremony has its own spiritual signification, and there is no ceremony in this whole action lacking its own spiritual signification.' Every physical activity, whether by the minister in setting apart the elements or in handling them, or by the participant in receiving them, has its spiritual equivalent. As the minister fulfils his role, 'Christ is busy doing all these things spiritually to your soul.' When the believer's mouth takes the bread and the wine, 'the mouth of your soul takes the Body and Blood of Christ, and that by faith.'[9]

The conjunction of the elements and what they signify

Bruce so far has hinted that his understanding of what takes place at the Supper is more Calvinian than Zwinglian. As he develops his explanation of what takes place at the Supper his agreement with Calvinist distinctions becomes even more clear.

Bruce admitted that the conjunction between the bread and the Body of Christ and the wine and the Blood of Christ is difficult to understand. He acknowledged that it was easier to point out what he did not mean than it was to say what he did mean. An observer can clearly see that the signs (bread and wine in the Supper) and the thing signified (Christ) are not conjoined locally (not in the one place), corporally (they don't touch one another) or visibly (both cannot be seen). In addition, the conjunction must correspond and agree 'with the nature of the Sacrament'. If the nature of the Sacrament does allow a conjunction, one still has to discover how far the conjunction can go.

For Bruce, the Sacraments were mysteries, and this nature of mystery required that the conjunction be 'a mystical, secret and spiritual' one. In order to understand the 'mysterious' nature of the Sacraments, one needs heavenly enlightenment by the Holy Spirit.

---

[8] Torrance, 77ff.
[9] Torrance, 78-79.

'Nothing that is taught in the Word and Sacraments will ever do you good or lift up your soul to heaven, unless the Spirit of God enlightens your mind, and makes you find in your soul the thing that you hear in the Word.'[10]

Bruce's use of the term 'mystery' is taken from Ephesians 5:32 where Paul calls the union between Christ and his people 'a great mystery', and if the whole is a mystery, it is appropriate to call a part (the union between Jesus and his people at the Lord's Supper) a mystery as well. Of course, the term 'mystery' can only be used if the participants in the Supper are engaged in more than mere remembering of Jesus and are also participating in real communion with him. Bruce's understanding here reflects the Scots Confession's affirmation: 'And so we utterly damn the vanity of those that affirm Sacraments to be nothing else but naked and bare signs…; and also, that in the Supper, rightly used, Christ Jesus is so joined with us, that he becomes the very nourishment and food of our souls.' This criticism indicates Bruce's rejection of a Zwinglian interpretation of the Supper and his agreement with Calvin.

The conjunction means that in every Sacrament, there are two features that have a 'relative and mutual respect to one another'. Concerning the relative feature, Bruce used the connection between the Word preached and the thing signified in the Sacrament to illustrate the connection between the sign and the thing signified. The listener can picture in his mind what is said in the sermon (for example, a reference to the king), even if he cannot understand how the connection is made because it is not a visible connection. Similarly, a partaker should realise that the Sacrament is a visible Word that conveys the thing signified to the mind in a similar manner to how the spoken Word conveyed the thing signified to the mind. Therefore, when the person observes the element of bread, its signification will come into his mind and he will think of the body of Christ. This can happen because there is an analogy between the sign and the thing signified. Bread nourishes the physical body, Christ nourishes 'both body and soul to life everlasting'.

The second feature in the conjunction 'consists in a continual and mutual concurring of the one with the other, in such a way that the

---

[10] Torrance, 82. Bruce's comments here merely reflect what is stated in the Scots Confession regarding human inability to understand what was occurring at the Lord's Supper ('yet we affirm that the faithful in the right use of the Lord's Table have such conjunction with Christ Jesus, as the natural man cannot comprehend').

sign and the thing signified are offered both together, received together at the same time, and in the same action, the one outwardly, the other inwardly; if you have a mouth in your soul, which is faith, to receive it.'[11] A believer has two mouths, as it were: his physical mouth eats the bread and drinks the wine; the mouth of his soul feeds on Christ by faith.

Objections to this conjunction

Bruce was aware of objections to his teaching, at that time from Roman Catholic sources.[12] One objection was to his emphasis that the only perception of Christ in the Supper is a spiritual one. His opponents argued that his teaching made the Supper superfluous because Christ could be received by faith when the Word was preached. Since he could be received then, what further need was there for the Supper? Bruce admitted that believers received nothing different in the Sacrament than what they received from the preached Word. It is the case that even if a believer ascends to heaven he cannot receive a greater Christ than what he receives in the Word. Yet Bruce did not allow that this reality meant that the Supper was unnecessary. When a believer takes part spiritually in the Supper he obtains a better hold on Christ and receives more of Christ. Bruce compares the Christ received in preaching as being like what a person can hold between his finger and his thumb whereas the Christ he receives in the Supper (which would have been preceded by preaching) is like what a person can hold in his whole hand.[13]

Bruce also noted another weakness in the argument that since Christ was received in the Word, what need was there to partake of him additionally in the Supper? That argument would prove that a person only needed to receive Christ once and there would be no need to have further receptions of Christ. But a believer grows each time he takes part

---

[11] Torrance, 52.

[12] Subsequent Roman Catholic criticism appeared in 1593, when a Roman Catholic priest, William Reynolde, published a volume partly in reply to Bruce's book called *A Treatise Conteyning the True Catholike and Apostolike Faith of the Holy Sacrifice and Sacrament Ordeyned by Chriſt at his laſt Supper. Vvith a declaration of the Berengarian hereſie renewed in our age: and an Anſwere to certain Sermons made by M. Robert Bruce Miniſter of Edinburgh concerning the matter.* Bruce was defended and Reynolde criticised in an appendix to a volume written in 1602 by Alexander Hume, Maister of the high Schoole of Edinburgh, called *Of the True and Catholik meaning of our Sauiour his words, this is my bodie, in the inſtitution of his laſte Supper through the ages of the Church from Chriſt to our owne dayis.*

[13] Torrance, 84-85.

in the Supper. Each time he comes, his faith is augmented, he increases in understanding, in knowledge, in capability of receiving, and in feeling,[14] since it is the same Christ that is given on subsequent occasions.

A second objection concerned the judgement that comes on an unbeliever who takes part in the Supper. It was claimed that since an unbeliever could not receive Christ in a spiritual manner, he could not be capable of eating and drinking unworthily, and therefore would not be guilty of the Body and Blood of Christ. Bruce responds that the failure of such to eat and drink by faith was an expression of unworthy partaking and made them guilty. He illustrates his response by noting that an earthly prince would be offended if a subject trampled on his seal just as if he had trampled on him in person. Therefore, although the wicked cannot eat in a spiritual way, they can be guilty of treating Christ in an unworthy manner. Bruce appeals for support to the passages in Hebrews 6:6 and 10:29 where apostates are condemned for despising Christ.

A third objection was that since the thing signified (body and blood of Christ) is always attached to the sign, then evil persons must eat Christ when they eat the bread and drink the wine. Bruce does not deny that Christ is present when the elements are taken but notes that it is possible for him not to be received. Christ is also present when the Word is preached, indeed is offered to all who hear, yet all who hear do not take him. Similarly, he is offered truly in the bread and wine to all who partake, but the mere partaking in a physical way does not indicate that a person has also eaten in a spiritual way. If they fail to benefit spiritually, the fault is theirs and not God's because he is not bound to give what they refuse to take. Nevertheless, if a person does receive Christ in a spiritual way, the reason is because of God's grace.[15]

The means that bring about this conjunction

Bruce regarded a true appreciation of the Lord's Supper as evidence of great theological attainment. This appreciation included the application of Christ to the soul, and if a person possessed it, he was a 'great theologian'. It is not enough to know about Christ, there has to be personal experience of him. 'For the right application of Christ to the sick soul, to the wounded conscience, and the diseased heart,

---

[14] Torrance, 85-86.
[15] Torrance, 88-89.

is the fountain of all our felicity, and the well-spring of all our joy.'[16]

Possession of Christ is possession of spiritual life. The outworking of spiritual life in the soul is parallel or similar to the outworking of physical life in the body, although the influences of spiritual life are far greater than those of physical life. In order for a person to have this conjunction, two activities must take place. First, God must work through the Holy Spirit and, second, we must have faith.[17]

How can a believer on earth receive the body of Christ since the body of Jesus is in heaven? Obviously there is a great distance between the believer on earth and Jesus in heaven. It is important for a believer to realise that this distance does not deprive him of the title he has to Christ. 'The distance of place does not hurt my title or my right. If any of you [in Edinburgh] has a piece of land lying in the farthest part of Orkney, if you have a good title to it, the distance of place cannot hurt it.'[18] A believer does not get Christ in the Supper because he ascends to heaven and plucks Christ from there. Instead, he gets Christ because he already possesses a permanent title to him; the right to the title was given in the Word, and in the Supper the believer receives confirmation of his entitlement. 'Therefore distance of place does not hurt, and nearness of place does not help, the certainty of my title.' Even if Jesus were to descend from heaven and touch a person, this touch would be of no benefit if the recipient had no title to Christ.

The contact that a believer has with Christ is not one between his body and Christ's body. Instead, it is contact between his soul and Christ's body. The cord that stretches between Christ in heaven and the soul of the believer on earth is the Holy Spirit. Just as the sun in the sky reaches us by its beams, so Christ in heaven reaches the believer by his Spirit. This contact by the Spirit on Christ's part is invisible. Therefore we are not to think that we can sense how it works, although we can sense the effects of it. Instead we are to remember that the Spirit, because he is divine, is infinite and 'it is as easy for the Spirit to join Christ and us, no matter how distant we may be, as it is for our soul to link our head and the feet of our body, though they

---

[16] Torrance, 90.

[17] Torrance, 91.

[18] Torrance, 92. The Scots Confession avers: 'And yet, notwithstanding the far distance of place, which is between his body now glorified in the heaven, and us now mortal in this earth, yet we most assuredly believe, that the bread which we break is the communion of Christ's body, and the cup which we bless is the communion of his blood.'

be separated from one another'. The Spirit is a ladder that conjoins us to Christ (just as Jacob's ladder reached from the ground to heaven).[19]

Faith, for Bruce, was not merely an intellectual persuasion, but included personal assurance of salvation. This assurance was the normal outcome of self-examination and prepared a person for participating at the Lord's Supper. It was what distinguished the faith of true Christians from the general faith of the Roman Catholics and from various sects.[20] It was also an assurance that could increase as long as the believer ensured that he maintained a good conscience towards God.

Yet Bruce was aware that some believers were possessed by doubts, with some of these periods of doubt being prolonged and severe. He recognises the hand of God in these times and gives two reasons for this divine permission. First, God lets some of his people taste the bitterness of sin in order to humble them and see how ugly sin is. Second, he allows such experiences in order for them to appreciate in a measure what Christ experienced in Gethsemane and realise how much they are indebted to him.

For Bruce, the opposite of faith was not doubt but despair. It was possible for faith and doubt to exist in the one heart, but it was impossible for faith and despair to co-exist. Despair means without hope, and faith cannot exist where there is no hope.

Doubt arises when a person does not immediately repent of sin. Within each believer, there remains much indwelling sin which is never idle. Each sin will banish light and hurt the conscience. When the conscience is hurt, the believer's light is dimmed and doubt arises. In fact, doubt would be much greater if God did not usually lead his people to repentance when they sinned. The way to deal with doubt was by focusing on the mercy of God. A small degree of faith was sufficient to allow participation in the Lord's Supper.[21]

---

[19] Torrance, 93-95. Bruce repeats the necessity of a title and the work of the Spirit in pages 101-106. He uses the incident of the woman with the issue of blood who was healed by Jesus. She was not healed because she touched him physically but because of her faith. The hand that touched the hem depicted the hand of her soul touching Christ by faith. Note also the emphasis of the Scots Confession regarding the necessity of the work of the Holy Spirit: 'but this union and communion which we have with the body and blood of Christ Jesus in the right use of the sacraments, is wrought by operation of the Holy Ghost, who by true faith carries us above all things that are visible, carnal, and earthly, and makes us to feed upon the body and blood of Christ Jesus, which was once broken and shed for us, which now is in the heaven, and appeareth in the presence of his Father for us.'

[20] Torrance, 180-81.

[21] 'You see in what points every one of you ought to be prepared: you must be endowed with this love, and with faith, and if you have these in any small degree, go forward boldly to hear the Word, and to receive the Sacrament. This is the preparation that we allow' (Torrance, 198).

Concluding reflections

Four comments can be made about Bruce's treatment of the Lord's Supper.

First, given the importance of participation for a true believer and the necessity of counter-acting at that time the false practices of the Roman church, it is surprising that Bruce did not suggest more frequent occasions of the Lord's Supper. The aim at that time in Scotland was for the Supper to be held quarterly in cities, although many churches did not achieve this target. Yet since the Supper is such an effective means of conveying spiritual blessing from Christ, one would assume that the logical consequence for Bruce would be more numerous occurrences of the Supper. Frequent observance would also have helped develop a spiritual bond between members of his congregation. A third argument for more frequent commemorations is that a good way to remove superstitious notions connected to the Supper is more regular practising of the scriptural way. Yet Bruce does not suggest any adjustments to the ecclesiastical practice of the time concerning frequency.

Second, we can learn from Bruce of the importance of understanding Christology as we prepare for, preach about and participate in the Lord's Supper. Whatever else may be said about Bruce's view, it is clear that Christ is central. Christians anticipate that they are going to meet with the Lord Jesus at the Supper. For many of them today, their focus is on themselves as they intend to remember him, and their concern, rightly, is to prepare themselves for the occasion. Yet few seem to give thought to what such a meeting involves for the deity of Jesus and for his risen and glorified humanity – as God he possesses omnipresence, as risen and glorified man he is confined to one place at a time, so in what way(s) does he meet with his followers as they remember him? Nor do they consider the role performed by the Holy Spirit in bringing together the ascended Lord and his people as they meet around his table. Bruce's work attempts to answer such questions. In doing so, we have seen that Bruce continued the teaching of Calvin concerning the spiritual presence of Christ at the Lord's Supper, teaching that was expressed in the Scots Confession. At the Supper, real communion takes place between Jesus (as divine and human) and his people; it is achieved by the work of the Holy Spirit, although the Saviour's body does not leave heaven and the believer's body does not leave earth. Yet the distance between them is not a barrier and believers do not merely gather to think about an absent Lord. Instead they come together to meet *with* him and receive *from* him.

Third, Bruce's work challenges us regarding the seriousness of taking part in a communion service. Such participation involves preparation of heart by self-examination *before* the Supper, which by definition requires a meaningful searching of one's heart. A serious participation also requires careful attention to what occurs *during* the Supper. The minister, according to Bruce, has to perform certain actions which have symbolic force and which will help observant participants as they sit at the Table. The participants had to observe the actual breaking of the bread and the pouring of the wine by the minister because they illustrated what had happened to Jesus when he died. It is the case that many expositors do not accept that these actions have any symbolic value and are not essential to a Biblically authentic ordinance. Today it is common for bread to be cut and wine to be poured into cups before the service begins and outside the location where the service takes place. Nevertheless actions at the Supper convey a message; for example, if the minister behaves in a casual manner, and is imitated by his congregation, he will contribute to an irreverent service; or if participants ignore the sharing of the elements and merely focus on their own participation, they can give the impression that fellowship is not occurring at the horizontal level and that brotherly love is unimportant.

Fourth, Bruce's explanation stresses the reality that the Lord's Supper has aspects beyond human explanation. His use of the term 'mystery' may be questionable, given that in the New Testament it usually refers to truths that were revealed by God to his apostles and prophets. Nevertheless, in the Lord's Supper we are engaging in communion with a Saviour whom we cannot see, who is present with his people in the fullness of his Person, who is united to them by the Holy Spirit, who conveys to them spiritual blessings through one of his chosen means of grace, who uses it as part of the process of developing his own image within their hearts, and who through it draws them onwards in their journey towards heaven. We can close this examination of Bruce's view of the Lord's Supper by borrowing J. I. Packer's description of mystery (given in another context): mystery 'means a reality distinct from us that in our very apprehending of it remains unfathomable to us: a reality which we acknowledge as actual without knowing how it is possible, and which we therefore describe as *incomprehensible.*'[22] I suspect Bruce would have agreed with such a description of what occurs at the Lord's Supper.

---

[22] J. I. Packer, 'What Did the Cross Achieve?' in J. I. Packer and Mark Dever (2007), *In My Place Condemned He Stood*, Crossway, 57.

6

Glory, Glory Dwelleth in Immanuel's Land

Guy M. Richard

Thomas Goodwin (1600-1680) tells the story of a memorable occasion in the 1620s when he attended a lecture given by the Puritan evangelist John Rogers on the topic of the importance of Scripture. According to Goodwin, Rogers spoke with such forcefulness and with such gravity on this occasion that the church was turned into 'a mere Bochim [i.e., a place of weeping, from Judges 2:1-5], the people [were] generally… deluged with there [sic] own tears'. Goodwin himself was so affected that he 'was fain to hang a quarter of an hour upon the neck of his horse weeping before he had power to mount'.[1]

I mention this story because it reminds me of my experience with Principal Donald Macleod at the Free Church of Scotland College in Edinburgh. When Principal Macleod lectured on the person and work of Christ, the effect was much the same as it was in Goodwin's story. The classroom was frequently transformed into a 'mere Bochim', and those of us in attendance were often forced to 'hang' upon our desks for a few minutes before we had the power to collect our things and move along. There was an evident forcefulness in Macleod's lectures on Christology, a *distinctive* forcefulness that differentiated them from his other lectures. They had the same breadth and depth of scholarship, the same flair

---

[1] Cited in Francis Bremer and Ellen Rydell, 'Performance Art? Puritans in the Pulpit', *History Today* 45:9 (September 1995), 53.

for practical application, and the same tendency to controversy (!) that characterized all of Principal Macleod's addresses. But these lectures on Christology carried a special *gravitas*, or weightiness, that impressed upon his students an overwhelming sense of the beauty and magnificence of Christ. This, more than anything else, is what stands out in my mind when I think of Donald Macleod's life and ministry.

And it is this same emphasis on the beauty and magnificence of Christ that characterized the life and ministry of Samuel Rutherford (1600-1661) and gave it its distinctive forcefulness as well. Anyone who has read Rutherford's *Letters* will know this.[2] From the opening pages, the *Letters* reveal the heart of a man who is deeply in love with the Lord Jesus Christ. For Rutherford, Jesus is the 'soul-delighting, lovely Bridegroom'; the 'fairest, the sweetest, the most delicious Rose of all His Father's great field'; the 'lovely, beautiful, and glorious Friend'; the 'Chief among ten thousands, the fairest among the sons of men'; the 'Rose of Sharon'; the 'Paradise and Eden of the saints'; and the 'Pearl' of great price who alone is 'altogether lovely'.[3]

Such an emphasis on the beauty of Christ has endeared Rutherford and the *Letters* to Christians the world over ever since the seventeenth century and has ensured that they would be kept in print ever since their original publication in 1664. It is also the reason why Rutherford's contemporary, Richard Baxter, once said of the *Letters*: 'Hold off the Bible, such a book the world never saw.' And it is the reason why the great Charles Spurgeon said: 'When we are dead and gone let the world know that Spurgeon held Rutherford's letters to be the nearest thing to inspiration which can be found in all the writings of mere men.'[4] In the *Letters*, we see a Christ-enraptured man seeking to lift Jesus up in the estimations of those to whom he is writing. When one reads them, one cannot help but see why they have been so cherished and why there have been nearly 100 different editions of them in at least five different languages over the last 350 years.

Rutherford's zeal for the beauty and majesty of Christ can be seen in more than just his *Letters*, however. His preaching ministry quite obviously demonstrated this pervading characteristic as well. Robert Wodrow tells the story of an English merchant who once visited Scotland and upon his return back home gave an account

[2] The *Letters of Samuel Rutherford*, ed. A.A. Bonar (Edinburgh and London: Oliphant Anderson & Ferrier, 1891), contains 365 letters written by Rutherford over the course of his lifetime to many of his friends and parishioners. More recent editions are still available today.
[3] Rutherford, *Letters*, 78, 89, 106, 137, 184, 254, 309, 446, 556, 637.
[4] A.A. Bonar, 'Sketch of Samuel Rutherford', in *Letters*, 24-5; Charles Spurgeon, *The Sword and the Trowel*, June 1891.

of the preaching he had heard while on his northern tour. After hearing Robert Blair in St. Andrews, the merchant described him as a 'sweet, majestic-looking man who showed me the majesty of God'. David Dickson, in Irvine, was said to be 'a well-favoured, proper old man, with a long beard', who 'showed me all my heart'. But Samuel Rutherford was distinguished from all the others as a 'little, fair man', who 'showed me *the loveliness of Christ*'.[5]

Hughes Old has reminded us that God dispenses his gifts to ministers according to a great variety. In the sixteenth century, it was said that 'none thundered more loudly than [William] Farel, none piped more sweetly than [Pierre] Viret, none taught more learnedly than Calvin.' In the seventeenth century, Richard Sibbes was said to be able 'to unfold the mysteries of the gospel in a sweet and mellifluous way'—such that he was ever after known as 'the Sweet Dropper' by those who heard him.[6] So it appears that Rutherford's unique gift as a preacher was to demonstrate the loveliness of Christ to all who came under the influence of his ministry.

In this article I would like to uncover the reasons why this emphasis on the loveliness of Christ so permeated Rutherford's life and ministry. Why *this* emphasis, as opposed to some other? What is it about Rutherford that produced in him an overwhelming love for Christ, to such a degree that he stands head and shoulders above others of his contemporaries in this area? In an attempt to answer these questions, this article will look at how several unique views in Rutherford's theology coalesced with his own unique experiences to produce in him this all-consuming love for Christ. We will look first at Rutherford's unique understanding of the supremacy of God and then turn our attention to his unique understanding of the sinfulness of man.

The Supremacy of God

R.A. Finlayson, in his essay on 'John Calvin's Doctrine of God', claims that 'the first word' in the theology of the Genevan Reformer is God. Calvin, he says, begins with the doctrine of God and assigns it priority of place in his thinking but does so in a way that differentiates his system of thought from all others. Calvin's theology not only gives 'prime place to the doctrine of God', but it 'accepts the implications

---

[5] Bonar, 'Sketch of Samuel Rutherford', in *Letters*, 5-6, emphasis original.

[6] Hughes Old, *The Reading and Preaching of the Scriptures in the Worship of the Christian Church*, vol. 4, *The Age of the Reformation* (Grand Rapids, MI: Eerdmans, 2002), 274.

of the doctrine in every sphere of thought and life'.[7] In other words, it is not only true, for Calvin, that God is God in a most general sort of way, but it is true in every specific area of life. There is no sphere— or, to borrow the well known words of the nineteenth-century Dutch Calvinist Abraham Kuyper, there is no 'square inch in the whole domain of our human existence'—over which God is not sovereign.[8] So thoroughgoing is this emphasis on sovereignty in Calvin that many scholars, like B.B. Warfield, for instance, have argued that it is *the* fundamental principle (or *principium*) of his theology.[9]

What can be said of Calvin, however, can also be said of those who have followed after him. Calvinism, like its namesake, is distinguished from other systems of thought by its doctrine of the supremacy of God in all of life. When seen in this light, Rutherford's emphasis on the supremacy of God should not surprise us. He stands well within the mainstream of Calvinist thinking,[10] and so we would rightly expect him to hold to a high view of the sovereignty of God. But in Rutherford we have an example of one who may hold to an even higher view of divine sovereignty than does Calvin, if only because many of the distinctive themes that are plainly set forth in Rutherford's theology appear only vaguely or by implication, if at all, in Calvin. In this section, we will explore some of these distinctive themes in Rutherford in more detail,

---

[7] R.A. Finlayson, 'John Calvin's Doctrine of God', in *Puritan Papers*, vol. 3: 1963-1964, ed. J.I. Packer (Phillipsburg, NJ: P&R, 2001), 119-120.

[8] Kuyper's full comment is: '[N]o single piece of our mental world is to be hermetically sealed off from the rest, and there is not a square inch in the whole domain of our human existence over which Christ, who is Sovereign over *all*, does not cry: "Mine!"' His statement is arguably the climax of his inaugural address given on the occasion of the dedication of the Free University of Amsterdam in October 1880. See Abraham Kuyper, 'Sphere Sovereignty', in *Abraham Kuyper: A Centennial Reader*, ed. James D. Bratt (Grand Rapids, MI: Eerdmans, 1998), 488.

[9] See B.B. Warfield, 'Calvinism', in *Calvin and Calvinism*, vol. 5, *The Works of Benjamin B. Warfield* (1932; Grand Rapids, MI: Baker Book House, 2000 reprint), 354. Warfield's actual language states that 'the fundamental principle of Calvinism....lies in a profound apprehension of God in His majesty.' More recently, John Piper has also argued that 'the fundamental issue for John Calvin—from the beginning of his life to the end—was the issue of *the centrality and supremacy and majesty of the glory of God*' (Piper, *John Calvin and His Passion for the Majesty of God* [Wheaton, IL: Crossway, 2009], 16).

[10] Some scholars have claimed that Rutherford is a 'hyper-Calvinist'. One even goes so far as to label him an 'extreme hyper-Calvinist'. And though these scholars do not attempt to define what they mean by the slippery term, it would appear that they intend to suggest that Rutherford stands well outside the mainstream of Calvinistic thought. See T.F. Torrance, *Scottish Theology: From John Knox to John McLeod Campbell* (Edinburgh: T&T Clark, 1996), 109-110; and M. Charles Bell, *Calvinism and Scottish Theology: The Doctrine of Assurance* (Edinburgh: Handsel Press, 1985), 70-84, especially 83-4. The current author has argued that this understanding of Rutherford is in fact quite false. Rutherford stands squarely within the tradition of Calvin (Guy M. Richard, *The Supremacy of God in the Theology of Samuel Rutherford* [Milton Keynes: Paternoster, 2008]).

looking particularly at his view of the supremacy of the divine will and its application to the specific areas of salvation and suffering.

The Supremacy of God's Will

In continuity with medieval scholastics like John Duns Scotus (c.1270-1308) and William of Ockham (c.1280-1349), Rutherford is a voluntarist in his understanding of God. This simply means that he believes that the divine will exercises sovereignty over the divine intellect or, in other words, that the will of God is free to function without any compulsion or constraint of any kind.[11] God's will is its own rule. It always and only chooses what it pleases. Nothing forces it or directs it to choose one thing over another.[12] In order to show how voluntarism manifests itself in Rutherford's theology, we will need to examine in more detail the distinctions that he makes between the will of God *ad intra* and *ad extra*, on the one hand, and between omnipotence and sovereignty, on the other.

The distinction between *ad intra* and *ad extra* is a scholastic distinction designed to express the difference between the divine will as it is within God himself and as it is directed toward us and is known by us. The will of God as it is within God himself—i.e., *ad intra*—is necessarily bound by the divine nature. God must will his own existence by necessity of nature. He must also love himself and beget and love the Son by necessity of nature. God cannot will himself into non-existence or choose to hate himself or the Son, because the nature of God constrains the will of God *ad intra*.[13] But other things, outside of himself—i.e., *ad extra*—God wills freely and without any compulsion at all, even from his own nature.

What this means is that God is good, merciful, and just in and of himself, and must will accordingly with respect to himself (*ad intra*). But he is under no obligation to be good, merciful, and just toward his creatures (*ad extra*). He can will whatever he wants to will in regard to them. As Rutherford says:

---

[11] The name 'voluntarism' is derived from the Latin word for 'will', *voluntas*. For more on voluntarism and its opposite, intellectualism, see Frederick Copleston, *A History of Philosophy*, 9 vols. (New York: Doubleday, 1993), II, 382-3, 529-33, 538-41.

[12] Rutherford does believe that the divine will is subject to certain constraints. For instance, he acknowledges that the divine intellect *precedes* the will and *exercises restraint* upon it, insofar as the will is only able to choose from those things that are contained in or known by the divine intellect (Samuel Rutherford, *Examen Arminianismi* [Utrecht, 1668], 173). He even goes so far as to suggest that the intellect inclines the will to certain courses of action (for more on this, see the current author's discussion in *The Supremacy of God in the Theology of Samuel Rutherford*, 136-8). But this is as far as Rutherford goes.

[13] Samuel Rutherford, *The Covenant of Life Opened* (Edinburgh, 1655), 29-31.

God is good in creating the world, in giving faith to Peter, and in communicating being and goodness with his creatures,…[but] he could have been "not-good," in this way, if he would not have created the world and would not have given faith to Peter, and if he would have annihilated the creatures.[14]

God's will is sovereign. He is not bound in what he wills *ad extra* by some preconceived notion of what is good. What he wills is good simply because he wills it.

Such an understanding of divine sovereignty may be precisely what Calvin himself embraces, although it seems impossible to say so with absolute certainty. In the *Institutes*, Calvin makes the following claims about the divine will, which *prima facie* sound identical to Rutherford's comments:

> [God's] will is, and rightly ought to be, the cause of all things that are. For if it has any cause, something must precede it, to which it is, as it were, bound; this is unlawful to imagine. For God's will is so much the highest rule of righteousness that whatever he wills, by the very fact that he wills it, must be considered righteous. When therefore, one asks why God has so done, we must reply: because he has willed it. But if you proceed further to ask why he so willed, you are seeking something greater and higher than God's will, which cannot be found.[15]

Calvin is clearly open to voluntaristic interpretation, more so than are others of his contemporaries like Wolfgang Musculus and Peter Martyr Vermigli.[16] But he is not nearly as explicit in his language as is Rutherford. There is no doubt where Rutherford comes down on this question.

The second important distinction that Rutherford makes in regard to the divine will is the distinction between omnipotency and sovereignty. Whereas omnipotency is 'what the Lord *can doe* [sic]', sovereignty is more than that; it includes the divine will: 'Soveraignty [sic] is not only his holy Nature what he can doe and so supposeth

---

[14] Rutherford, *Examen Arminianismi*, 146. See also Rutherford, *Covenant of Life Opened*, 27-34; and idem, *Disputatio scholastica de divina providentia* (Edinburgh, 1649), 342, 345.

[15] John Calvin, *Institutes of the Christian Religion*, ed. J.T. McNeill, trans. and indexed F.L. Battles (Philadelphia: Westminster, 1960), III.xxiii.2, 949.

[16] Some scholars have argued that Calvin is a voluntarist who is influenced more by Duns Scotus than by Aquinas. Among them are Albrecht Ritschl, Henri Bois, Williston Walker, and Reinhold Seeberg. See, e.g., François Wendel, *Calvin: The Origins and Developments of his Religious Thought*, trans. P. Mairet (London: Collins, Fontana Library, 1965), 127ff; and T.F. Torrance, *The Hermeneutics of John Calvin* (Edinburgh: Scottish Academic Press, 1988).

his Omnipotency, but also what he doth freely, or doth not freely, and doth by no natural necessity, and so it includes his holy supreme Liberty.' For Rutherford, it is not only true that God *is able* to do as he pleases (omnipotency) but that God *actually does* as he pleases (sovereignty), and, in doing so, his 'holy Will [is] essentially wise and just, [and] is a Law and Rule to himself'.[17]

So, what does all this mean? It means, in the first place, that in Rutherford's theology God's will is the ultimate cause of all things. Nothing outside of God lives or moves or has its being apart from the divine will. As we will soon see, this is important in shaping Rutherford's views of suffering. But in the second place, it also means that in Rutherford's theology God is supreme in such a way that he always and only does as he pleases, without anything, either within himself or outside of himself, directing or compelling him to do it. God elects, creates, allows his creatures to fall into sin, and is just and merciful toward his creatures because he chooses to do these things. No necessity of any kind requires him to do them. He could have chosen not to do these things or to do their opposites, and he still would have been good, just, and merciful in and of himself.

The Supremacy of God's Will in Salvation

Rutherford's commitment to a high view of the sovereignty of God is further reflected in his advocacy of supralapsarianism and in his denial of the absolute necessity of the atonement of Christ. We will take up these two topics in this section, beginning with the former, in order to demonstrate further some of the ways in which Rutherford was unique in his understanding and convictions.

Supralapsarianism is the name given to the particular predestinarian view that sees the object of God's predestination as mankind not yet created and not yet fallen into sin. According to the supralapsarian scheme, God first chooses the end result that he wants (i.e., God chooses to have a people for his own possession), and then he chooses the means by which he will bring that intended result to pass (i.e., he chooses to create them, to allow them to fall into sin, and to be redeemed by the cross of Christ). This view derives its name from the Latin phrase *supra lapsum*, which means 'above or prior to the fall', because it locates God's decree to elect and reprobate prior to his decrees to create and to permit the fall. Supralapsarianism is distinguished

---

[17] Samuel Rutherford, *Influences of the Life of Grace* (London, 1659), 33.

from infralapsarianism, the view that sees the object of predestination as mankind already created and fallen into sin. Infralapsarianism comes from the Latin phrase *infra lapsum*, which means 'below or subsequent to the fall'. As its name suggests, it locates the decree of election and reprobation after (or subsequent to) the decrees to create and to permit the fall. In other words, infralapsarianism states that God first decides to create a people and to allow them to fall into sin and, then, he decides to choose a people for his own possession out of the mass of fallen mankind.[18]

These two approaches to the ordering of the divine decrees within the mind of God became a matter for debate in the seventeenth century, with ministers and theologians clearly pronouncing which side of the fence they were on.[19] Rutherford took up his place on the supralapsarian side. This fact is well documented in the secondary literature. But until John Coffey's important book on Rutherford,[20] the only references that were given to support the claim were inconclusive in determining Rutherford's true lapsarian position.[21] The reality is that supralapsarianism is set forth only implicitly in the majority of Rutherford's writings and explicitly only in two of his most obscure works.

The first of these obscure works is an unpublished manuscript discourse on Ephesians 1:4, written in Rutherford's own hand. It contains the most explicit statement of Rutherford's supralapsarianism. Here, Rutherford clearly reveals his conviction that election stands

---

[18] For more on the meanings of supralapsarianism and infralapsarianism, see Richard A. Muller, *Dictionary of Latin and Greek Theological Terms: Drawn Principally from Protestant Scholastic Theology* (Grand Rapids, MI: Baker, 1985), 155, 234-5, 292.

[19] For more on the seventeenth-century supralapsarian-infralapsarian debate, see Karl Barth, *Church Dogmatics*, ed. G.W. Bromiley and T.F. Torrance, 4 vols. (Edinburgh: T&T Clark, 1936-1975), II/2, 127-45; William Cunningham, *Reformers and the Theology of the Reformation* (1862; Edinburgh: Banner of Truth, 1989), 358-71; Herman Bavinck, *The Doctrine of God*, trans. W. Hendriksen (Edinburgh: Banner of Truth, 1977), 382-94; and G.C. Berkouwer, *Divine Election*, trans. H. Bekker (Grand Rapids, MI: Eerdmans, 1960), 254-77.

[20] Coffey, *Politics, Religion and the British Revolutions: The Mind of Samuel Rutherford* (Cambridge: Cambridge University, 1997).

[21] E.g., David A.S. Fergusson, 'Predestination: A Scottish Perspective', *Scottish Journal of Theology* 46 (1993), 465-66. Here Fergusson cites *The Covenant of Life Opened* and Rutherford's catechism, both of which could be read from an infralapsarian point of view. John Macleod makes no mention of any of Rutherford's works to substantiate his claims of supralapsarianism (*Scottish Theology in Relation to Church History since the Reformation* [Edinburgh: Publications Committee of the Free Church of Scotland, 1943], 70). James Walker does list several quotations from Rutherford which do seem to favor a supralapsarian scheme. But because Walker does not disclose the sources of his quotations, the original contexts cannot be examined in greater detail to determine how much, if any, of what Rutherford says in these quotations could apply to the temporal *ordo salutis* and not just the eternal order of the decrees (*The Theology and Theologians of Scotland 1560-1750* [Edinburgh: Knox Press, 2nd edition. 1982], 50-51).

logically prior to every decree. 'Some', he says, believe 'our election to be both after the decrees of creating us and permitting us to fall into sin. [But] we prove that God's electing of us cannot be after the consideration of our creation and fall.'[22] The second obscure work is the *Examen Arminianismi*—an extremely rare collection of Rutherford's theological lectures given at St. Andrews University and published in the Netherlands after his death. Here again, Rutherford unambiguously reveals his supralapsarianism, this time by stating that 'the object of predestination is mankind which is about to be but is not yet created [*homo creandus et nondum creatus*]'.[23]

The reason that Rutherford gives for embracing supralapsarianism is his understanding of the sovereignty of God and, particularly, of the sovereignty of the will of God. The divine decree to elect (and reprobate) must be prior to the decrees to create and allow the fall, because, to Rutherford's way of thinking, election cannot be based on anything except God's sovereign choice. If the infralapsarians are right, and the divine decree to elect and reprobate occurs after the decrees to create and allow the fall, then election is no longer based on God's sovereign choice alone but is, at least partially, based on something that is foreseen in his creatures (i.e., their choice to sin). Election would then become a divine response to human failure. In this way, Rutherford says, infralapsarianism concedes far too much to Arminianism by making 'God look out of himself for determining his will' and, thus, destroying the 'all sufficiencie' of God by making him 'go forth of himself, seeking knowledge from things without him, as we [who are mere creatures] doe'.[24]

While there can be no doubt that Rutherford embraces the supralapsarian position, the same cannot be said about his predecessor John Calvin. Scholars are divided as to whether Calvin is supralapsarian or infralapsarian.[25] The uncertainty stems from the fact that there are

---

[22] Rutherford, unpublished manuscript, University of Edinburgh Library, La.II.394, 5.

[23] Rutherford, *Examen Arminianismi*, 272.

[24] Rutherford, unpublished manuscript, La.II.394, 8.

[25] Among those who see Calvin as infralapsarian are, Francis Turretin, *Institutes of Elenctic Theology*, trans. G.M. Giger, ed. J.T. Dennison, Jr., 3 vols. (Phillipsburg, NJ: P&R, 1992-7), 4.9.30, I, 349-50; and Henri Blocher, 'Calvin infralapsaire', *La Revue Réformée* 31 (1980), 273. Among those who see Calvin as supralapsarian are, Karl Barth, *Church Dogmatics*, II/2, 127-8; Edward A. Dowey, *The Knowledge of God in Calvin's Theology* (Grand Rapids, MI: Eerdmans, 1994), 186-7; J.T. McNeill, in Calvin's *Institutes* II.xii.5, 469n5; G.C. Berkouwer, *Divine Election*, 257; Paul K. Jewett, *Election and Predestination* (Grand Rapids, MI: Eerdmans, 1985), 89; and, most recently, J.V. Fesko, *Diversity Within the Reformed Tradition: Supra- and Infralapsarianism in Calvin, Dort, and Westminster* (Greenville, SC: Reformed Academic Press, 2001), especially 81-106.

clear elements of both in his theology. As Richard Muller remarks, 'Calvin sometimes speaks as if the object of predestination is fallen humanity in need of redemption, sometimes as if the decree is radically prior, given God's predestining of the fall itself.'[26] Another part of the problem in discerning where Calvin comes down on this issue arises from the simple fact that he lived in the century before it became a matter of serious debate within the church. So we should not be surprised that Calvin is less explicit than is Rutherford. But the fact remains that while Rutherford is clearly supralapsarian, Calvin is not and may actually be infralapsarian.

One other logical outflow of Rutherford's view of the sovereignty of the divine will can be seen in his unique understanding of the justice and mercy of God and their relation to the atonement of Christ. As we mentioned earlier, Rutherford believes that justice is a divine attribute *ad intra* and that God is required to exercise that justice within himself but that he is in no way required to exercise it *ad extra*, toward his creatures. This means that God is not required by any necessity of his own nature to punish our sin. It is something he chooses to do; but that choice is voluntary, and God could have made the opposite choice had he been so inclined. Rutherford states: 'Justice (as manifested to us) is a voluntary decree of God to punish sinners.'[27] While Rutherford acknowledges that God has chosen to be just and to punish sin in actuality, his point is that no essential necessity—i.e., no necessity resulting from his nature— forces this choice upon him. It is wholly voluntary.

Likewise, Rutherford says, mercy is also voluntary in God: 'Mercy floweth not from God essentially, especially the mercy of Conversion, Remission of sins, [and] Eternal life, but of meer Grace; for then God could not be God, and deny these favours to Reprobats [sic].'[28] Rutherford is saying that if God is required by necessity of his own nature to be merciful to his creatures (*ad extra*), he would then be required to act mercifully to all people, both elect and reprobate, and, thus, to remove the hardness of every heart. But, according to Rutherford, this would contradict the justice of God, because 'the Attribute of Justice is as essential as Mercy'. One attribute cannot take precedence over the other. If one is essential, they both must be.

---

[26] Richard A. Muller, *Post-Reformation Reformed Dogmatics: The Rise and Development of Reformed Orthodoxy, ca. 1520 to ca. 1725*, 4 vols. (Grand Rapids, MI: Baker Academic, 2003), I, 127.

[27] Samuel Rutherford, *Fourteen Communion Sermons*, ed. A.A. Bonar (Glasgow: Glass & Co, 1877), 30.

[28] Samuel Rutherford, *The Tryal and Triumph of Faith* (London, 1645), 17.

In Rutherford's estimation, the intellectualist position (which is the opposite of his voluntarism) wrongly places divine justice above divine mercy by suggesting that God must punish sin by necessity of nature but that he does not have to show mercy until and unless he decides to do so. For Rutherford, God is either free to do as he pleases in regard to both, or he is required to exercise both by necessity of nature. There can be no middle ground.

Coordinate with Rutherford's denial of the necessity of justice and mercy in God is his denial of the absolute necessity of the atonement of Christ. Not only is God free to choose to punish sin or not to punish sin and to show mercy or not to show mercy, he is also free to choose to forgive sins by way of the cross of Christ or by some other way:

> *God*, if wee speake of his absolute power [or, his omnipotency], without respect to his free decree [his sovereignty], could have pardoned sinne without a ransom, and gifted all *Mankind* and fallen *Angels* with heaven, without any satisfaction of either the sinner, or his Surety; for he neither punisheth sin, nor tenders heaven to *Men* or *Angels* by necessity of nature...but freely.[29]

For Rutherford, there is no absolute necessity that Christ should die upon the cross. God could have chosen to forgive sins in some other way, either by sweeping sin under the rug or by divine fiat or by having us jump through hoops with our eyes closed.

Rutherford clearly believes that God has chosen to be just toward his creatures by choosing to punish their sin. He also believes that God has chosen to be merciful toward his creatures by forgiving their sins by way of the cross of Christ. And he believes that Christ has chosen to die on the cross in order that that mercy might be extended to the elect. But the point is that Rutherford believes that all these choices are wholly voluntary for God. No necessity of any kind compels or constrains him to make them. He freely chooses to be just, to be merciful, and to forgive by way of the cross.

The Supremacy of God's Will in Suffering

Rutherford's commitment to a high view of the sovereignty of God is also reflected in his view of suffering. All suffering, for Rutherford, is ultimately the result of God's sovereign choice. Here again, God

---

[29] Samuel Rutherford, *Christ Dying and Drawing Sinners to Himselfe* (London, 1647), 7-8.

does as he pleases, and what he does is always right for the simple fact that he does it. The proper response of the Christian to suffering is, therefore, to bow the knee and humbly to submit, which is precisely Rutherford's counsel to Lady Jane Campbell on the occasion of the death of one of her children:

> I believe faith will teach you to kiss a striking Lord; and so acknowledge the sovereignty of God (in the death of a child) to be above the power of us mortal men, who may pluck up a flower in the bud and not be blamed for it. If our dear Lord pluck up one of His roses, and pull down sour and green fruit before harvest, who can challenge Him? For He sendeth us to His world, as men to a market, wherein some stay many hours, and eat and drink, and buy and sell, and pass through the fair, till they be weary; and such are those who live long, and get a heavy fill of this life. And others again come slipping in to the morning market, and do neither sit nor stand, nor buy nor sell, but look about them a little, and pass presently home again; and these are infants and young ones, who end their short market in the morning, and get but a short view of the Fair. Our Lord, who hath numbered man's months, and set him bounds that he cannot pass (Job xiv.5), hath written the length of our market, and it is easier to complain of the decree than to change it.[30]

We may not be able to fathom God's mysterious will for our lives, but we should rest content nonetheless in what he has sent our way, because 'it is certain [that it] is not only good which the Almighty hath done, but it is *best*'.[31]

God sovereignly establishes the *fact* of suffering in our lives, according to Rutherford, and he also sovereignly allocates the *amount* of suffering that each person will face. Thus, in giving the reason for why some Christians suffer more here on earth than others do, Rutherford explicitly points to the sovereign will of God:

> Why some of the Saints are carried to *Abraham's* bosome, and to heaven in *Christ's* bosome, and for the most, feast upon sweet manifestations all the way, and others are oftner in the *hell* of soule-trouble, then in any other condition, is amongst the depths of holy Soveraignty. (1) Some feed on honey, and are carried in *Christ's* bosome to heaven; others are so quailed and kept under water, in the flouds of wrath, that their first smile of joy is when the one foot is on the shore, and when the morning of eternities Sunne dawnes in at the window of the

---

[30] Rutherford, *Letters*, 97-8.
[31] Rutherford, *Letters*, 103-4.

soule. Some sing, and live on sense all the way; others sigh, and goe in at heavens gates weeping, and *Christs* first kisse of glory dryes the tears off their face. (2) *Christ* walkes in a path of unsearchable liberty, that some are in the suburbs of heaven, and feele the smell of the dainties of the *Kings* higher house, ere they be in heaven; and others, children of the same Father, passengers in the same journey, wade through hell, darknesse of fears, thornes of doubtings, have few love-tokens till the marriage-day.[32]

Rutherford's comments may sound like the less-than-helpful advice of a man who has never experienced hardship to any real degree, but such is actually not the case. Rutherford knew all too well what it was to suffer. From the time that he began as Regent of Humanity at the University of Edinburgh in 1623, Rutherford endured constant humiliation and affliction. In 1626, he was the centre of a public scandal involving his future wife Eupham Hamilton (about which more will be said in the next section). Besides undergoing a public trial and the consequent removal from office that resulted from this scandal, Rutherford also faced the loss of at least eight children, his wife, his mother, many members of his congregation, and his own ill health.

Out of at least nine children that were born to him, only one survived him; eight died in infancy.[33] His wife—whom he calls the 'delight of mine eyes'—died near the end of his third year in Anwoth (only the fifth of their marriage), after a thirteen-month struggle with an illness that Rutherford later described as an 'exceeding great torment night and day'.[34] Her death left him with such a great 'wound' that even four years later Rutherford would say that it was 'not yet fully healed and cured'.[35] Yet he never wavered in ascribing this hardship to the will of God and in praising him for it: 'The Lord hath done it; blessed be His name.'[36]

During his wife's illness, Rutherford himself struggled with a tertian fever 'for the space of thirteen weeks' and was unable to carry out many of his pastoral duties. In his *Letters*, he laments that 'life was never so wearisome' as it was for him at this juncture.[37] Poor health would again plague Rutherford during the Westminster Assembly (a fact that makes his prodigious accomplishments there all the more amazing) and during the

---

[32] Rutherford, *Christ Dying*, 50.
[33] Coffey, *Politics, Religion and the British Revolutions*, 39-40, 50, 53, 60.
[34] Rutherford, *Letters*, 50, 53, 100.
[35] Rutherford, *Letters*, 100.
[36] Rutherford, *Letters*, 53.
[37] Rutherford, *Letters*, 50, 53-4.

early 1650s, in the initial stages of the Protester-Resolutioner controversy. And, as his *Letters* reveal, he endured the countless losses and crosses of members of his congregation and sought to minister comfort to them in the midst of their tragedies, all the while enduring his own adversities.

Were this the extent of Rutherford's sufferings, it still would be more than most people face in their lifetimes and would still provide him sufficient grounds to speak to us about how we should handle adversity. But this is not the extent of his sufferings. Following the publication of his first theological treatise, *Exercitationes apologeticae pro divina gratia* in 1636, Rutherford was called before the Court of High Commission in Edinburgh, found guilty of non-conformity, and exiled to Aberdeen for the next eighteen months. In Aberdeen, he was kept at a great distance from his congregation, forbidden from preaching—which he says was his 'one joy out[side] of heaven'—and openly preached against in his hearing and insulted by passers-by in the streets.[38] Though the signing of the National Covenant in February 1638 temporarily released him from his persecutions and enabled him to return to his beloved Anwoth, it did not provide permanent emancipation. With the restoration of King Charles II in 1660, the persecution resumed near the end of Rutherford's lifetime. The Committee of Estates declared that Rutherford's *Lex, Rex* was 'a book inveighing against monarchie, and laying ground for rebellion' and, therefore, was to be recalled and burned in both Edinburgh and St. Andrews. Rutherford himself was removed from his positions in the university as a professor of divinity and principal of St. Mary's College, deprived of his pastoral charge in the church, divested of his stipend, and placed under house arrest. He was charged with treason and called to appear before parliament to respond to the allegation. Many of his friends feared he would face execution along with James Guthrie and Archibald Campbell, the Marquis of Argyll.[39] Rutherford himself said that 'he would willingly dye on the scaffold...with a good conscience'.[40] But before he could do so, he once again became ill and was prevented from answering parliament's summons by what he referred to as an earlier and more important 'summons before a superior Judge and judicatory'. His message to parliament was: 'I behove to answer my first summons; and, ere your day arrive, I will be where few kings and great folks come.'[41] Rutherford died shortly thereafter, near the end of March 1661.

[38] Gilmour, *Samuel Rutherford*, 82, 83.

[39] Robert Baillie, *Letters and Journals*, ed. David Laing (Edinburgh: Robert Ogle, 1841), III, 447, 467, cited in Coffey, *Politics, Religion and the British Revolutions*, 60-61.

[40] Robert Wodrow, *Analecta: or, Materials for a History of Remarkable Providences; Mostly Relating to Scotch Ministers and Christians*, 3 vols. (Edinburgh: Maitland Club, 1842-3), I, 165-6.

[41] Rutherford, *Letters*, 20.

Summary

Rutherford's voluntarism, his supralapsarianism, his views of the non-necessity of justice and mercy in God and of the non-necessity of the atonement of Christ, and his understanding and experience of suffering all reveal his commitment to a high doctrine of the sovereignty of God. Although Rutherford evidently stands within the mainstream of Calvinist thinking, his views of divine sovereignty would appear to be even stronger at many points than those of Calvin himself, if only because Calvin's own views in several of the abovementioned areas are less than explicit. The impact that this high conception of God has in Rutherford's experience can be seen only when it is juxtaposed with his understanding of the sinfulness of sin.

The Sinfulness of Sin

If there is one thing that Rutherford knew for sure it was the fact that he was a sinful man. This was not just a theological truth for Rutherford; it was an experiential one: 'no man knoweth what guiltiness is in me so well as these two, who keep my eyes now waking and my heart heavy, I mean (1) my heart and conscience, and (2) my Lord, who is greater than my heart'.[42] For his entire life, Rutherford maintained a profound awareness of and sensitivity to the sinfulness of his own sin. This can be seen clearly in his *Letters*, where he repeatedly refers to the 'body of sin and corruption', the 'guiltiness', 'abominable vileness', 'sink of corruption', and 'sour fruits of sin' that he finds within himself.[43] Even at the end of his lifetime, Rutherford would look back in regret at his 'unseen and secret abominations' and be deeply troubled at the prospect that they were 'no small reproach to the holy name and precious truths of Christ'.[44]

Rutherford's profound sensitivity to his own sinfulness was instilled in him from the time of his conversion, a conversion which seems to have been brought about by the public scandal that involved his future wife. In 1626, while Rutherford was serving as Regent of Humanity for the University of Edinburgh, he was accused of fornication by the university's Principal John Adamson. Edinburgh's city records for February 3, 1626, record Adamson's charge: 'Mr Samuell Rutherfuird, regent of humanitie, hes fallin in furnicatioun with Euphame

---

[42] Rutherford, *Letters*, 139.
[43] Rutherford, *Letters*, 177, 303, 313, 332, 535.
[44] Rutherford, *Letters*, 701.

Hamiltoun, and hes committit ane grit scandle in the college [sic].'[45] Unfortunately, this account does not completely square with the university's record, which somewhat vaguely states that Rutherford 'having incurred some scandal on account of irregular marriage found it prudent to resign his office'.[46]

Because of the questions arising from the two differing accounts and because the details lying behind Adamson's charge are nowhere given, a great debate has ensued over the years as to what exactly happened. Those who dismiss Adamson's charge against Rutherford do so largely on the basis of the difficulty they have in believing that Rutherford could commit fornication one year and then be appointed minister in Anwoth the next.[47] While this is a legitimate point that ought not to be treated cavalierly, it, nevertheless, seems best to conclude with John Coffey that Adamson's charge was in fact correct. Coffey has shown that extending 'such leniency' as would have been required to appoint Rutherford to Anwoth in spite of his sin was not unheard of in the church at that time. What is more, he has offered five reasons for supporting the accuracy of Adamson's charge, the most convincing of which is the fact that the committee, which was formed to investigate the charge and appoint a replacement for Rutherford in the event that the charge proved to be justified, did in fact appoint a replacement, suggesting that they did find in fact find that Adamson's charge was accurate.[48]

Most of Rutherford's biographers acknowledge that this scandal forced Rutherford to come face to face with the corruption in his own heart like never before. As a result, he appears to have experienced Christian conversion. Even some of the biographers who deny the charges of fornication still trace his conversion to this point in time. Andrew Thomson, for instance, says that it is 'far from unlikely' that the 'bitter hours associated with this passage in Rutherford's life... led him into trains of thought and self-reflection which ended in his coming under the supreme power of the religion of Christ'.[49] And

[45] Marguerite Wood, ed., *Extracts from the Records of the Burgh of Edinburgh, 1604 to 1626* (Edinburgh: Oliver & Boyd, 1931), 296.

[46] Andrew Dalzell, *History of Edinburgh University* (Edinburgh: Edmonston and Douglas, 1862), II, 84.

[47] See Andrew Thomson, *The Life of Samuel Rutherford* (Glasgow: Free Presbyterian, 1988), 13; Gilmour, *Samuel Rutherford*, 29; Thomas Murray, *The Life of Rev. Samuel Rutherford* (Edinburgh: Oliphant, 1828), 18-21; and Kingsley G. Rendell, *Samuel Rutherford: A New Biography of the Man & his Ministry* (Fearn, Ross-shire: Christian Focus, 2003), 21-2.

[48] Coffey, *Politics, Religion and the British Revolutions*, 38.

[49] Thomson, *Life of Samuel Rutherford*, 13.

Marcus Loane adds, perhaps a little more cautiously, that 'this phase of his career...seems to have marked the time when he entered into the peace and joy of a saving experience of Christ'.[50] If Rutherford's biographers are right that this point did in fact mark his conversion, then this, plus the fact that Rutherford later married the woman that he was involved with, could help to explain why he might have been shown leniency and appointed as minister in Anwoth only a little over a year after committing what would have been a serious sin in the eyes of the church.

One of the most convincing reasons for tracing Rutherford's conversion to the time of the fornication scandal is that this event sets the paradigm for the remainder of Rutherford's Christian life. From this point on, Rutherford's Christianity becomes deeply experiential, which one would expect to find following conversion, especially a conversion brought on by a public humiliation of the order that he endured. From this point on, Rutherford's Christian life becomes very much like the Apostle Paul's. His 'Damascus road' conversion (à la Acts 9) ensured that he, like Paul, would ever after see himself as 'the chief of sinners' (1 Timothy 1:15) and that he, like Paul, would be overwhelmingly grateful for the rest of his life because of what Christ had accomplished on the cross on his behalf (Romans 7:24-5).

The Loveliness of Christ

It is Rutherford's high view of the sovereignty of God together with his high and profoundly experiential view of the sinfulness of his own sin that led Rutherford to be deeply passionate about Christ. And although it is true, as B.B. Warfield states, that Calvinism in general is characterized not simply by a high view of God's sovereignty but also by a high view of sin and a personal appropriation of the work of Christ,[51] it is *distinctively* true of Rutherford because of his view of the sovereignty of God and because his understanding of depravity was not just doctrinal or theoretical but *profoundly* experiential and personal. Rutherford knew that God was not required to forgive his sins and that Christ was not required to offer his life as a ransom on

---

[50] Marcus L. Loane, *Makers of Religious Freedom in the Seventeenth Century* (London: InterVarsity, 1960), 60. Rutherford himself confesses that he was a fool in his youth because he never opened the gate leading to the way to heaven until he was advanced in years: 'I suffered my sun to be high in the heaven, and near afternoon, before ever I took the gate by the end' (Rutherford, *Letters*, 364).

[51] See, e.g., B.B. Warfield, *The Plan of Salvation* (Grand Rapids, MI: Eerdmans, reprint, 1984), 96-104. See also Calvin, *Institutes* II.xvi.2-3, 504-6.

his behalf. The fact that God freely chose to do this for him, despite his own obvious unworthiness, produced in Rutherford a deep sense of love and gratitude. This love and gratitude was especially aimed at Christ, whom Rutherford saw as the incredible vehicle through which he himself received mercy instead of justice. The fact that Christ would voluntarily give his life for a vile sinner like himself—when there was no necessity that he do so—had a tremendous impact upon Rutherford.

This impact was so great that, for the rest of his days, Rutherford would look upon Christ as a 'precious and never-enough exalted Redeemer'.[52] He did not believe that Christ was given anywhere near the glory and honor that he deserved, either in his own life or in the lives of others. He lamented this, and he longed to raise all people's estimation of Christ. It especially grieved him to see the world running after other things instead of Christ and cheapening Christ by placing other things ahead of him:

> O if I could raise the market for Christ, and heighten the market a pound for a penny, and cry up Christ in men's estimation ten thousand talents more than men think of Him! But they are cheapening Him, and crying Him down, and valuing Him at their unworthy halfpenny; or else exchanging and bartering Christ with the miserable old fallen house of this vain world.[53]

In Rutherford's estimation, it was impossible to exalt Christ too highly or to give him too high a place:

> [Christ] cannot be set too high; nay, if there were ten thousand times ten thousand heavens, and each to be above another, and Christ to be set in the highest of them all; yet were He too low. Alas! He is too little thought of! He is like the field where the pearl is, that men go over, and tread upon the grass that grows above it, and yet they ken it not. Men tramp upon this pearl, and yet they know not what they are doing. Fy! fy! earthly man that thou art! Wilt thou put a cow or a sheep in thy affection beyond thy salvation? Fy for shame for evermore, that men set their lusts above Him! And O, fy for shame! that you should set your new-come-over lord, Willful-will, above the old eternal Lord, the Ancient of days, Jesus Christ. O! how is Christ put out of His place?[54]

---

[52] Rutherford, *Letters*, 656.
[53] Rutherford, *Letters*, 154.
[54] Rutherford, *Communion Sermons*, 18.

Rutherford believed that everything in all creation paled into insignificance when compared to Christ. If one could imagine the 'beauty of ten thousand thousand worlds of paradises, like the garden of Eden', all wrapped up into one; or if one could capture the beauty of 'all trees, all flowers, all smells, all colours, all tastes, all joys, all sweetness, all loveliness' contained in the world; it would still 'be less to that fair and dearest Well-beloved, Christ, than one drop of rain to the whole seas, rivers, lakes, and fountains of ten thousand earths'.[55] Even heaven was nothing to Rutherford when compared with the glory of Christ. In fact, Rutherford frequently went so far as to say that heaven without Christ would not be heaven at all but would be more like hell instead.[56] Such was the loveliness of Christ in his estimation.

Conclusion

It has been suggested that the main passion of a man's lifetime is frequently strongest in the days and hours leading up to his death, especially if that passion carries an eternal significance.[57] Death has a way of clarifying the mind, of calling us back to things of first importance and lasting significance. Such was certainly the case for Rutherford. His passion in life was to see Christ in all his beauty and splendor and to share what he saw with everyone with whom he came in contact; and this was his passion as he lay dying in 1661. When four members of his presbytery came to visit him a few weeks before he was to die, he pointed them to Christ just as he had done throughout his ministry, saying:

> My Lord and Master is the Chief of ten thousand of thousands; none is comparable to Him in heaven or in earth. Dear brethren, do all for Him: pray for Christ, preach for Christ; feed the flock committed to your charge for Christ: do all for Christ: beware of men-pleasing, there is too much of it among us.[58]

When Robert Blair, his companion in the ministry at St. Andrews, asked him, 'What think ye now of Christ?', Rutherford again replied true to form: 'I shall live and adore Him. Glory, glory to my Creator and Redeemer for ever. Glory shineth in Immanuel's Land.'[59]

---

[55] Rutherford, *Letters*, 446.

[56] See, e.g., Rutherford, *Letters*, 154, 398, 448, 550, 574.

[57] See, e.g., Gilmour, *Samuel Rutherford*, 229.

[58] Gilmour, *Samuel Rutherford*, 230.

[59] Bonar, "Sketch of Samuel Rutherford," in *Letters*, 20-21.

According to Andrew Bonar, the last few days of Rutherford's life were full of rapturous exclamations about Christ. 'I shall see Him as He is!', Rutherford said, 'I shall see Him reign, and all His fair company with Him.' Referring to 1 Corinthians 1:30, Rutherford declared, 'I close with it! Let Him be so. He is my all and all….If He should slay me ten thousand times I will trust.' On several occasions he asked for 'a well-tuned harp', as though he were ready right then 'to join the redeemed in their new song'. When he did at last draw his final breath, near the end of March 1661, his last words were exactly what we would expect, given the overall bent of his life to demonstrate the beauty and majesty of Christ: 'Glory, glory dwelleth in Immanuel's land!'[60]

As it was in life, so it was in death for Rutherford. He was a man wholly consumed with the loveliness of Christ. His high view of the sovereignty of God—i.e., his voluntarism, his supralapsarianism, his denial of the absolute necessity of justice and mercy in God and of the atonement of Christ, and his view of suffering—indicated to him that God was not compelled in any way whatsoever in any of his dealings with mankind. He did not have to punish sin or to be merciful toward sinners. He did not have to forgive sin or to forgive it by way of a cross. And Christ did not have to die on the cross in order to purchase forgiveness for his people. The fact that God did choose to be just and merciful and the fact that Christ did choose to die in order to secure divine mercy demonstrated to Rutherford God's overwhelming love for his people—of which Rutherford himself was one. This love found its ultimate expression in the person and work of Jesus Christ, the one whom the Bible calls Immanuel, God with us. When this understanding of God's sovereign freedom—especially as it was expressed in Christ—joined together with Rutherford's high view of his own unworthiness, it produced in him an overwhelming love and preoccupation with the beauty and magnificence of Christ. For Rutherford, glory really did dwell in *Immanuel's* land.

[60] Bonar, "Sketch of Samuel Rutherford," in *Letters*, 21-2.

7

William Cunningham and
the Doctrine of the Sacraments

Michael W. Honeycutt

'We believe that there is scarcely any subject set forth in the
Confessions of the Reformed churches...less understood than this of
the sacraments; and that many even of these who have subscribed
these Confessions, rest satisfied with some defective and confused
notions on the subject of baptism, and on the subject of the Lord's
Supper....'[1]

Introduction

On the day in 1845 when William Cunningham was appointed to
the Chair of Ecclesiastical History at New College in Edinburgh, a
friend offered her congratulations and spoke of the satisfaction felt
throughout the Free Church of Scotland at the news. 'Well,' replied
Cunningham, 'I'm told that some people are opposed to it on this
ground, that I have no imagination. Don't you think a want of
imagination is rather a good feature in a historian?'[2]

As Cunningham assumed his new post, his 'lack of imagination'
suited his pedagogical intentions well. His plan was not to speculate
about possible influences on the historical doctrines of the Church but
instead to measure those doctrines against the boundaries of Scriptural

---

[1] W. Cunningham, *The Reformers and the Theology of the Reformation* (1862; reprint, Carlisle,
Pennsylvania: Banner of Truth, 1979), 238-39.
[2] J. MacKenzie and R. Rainy, *Life of William Cunningham, D. D.* (London, 1871), 225.

proclamation.[3] As he explained to his students in the introductory lecture on Church History, the main purpose of his lectures was to

> make the history of the church subservient to the purpose of assisting you to form clear and definite conceptions of the real meaning and import of the revelation which God has given us, and of the best mode of explaining, illustrating, and defending the truths which it unfolds. With this view, and, as it is necessary to make a selection among the vast variety of subjects which the history of the church embraces, the more formal lectures of the course will be restricted almost wholly to the history of theology, properly so called—that is, of the doctrines taught in Scripture, or professedly deduced from it, and of the discussions to which they have given rise....[4]

Guiding seminary students to a better understanding of Scripture was, to Cunningham, the primary purpose of all theological education, including the teaching of Church history. For that reason, he intended to hold past theological discussions up to the 'lamp of divine truth' to determine the extent to which they concurred with the 'unerring standard of the Word of God.'[5]

Cunningham was well aware that historical theologians on the Continent refrained from this kind of evaluation. And he respected what he understood to be their concern that polemics tended to corrupt the truth of history. As he put it, 'controversial discussion is at all times attended with some danger.' But, he argued,

> it must not be forgotten, that in regard to most...of the controversies which have agitated the church and influenced the progress of opinion, there was a right and a wrong side, even when neither party in the controversy may perhaps have been wholly right or wholly wrong, and that an investigation into the precise opinions which may, in point of fact, have been held and advocated by the different parties, is really important and valuable only in so far as it affords materials which may furnish some assistance in estimating aright the truth, the importance, and the relative bearings of the opinions that may have been broached.[6]

---

[3] Cunningham's reputation for a 'want of imagination' derives from his straightforward style of preaching, unembellished by the use of illustration and figurative language as were the sermons of the popular preachers of the day; here, however, Cunningham cleverly fills that phrase with a new meaning, turning it into a positive trait.

[4] Cunningham, *Introductory Lecture on Church History*, 7 November 1850 (Edinburgh, [1850]), 64-66.

[5] ibid., 68.

[6] ibid., 70.

Rather than simply lecturing on the history of doctrine, then, Cunningham would do so polemically while focusing on the leading controversies of the Church in the past. To make this even more beneficial to his students and to the Church, he would focus on 'those subjects of discussion which still continue to divide the opinions of men and churches'.[7]

One subject that will always divide the opinions of the Church Militant is that of the sacraments. Today, various views of the nature, purpose, and efficacy of the sacraments continue to divide Protestant from Catholic and Protestant from Protestant. Even within Protestant traditions as narrowly circumscribed as the Reformed Churches, uniformity of opinion is difficult, if not impossible, to come by.

Some of Cunningham's more mature writing addressed the doctrine of the sacraments. Near the end of his life, between 1855 and 1860, Cunningham edited the *British and Foreign Evangelical Review*, a journal of high academic standard. Among the numerous articles he contributed to the journal, one was entitled, 'Zwingle and the Doctrine of the Sacraments.' This, according to Donald Macleod, includes 'probably the best treatment of the Lord's Supper in the English language'.[8] It also includes an insightful, thought-provoking defence of the Westminster standards against the charge of baptismal regeneration.

'Zwingle and the Doctrine of the Sacraments' and Cunningham's *Historical Theology* (largely his class lectures) contain most of what Cunningham has left the Church on the sacraments. Although written in the nineteenth-century context of a rising wave of anti-Catholicism and the Roman Catholic tendencies of the High Church Anglican movement known as Tractarianism (or the Oxford Movement), Cunningham's arguments are equally valid for the Church today. Debate over the nature of the grace bestowed in baptism continues within and among the Reformed Churches, for example; and many within these bodies would be surprised to discover what all they are embracing when they claim John Calvin's doctrine of the Lord's Supper as their own.

Before Cunningham sought to defend a Protestant and Reformed understanding of the sacraments, he provided just enough history (and

---

[7] ibid., 64-66.
[8] D. Macleod, *A Faith To Live By: Studies in Christian Doctrine* (Fearn: Christian Focus Publications, 1998), 251.

no more) in his class lectures to point out the fact of their doctrinal and practical corruption. In the New Testament, he argued, very little prominence is given to the sacraments; certainly nothing is there that gives any basis for Roman Catholic and Tractarian views on the nature, purposes, and results. Church fathers of the second and third centuries, however, began to exaggerate these very things, evidencing a tendency to 'make great mysteries of the sacraments'.[9] Cunningham referenced one such passage in the first *Apology* of Justin Martyr, the earliest of the fathers not contemporary with the apostles. Rather than quoting it, though, he simply pointed out the ambiguity of the passage by noting that Catholics see transubstantiation there, Lutherans see consubstantiation, and most others see neither transubstantiation nor consubstantiation. Like 'many other passages in the writings of the fathers,' he continues, 'it really has no definite meaning; and that if we would call up its author, and interrogate him on the subject, he would be utterly unable to tell us what he meant when he wrote it.'[10]

The declension from biblical teaching on the sacraments began in earnest just before the end of the third century. At that time, the fathers started to identify the sign with the thing signified. This led to the practice of ascribing to the sacraments a kind of inherent efficacy or power to confer what they merely represented or symbolized. Baptism, for instance, came to be seen as the occasion and instrumental cause of forgiveness of sin and regeneration. Before this time, those who linked baptism with salvation in some way did so '*upon the assumption*' that faith 'existed and was expressed or embodied in the reception of baptism'.[11] This assumption, however, was gradually 'lost sight of, and they began to talk as if baptism of itself necessarily implied all this.'[12] Not that the principles of the *opus operatum*[13] or the absolute necessity of baptism to salvation can be shown to have been widely or distinctly held by the fathers of the third century. That would not happen until the fourth. But both principles were already there in seed form.

[9] W. Cunningham, *Historical Theology: A Review of the Principal Doctrinal Discussions in the Christian Church since the Apostolic Age*, vol. 1 (1882; reprint, St. Edmonton: Still Waters Revival Books, 1991), 202.

[10] Cunningham, *Reformers*, 232.

[11] Cunningham, *Historical Theology*, vol. 1, 203.

[12] ibid.

[13] From the *New Catholic Dictionary*: *opus operatum* [like *ex opere operato*] is a 'technical phrase used by theologians since the 13th century to signify that the sacraments produce grace of themselves; [it] is used to signify the objective character of the sacraments as producers of grace in opposition to the subjectivism of the Reformers.

Not surprisingly, alongside these aberrant principles appeared the aberrant practice of delaying baptism. It became common, in fact, during the third and fourth centuries, for those who professed conversion to postpone their baptism until they believed they were near death. This they did under the commonly held notion, as Cunningham put it, that 'baptism conferred the remission of all past sins, and thus, as it were, cleared off all scores, and prepared them for death and heaven. This erroneous and most dangerous notion was not, indeed, directly countenanced by the doctors of the church, but there must have been something in the common mode of stating and explaining the nature and the efficacy of baptism which naturally led to the adoption of it.'[14]

During the fourth, fifth, and subsequent centuries of the middle ages, the doctrines of the sacraments that now separate Protestants from Catholics were largely developed. By the end of the fourth century, for example, ambiguity regarding the import of baptism was cleared up as the fathers began to proclaim the doctrine of the absolute necessity of baptism to salvation. By the end of the ninth century, the French monk Paschasius Radbertus 'reduced the fluctuating expressions long in use concerning the body and blood of Christ in the holy supper, to [the] theory of transubstantiation.'[15] And by the end of the Middle Ages, the scholastic theologians had so developed the doctrines regarding the nature, design, and effects of the sacraments that 'Christianity was looked upon by the great body of its professors as a system which consisted in, and the whole benefits were connected with, a series of outward ceremonies and ritual observances.'[16] These declarations of the ancient and medieval Church on the sacraments were then made official by the Council of Trent in the sixteenth century.

In Defence of William Cunningham and His Doctrine of the Lord's Supper

Only against this historical backdrop does Cunningham's oft-cited criticism of his theological hero, John Calvin, make sense:

We have no fault to find with the substance of Calvin's statements in regard to the sacraments in general or with respect to baptism; but we cannot deny that he made an effort to bring out something like

---

[14] Cunningham, *Historical Theology*, vol. 1, 204.
[15] ibid., 206.
[16] Cunningham, *Historical Theology*, vol. 2, 122.

a real influence exerted by Christ's human nature upon the souls of believers, in connection with the dispensation of the Lord's Supper—an effort which, of course, was altogether unsuccessful, and resulted only in what is about as unintelligible as Luther's consubstantiation.[17]

Though Calvin denied, of course, the doctrine of transubstantiation and posited a view distinct from consubstantiation, he was, according to Donald Macleod, 'mentally conditioned by medievalism and simply could not shake off the idea that somehow the "thing", the body of Christ, was present in the sacrament.'[18] 'This,' according to Cunningham, 'is perhaps, the greatest blot in the history of Calvin's labours as a public instructor....'[19]

As might be imagined, Cunningham's critique of Calvin's view of the Lord's Supper has not gone unnoticed. Perhaps the most noteworthy challenge to that critique in our day comes from the pen of Keith Mathison in *Given for You: Reclaiming Calvin's Doctrine of the Lord's Supper*. A work that is both polemical and pastoral, it has no doubt fostered a renewed appreciation for the Lord's Supper that has long been lacking, even, surprisingly, in Reformed circles.[20] Mathison's main argument, in his words, is this:

> During the sixteenth and seventeenth centuries two distinct views of the Lord's Supper gained some measure of confessional authority in the Reformed church. The first traces its roots to John Calvin, while the second traces its roots to Ulrich Zwingli's successor, Heinrich Bullinger. Zwingli's own strictly memorialist view was generally disowned by the Reformed churches and confessions of the sixteenth century. However, from the seventeenth century onward, it has gradually become the dominant view in the Reformed church.... It is the thesis of this book that the gradual adoption of Zwingli's doctrine has been a move away from the biblical and Reformed view of the Lord's Supper. This book will argue that Calvin's doctrine of the Lord's Supper is the biblical doctrine, the basic doctrine of sixteenth-century Reformed churches, and the doctrine that should be reclaimed and proclaimed in the Reformed church today.[21]

---

[17] Cunningham, *Reformers*, 240.

[18] Macleod, *A Faith To Live By*, 251.

[19] Cunningham, *Reformers*, 240.

[20] Robert Peterson, one of my colleagues at Covenant Theological Seminary, in fact, has used this as a textbook and has said as much.

[21] K. A. Mathison, *Given for You: Reclaiming Calvin's Doctrine of the Lord's Supper* (Phillipsburg: P&R Publishing, 2002), xv-xvi.

History does reveal that the Reformed Church has in large part departed from the fullness of Calvin's doctrine of the Lord's Supper. In truth, few understand that his doctrine includes more than simply subscribing to some form of the spiritual presence of Christ in the Supper. But, two concerns with Mathison's thesis should be raised. First, some suggest that his definition of Calvin's doctrine presents a higher sacramentalism than can be found in Calvin. Certainly his embrace of John Williamson Nevin's view of the Lord's Supper, for example, encourages that conclusion. This concern, however, has been ably handled elsewhere and will not be further addressed here.[22] Second, the same history that reveals some level of departure from Calvin's view of the Lord's Supper does not indicate that the swing has reached the so-called 'strictly memorialist' view of Zwingli. Mathison's labelling, then, of certain Reformed theologians as Zwinglian tends both to disenfranchise them and to categorize them in a way they themselves would not recognize.[23]

Unfortunately, this is the case for Cunningham and all who follow him in his understanding of the Lord's Supper. Mathison concludes his section on Cunningham with these words: 'Essentially, then, what we find in Cunningham is the eucharistic doctrine of Zwingli.'[24] Since Mathison defines Zwingli's position as 'essentially a commemoration of the death of Christ', this can only mean that Cunningham, like Zwingli, believed in a 'purely symbolic memorialism'.[25] And *Given for You* does depict Cunningham in a way that would indicate he believed the Lord's Supper to be a mere sign or testimony of spiritual blessing. For example: 'According to Cunningham the sacraments are symbols that "merely signify or represent…spiritual blessings…." In the Lord's Supper, therefore, God "is just telling us that Christ's body was broken, and that his blood was shed, for men…."'[26] These are indeed Cunningham's words, but not all of them. In the same article from which these quotations are taken, 'Zwingle and the Doctrine of

---

[22] L. Duncan, 'True Communion with Christ in the Lord's Supper: Calvin, Westminster and the Nature of Christ's Sacramental Presence,' *The Westminster Confession into the 21st Century: Essays in Remembrance of the 350th Anniversary of the Westminster Assembly*, vol. 2, ed. by L. Duncan (Fearn: Christian Focus Publications, 2004), 429-75.

[23] A more nuanced and thus more helpful way to categorize Reformed theologians with respect to their views of the Lord's Supper can be found in Duncan, 'True Communion with Christ in the Lord's Supper,' *The Westminster Confession into the 21st Century*, 431-34.

[24] Mathison, *Given for You*, 166. Mathison does acknowledge Cunningham's view is a modified Zwinglianism, 'but it is Zwinglianism nonetheless. '

[25] ibid., 4, 176.

[26] ibid., 166.

the Sacraments,' Cunningham argues that not even Zwingli was that 'Zwinglian' – at least not at the end of his life:

> in the last work which he wrote…, the 'Exposito Fidei,' he gave some indications, though perhaps not very explicit, of regarding the sacraments not only as signs but as seals,—as signs and seals not only on the part of men, but of God,—as signifying and confirming something then done by God through the Spirit, as well as something done by the receiver through faith. This is the great general principle which has been usually held by Protestants upon the subject, and is commonly regarded as constituting the leading point of difference between what is often represented as the Zwinglian doctrine of the sacraments being only naked and bare signs, and that held by the Protestant churches.[27]

Elsewhere, in that same article, Cunningham distances himself from the memorial view: 'the sacraments…are signs and seals of the covenant of grace…not only signifying or representing Christ and the benefits of the new covenant, but sealing or confirming them, and in some sense applying them, to believers.'[28] They are, in other words, 'means of grace', 'institutions which God intended and appointed to be, in some sense, the instruments or channels of conveying to men spiritual blessings, and in the due and right use of which men are warranted to expect to receive the spiritual blessings they stand in need of.'[29]

This of course is not *fully* Calvin's position; Cunningham in fact believed 'the discussion of the kind and manner of the presence of Christ' in the Lord's Supper (a significant aspect of Calvin's doctrine) to be 'one of the most useless controversies that ever was raised'.[30] But, it is exactly contrary to what Mathison has described as Zwingli's position: 'Zwingli,' he argued, 'completely rejected the idea of the

---

[27] Cunningham, *Reformers*, 228. As Ligon Duncan has noted, Zwingli denied the memorial view explicitly: "Zwingli asserted on one occasion, 'If I have called this a commemoration, I have done so in order to controvert those who would make of it a sacrifice…. We believe that Christ is truly present in the Lord's Supper; yea, that there is no communion without such presence…. We believe that the true Body of Christ is eaten in Communion, not in a gross and carnal manner, but in a spiritual and sacramental manner by the religious, believing, and pious heart.' See W. P. Stephens extremely helpful survey of Zwingli on the sacraments in *The Theology of Huldrych Zwingli* (Oxford: Clarendon, 1986), 180-93, 218-59." 'True Communion with Christ in the Lord's Supper,' *The Westminster Confession into the 21ˢᵗ Century*, 431-32, fn. 5.

[28] Cunningham, *Reformers*, 245.
[29] ibid., 260.
[30] ibid., 289.

sacrament as means of grace.'[31] Cunningham, himself, is quick to call this an error in Zwingli's thinking, an error resulting from over-reaction to sacramentalism: when leaning away from 'the unintelligible and mystical' towards 'what was clear, definite, and practical', he 'did not stop precisely at the right point and…carried the work of demolition too far.' He 'came short indeed of the truth in his doctrine as to the nature and efficacy of the sacraments, by not bringing out fully what God does, or is ready and willing to do, through their instrumentality, in offering to men and conferring upon them, through the exercise of faith, spiritual blessings.'[32]

In one sense, it is easy to see why Cunningham might be identified with Zwingli on the doctrine of the sacraments. In the same article that he strongly criticizes Calvin, he highly praises Zwingli, whose contribution to a Protestant expression of the sacraments is unparalleled in Cunningham's eyes. It was Zwingli, Cunningham writes, who 'entirely threw off the huge mass of extravagant absurdity and unintelligible mysticism which, from a very early period, had been gathering round the subject of the sacraments, and which had reached its height in the authorised doctrine of the Church of Rome.'[33] This, he continues, was 'one of the most important… achievements which the history of the church records,' an achievement that Luther never reached, either in his understanding of baptism or the Lord's Supper, and one that Calvin never reached in his understanding of the Lord's Supper.[34] This is indeed very high praise for Zwingli; it does not, however, make of Cunningham a Zwinglian.

Another, earlier, response to Cunningham's criticism of Calvin's view of the Lord's Supper is found in the article, 'Calvin Defended against Drs. Cunningham and Hodge.' Appearing in *The Southern Presbyterian Review* in 1876, it was written by the fiery John Adger in the wake of the sacramental debate between Princeton's Charles Hodge and Mercerburg's John Williamson Nevin. In that debate, Nevin had argued for a return, in the Reformed Church, to what he understood to be a fully Calvinistic understanding of the Lord's Supper. Hodge, like Cunningham, was less than enamoured with the entirety of Calvin's position and argued instead for a middle position

---

[31] Mathison, *Given for You*, 63.
[32] Cunningham, *Reformers*, 229-30.
[33] ibid., 228.
[34] ibid., 228.

Michael W. Honeycutt

between that of Calvin and Zwingli.[35] Adger, who held the chair of Church History at Columbia Seminary in South Carolina, sought to promote Calvin's position and openly sided with Nevin against Hodge in his annual lectures on the Lord's Supper.[36]

Hodge and Cunningham were considered by some to be the two great theologians of their day, and Adger takes them both to task in 'Calvin Defended against Drs. Cunningham and Hodge.' He devotes most of his article, however, to Cunningham, whom he believes has been 'not a little disparaging to the great Genevese'.[37]

According to Adger, Cunningham had levelled five charges against Calvin. First, 'The Reformer's views were not strictly his own—the product of his own calm and unbiased investigation and reflection, but were reached under the control of a reactionary influence from Zwingle's genius, or at least from Zwingle's extravagance.'[38] Mostly true. Cunningham was more cautious in his language, but he did believe that the general tendency among the Reformers was to overreact to Zwingle's oversimplification of the sacraments as a result of his over-reaction to the doctrine of the Church of Rome. 'This,' Cunningham believed, 'appears more or less even in Calvin....'[39]

Second, 'Calvin, under this influence, went astray and approximated Rome.' True again. But not in the way Adger understands it or states it. Cunningham's actual statement was that Calvin 'approximated somewhat *in phraseology* to the Romish position', and he cites two examples of this. The first has been noted already.[40] It was the second, apparently, that elicited Adger's impassioned but unnecessary response. Cunningham had pointed out that Calvin, in 'Antidote to the Council of Trent', suggests a sense in which the sacraments contain the grace they signify (*sacramentis contineri gratiam quam figurant*).[41]

---

[35] Mathison, *Given for You*, 148.

[36] ibid., 159.

[37] J. Adger, 'Calvin Defended Against Drs. Cunningham and Hodge,' *Southern Presbyterian Review* 27 (January 1876), 135.

[38] Adger, 'Calvin Defended,' 135.

[39] Cunningham, *Reformers*, 240.

[40] Calvin 'made an effort to bring out something like a real influence exerted by Christ's human nature upon the souls of believers, in connection with the dispensation of the Lord's Supper....' (Cunningham, *Reformers*, 240). This is more than Cunningham was comfortable with, but a far cry from the Roman Catholic doctrine of transubstantiation. It approaches Rome only in the sense that there are hints of vague commonality in the language – Rome spoke of the sacramental elements becoming the body of Christ; Calvin spoke of Christ's body being made present to us in the Lord's Supper by the Spirit.

[41] Cunningham, *Reformers*, 261.

Adger countered this, arguing that Calvin disagreed profoundly with Rome, 'denouncing as "fatal and pestilential this sentiment—that the sacraments have a kind of secret virtue." In fact he says, in his own forcible way, that "it is plainly of the devil."'[42]

Cunningham, if he had even a drop of Baptist blood in that Presbyterian heart of his, would gladly give a hearty 'amen' to that. He had said the very same thing when he qualified his earlier statement: Calvin 'asserts also that those who allege, that by the sacraments grace is conferred upon us when we do not put an obstacle in the way, overturn the whole power of the sacraments....'[43] What's more, 'he distinctly admits that the sacraments are instrumental causes of conferring grace upon us, though the power of God is not tied to them, and though they produce no effect whatever apart from the faith of the recipient.'[44] Adger's second charge was, in the end, no charge at all.

Third, 'Acting along with Zwingle's reactionary influence...there was another perverting element—a rather weak desire to keep on friendly terms with Luther.'[45] True and false. True, in that Cunningham believed Calvin's desire to remain on good terms with Luther did influence (within the boundaries of conscience[46]) his doctrine of the Lord's Supper. False, in that Cunningham did not speak of a 'weak' desire to keep on friendly terms with Luther. It was, instead a noble quality in Calvin 'for which he usually gets no credit—viz., an earnest desire to preserve unity and harmony among the different sections of the Christian church.'[47] Adger's attempt, then, to undermine Cunningham's argument at this point by giving examples to show that Calvin was no 'boot-licker to Luther', once again, misses the point.[48]

Fourth, 'All this gave rise to a dishonest effort on Calvin's part to bring out of Scripture what was not in Scripture.' False. This is an argument from silence. And Cunningham was not silent about the shortcomings of others. Nor was he subtle. If Cunningham believed Calvin to be dishonest on this point, he would have said so in no uncertain terms.

---

[42] Adger, 'Calvin Defended,' 137-38.

[43] Cunningham, *Reformers*, 261. Adger had cited John Calvin's *Institutes of the Christian Religion* (4. 14. 14) where he rejected the notion that the sacraments contain 'some sort of secret powers' so that they 'confer grace, provided we do not set up a barrier of mortal sin.'

[44] Cunningham, *Reformers*, 261.

[45] Adger, 'Calvin Defended,' 135.

[46] Cunningham, *Reformers*, 240. Cunningham's words are 'approximate *as far as he could.*'

[47] ibid.

[48] Adger, 'Calvin Defended,' 151.

Fifth, 'The result was…a theory as unintelligible as Luther's consubstantiation.' True. Cunningham said this, and Adger accurately interpreted what he said. But it cannot escape notice that the complexity of Calvin's doctrine of the Lord's Supper is obvious from the numerous debates, articles, and books it has produced. Probably the most difficult and debated element of Calvin's view is exactly what concerned Cunningham – the idea that somehow in the sacrament the Spirit of God lifts us up to heaven so that we truly, though in a non-corporeal way, partake in the human nature of Christ (what Church historian David Calhoun affectionately refers to as the 'miracle of transportation' as opposed to the 'miracle of transubstantiation'). This is far more than what many Reformed folk embrace when they speak of the 'spiritual presence' of Christ in the sacrament.

It is also far more than what Calvin, himself, could explain. In his own words, 'if anyone should ask me how this takes place, I shall not be ashamed to confess that it is a secret too lofty for either my mind to comprehend or my words to declare. And, to speak more plainly, I rather experience than understand it.'[49] It does seem 'unbelievable,' he acknowledged, 'that Christ's flesh, separated from us by such great distance, penetrates to us, so that it becomes our food….'[50]

It was this aspect of Calvin's doctrine of the Lord's Supper that was 'unintelligible' to Cunningham. He never accepted it, and he viewed it as perhaps the greatest error in Calvin's theology. Nevertheless, Cunningham was no Zwinglian, as that term is often used, and when it's all said and done, Cunningham affirmed many of the central Calvinian teachings on the Lord's Supper. He held views in fact that were in perfect accord with the Westminster Confession 'and thus,' as Ligon Duncan writes, 'ought to be esteemed as part of the Reformed consensus on the Supper.'[51]

William Cunningham's Defense of the Westminster Standards and its Doctrine of Baptism

In 1828, not long after Cunningham was licensed to preach by the Church of Scotland at the ripe old age of twenty three, he wrote to a friend about the doctrines to which he had just expressed his solemn consent. 'With regard to the Confession of Faith,' he stated, 'I think

---

[49] J. Calvin, *Institutes of the Christian Religion*, 4. 17. 32.

[50] ibid., 4. 17. 10.

[51] Duncan, 'True Communion with Christ in the Lord's Supper,' *The Westminster Confession into the 21ˢᵗ Century*, 448.

I can say sincerely, that I believe the whole doctrine contained in it. I believe to be true every doctrine which is really and expressly asserted in it....'[52] Afterwards, he devoted much of his public career as a Churchman to expounding and defending that document as a true expression of biblical teaching.

Twenty years after Cunningham's ordination, in 1848, an incident in England triggered what he viewed as a challenge to the doctrine of baptism contained within the Westminster standards. Henry Philpotts, the Bishop of Exeter, refused to install George Cornelius Gorham as rector of the tiny village of Brampford Speke, citing 'unsoundness' concerning baptismal regeneration.[53] Philpotts, an Anglo-Catholic, and Gorham, an outspoken Calvinistic Evangelical, 'had already clashed over the subject of baptism, Gorham insisting that it was no doctrine of the Church of England that baptism "regenerated" anyone, and Philpotts using Tractarian arguments to insist otherwise.'[54] More importantly for Cunningham, Philpotts, in that same year, asserted in writing that a number of the confessions of the Reformed churches, including the Helvetic, the Augsburg, the Saxon, the Belgic, and the Catechism of Heidelberg, taught the doctrine of baptismal regeneration, agreeing with the Church of Rome and the Church of England. That same allegation was then levelled against the Shorter Catechism.[55]

Cunningham did believe that there was a general tendency among the early Protestant confessions, both during the Reformation and in the seventeenth century, to magnify the value and efficacy of the sacraments. The charge that they taught baptismal regeneration, however, was a 'most extraordinary blunder'.[56] Moreover, 'there is nothing in the "Shorter Catechism" which gives any countenance to this notion, or, indeed, conveys any explicit deliverance as to the bearing of baptism upon infants.'[57]

---

[52] MacKenzie and Rainy, *Cunningham*, 41.

[53] A. C. Guelzo, *For the Union of Evangelical Christendom: The Irony of the Reformed Episcopalians* (University Park: The Pennsylvania State University Press, 1994), 57.

[54] ibid.

[55] Cunningham, *Reformers*, 241. In our day, Church historian David Wright has renewed this argument. 'The Westminster divines,' he writes, 'viewed baptism as the instrument and occasion of regeneration by the Spirit, of the remission of sins, of ingrafting into Christ (cf. 28:1). The Confession teaches baptismal regeneration' (D. Wright, 'Baptism at the Westminster Assembly,' *The Westminster Confession into the 21st Century*, vol. 1, 169). Others, today, associated with the so-called Auburn Avenue Theology or Federal Vision, have also argued for the possibility of some form of baptismal regeneration within the Westminster standards.

[56] Cunningham, *Reformers*, 241.

[57] ibid., 242.

Michael W. Honeycutt

This last statement hints at Cunningham's sometimes-straightfor-
ward, sometimes-complex defence of the Westminster standards. In
essence, he contends that the Reformers and the Westminster divines
reflected in their Confessions the understanding that 'the sacraments
were instituted and intended for believers, and produce their appropriate beneficial effects, only through the faith which must have previously existed, and which is expressed and exercised in the act of partaking them.'[58] So, while the Shorter Catechism teaches that infants of
members of the visible Church are to be baptized, when it speaks of
the effects of baptism it refers to believing recipients. Understood in
this light, the Shorter Catechism allows no room for baptismal regeneration. Baptismal regeneration, in fact, assumes the mistaken notion
'that the general description given of the import and object of baptism…is intended to apply to every case [believer and infant] in which
the outward ordinance of baptism is administered.'[59]

Cunningham realized that this represented a paradigm shift in
understanding for those accustomed to seeing baptism ordinarily
administered to infants. In his words, 'This mode of contemplating
the ordinance of baptism is so different from what we are accustomed
to, that we are apt to be startled when it is presented to us, and find
it somewhat difficult to enter into it.'[60] Nevertheless, the Confessions
of the Reformers and then the Westminster Divines, when addressing
'the general object and design of baptism…in the abstract,…have in
their view…only *adult* baptism, the baptism of those who, after they
have come to years of understanding, ask and obtain admission into
the visible church by being baptized.'[61] Infant baptism is not in their
sights.

The Reformed Confessions did this partly because of their historical
context. In conversation with their Roman Catholic opponents,
they sought to accommodate themselves to the manner in which
the Council of Trent presented the subject. And, interestingly, the
Tridentine decrees and canons described the process of justification
(which in Roman Catholicism asserts baptism as the instrumental
cause of regeneration) as it relates to adults. In other words, those who
have become adults and who then embrace Christianity and apply to
be baptized are the ones in consideration.

[58] ibid., 244.
[59] ibid., 242.
[60] ibid., 245.
[61] ibid.

The Reformers, as a result, also assumed adult baptism in their Confessions. It was for this reason, in fact, that they sometimes spoke in a way that seemed almost to identify baptism and regeneration. Not because they asserted the Roman Catholic principle of an invariable connection between the outward ordinance and the spiritual blessing (which they rejected). But because adult baptism, if not 'a hypocritical profession', was, '*in every instance*, according to the general doctrine of Protestants,... the sign and seal of a faith and regeneration *previously existing*,—already effected by God's grace....'[62]

Cunningham acknowledged that by assuming adult baptism in their Confessions, the Reformers' descriptions of the sacraments, if pressed, might seem to discountenance infant baptism. This, obviously, was never their intent, and they strenuously defended its lawfulness and obligation against the anti-paedobaptist position of the Anabaptists. But they viewed infant baptism as holding a 'somewhat peculiar and supplemental position'. As Cunningham noted, the 'general tenor of Scripture language upon the subject of baptism applies primarily and directly to the baptism of adults' and it is 'necessary, therefore, to form our primary and fundamental conceptions of the objects and effects of baptism...from the baptism of adults and not of infants.'[63]

The Westminster Confession, like the Reformed Confessions of a century before, addressed adult baptism when speaking of efficacy. This is evident in the statements of the Confession and Catechisms, as will be seen, but also in the statements of some of the more important

---

[62] ibid., 248; Cunningham, *Historical Theology*, vol. 2, 126.

[63] Cunningham, *Historical Theology*, vol. 2, 144. 'The Reformed divines, not holding the doctrine of baptismal regeneration, did not regard the baptism of infants as being of sufficient importance to modify the general doctrine they thought themselves warranted to lay down with respect to the sacraments, as applicable to adult baptism and the Lord's Supper. And it is...instructive to notice, that the adoption, by the Lutherans, of the doctrine of baptismal regeneration led them to be much more careful of laying down any general statements, either about the sacraments or about baptism, which virtually ignored the baptism of infants. They are much more careful than the Reformed divines, either expressly and by name to bring... infant baptism into their general definitions or descriptions, or, at least, to leave ample room for it, so that there may be no appearance of its being omitted or forgotten. It may be worthwhile to give a specimen of this. [Johann Franz] Buddaeus, one of the best of the Lutheran divines,... in treating of the effect of baptism, which, he says, may also be regarded as the end or object of the ordinance, lays it down, that it is "with respect to infants, regeneration, and with respect to adults, the confirming and sealing...of the faith of which they ought to be possessed before they are admitted to baptism." In contrast with this, many of the Reformed divines asserted, without any hesitation, that the great leading object and effect of the sacraments and, of course, of baptism as well as of the Lord's Supper, was just the...confirming and strengthening of the faith, which must, or, at least, should, have existed in the case of adults before either sacrament was received' (Cunningham, *Reformers*, 263-64).

Westminster divines. Cunningham cites two: Samuel Rutherford (*Due Right of Presbyteries*) and George Gillespie (*Aaron's Rod Blossoming*). Before quoting them, he notes their qualifications: 'Rutherford and Gillespie are literally and without any exception, just the two very highest authorities that could be brought to bear upon a question of this kind, at once from their learning and ability as theologians, and from the place they held and the influence they exerted in the actual preparation of the documents under consideration.'[64]

From Rutherford:

> 1. Baptism is not that whereby we are entered into Christ's mystical and invisible body as such, for it is presupposed we be members of Christ's body, and our sins pardoned already, before baptism come to be a seal of sins pardoned. But baptism is a seal of our entry into Christ's visible body, as swearing to the colours is that which entereth a soldier to be a member of such an army, whereas, before his oath, he was only a heart friend to the army and cause.

> 2. Baptism, as it is such, is a seal, and a seal—as a seal,—addeth no new lands or goods to the man to whom the charter and seal is given, but only doth legally confirm him in the right of such lands given to the man by prince or state. Yet this hindreth not, but baptism is a real legal seal, legally confirming the man in his actual visible profession of Christ, remission of sins, regeneration, so, as though before baptism he was a member of Christ's body, yet, *quoad nos* [with respect to us], he is not a member of Christ's body visible, until he be made such by baptism.[65]

From Gillespie:

> The papists hold that the sacraments are instrumental to confer, give, or work grace, yea, *ex opere operato*, as the schoolmen speak. Our divines hold that the sacraments are appointed of God, and delivered to the church as sealing ordinances, not to give, but to testify what is given, not to make, but to confirm saints. And they not only oppose the papist's *opus operatum*, but they simply deny this instrumentality of the sacraments, that they are appointed of God for working or giving grace where it is not. This is so well known to all who have

---

[64] Cunningham, *Reformers*, 279.
[65] ibid.

studied the sacramentarian controversies, that I should not need to prove it….[66]

These authorities were only auxiliary support, however, to Cunningham's main argument – the actual statements of the Westminster standards. Beginning with the Shorter Catechism, Cunningham asserted that its doctrine of baptism can only be properly grasped after its description of the sacraments in general is understood. The Westminster divines, as was typical for authors of the Reformed Confessions, gave as a definition or description of the sacraments (in the abstract) only that which applied equally to both the Lord's Supper and baptism. Put another way, 'all that is said about a sacrament not only may, but must, be applied both to baptism and the Lord's Supper, as being in all its extent true of each of them.'[67] So, to the question, 'What is a sacrament?' the Shorter Catechism answers: 'A sacrament is a holy ordinance instituted by Christ, wherein, by sensible signs, Christ and the benefits of the new covenant are represented, sealed, and *applied to believers*.'[68] Then, to the question, 'What is baptism?' the Shorter Catechism answers: 'Baptism is a sacrament, wherein the washing with water, in the name of the Father, the Son, and the Holy Ghost, doth signify and seal our ingrafting into Christ, our partaking of the benefits of the covenant of grace, and our engagement to be the Lord's.'[69]

Putting these two together leads to the conclusion that 'this description of baptism applies fully and in all its extent, only to those who are possessed of the necessary qualifications or preparations for baptism, and who are able to ascertain this.'[70] In other words, the Shorter Catechism's description of baptism is written with believers in mind, not all who are baptized. Only those who are baptized after they have become believers are 'capable of ascertaining that they have been legitimately baptized, *and…are in consequence able to adopt the language of the catechism*' in its general description of baptism.[71] Its statement, then, that 'baptism signifies and seals *our* ingrafting into Christ, etc., must mean, that it signifies and seals the ingrafting into Christ OF THOSE OF US who have been ingrafted into Christ by faith.'[72]

---

[66] ibid., 280.
[67] ibid., 242.
[68] *WSC* 92.
[69] *WSC* 94.
[70] Cunningham, *Reformers*, 243.
[71] ibid.
[72] ibid., 244.

Michael W. Honeycutt

The Westminster divines, then, like the authors of the earlier Reformed Confessions, regarded infant baptism as a

> peculiar, subordinate, supplemental, exceptional thing, which stands, indeed, firmly based on its own distinct and special grounds, but which cannot well be brought within the line of the general abstract definition or description of a sacrament, as applicable to adult baptism and the Lord's Supper.... This, again, implies an admission that the definition given of a sacrament does not apply fully and in all its extent to the special case of infant baptism; while it implies, also, that the compilers of the catechism thought it much more important, to bring out fully, as the definition of the sacrament, all that could be truly predicated equally of adult baptism and the Lord's Supper, than to try and form a definition that might be wide enough and vague enough to include infant baptism....[73]

Moving from the Shorter Catechism to the Larger Catechism, Cunningham answers a potential challenge to his argument. There a sacrament is described as 'an holy ordinance instituted by Christ, in His church, to signify, seal, and exhibit *unto those that are within the covenant of grace*, the benefits of His mediation, to strengthen and increase their faith....' According to the prevailing views at the time of the Westminster Assembly and in accordance with Scripture, the expression, 'those that are within the covenant of grace' might encompass the children of believing parents. But this extended sense is not being used here because 'this sentence goes on immediately, without any change in the construction, and without any indication of alteration or restriction in regard to the persons spoken of, to say, that the sacraments were instituted "to strengthen and increase THEIR faith,"—implying, of course, that the persons here spoken of had faith before the sacraments came to bear upon them, or could confer upon them any benefit.'[74]

Moving to the Confession of Faith, Cunningham demonstrates that it is consistent with both the Shorter and Larger Catechisms, though not as explicit in its language:

> The Confession[75] lays it down as the first and principal...object of the sacraments, of both equally and alike, 'to represent Christ and

---

[73] ibid., 250.
[74] ibid., 251.
[75] *WCF* 27. 1.

126

His benefits, and to confirm our interest in Him,'—this last clause implying, that those for whom the sacraments were intended, have already and previously acquired a personal interest in Christ, which could be only by their union to Him through faith. It further[76] in speaking still of the sacraments, and, of course, of baptism as well as the Lord's Supper, asserts that 'the word of institution contains a promise of benefit to worthy receivers;' and worthy receivers, in the full import of the expression, are, in the case of adult baptism, believers. In the next chapter, the twenty-eighth, the description given of baptism manifestly applies only to believing adults. It is there described as a 'sacrament of the New Testament, ordained by Jesus Christ, not only for the solemn admission of the party baptized into the visible church, but also to be unto him a sign and seal of the covenant of grace, of his ingrafting into Christ, of regeneration, of remission of sins, and of his giving up unto God, through Jesus Christ, to walk in newness of life.' It is quite true that infants, as well as adults, though incapable of faith, must be ingrafted into Christ, and must receive regeneration and remission; and that without this, indeed, they cannot be saved. But the statement in the Confession plainly assumes, that each individual baptized not only should have the necessary preliminary qualifications, but should be himself exercised and satisfied upon this point; and should thus be prepared to take part, intelligently and consciously, in the personal assumption of the practical obligations which baptism implies.[77]

The Confession of Faith, then, is in harmony with the Shorter and Larger Catechisms. All teach the general position 'that the sacraments are intended for believers; that participation in them assumes the previous and present existence of faith in all who rightly receive them; and that they produce their appropriate, beneficial effects only through the operation and exercise of faith in those who partake in them.'[78]

It follows from this that baptism does not produce or bestow justification and regeneration – either in an auxiliary or an instrumental way. Baptism has its intended effect only after the participant already possesses justification and regeneration. Baptism, in other words, like the Lord's Supper, conveys sanctifying grace, not the initial grace of salvation. As Cunningham puts it:

[76] *WCF* 27. 3.
[77] Cunningham, *Reformers*, 262-63.
[78] ibid., 263
[79] ibid., 272-73.

the spiritual blessings which the sacraments may be instrumental in conveying, can be those only which men still stand in need of, with a view to their salvation, after they have been justified and regenerated by faith. And these are the forgiveness of the sins which they continue to commit, a growing sense of God's pardoning mercy, and grace and strength to resist temptation, to discharge duty, to improve privilege, and to be ever advancing in holiness;—or, to adopt the language of the 'Shorter Catechism,'…they are 'assurance of God's love, peace of conscience, joy in the Holy Ghost, increase of grace and perseverance therein to the end. '[79]

The main purpose of both sacraments, then, is to convey these blessings to those who have already believed and 'to do this mainly, if not solely, by strengthening and confirming their faith'.[80] The nineteenth chapter of the Confession declares this explicitly: with respect to saving faith, it says, '"it is ordinarily wrought by the ministry of the word, by which also, and by the administration of the sacraments and prayer, it is increased and strengthened." Here the increasing and strengthening of saving faith, previously produced and already existing, is ascribed to the administration of the sacraments, and of course is predicated equally and alike of baptism and the Lord's Supper….'[81]

By increasing a faith that already exists, the sacraments convey, not a grace that initiates salvation, but one that encourages and nourishes a salvation that has already begun. Baptism does not impart regeneration. This was the testimony of the documents of the Westminster standards and the testimony of some of Scotland's leading divines. George Gillespie, one of the more important members, it will be remembered, of the Westminster Assembly, stated it this way: 'Protestant writers do not only oppose the *opus operatum*…, but they oppose…all causality or working of the first grace of conversion and faith in or by the sacraments, supposing always a man to be a believer and within the covenant of grace before the sacrament, and that he is not made such, nor translated to the state of grace in or by the sacrament.'[82] Thomas Erskine, one of the great Scottish theologians of the early part of the eighteenth century, said this: 'The sacraments are not converting but confirming ordinances; they are appointed for

---

[80] ibid., 273-74.
[81] ibid., 275. The Larger Catechism uses similar language: 'to strengthen and increase their faith and all other graces….' (Q. 162).
[82] Cunningham, *Reformers*, 281.

the use and benefit of God's children, not of others....'[83] And John Erskine, 'probably the greatest divine in the Church of Scotland' in the latter part of the eighteenth century, wrote these words: 'Baptism, then, is a seal of spiritual blessings; and spiritual blessings it cannot seal to the unconverted.'[84]

Conclusion

It must be obvious by now that Cunningham's teaching on the sacraments is more a defence of a certain Protestant and Reformed understanding of the sacraments than a careful, balanced, detailed description of that understanding. In modern parlance, he was 'hard-wired' toward polemics, and here that is very evident. With respect to the doctrine of the sacraments, he takes on the 'unintelligible' arguments of Luther and Calvin, the 'absurd' arguments of Roman Catholics and Tractarians, the 'seemingly plausible' arguments of the anti-paedobaptists, and even the 'careless' arguments of paedobaptists who rest contented with obscure and defective notions. He also, of course, takes on the detractors of Zwingli, and, at times, Zwingli himself.

A full-orbed understanding of Cunningham's views of the sacraments, then, must take into consideration, not only what he said his beliefs were, but also what he said they were not. He was not, for example, Roman Catholic, because he believed that union with Christ through faith was the way of salvation. And the scholastic 'sacramental system' distracted from that salvation by emphasizing dependence on outward ordinances. At the same time, though, he was not in full agreement with Calvin, whose sacramental views at times were too

---

[83] ibid., 282.

[84] ibid., 283. The question naturally arises, 'what about the grace of baptism for those baptized in infancy?' The Confession of Faith puts it this way: 'The efficacy of Baptism is not tied to that moment of time wherein it is administered; yet, notwithstanding, by the right use of this ordinance, the grace promised is not only offered, but really exhibited, and conferred, by the Holy Ghost, to such (whether of age or infants) as that grace belongeth unto, according to the counsel of God's own will, in His appointed time' (*WCF* 28:6). Richard D. Phillips has helpfully commented on these words: 'Doesn't the *Confession* insist...that baptism was effectual in conveying grace when the church-raised convert finally believed? Yes, it does, but that grace is *sanctificational* to him *in response* to the faith that finally saved him. The same thing happened to the former Hindu when he was baptized [as an adult]. Having believed, he was edified by the grace of his baptism just as the other man was edified through his baptism administered so long beforehand.' 'A Response to "Sacramental Efficacy" in the Westminster Standards,' *The Auburn Avenue Theology: Pros & Cons*, ed. by C. E. Beisner (Fort Lauderdale: Knox Theological Seminary, 2004), 250.

high and too confusing, or with Zwingli, whose views at times were too low and too clear.

It would be simplistic, then, and inaccurate to label Cunningham 'Zwinglian'. There is one point, however, at which Cunningham may seem to lean in that direction: his defence of the Westminster standards against baptismal regeneration. Because he is consistent in his emphasis on adult baptism and the faith that is necessary for baptism to have its intended effect, he does at times look one-sided. Mitigating this, though, is Cunningham's explicit statement that 'the sacraments are to be regarded as signs and seals on the part of God as well as of man'.[85] In addition to this, it helps to understand that Cunningham did not shut the door completely to the notion that baptism may confer some kind of grace to infants, who, of course, do not have the faith that is ordinarily necessary to receive the blessings of that sacrament. He simply believes that Scripture does not provide enough information to enable us to describe the efficacy of baptism in the case of infants, whereas Scripture is clear in the case of adults.[86]

It seems only appropriate to end this review of Cunningham's view of the sacraments with his own words. Though the sentences are at times long and the words occasionally antiquated, the motivation of this man's heart cannot be obscured.

> We have now stated the substance of what is…set forth in the Westminster Standards, concerning… the sacraments. And we have done so under the influence of a strong desire…to avoid the very common and injurious tendency, either, directly to overrate the value and efficacy of the sacraments, or to furnish…encouragements to others to overrate them, by leaving our statements on these subjects in a condition of great vagueness and confusion. Any attempts to assign to them greater dignity, value, and efficacy than we have ascribed to them, or to invest them with a deeper shade of mystery, are, we are persuaded, not only unsanctioned by Scripture, but… fitted to exert an injurious influence upon the interests of truth and holiness. The strong natural tendency of men to substitute the tithing of mint, anise, and cumin, for the weightier matters of the law,— to substitute the observance of outward rites and ceremonies for the diligent cultivation of Christian graces and the faithful discharge of

---

[85] Cunningham, *Reformers*, 287.

[86] Cunningham, *Historical Theology*, vol. 2, 150. Because Cunningham believes that infants can be saved before baptism takes place, he is not here embracing baptismal regeneration (ibid., 150, 152).

Christian duties,—is strengthened by everything which...either adds to the number of the rites and ceremonies which God has prescribed, or assigns even to prescribed rites an importance and an efficacy beyond what He has sanctioned. In the second of these ways, as well as in the first, the truth of God has been grievously perverted, and the interests of practical godliness have been extensively injured. Almost the only rites and ceremonies permanently binding upon the Christian church are baptism and the Lord's Supper; and these have been in every age so distorted and perverted by exaggeration and confusion, as to have proved...the occasions of fearful injury to men's souls. It is true that men have sometimes exhibited a tendency to go to the opposite extreme, to depreciate instituted ordinances, and to reduce their importance, value, and efficacy below the standard which the word of God sanctions. But the tendency to overvalue the sacraments, and to make the observance of them a substitute...for things of much greater importance, is far more common and far more dangerous; more dangerous...because it is more likely to creep in, and to gain an ascendancy in men's minds, and because, when yielded to and encouraged, it exerts a more injurious influence upon the highest and holiest interests, by wrapping men in strong delusion in regard to their spiritual condition and prospects, and leading them to build their hopes of heaven upon a false foundation.[87]

---

[87] Cunningham, *Reformers*, 288-89.

Systematic Theology

8

'More Than That' –
Christ's Exaltation and Justification[1]

Richard B. Gaffin, Jr.

The Issue

1. 'The riches of Christ,' according to the apostle Paul, are 'unsearchable' or, as we may also translate, 'fathomless,' 'boundless' (Eph. 3:8).[2] The work of Christ, manifesting as it does 'the manifold wisdom of God' (v. 10), is so multifaceted that in its totality it cannot be known fully or exhaustively. At the same time Paul's prayer for the church reflects his confidence that by the power of the Spirit it will comprehend these multiplex and ultimately unfathomable riches in something of their full dimensions, that it will in fact 'know the love of Christ that surpasses knowledge' (vv. 18-19; cf. v. 16). What is bounded by incomprehensibility may also be known, truly and adequately.

The 'mystery' that the gospel is (vv. 3-7, 9), Paul makes clear elsewhere, has had its centre – what is 'of first importance'– revealed in Christ's death and resurrection for human sin (1 Cor. 15:3-4). Tethered to that centre, then, the ongoing task before the church is to appropriate that

---

[1] This chapter builds on a lecture given at the Sixth Annual International Conference on the Work of the Westminster Assembly on the general theme 'The Priestly Office of Our Lord,' held at the Reformed Presbyterian Theological Seminary, Pittsburgh, Pennsylvania, USA on June 26-27, 2009. Its expansion here is offered in appreciation for Donald Macleod and his ministry to the church over the years.

[2] Unless otherwise noted all Scripture quotations will be from the English Standard Version (ESV), occasionally with slight modifications of my own.

mystery in terms of its richly abundant aspects together with their inter-relationships as revealed in Scripture. This chapter explores one such aspect or facet of Christ's work that has not received as much attention as some others and certainly not, it is fair to say, the attention it warrants.

The confessionally privileged summary of Christ's work in the Westminster standards provides a useful point of departure. There his work as Mediator, or Redeemer, is presented in terms of his three-fold office of prophet, priest and king. The Larger and Shorter Catechisms do so along with making the distinction between his two states, his humiliation and subsequent exaltation.[3] Given these categories the question may be posed how Christ's work as priest[4] relates to the justification of believers, a question that subdivides into two, one concerning Christ as high priest in his state of humiliation and their justification, the other, Christ as high priest in his state of exaltation and their justification. The latter is our interest in this chapter.

This question requires further focusing. The relevance for justification of Christ's exaltation may be considered either in terms of its initiation, in the event of his resurrection, or in terms of the consequent state that results from the resurrection together with the ascension, his heavenly session. Both these aspects, for instance, are arguably within the purview of Romans 4:25: Jesus 'was delivered up for our trespasses and raised for our justification.' Whether or not utilizing an existing pre-Pauline formulation, this summary statement captures the heart of much of the argumentation of the letter to that point and lays a foundation for what follows – particularly as we will see in 8:33-34 – concerning Christ's work as it bears on justification. The one aspect, the significance for justification of Christ's continuing exaltation state rather than its initiation in the resurrection, is the focus of the reflections that follow.[5]

---

[3] *Larger Catechism*, 42-56; *Shorter Catechism*, 23-29. This distinction is implicitly redemptive- or covenant-historical at its core. Cf. the general observation of Geerhardus Vos, Reformed theology 'has from the beginning shown itself possessed of a true historic sense in the apprehension of the progressive character of the deliverance of truth. Its doctrine of the covenants on its historical side represents the first attempt at constructing a history of revelation and may be justly considered the precursor of what is at present called biblical theology' (*Redemptive History and Biblical Interpretation. The Shorter Writings of Geerhardus Vos* [ed. R. Gaffin, Jr.; Phillipsburg, NJ: P&R, 1980/2001], 232); cf. my 'Biblical Theology and the Westminster Standards,' *Westminster Theological Journal* 65 (2003): 165-79.

[4] Throughout 'priest' and 'high priest' referring to Christ will be used interchangeably, permissible in the light of biblical usage (specifically in Hebrews), whatever differences of accent there may be between the two designations.

[5] Elsewhere I have addressed in some detail, particularly in Paul's theology, the significance for justification of the event of the resurrection. Christ's own justification, based on his obedience

But, it might be objected or at least asked at this point, are such reflections relevant or even appropriate? What can Christ's present exaltation activity, as high priest, possibly have to do with justification? Isn't that priestly relevance exhausted by what he accomplished in his state of humiliation? Specifically, isn't his priestly work for our justification finished – completed by his obedience, culminating in the propitiatory sacrifice of his death? Doesn't that obedience, so far as our justification is concerned, constitute the righteousness, finished and sufficient, that is imputed to us as it is received solely by faith? Doesn't this imputed priestly accomplishment not only secure the remission of all our sin, past, present and future, but also entitle believers to eternal life, to blessings that are nothing less than eschatological, and do so infallibly?

Given the finished, once-for-all finality of Christ's work as priest for our justification in his state of humiliation, it might even be insisted further, how is it at all meaningful to view his exalted priestly activity as relevant and thus necessary for justification? If Christ's work for justification, as well as justification itself, is past and settled, how can we say that justification is somehow dependent on or conditioned by his present activity?

These questions are certainly prompted by and express important biblical truths, realities in fact that are at the heart of the gospel. In fact, without those realities there is simply no gospel and nothing said here or elsewhere may be allowed to eclipse or otherwise compromise them. At the same time, however, with the truth of the settled reality of the believer's justification established and maintained, there is nonetheless a further reality, also integral to justification, to consider.

2. The Westminster standards stipulate, true to Scripture as we will presently confirm for ourselves, that the priestly work of Christ in

---

culminating in his death (Phil. 2:8), is effected in his resurrection as a *de facto* judicially declarative event ('... justified in the Spirit,' 1 Tim. 3:16, where the reference, almost certainly, is to the Holy Spirit's activity in raising Jesus from the dead). For Christians, his justification becomes theirs, when united, by faith, to the resurrected, that is, the now justified Christ, his righteousness is reckoned as theirs or imputed to them. See my *'By Faith, Not By Sight.' Paul and the Order of Salvation* (Milton Keynes, England: Paternoster, 2006), 84-92 and *Resurrection and Redemption. A Study in Paul's Soteriology* (2nd ed.; Phillipsburg, NJ: P&R, 1987), esp. 119-24. While my reflections in this chapter move in a different direction than those of Peter Stuhlmacher, I acknowledge the stimulus, particularly in pointing up the link between Romans 4:25 and 8:34, of his, "Christus Jesus ist hier, der gestorben ist, ja vielmehr, der auch auferweckt ist, der zur Rechten Gottes ist und uns vertritt," in eds. F. Avemarie and H. Lichtenberger, *Auferstehung – Resurrection* (Tübingen: Mohr Siebeck. 2001), 351-61.

his state of exaltation, his heavenly high priestly activity, consists in his intercession, his active intercessory presence, at the right hand of God.[6] If, then, we take this heavenly high priestly intercession as a further point of departure, the question of the bearing of Christ's exaltation on justification becomes, more specifically, if and, if so, how this present intercession pertains to justification.

An avenue for answering these questions from Scripture opens in Chapter 11 of the *Westminster Confession of Faith* (on justification). There, in affirming that God continues to forgive the sins of those who are justified, section 5 speaks of their being in 'the state of justification,' a state, further, from which 'they can never fall.' A couple of things are immediately apparent from this language. Generally considered, justification is to be seen not only as a past event for believers but also, as such, has present significance for them, an ongoing, even daily relevance for their lives.

This language also raises a related question, how is it that those already justified are sustained in that state? How are they kept, infallibly, from falling from it? This question is as important as it is vitally practical, for it is apparent that if already having been justified does not result in a state of being permanently and irrevocably justified, one's justification at best remains uncertain and so beset with anxiety. So, the language of the *Confession* prompts asking, what is it that keeps believers from losing their justification? What assures them that they will not?

In this respect, then, justification is a present issue for believers. In passing, it is of interest to note that in a similar vein, Calvin, for instance, in the course of his lengthy treatment of justification in Book 3 of the *Institutes*, entitles chapter 14, 'The Beginning of Justification and its Continual Progress,' where he also writes, 'Therefore, we must have this blessedness [justification] not just once but must hold to it throughout life' (3:14:11).[7] The question, prompted by the *Confession*, as we may

---

[6] Is this intercession the reality that he is there, his presence itself as inherently intercessory, or is his intercession additional to his presence, a specific and ongoing praying activity? That much-mooted question, with the respective arguments for each view, need not be entered into here. Notably, the answer to question 55 of the *Westminster Larger Catechism* ('How doth Christ make intercession?') appears to include both aspects: 'Christ maketh intercession, by his appearing in our nature continually before the Father in heaven, in the merit of his obedience and sacrifice on earth, declaring his will to have it applied to all believers; answering all accusations against them, and procuring for them quiet of conscience, notwithstanding daily failings, access with boldness to the throne of grace, and acceptance of their persons and services.'

[7] *Institutes of the Christian Religion* (trans. F. L. Battles, Philadelphia: Westminster, 1960), 1:768, 778.

also put it, is how justification relates to the present, to the ongoing circumstances of the Christian life. Or, yet again, what is involved in 'progressing' (Calvin) or, in other terms, persevering in justification? To speak of 'the state of justification' and of 'never fall[ing] from' that state raises the issue of justification and perseverance.[8]

Tying together the strands of our reflections to this point, the question before us is this: how does Christ's priestly work in his state of exaltation, specifically his heavenly high priestly intercession, relate to the believer's persevering in 'the state of justification'? Or, more pointedly, as we will presently see, Scripture teaches us better to ask that question and then also answers it, how is that intercession essential for our persevering in the state of justification?

Romans 8:33-34

1. Of a number of passages that address this question (several in Hebrews will be noted as well below), none is more a key than Romans 8:33–34. None answers it in a more decisive and encouraging way: 'Who shall bring any charge against God's elect? It is God who justifies. Who is to condemn? Christ Jesus is the one who died – more than that, who was raised – who is at the right hand of God, who indeed is interceding for us.'

Since we are orienting our discussion to the outlook of the Westminster standards, it is worth noting that the *Confession* as originally published (1647) does not include these verses among those cited in chapter 11:5 to support the state of justification statement. However, in *Larger Catechism*, 77 ('Wherein do justification and sanctification differ?'), it is the only passage cited to support the statement that justification 'equally frees all believers from the revenging wrath of God, and that perfectly in this life, *that they never fall into condemnation*' (emphasis added). And earlier in *Larger Catechism* 55 ('How doth Christ make intercession?'), it is the sole passage used to establish the truth that Christ's present intercession for believers is effective in 'answering all accusations against them'. So, we should not hesitate to say that it would certainly have been appropriate to cite Romans 8:33-34 in *Confession*, 11:5.[9]

---

[8] This provides a reminder that, given the total depravity of sinners, the other four petals of the Calvinistic TULIP stand or fall together; no one exists without entailing each of the others.

[9] These verses have been added at this point in the revision of the proof texts adopted by the Orthodox Presbyterian Church (in North America). The original proof texts for the statement in 11:5 are Luke 22:32; John 10:28; Hebrews 10:14. Elsewhere in the standards (*Confession of Faith*, 8:4, 8), v. 34 is cited in support of references to Christ's intercession.

Romans 8 as a whole peaks to a closing crescendo in verses 38-39. Its final section begins with the rhetorical questions of verse 31, 'What then shall we say to these things? If God is for us, who can be against us?' 'These things' refer most directly to what Paul has just asserted (vv. 29-30): the ultimate goal of God's predestinating purpose is realized in our conformity to the image of his Son as firstborn brother, and that conformity, culminates, through our justification, in our glorification.

In the second of these questions in verse 31, 'for us' and 'against us' are fairly seen as at least including a legal or forensic overtone; they suggest a judicial proceeding. That a judicial scenario is in view is put beyond question by the related questions, also rhetorical, at the beginning of verses 33 and 34, respectively: 'Who will bring any charge against God's elect?'; 'Who is the one that condemns?' Plainly at stake are issues that concern justification, in view here in terms of its forensic antithesis, condemnation, and these issues are clearly a matter of *present* concern.

These questions, in turn, have their answers in the latter halves of these two verses, where verse 34b is best understood as reinforcing and explaining verse 33b. While there is some debate among commentators, a synthetic or progressive parallelism between the later halves of verses 33 and 34 is their most plausible construal. Several further points may be noted.

First, we are told simply, elementally, 'God is the one who justifies'(v. 33b). That is the decisive bottom line; that settles the issue. Verse 34b, then, goes on to expand on God's activity *as Justifier as it is in view here*. 'Christ Jesus,' Paul says, 'is the one who died – more than that, who was raised, who also is at the right hand of God, who indeed is interceding for us.' What or, better, *who* expounds God as the God who justifies is Christ and God's work through him in view here.

Noteworthy, further, is how, according to verse 34, Christ is said to be relevant, even decisive, for justification and its maintenance, for maintaining, we may say, 'the state of justification.' His death is mentioned first, and an understandable reaction may well be, 'Yes, of course. Christ died for our sins so that we might be justified.' Paul has already made that abundantly clear in Romans, for instance, back in 3:24-26: the propitiation effected by his blood is such that God might be 'just and the justifier of those who believe in Jesus'; in 5:9: 'we have now been justified by his blood'; in 5:18-19: his righteousness and obedience, focused in his death, leads to justification by grounding it,

IMPORTANT

by establishing the basis of justification. There is also an unmistakable allusion to his death as it bears on justification in the immediate context (v. 32), 'he who did not spare his own Son but gave him up for us all.' The argument in Romans to this point is clear: the obedience of Christ, culminating in his propitiatory death for sin, is the righteousness that grounds the believer's justification.

Here, however — and this is striking – Paul does not stop with Christ's death. In the matter of his work, as it is *pertinent to justification*, his death is not punctuated with a period. Paul instead continues, 'more than that, ...' 'More than that'? More than Christ's death, past and definitive as it is, concerns our justification?

'Yes,' it appears, is to be the answer, for Paul goes on to speak of Christ's resurrection and, with that, of the enduring consequences of his resurrection, in other words, of his state of exaltation at God's right hand. This provides the important reminder that in the matter of our justification and salvation, we must not so focus on the death of Christ, the priestly work of Christ in his state of humiliation, as precious and essential as that atoning sacrifice is, that we fail to appreciate 'the fact that Jesus' death would have been of no avail in fulfilling the ends in view apart from the resurrection.'[10] Paul could hardly be more pointed to that effect when he says elsewhere, 'And if Christ has not been raised, your faith is futile and you are still in your sins' (1 Cor. 15:17). Apart from Christ's resurrection, there is no justification. How that is so is what, in part, we are in the midst of considering.

Here we are pointed to what is *presently* the case for justification, and, in this passage at least, that present reality is where the emphasis lies. Specifically, the focus is on the continuing intercessory presence of the resurrected Christ at God's right hand, an intercessory presence said to be, echoing the question of verse 31, 'for us.' Relevant to the believer's justification, Paul is saying, is not only what Christ has done in the past on earth, as absolutely crucial as that is, but also what he is doing now, presently, in heaven.

According to this passage, then, justification is bound up with Christ's ongoing intercessory presence. That is so in the sense that our remaining, infallibly, in 'the state of justification,' our not being separated from the love of God in Christ, not even by death or whatever else the future brings (vv. 35, 37–39), depends upon this continuing and unfailing intercession. Christ exalted to God's right hand is there

---

[10] J. Murray, *The Epistle to the Romans* (Grand Rapids: Eerdmans, 1959), 1: 306-07.

as the permanently efficacious and ever-availing exhibition of that finished and perfect righteousness that is ours.

With an eye to the wider context in Paul, the overall picture is this: Christ's righteousness has been imputed to believers once for all.[11] So, in view of this passage, that irrevocable reckoning continues to be reaffirmed in the face of whatever challenges to it by whomever (v. 33a). As it could be put, the imputation of Christ's righteousness is continually being revalidated or confirmed by the 'God who justifies' without it ever having expired or becoming invalid, even for an instant. Christ is present in that place of ultimate and final judgment as the righteousness which he 'became for us ... from God' (1 Cor. 1:30), and that is the answer, ever effective, to any charge brought against already justified believers. He is there, at God's right hand, as Calvin says on our passage, 'that he may be a perpetual advocate and intercessor in securing our salvation.'[12]

So, concerning justification and the priestly work of Christ in his state of exaltation, we are brought to this basic conclusion: his perpetual heavenly advocacy is in the interests of justification in that it maintains believers in 'the state of justification'.

2. We may reflect further on this conclusion by addressing a question implicit in it: why does the exalted Christ intercede for those already

---

[11] Proponents of the New Perspective on Paul characteristically hold that the imputation of Christ's righteousness is a dogmatic construct alien to Paul, read into him by the Reformation and post-Reformation Reformed and Lutheran orthodoxy. Here I can do no more than indicate in the briefest fashion and without interacting with this view that the contrary is the case. Prominent in the argumentation for the justification of the ungodly in Romans 4 is the counting or reckoning of faith as righteousness (vv. 3, 5-6, 9-10, 22-24), whether for old (Abraham, David) or new covenant believers. But faith for Paul is never an end in itself; faith itself does not constitute the righteousness that justifies. Rather, the integrity and efficacy of faith is in its object, as it looks away from itself; faith in that sense is extraspective. Specifically for Paul, justifying faith is manifestly faith in Christ (e.g., Rom. 3:22; Gal. 2:16; 3:22; Phil. 3:9), so that the reckoning of faith as righteousness is the reckoning of Christ's righteousness to faith (cf. 'Christ ... our righteousness,' 1 Cor. 1:30). This conclusion is reinforced by the striking metonymic use of 'faith' in the context of the related treatment of justification in Galatians 3:23, 25, where 'until the coming faith' and 'now that faith has come' function for 'Christ came' ('until Christ came,' v. 24). So thoroughly is justifying faith bound to its object not only for its validity but also for its very meaning that for Christ to come 'in the fullness of time' (4:4) is for faith to come – even in view of the proleptic exercise of justifying faith (by way of the covenant promise, e.g., Abraham, 3:6-9) before his coming (a *fides quae* sense, 'the faith' as a body of belief or doctrine, is excluded here). For a recent and aggressive New Perspective construal, see N. T. Wright, *Justification. God's Plan & Paul's Vision* (Downers Grove: IVP Academic, 2009), 105, 142 ('the imputation of Christ's righteousness' is a 'sub-Pauline idea'), 158, 206, 213, 217, *passim*.

[12] J. Calvin, *Commentaries on the Epistle of Paul the Apostle to the Romans* (trans. J. Owen; Grand Rapids: Eerdmans, 1948), 325.

justified? Better, why does he *have* to? Why is his perpetual prayer presence at God's right hand for the elect (v. 33) *necessary* to preserving their justification? Why after all that he has done in suffering and dying for them, the righteous for the unrighteous, why can't he, as it were, just sit back and watch and enjoy the rewards of his obedience? Again, why *must* he pray for 'God's elect'?

The question may, in fact *must*, be put just that strongly because while the work of Christ as Redeemer is always gratuitous in the sense of being free and undeserved for those who benefit from it, it is never gratuitous in the sense of being unnecessary or redundant. The necessity of this gratuitous intercession of the exalted Christ is plain from the fact that it exists, simply because, as we are told here, it is happening and will continue to happen. Christ does what is necessary for our salvation and its maintenance. He is not presently involved, we may be sure, in doing what is unnecessary.

What explains the necessity of this present intercession in heaven for our justification? What occasions that necessity? That question prompted by our passage can be addressed by raising another. In parallel fashion verses 33a and 34a refer in an indefinite fashion to one who brings a charge against or accuses the elect, someone not otherwise identified who undertakes to condemn them.[13] Is this accusation, this judicial effort, only hypothetical, or at the most potential, or alternatively, is it actual? Are the questions rhetorical in the sense that they anticipate a response like, 'No, no one does that, especially since Christ has died for our sins and we are already justified.' Or, as they are rhetorical, do they have in view a present reality, a real state of affairs? The answer is surely the latter, what is actually the case, because, as we have seen, Christ's intercession, as real and actual as it is hardly unnecessary or redundant, is the response to this accusing, this effort to condemn.

Who, then, concretely is the accuser (v. 33), the one who condemns (v. 34)? The immediate context does not provide an answer, but surely within the broader context of Scripture, we should think here, first of all, of Satan. The scenario pictured in Revelation 12 particularly comes to mind. There 'the great dragon ..., the ancient serpent, who is called the devil and Satan, the deceiver of the whole world,' has, with his angels, been 'thrown down.' Nonetheless, he still remains *the accuser of [the] brothers ..., who accuses them day and night before our God*' (vv. 9-10).

---

[13] Verse 34a is best translated,'Who is the one who condemns?' or 'Who is he that condemns?' (NIV).

According to 1 Peter 5:8, 'Your adversary the devil prowls around like a roaring lion, seeking someone to devour.' 'Someone' here should not be read indiscriminately or without any differentiation. In view primarily, perhaps exclusively, is the church ('*your* adversary'). The devil, we may say, has little or lesser concern about the destruction of those who belong to him and serve him, the doomed angels (2 Pet. 2:4; Jude 6) and people who presently have not yet or never will be 'delivered ... from the domain of darkness and transferred ... into the kingdom of his beloved Son' (Col. 1:13). Rather, as a 'high priority agenda item' he is intent particularly, however desperately, on destroying the church and uses every device, forensic and accusatory efforts among them, toward achieving that end.

So, we ought in our passage to think primarily of the Evil One, the Tempter that he is, and all who conspire with him in never tiring of challenging the Christian's justification and its settled certainty, of trying to destroy its present and continuing reality by bringing about a fall from 'the state of justification'. Additionally, there is every good reason to think here as well of the situation where perhaps, under the stressful circumstance of 'the sufferings of the present time' (Rom. 8:18) and as they continue to sin, Christians themselves may succumb to the temptation to doubt their justification, to question whether they are in a 'state of justification'.

In the face of these all too present threats, destructive in their tendency, Paul assures the church by directing attention not only to Christ crucified but also, 'more than that,' to Christ as he is now, presently, 'at the right hand of God.' His abiding presence there 'for us', in that place of final judgment, permanently refutes and nullifies every challenge against our justification and so all doubts about it. And that 'answer' that the living Christ is and provides in the face of every conceivable accusation against the elect, it should not be missed – to address a persisting misconception – is not the perpetual re-sacrificing of himself before a God who is in constant need of being re-propitiated. Rather, that 'answer'– Christ in his intercession – is provided, in his infinite love for us, by God the Father himself, 'who did not spare his own Son but gave him up for us all' (v. 32).

To recapitulate using the central threads of the argument in Romans that bear on our topic: Romans 8 opens on a note of confident certainty, 'There is therefore now no condemnation for those who are in Christ Jesus.' This is the negative echo of the positive declaration in 5:1, summarizing much of the argument in 3:21–4:25: Christians, by faith, have been justified, and since that is the case, through Christ, they are at peace with God and have 'access to the grace in which [they] stand'. They are in a state of grace, yes, 'the state of justification,' a state so settled that it carries with it the 'hope of the glory of God', a hope as it includes their own future glorification that does not 'put to shame' (v. 5). The air of unshakeable confidence and certainty here is unmistakable.

With that noted and always in the background, our passage brings into view that this state of grace, the state of justification, however settled and certain, continues to be threatened or challenged. In the face of those threats, Christ is the living and abiding embodiment of the righteousness, already irrevocably imputed to believers. As such he continues to avail for the justification of those God has already predestined and justified (vv. 29-30), in the sense that he sustains them in their justified state. And he does that sustaining and preserving work with unwavering faithfulness, just as he, their righteousness, has and always will, ever since each of those elect was first united to him by faith. Because of this, his highly priestly intercession in his state of exaltation, they cannot and will not ever fall from 'the state of justification'.

Hebrews

Some prominent aspects of the teaching of the Book of Hebrews amplify and reinforce the heavenly, judicially-oriented intercessory scenario in Romans 8. The scope of Hebrews as a whole, or at least in large part, is captured by two verses: 13:22 and 8:1. As the document draws to a close, 13:22 reads, 'I urge you, brothers, bear with this [the] word of exhortation, for I have written to you briefly.' As more careful exegesis will show, here 'the word of exhortation' is best taken to refer to the document as a whole. By the writer's own characterization, then, Hebrews is basically hortatory. It is not a doctrinal treatise but essentially parenetic, though it undeniably contains considerable and profound teaching concerning Christ's person and work.[14]

---

[14] As it has been neatly put, in Hebrews 'thesis serves parenesis'; '... in Hebrews parenesis takes precedence over thesis in expressing the writer's purpose' (W. Lane, *Hebrews 1–8* [*Word Biblical Commentary*, vol. 47A; Dallas: Word Books, 1991], c). 'The writer was obviously a theologian before he wrote the Epistle; he had in mind a well defined doctrinal system.' At the same time, 'It [the document] expresses a firm belief in the efficacy of *doctrine* as a means of grace... In Hebrews doctrine is never introduced for its own sake; ...' (G. Vos, *The Teaching of the Epistle to the Hebrews* [Grand Rapids: Eerdmans, 1956], 69, italics original).

'Now the main point in what we are saying is this: we have such a high priest, one who is seated at the right hand of the throne of the Majesty in heaven, a servant in the sanctuary, in the true tent that the Lord set up, not man' (8:1-2). What is the intended range of 'main point'?[15] Plausibly, it covers the large central section, 4:14–10:31. But considering that Christ as high priest comes into view on either side of this section, at 2:17–3:1, in fact pointing back all the way to 1:3, on the one side and at 13:11ff. on the other, it does not seem too far off the mark to apply 8:1-2 to the entire book. In the writer's own view, then, the heavenly high priestly ministry of Christ is the main point of Hebrews as a whole.

So, 13:22 and 8:1-2 are, as it were, the axes around which the study of Hebrews as whole ought to revolve. These verses define the matrix within which the writer develops his teaching; they set the parameters that fix the area of his overall concern. A helpful approach to Hebrews is to view it as a 'world of exhortation', in which the heavenly high priestly ministry of Christ is the 'main point'.[16]

This conclusion prompts a question. If Christ is exalted high priest, with all that entails in terms of his present redemptive triumph, of his accomplishment of a salvation that is settled and secure, why the exhortation, why the need for the imperatives that in fact permeate the document? As we might put it, if the heavenly high priestly ministry is its 'main point', why is the book as a whole a 'word of exhortation'?

The answer to this question lies in recognizing that in Hebrews the imperatives are, so to speak, indicative of an indicative. That is, the exhortation that permeates the document points to a state of affairs, to a basic aspect of the present circumstances of the church. The writer, in other words, does not contemplate Christ's priestly ministry in the abstract but in light of the present situation of the church. He considers Christ as high priest in terms of the present circumstances of the church, circumstances for which the pervasive parenesis (exhortation) is not only relevant but necessary.

What, in the author's view, is that situation, those basic circumstances? The answer in large part is provided in the section, 3:7–4:13, where, in an interpretive handling of Psalm 95:7-11 with the inclusion of Genesis 2:2, he makes a large scale redemptive-historical

---

[15] As κεφάλαιον is better translated here.

[16] In the overall profile of New Testament teaching, while the concept of Christ's priestly work is plainly taught elsewhere (for instance, as we have seen, in Romans 8:33-34), Hebrews is the only document that explicitly calls Christ 'priest,' 'high priest.'

comparison between old covenant Israel and the new covenant church. He does that by drawing the analogy at a specific point in Israel's history, to the experience of the wilderness generation.[17] This comparison has two sides to it. On the one hand, the church has had a real experience of salvation from the guilt and power of sin promised in the gospel, of the eschatological deliverance pictured by Israel's exodus from Egyptian bondage.

At the same time, on the other hand, just as Israel in the wilderness, freed from slavery, had not yet entered into the promised land (the 'rest' of Canaan; see, e.g., Deut. 12:9-10; Josh. 1:13-15), so New Testament believers do not yet enjoy God's 'rest' (4:9), eschatological salvation in its full and final form. Though their present possession of salvation is certain and secure, they have not yet attained to an experience of it that is unthreatened and unchallenged. As the people of God, their present circumstances between Christ's ascension and return (e.g., 9:26, 28), are such that trials and hardships are pervasive. Categorically, these are 'the sufferings of the present time' (Rom. 8:18). As such they are testings that carry with them and conspire together toward the ultimate temptation, as Israel faced in the wilderness, to abandon their faith and rebel against God in unbelief.[18] This present wilderness identity and circumstances of the New Testament church provides the rationale, indeed the necessity, for the writer's repeated exhortations.

Accordingly, 3:12-14 for instance is addressed not to unbelievers but to the church ('brothers'), to all, not just some, who have made Christian confession (4:14; 10:23). 'Take care, brothers, lest there be in any of you an evil, unbelieving heart, leading you to fall away from the living God. But exhort one another every day, as long as it is called "today," that none of you may be hardened by the deceitfulness of sin. For we share in Christ, if indeed we hold our original confidence firm to the end.'

---

[17] For some expansion of the comments here on the writer's use of this analogy, see my 'A Sabbath Rest Still Awaits the People of God,' in C. Dennison & R. Gamble, eds., *Pressing Toward the Mark. Essays Commemorating Fifty Years of the Orthodox Presbyterian Church* (Philadelphia: The Committee for the Historian of the Orthodox Presbyterian Church, 1986), 33-51, esp. 34-41.

[18] The link between suffering and temptation – explicit for Christ, implicit for Christians – comes into view for the first time in 2:18, which, following Vos, should be translated, 'Since he was tempted in what he suffered, he is able to help those who are being tempted' (*Teaching*, 102; ed. R. Gaffin, Jr., *Redemptive History and Biblical Interpretation. The Shorter Writings of Geerhardus Vos* [Phillipsburg, NJ: P&R, 1980], 145). Suffering is in view specifically on its ethical side, as giving rise to temptation; they are 'temptation-sufferings' (Vos). Cf. the similar link between 'weaknesses' and temptation in 4:15.

Richard B. Gaffin, Jr.

Here verse 14 seems particularly pertinent to our topic, justification. Syntactically, the perfect indicative of the main clause ('we have been made partakers of Christ') is linked with a future conditional clause ('if we hold fast ... to the end'; cf. v. 6c). A perfect (past) indicative is contingent on a future condition. This reflects grammatically what can be characterized as the conditioned certainty, the 'contingent confidence',[19] taught throughout Hebrews.

The notion of being a 'partaker' or 'sharer' of Christ is the close, if not exact, equivalent of union with Christ in Paul. While the writer does not develop teaching on justification as does Paul, on the assumption that union and justification are inseparable in that teaching (cf. Philippians 3:8-9: 'that I might gain Christ and be found in him, not having a righteousness of my own ...'), there does not seem to be any good reason for excluding its substance here. Verse 14, then, amounts to saying, 'we are in Christ and have been justified in him, if we hold fast to the end.' Here, to honour the language of the text, being justified, being in a state of justification, is, in effect, conditioned on perseverance; justification by faith is contingent on persevering in faith.[20]

With this observation comes a further question, as pressing as it is practical, where are Christians, 'partakers of Christ,' to find the resources for holding fast, for persevering in faith? With just that question in view, the writer ultimately directs his readers, notably, not to their faith or to perservering efforts, of whatever sort, praying or otherwise, but to his 'main point.' He draws their attention to Christ their high priest in heaven and to *his* praying, to Christ, who 'after he has appeared once for all at the end of the ages to put away sin by the sacrifice of himself, ... has entered .. into heaven itself, now to appear in the presence of God on our behalf [for us]' (9:26, 24). There, in that heavenly sanctuary and place of final justice, Christ is 'able to save to the uttermost those who draw near to God through him, since he always lives to make intercession for them' (7:25). Because of that intercession, because of its unfailing efficacy, they hold fast to the end, they persevere in faith, they do not cease being partakers of Christ, they continue infallibly in 'the state of justification'.

---

[19] D. Johnson, in unpublished lecture notes on this passage for NT311 General Epistles and Revelation taught at Westminster Seminary California, 1987, 70.

[20] Another reminder that in the Calvinist TULIP, the 'I' (irresistible grace), as it includes justification and the faith that justifies, does not exist apart from, indeed includes, the 'P.'

One of the passages cited in the *Westminster Confession*, 11:5 for 'the state of justification' statement is Luke 22:32. There, shortly before going to the cross, Jesus informs Peter that Satan would like to 'sift you like wheat,' but then, he assures him, 'I have prayed for you that your faith may not fail.' The efficacy of that prayer is documented by the sequel. Despite his grievous lapse in denying Jesus, ultimately Peter's faith, the New Testament record makes clear, did not fail. He persevered in faith; he did not fall from the state of justification but persevered in it.

Paul and Hebrews together assure the church: what Jesus did so efficaciously in the past on earth, still in his state of humiliation, in praying for Peter, he is presently doing in heaven for all who belong to him, now with the settled efficacy that marks his state of exaltation. Because he is praying for them, despite their sins and lapses and yielding to temptation, as no accusation against them can stand, so their faith does not and will not fail.

One other New Testament instance of this heavenly intercession, dramatic and poignantly powerful, is present at the close of Acts 7, in the account of Stephen's appearance before a hostile Sanhedrin. In that earthly court justice grinds inevitably to its sickening miscarriage; Stephen is taken out and stoned to death (vv. 58-60). But the narrative discloses the full dimensions of what is taking place, not only on earth but also in heaven, there at God's right hand in the place where ultimate justice is rendered. One detail in this scenario is most remarkable: Stephen saw 'Jesus standing at the right hand of God'(v. 55). That detail is so striking that we are told not only that Stephen saw it but also that he exclaimed, 'Behold, I see the heavens opened, and the Son of Man standing at the right hand of God' (v. 56).

Elsewhere in Scripture Christ or Jesus exalted, sometimes identified as the Son of Man, is always and repeatedly pictured, either with explicit reference or implicit allusion to Psalm 110:1, as *sitting* at God's right hand, in a place of rule and authority (Matt. 22:44 and parallels; Matt. 26:64 and parallels; Acts 2:34; Eph. 1:20; Col. 3:1; in Heb., 1:3, 13; 8:1; 10:12; 12:2). But here, in this sole instance in Scripture, Jesus, the exalted Son of Man, is *standing*. The meaning of that is hardly in doubt. There in that heavenly forum, in that place of final judgment, the judge becomes the advocate, the king is also the intercessor. Jesus, the Saviour of sinners, stands up for Stephen and in doing so makes good now in heaven, as crown witness for the defence, on his promise to everyone of his disciples made during his earthly ministry that 'everyone who confesses me before men, I will also confess him before my Father who is in heaven' (Matt. 10:32).[21]

Conclusion

Why then is it that believers will not, in fact, cannot cease being justified? Why is it that they cannot lose their justification, that they 'can never fall from the state of justification'? Because of their election, settled, sovereignly and irreversibly, 'before the foundation of the world' (Eph. 1:5)? Yes, of course; that is indicated in the Romans 8 passage, in verse 29, and clearly taught elsewhere in Scripture. Because of Christ's perfect righteousness imputed to them once for all as it is received solely by faith? Again, of course; nothing could be clearer, for instance, from Paul's teaching in Romans and elsewhere.

But also – and this is no less essential, no less a component integral to our justification – because of or, to put it negatively, not without, Christ presently at God's right hand, continuing there to intercede for them.[22] As we have seen, the necessity of that intercession stems from two related considerations: the continuing sinfulness of 'God's elect' (Rom. 8:33) and their need to persevere in faith. His intercessory presence is the constant and enduring refutation of every accusation that because they continue to sin they deserve condemnation; it involves as well the ongoing application of 'the propitiatory power of his sacrifice' for the continuing forgiveness of their sins.[23] That

---

[21] *Larger Catechism*, 145 cites vv. 56-57 to support 'stopping our ears against *just defense*' as one of the sins forbidden in the ninth commandment (italics added).

[22] Noteworthy here is the linking together of multiple factors in *Larger Catechism*, 79 in answer to the question, one plainly pertinent to our inquiry, 'May not true believers, by reason of their imperfections, and the many temptations and sins they are overtaken with, fall away from the state of grace?': 'True believers, by reason of the unchangeable love of God, and his decree and covenant to give them perseverance, their inseparable union with Christ, his continual intercession for them, and the Spirit and seed of God abiding in them, can neither totally nor finally fall away from the state of grace, but are kept by the power of God through faith unto salvation.'

[23] Vos comments on Hebrews 2:17, 'It should be observed in this connection ['the priestly succour' to the tempted in v. 18] that ἱλάσκεσθαι does not here denote the single act of atonement on the cross, but the subsequent activity whereby the Saviour continually applies the propitiatory power of His sacrifice' (*Shorter Writings*, 145); 'The reference is not to the sacrifice of Calvary, but to the intercessory work of Christ as priest which is now being exercised in heaven' (*Teaching*, 102). Commentators, characteristically, do not follow Vos on this point and instead see a reference to Christ's propitiatory death. However, I find his proposal plausible, even persuasive, in view of (a) the immediate context (14-16), where, as Vos points out, death appears to be included in being 'made like his brothers in every respect' as prerequisite for his being 'a merciful and faithful high priest' (*Shorter Writings*, 154, 218), as well as (b) the progressive or

intercession infallibly ensures that their justifying faith is a persevering faith. Their justification, their continuing infallibly in 'the state of justification', depends not only on their election from eternity in Christ, not only on what he has done for them in the past, but also on what he is doing and will continue to do for them until he comes again.

The justification of God's elect is unshakably secure because, in a sentence, Jesus Christ is 'the same yesterday, today and forever' (Heb. 13:8). Despite the way it is often read, this is not, at least in the first place, a proof text for Christ's divine immutability, that as God he is unchanging, though that attribute is surely in the background (see, for instance, 1:10-12).[24] Rather, it is most likely an affirmation of his unwavering fidelity, his abiding reliability as high priest – in his once-for-all sacrifice in the past on earth and in his ongoing present and future (cf. 7:25) intercession in heaven. That is as good a note as any to bring these reflections to a close. 'Jesus Christ – the same yesterday, today and forever.' This, first and finally, is what Christians need to know about their justification when they consider Christ as their priest, not only in his state of humiliation but also in his state of exaltation.

---

continuous aspect of the present tense infinitive. This understanding in no way takes away from the propitiatory efficacy and finality of Christ's once-for-all sacrificial death, about which the writer is not only clear but emphatic elsewhere, for instance, in 9:26, 28; 10:12, 14.

[24] '[N]ot ... the external existence of Christ' (J. Calvin, *Commentaries of the Epistle of Paul the Apostle to the Hebrews* [trans. J. Owen; Grand Rapids: Eerdmans, 1948], 345; 'not ... an acclamation of Jesus' timeless ontological immutability' (W. Lane, *Hebrews 9–13* [*Word Biblical Commentary*, vol. 47B; Dallas: Word Books, 1991], 528).

9

Spirit-Baptism and The Clash of the Celts

Derek W. H. Thomas

On the scale of things, Donald Macleod's *The Spirit of Promise* is a modest little book amounting to little more than a hundred pages.[1] Most of its contents first appeared as editorials in the *Free Church Monthly Record* in the 1970s and early 80s. I vividly recall reading them and taking notes in one of many notebooks – notebooks that have proven invaluable to me over the subsequent years. The articles were racy, provocative and insightful, focusing on (sometimes admittedly bizarre) views of the Holy Spirit: the baptism of the Spirit, the sealing of the Spirit, the continuity-cessation of the charismata, guidance and so on. A particularly memorable line still lingers in my brain (in an article on the leading of the Spirit) to the effect that the preacher who claims his choice of text is God's will for the congregation is 'arrogant'.[2]

Macleod's principal target in some of these articles was 'The Doctor', my fellow-countryman and Dean of all things evangelical and Reformed for the best part of mid-twentieth century? I refer, of course, to 'Doctor' Martyn Lloyd-Jones whose views on Spirit-baptism as a post-conversion experience aroused great interest in the wake of similar (though essentially different) views among Keswick, Pentecostal/ charismatic and Perfectionist schools of thought. According to Lloyd-

---

[1] Donald Macleod, *The Spirit of Promise* (Fearn, Tain: Christian Focus Publications, 1986).
[2] Ibid., 67.

Jones, the baptism of the Spirit 'is an experience of the Spirit which gives the full assurance of faith and is to be identified with the sealing of Ephesians 1:13.' He continued his line of thought by adding that such an experience 'results in power and boldness which are the prerequisites for truly effective Christian witness'.[3]

Criticism of a fellow Celt on Macleod's part was (and remains) a risk-laden strategy even if, for my part, the Scot had the better exegesis of the relevant biblical texts. But a particular sentence stands out, one upon which we will reflect in the course of this chapter. On the theological importance and implications of the indwelling of the Spirit in the life of the believer, Macleod wrote the following:

> ...to be in Christ means to have communion with Him and this in turn means that we share fully in all that He has. The most precious of all His endowments, surely, is the full and overflowing indwelling of the Holy Spirit.[4]

And on Spirit-baptism in particular he added:

> The importance of a doctrine cannot be measured, however, by the frequency with which a precise wording occurs in Scripture. Otherwise the doctrine of the Trinity would have to be dismissed as quite secondary. Holy Spirit baptism is only one of several designations for that all-important initiatory experience by which the Holy Spirit comes to take up residence in the believer; and as such it rivals union with Christ as the single most important concept in the Christian doctrine of salvation.[5]

Macleod viewed receiving the Spirit, Spirit-baptism (baptism *with* or *in* rather than *by* the Spirit) and being filled by the Spirit as one and the same:

> It is surely clear that no one can claim the authority of the New Testament for distinguishing between receiving the Spirit, on the one

---

[3] D. Martyn Lloyd-Jones, *Joy Unspeakable: The Baptism and Gifts of the Holy Spirit* (Eastbourne: Kingsway Publications, 1995), 67. There have been attempts to limit the Doctor's remarks to preachers – preachers in times of revival to be more exact – but it is difficult not to conclude from the Ephesian sermons that he meant this as an experience for every Christian at all times.

[4] *The Spirit of Promise*, 7.

[5] Ibid., 1. In a similar way, Sinclair Ferguson writes: 'the model we employ for structuring the Spirit's ministry should be that of union with Christ' (Sinclair B. Ferguson, *The Holy Spirit*, Contours of Christian Theology, Downers Grove, IL: Inter-Varsity Press [1996], 100).

hand, and being baptized or filled with the Spirit on the other. Equally clearly, no one can claim canonical authority for the form of words: 'All have received the Spirit, but not all have been baptized or filled with the Spirit.'[6]

Macleod's conclusion is based on a concatenation of both exegetical and theological arguments which we summarize in bullet-form here:[7]

• The Acts of the Apostles employs the verbs 'to baptize,' 'fill,' and 'receive' with respect to the Spirit interchangeably.

• Old Testament prophecies of the Spirit envisaged an environment in which every believer is a recipient of the fullness of the Spirit, something to which Luke draws attention in his account of Pentecost in Acts 2.

• The *coinherence* of the divine persons implies that to receive the Son is at the same time to receive the Father and the Spirit.

• Both Old and New Testaments perceive faith in terms of receiving the Spirit – hence Paul's question to the Galatians was, 'Did you receive the Spirit by works of the law or by hearing with faith?' (Gal. 3:2)[8], an inappropriate question *if* there existed a possibility of true faith without the Spirit's indwelling or baptism or fullness.

• To suggest Ephesians 1:13 teaches that faith and the sealing of the Spirit are chronologically separate entities (as in the KJV rendition, 'In whom also, *after ye believed*, ye were sealed with the Holy Spirit of promise') is based on a translational and contextual misreading of the passage.[9]

• In times of particular stress and difficulty, the New Testament *never* resorts to the ethical admonition, 'What you need now is the baptism/sealing of the Spirit.'

• A two-stage experience of the Spirit among the early disciples is explained by way of the fact that they 'straddled two dispensations and as such was utterly unique'.[10]

• The reception of the Spirit by the Samaritans in Acts 8, Cornelius at Caesarea in Acts 11, and the Ephesians in Acts 19 are examples that must be viewed redemptive-historically. Even if some of them had genuine faith before their reception of the Spirit as described in these

---

[6] Macleod, *The Spirit of Promise*, 3.

[7] Ibid., 3-10, 49-56, 83-91.

[8] All Scripture citations (apart from those in direct citations of other authors) are taken from The Holy Bible, English Standard Version® (ESV®), copyright © 2001 by Crossway.

[9] Macleod, *The Spirit of Promise*, 7, 49-56, 83-84.

[10] Ibid., 13.

passages,[11] their experience of the reception of the Spirit once again falls at a unique point in the history of redemption. In both locations there were 'Pentecost-like' events as the gospel moved beyond the boundary of Jerusalem and moved (as Luke programmatically indicates at the beginning of Acts) in the direction of 'Samaria and the ends of the earth' (Acts 1:8). What occurs at these locations is strategic in the development of the mission as announced in Acts 1:8.

In addressing the *sealing* of the Spirit, Macleod once again tackles 'the Doctor' head-on.[12] Lloyd-Jones took a position similar to some of the experiential theologians of the English Puritan movement – notably, William Perkins (1558–1602),[13] Thomas Goodwin (1600–1680),[14] Richard Sibbes (1577–1635),[15] Paul Bayne (d. 1617),[16] and an early version of John Owen (1616–1683), viewing the sealing of the Spirit as a post-conversion work of assurance rather than something which essentially belongs to regeneration. Richard Sibbes in particular influenced opinion regarding the sealing of the Spirit for many years, essentially viewing the seal (*sphragis*) in terms contextualized to the

---

[11] Macleod is open to the possibility that in the case of the Samaritans, their reception of the Spirit was the point at which they first believed. Whatever their experience was prior to this it was not one of saving faith in Jesus Christ (Ibid., 14-15). Sinclair Ferguson is of the opinion that in both Samaria and Ephesus we 'encounter believers (*i.e.* people already regenerated) who have not yet received (in the sense of being baptized with) the Spirit. This second stage is conceptually, and in these cases chronologically, separated and separable from regeneration' (*The Holy Spirit*, 82). In the case of the Ephesians, Ferguson believes Luke 'deliberately gives us a series of signals which indicate that he did not view these men as Christians in the New Testament sense' (Ibid., 83).

[12] *The Promise of the Spirit*, 49-56. For Lloyd-Jones' views, see D. Martyn Lloyd-Jones, *God's Ultimate Purpose: An Exposition of Ephesians One* (Edinburgh: Banner of Truth, 1978), 243-300; *Romans: An Exposition of Chapter 8:5-17 – The Sons of God* (Edinburgh: Banner of Truth, 1974), 148-398, especially 338-55.

[13] Perkins taught that sealing of the Spirit removed all doubt from the believer, begetting an assured 'trust and confidence' in the promises of God. See, *William Perkins, 1558-1602; English Puritanist: His Pioneer Works on Casuistry*, ed. Thomas F. Merrill (Nieuwkoop: B. DeGraaf, 1966), 50-51, cited by Sinclair Ferguson, *John Owen and the Christian Life* (Edinburgh: Banner of Truth, 1987), 117.n5; *The Workes of that Famous and Worthy Minister of Christ, Mr. William Perkins* (London: John Legatt, 1612), 1:104-05. See also, 'Introduction' by Joel Beeke to *The Works of Thomas Goodwin* (12 vols. 1861-66; repr. Eureka, CA: Tanski Publications, 1996), 15-22.

[14] Goodwin has most to say about the sealing of the Spirit in his *Exposition of the Epistle to the Ephesians* (sermons 13–17 on Ephesians 1:13-14), and *Of the Object and Acts of Justifying Faith* (Part II ['Of the Acts of Faith'], particularly Book II ['Of faith of assurance']). *The Works of Thomas Goodwin*, vol. 1:227-52, and vol. 8:338-419.

[15] See *The Works of Richard Sibbes*, ed. A. B. Grosart (6 vols., 1862-64; repr. Edinburgh: Banner of Truth, 1979-83), vol. 3:453ff.

[16] Paul Bayne, *An Entire Commentary vpon the whole Epistle of the Apostle Paul to the Ephesians* (London: Printed by M. F. for Milbourne and I. Bartlet, 1643), 80-81, cited by Ferguson, *John Owen and the Christian Life*, 117-18.

seventeenth century, namely, something which bears the image of a monarch. As Sinclair Ferguson explains, 'For him, therefore, the function of the seal of the Spirit was to stamp afresh on our lives the image of Jesus Christ.'[17] The sealing of the Spirit, in Sibbes' view, was a 'superadded work' and 'superadded confirmation' of the believer's faith.[18] Lloyd-Jones cites with evident approval Thomas Goodwin on the meaning of *sphragizō* ('sealed') in Ephesians 1:13:

> There is light that cometh and over-cometh a man's soul and assureth him that God is his, and he is God's, and that God loveth him from everlasting . . . It is a light beyond the light of ordinary faith . . . the next thing to heaven; you have no more, you can have no more, till you come thither . . . It is faith elevated and raised up above its ordinary rate, it is electing love of God brought home to the soul.[19]

Attaching the seal of the Spirit in this way to assurance rather than regeneration led some Puritans to advocate the possibility (one might even say given the high degree of those who professed not to be in possession of an assurance of faith, probability) of saving faith in the absence of the sealing work of the Spirit. This was a clear departure from Calvin's position a century earlier. Commenting on Ephesians 1:13, Calvin asks: 'Is it not the faith itself which is here said to be sealed by the Holy Spirit?' The answer is unequivocally in the negative:

> If so, faith precedes it. I answer, the effect of the Spirit in faith is twofold, corresponding to the two chief parts of which faith consists. It enlightens the intellect (*mens*) and also confirms the thinking (*animus*). The commencement of faith is knowledge; its completion is a firm and steady conviction, which admits of no opposing doubt. Each, I have said, is the work of the Spirit. No wonder, then, if Paul should declare that the Ephesians not only received by faith the truth of the gospel, but also were confirmed in it by the seal of the Holy Spirit.[20]

---

[17] Ferguson, *The Holy Spirit*, 181.

[18] Sibbes, *Works* 3:455. For additional sources, see Joel Beeke's 'Introduction' to *The Works of Thomas Goodwin* (Tanski edition), 1:14-22.

[19] *The Works of Thomas Goodwin*, 1:236. Cited in D. Martyn Lloyd-Jones, *Romans: An Exposition of Chapter 8:5-17 – The Sons of God*, 344.

[20] John Calvin, *Calvin's New Testament Commentaries: A New Translation*, 12 vols. eds. David W. Torrance and Thomas F. Torrance, Vol. 11, *Galatians, Ephesians, Philippians and Colossians*, trans. T. H. L. Parker (Grand Rapids, MI: Eerdmans, 1993), 1:13.

In a sermon on Ephesians 1:13-14, Calvin is even clearer:

> When we have once embraced God's grace by faith, so that we know that our Lord Jesus is he in whom we find all that is required to make us perfectly happy, it is very necessary for us to be established in this truth. And why? Let us notice how volatile men are. He that is best disposed to follow God will soon fall, for we are so frail that the devil will overcome us every minute of time, if God does not hold us up with a strong hand. And for that reason it is said that God manifests his power in upholding us when he has elected us to our Lord Jesus Christ. For if he did not fight for us, alas, what would become of us? We should be so absolutely confounded, and not by reasons of one stroke only, but there would be an infinite number of falls, as I said before. As soon as we were in the way of salvation, we would at once be turned out of it by our own frailty, lightness and inconsistency, if we were not restrained and if God did not so work in us that we might, by his Holy Spirit, overcome all the assaults of the devil and the world. Thus God's Spirit does a twofold work in us with respect to faith. For he enlightens us to make us understand things which otherwise would be hidden from us, and to receive God's promises with all obedience. That is the first part of his work. The second is that the same Spirit is pleased to abide in us and to give us perseverance, that we do not draw back in the midst of our way. That, then, is what St. Paul is handling now.
>
> It is as if he should say, My friends, you have known God's grace and had experience of it, and he has drawn you to obey his gospel. For you would never have come to it, if he had not shown himself merciful to you. But be sure of this also, that he increases his grace in that he gives you power to persevere in it. For had you continued only three days, or three years, or even more, God must needs have helped you in that, or else you would always have been tossed about like poor wretches at your wits' end, without any certainty at all, unless God had promised to take care of you and to guide you continually till you have come to the end of your way and have finished your course. That, therefore, is the reason why he says here they were sealed by the Holy Spirit.[21]

The Holy Spirit is, for Calvin, a guarantee of our inheritance not just in the sense of authenticating it, but also in the sense of *securing* that inheritance. By this understanding every true Christian must also necessarily be sealed with the Spirit.

---

[21] John Calvin, *John Calvin's Sermons on Ephesians* (Carlisle, PA: Banner of Truth, 1973), 73.

It is interesting to note that John Owen, after he had turned fifty years of age, could write in a treatise on *Communion with the God the Father, Son, and Holy Ghost*: 'I am not very clear on the certain particular intendment of this metaphor.'[22] Sinclair Ferguson comments on Owen's apparent interpretive reticence:

> [I]f Owen had the wisdom and courage to say, 'I am not completely certain what this text of Scripture means' we should not be slow to share his modesty. Indeed, it is one of the blessings of reformed theology's sense of the incomprehensible greatness of God that it recognizes we do not know all of the answers![23]

Ferguson explains that Owen in 1667 reasoned 'it is the promises of God, not the persons who receive them that are in view in the first instance in this sealing: God seals his promises to the believer.'[24] As a result, the believer enters into the enjoyment of these promises (assurance). But, as Ferguson further elaborates, Owen changed his mind on the meaning of seal of the Spirit. Published ten years after his death, in his magnificent treatise, *A Discourse on the Holy Spirit as Comforter*,[25] Owen writes with greater certainty as to the meaning of the seal of the Spirit:

> The effects of this sealing are gracious operations of the Holy Spirit in and upon believers but the sealing itself is the communication of the Spirit unto us.[26]

Clearly, Owen has moved away from viewing the sealing of the Spirit as something that belongs in the area of assurance to a view that sees the seal as belonging to the very foundation of what a Christian *is*: someone who is indwelt by the Holy Spirit. Noting the decades of Puritan discussion on the matter, Owen adds:

> It hath been generally conceived that this sealing with the Spirit is that which gives assurance unto believers, — and so indeed it doth, although the way whereby it doth it hath not been rightly apprehended; and,

---

[22] *The Works of John Owen*, ed. W. H. Goold (24 vols., 1850-53; repr. of vols. 1-16, Edinburgh: Banner of Truth, 1965), 2:242. Vols. 17-24 were reprinted as 7 vols., *An Exposition of the Epistle to the Hebrews* in 1991.

[23] Sinclair Ferguson, 'John Owen and the doctrine of the Holy Spirit' in *John Owen: The Man and His Theology*, ed. Robert W. Oliver (Darlington, England: Evangelical Press; Phillipsburg, NJ: P & R, 2002), 122.

[24] Ibid.

[25] *Works*, 4:353-419.

[26] Ibid., 404

therefore, none have been able to declare the especial nature of that act of the Spirit whereby he seals us, whence such assurance should ensue. But it is indeed not any act of the Spirit in us that is the ground of our assurance, but the communication of the Spirit unto us.[27]

Owen's volte-face

Why did Owen change his mind? Given the considerable weight of opinion expressed on the sealing of the Spirit in the first half of the seventeenth century, his reversal of opinion, though consonant with Genevan, sixteenth century opinion, rowed against the stream of his own era. It is interesting to follow, in summary, the lines of thought that brought about this change of mind.

In his earlier writings, Owen drew from the relevant texts in which the term 'seal' (*sphragis*) is used in relation to the Spirit (Eph. 1:13; 4:30 and 2 Cor. 1:21-22), Owen carefully explains his reasoning:

• If the sealing of the Spirit is assigned to a subjective, post-conversion experience of the Spirit, it is difficult to know what might be excluded from such an operation.

• '...it is not said that the *Holy Spirit seals us*, but that *we are sealed with him*; he is God's seal unto us.'

• The seal of the Spirit is integrally related to our union with Christ brought about by conversion.[28]

And it is at this point that Owen introduces an important Christological point: that Jesus is said to have been 'sealed' by the Father: 'For on him God the Father has set his seal' [John 6:27].[29] Owen adds: 'if we can learn aright how God the Father sealed Christ, we shall learn how we are sealed in a participation of the same privilege.'[30] Dismissing the various interpretations of John 6:27 (he cites one author as having mentioned ten), Owen makes the following observations:

• It is in his human nature and in discharging his office as the one who would provide spiritual bread – 'the food that endures to eternal life (John 6:27)' – that Christ is said to be sealed by the Father.

• This sealing results in a demonstration of Jesus' authority and power to provide what he has promised.

---

[27] Ibid., 405
[28] Ibid., 401.
[29] τοῦτον γὰρ ὁ πατὴρ ἐσφράγισεν ὁ θεός
[30] *Works*, 4:401.

• As a seal, it demonstrates that he is 'owned' by God, a public testimony of the Spirit's indwelling having been afforded at the time of Jesus' baptism, 'which was nothing but a public declaration that this was he whom God had sealed, and so owned in a peculiar manner.'[31]

• 'Wherefore, this sealing of the Son is the communication of the Holy Spirit in all fullness unto him, authorizing him unto, and acting his divine power in, all the acts and duties of his office, so as to evidence the presence of God with him, and his approbation of him, as the only person that was to distribute the spiritual food of their souls unto men.'[32]

And for Owen, what is true of the sealing of Jesus by the coming (baptism, filling) of the Spirit, must also be true *mutatis mutandis* of believers since by believing they are brought into union and fellowship with Jesus Christ. The Holy Spirit *himself* was given to the incarnate Son without measure, testifying as to his identity and purpose. Similarly, as believers are drawn into union with Christ, it is to the same end that the Spirit is given as a seal – to testify as to their renewed nature and purpose. Owen writes:

> In this state God owns them, and communicates unto them his Holy Spirit, to fit them for their relations, to enable them unto their duties, to act their new principles, and every way to discharge the work they are called unto.[33]

Owen, in the end, removed 'the suggestion of any theology of subsequence from his doctrine of the Christian life, without destroying the element of progression and development in the experience of God.'[34]

Westminster Confession
We should also note that the Westminster Confession also displays some ambivalence over the meaning of the sealing of the Spirit. In addressing the topic of assurance, the Divines assert the possibility of assurance, defined as 'an infallible assurance of faith founded upon the divine truth of the promises of salvation, the inward evidence of those graces unto which these promises were made, the testimony of the

---

[31] Ibid., 401-02.
[32] Ibid., 403.
[33] Ibid, 404
[34] Ferguson, *John Owen and the Christian Life*, 123.

Spirit of adoption witnessing with our spirits that we are the children of God, which Spirit is the earnest of our inheritance, whereby we are sealed to the day of redemption.'[35] Of interest are the proof-texts provided for the final clause, namely Ephesians 1:13-14, 4:30 and 2 Corinthians 1:21-22. In other words, the Confession views the possibility of the sealing of the Spirit as an experience of *assurance* which may occur sometime after regeneration and faith; and possibly not at all!

Sidestepping the vexed (and by now, somewhat tired) issue of the extent to which Calvin differs from Westminsterian theology,[36] on this point (the sealing of the Spirit) some tension certainly exists. Thomas Goodwin, after all, was a member of the Assembly and in a recent work, Robert Letham suggests that the Assembly 'accommodated' Goodwin's understanding of Ephesians 1:13-14.[37]

It is not that doubt should be expressed over post-conversion experiences of assurance. Even Calvin would not demur here. What is at issue is whether they should be labeled 'Spirit-baptism' or 'Spirit-sealing.' Reflecting on chapter 18 of the Westminster Confession, and speaking of the claim that experiences of assurance may be termed 'Spirit baptism,' Donald Macleod writes:

> Many people who claim to have had a subsequent Spirit baptism are, in fact, people in whose lives there has been a hiatus between conversion and assurance. They may easily feel that in that moment of assurance they have had some second overwhelming experience. It is very important that we should not deny the experience. I am simply denying the label. It is not Spirit Baptism.[38]

---

[35] Westminster Confession of Faith 18:2.

[36] I refer to the fact that Calvin defined assurance as 'of the essence of faith' (Institutes 3.2.7), whereas the Confession allows for the possibility of true faith devoid of assurance. This observation, however, is guilty of a category error: the *Institutes* is defining what faith is and the Confession is defining how faith is *experienced*. For a summary of this issue, see among others, Mark Dever, 'Calvin, Westminster and Assurance,' in *The Westminster Confession into the 21st Century: Volume One*, ed. J. Ligon Duncan (Fearn, Ross-shire: Mentor, 2003), 303-342; J. Beeke, *Assurance of Faith: Calvin, English Puritanism, and the Dutch Second Reformation* (New York: Peter Lang, 1991); Carl R. Trueman and R. Scott Clark eds., *Protestant Scholasticism: essays in Reassessment* (Carlisle: Paternoster, 1999).

[37] Robert Letham, *The Westminster Assembly: Reading Its Theology in Historical Context* (Phillipsburg, NJ: P & R, 2009), 285.

[38] Donald Macleod, *A Faith to Live By: Understanding Christian Doctrine* (Fearn, Ross-shire: Mentor, 1998), 158.

Replacing 'Spirit baptism' with the 'sealing of the Spirit' in the citation, Macleod would equally be unhappy with this attribution.

Christ and the Spirit

Following on from John Owen's observation with respect to the sealing of Christ in John 6, we return to our starting-point and Macleod's statement that Holy Spirit baptism is only one of several designations for that all-important initiatory experience by which the Holy Spirit comes to take up residence in the believer, rivaling union with Christ as the single most important concept in the Christian doctrine of salvation. It is time to investigate this further from both biblical and theological points of view. In doing so we are reflecting on the wider implications of the Spirit's initiatory baptismal/sealing/filling ministry – implications, as we shall see, that have cosmic, eschatological aspects.

To be 'in Christ' in New Testament (specifically, Pauline) terms is to employ a category of thought that encompasses several perspectives. As Richard Gaffin explains, 'in Christ' 'is either *predestinarian* (Eph. 1:4); *past* or *redemptive-historical*, the union involved in the once-for-all accomplishment of salvation, particularly in his death and resurrection; or *present*, the union involved in the actual possession or application of salvation, in that sense *existential* union.'[39] Focusing on the latter, 'union in the actual appropriation or application of salvation, the *ordo salutis* aspect of union,' Gaffin notes that in addition to being representative and legal, this union is also 'mystical' – involving what Paul calls a 'great mystery' (Eph. 5:32), the closest analogy being the relationship between husband and wife.[40] It is also *spiritual* because it involves the activity and indwelling of the Holy Spirit. Gaffin continues:

> As spiritual, that is, effected by the Holy Spirit, it is neither ontological (like that between the persons of the Trinity), nor hypostatic (like that between Christ's divine and human natures), nor psychosomatic (between body and soul in human personality), nor somatic (between husband and wife); nor is it merely intellectual and moral, a unity in understanding, affections and purpose.[41]

---

[39] Richard B. Gaffin Jr., *By Faith, Not by Sight: Paul and the Order of Salvation* (Milton Keynes, Bucks: Paternoster Press, 2006), 37.

[40] Ibid., 38.

[41] Ibid., 38-39.

And more pertinently:

> Because of his resurrection and ascension, the incarnate Christ ('the
> last Adam') has been so transformed by the Spirit and is now in such
> complete possession of the Spirit that he has 'become life-giving
> Spirit,' with the result that now 'the Lord [=Christ] is the Spirit'
> (1 Cor. 15:45; 2 Cor. 3:17). In view is a functional equation that does
> not efface personal distinction, a oneness in their activity of giving
> resurrection-life (1 Cor. 15) and eschatological freedom (2 Cor. 3),
> so that in the life of the church and within believers, Christ and the
> Spirit are inseparable, in fact, one. So, for example, in Romans 8:9-10
> 'you in the Spirit,' 'the Spirit in you,' you 'belonging to Christ' or
> 'of Christ' (close, perhaps equivalent to 'in Christ'), and 'Christ in
> you' are all inseparable facets describing a single union. Likewise, in
> Ephesians 3:16-17, to have 'his Spirit in your inner man' is for 'Christ
> ... [to] dwell in your hearts.'[42]

Thus, it may be said of the believer that in the Spirit:

- 'Christ [is] in you' (Col. 1:27)
-· 'I no longer live, but Christ lives in me' (Gal. 2:20)
- 'Your life is hid with Christ in God' (Col. 3:3).

These assertions are true because 'the last Adam became a life-giving
spirit' (1 Cor. 15:45), and better, 'Spirit' with a capital 'S.'[43] Subsequent
to Christ's resurrection and ascension, as Peter made so emphatically
clear at Pentecost, the Holy Spirit was poured out upon the church:
'This Jesus God raised up, and of that we all are witnesses. Being
therefore exalted at the right hand of God, and having received from
the Father the promise of the Holy Spirit, he has poured out this that
you yourselves are seeing and hearing' (Acts 2:32-33). As Gaffin puts it,
'"first-fruits" of the resurrection harvest, Christ is "life-giving Spirit";
as the life-giving Spirit he is the "first-fruits".'[44] And again, 'As "the life-

---

[42] Ibid., 39.
[43] Richard B. Gaffin Jr., ' "Life-Giving Spirit": Probing the Center of Paul's Pneumatology,'
in *Journal of the Evangelical Theological Society* 41.4 (December 1988), 579-80. Earlier, Gaffin
gives as his two reasons for viewing Pneuma as [Holy] Spirit, (1) the adjective πνευματικόν
[*pneumatikon*] in verses 44 and 46 plainly refers to the activity of the Holy Spirit, so its correlative
noun πνευμα in verse 45 refers to the person of the Holy Spirit; and (2), the last Adam did not
simply become πνευμα [*pneuma*] but life-giving πνευμα – the 'spirit' in view is an acting subject.
See page 577-78.
[44] Ibid., 578.

giving Spirit," (the resurrected and ascended) Christ is the one who baptizes with the Spirit.'[45] The presence of the Spirit in the life of the believer is therefore 'the first-fruits' of their full adoption to be realized in 'the redemption (= the resurrection) of the body' (Rom. 8:23), and the 'deposit' toward the resurrection body (2 Cor. 5:5). In his sealing activity as 'the Spirit of promise' he is the deposit on the church's 'inheritance' (Eph. 1:14).

In a similar way, Paul writes to the Corinthians and says, 'The Lord is the Spirit' (2 Cor. 3:17). The 'Lord' here is Christ (the antecedent in verse 13 is 'Christ').[46] The statement is pivotal to both Christology and pneumatology: it defines the fellowship that exists between the exalted Christ and the Spirit as well as the Spirit's role in establishing and nurturing the believer's existential union with Christ. Similarly, in short compass Romans 8:9-10 rings the changes by employing synonymous phrases – 'you ... in the Spirit ... the Spirit of God dwells in you ...belong to [Christ] ... Christ is in you.' These four phrases hardly describe different experiences distinct (experientially and chronologically) from each other, but the same reality in its multi-faceted dimensions.[47] And Sinclair Ferguson concurs:

> To have the Spirit is to have Christ; to have Christ is to have the Spirit. Not to have the Spirit of Christ is to lack Christ. To have the Spirit of Christ is to be indwelt by Christ (Rom. 8:9-11). There is clear ontological distinction, but economic or functional equivalence. In this sense, through the resurrection and ascension, Christ 'became life-giving Spirit'.[48]

Similarly, Paul's Trinitarian prayer in Ephesians 3 is to the effect that the Father 'may grant you to be strengthened with power through his Spirit in your inner being, so that Christ may dwell in your hearts through faith' (Eph 3:16-17). We are to view this as a statement of the functional (economic) equivalence of the Spirit's strengthening and Christ's indwelling, and this *because* the ascended Christ has become the 'life-giving Spirit' – 'the Spirit of God' who has become 'the Spirit of Christ' (Rom. 8:9).

---

[45] Ibid., 582.

[46] See Sinclair Ferguson, *The Holy Spirit*, 55. Contrary to what has been an emerging consensus in our time which views it as an application of Exodus 34:34 (just cited in verse 16) to the Spirit. This, at least, makes sense as to why 'Lord' is distinguished from 'Spirit' in verse 17, 'The Spirit of the Lord.'

[47] See Gaffin, 'Life-Giving Spirit,' 584.

[48] Ferguson, *The Holy Spirit*, 54.

All of this is of a piece with our Lord's final observation in the Upper Room prior to his 'exodus' (Luke 9:31). He is going away but he is also to come to them again – understood as a reference to the Spirit's New Covenant, post-Pentecost ministry as the vicar (personal representative agent) of Christ (John 14:3, 18-19, 28; 16:22). As J. D. G. Dunn puts it, with respect to the Spirit's economic ministry to us, the Spirit has been 'imprinted' with the character of Jesus.[49] Thus, in the inter-adventual age between the first and second appearings of Christ, the Holy Spirit's ministry is to highlight ('floodlight') Christ, so much so that his presence in the church (corporately and individually) is the presence of the ascended Jesus. In that sense, 'the Lord [= Christ] is the Spirit' elucidates the promise in the Upper Room: 'I will not leave you as orphans; I will come to you' (John 14:18).

It is important to view the Spirit's ministry in making Christ known to us on a personal as well as a corporate scale, particularly when it has become fashionable by New Perspective proponents to view the corporate (and ecclesial) dimension exclusively and at the expense of the personal. After all, Paul could say in Galatians, 'the Son of God who loved me and gave himself for me,' and 1 Timothy 1:13, 15, 'I … a blasphemer, a persecutor, and an insolent man … chief of sinners … obtained mercy.'

Spiritus Recreator

Two areas of consideration now come into view as we reflect on the role of the Spirit in our relationship to Christ: sanctification and eschatology. Nor are these two areas unrelate d; the goal of sanctification is conformity to the image of Christ – 'already' an on-going reality by virtue of our union with Christ but 'not yet' complete.

The Spirit's coming in a redemptive-historical sense – he 'comes' in response to the (historical) resurrection-ascension of Christ – highlights the eschatological character of redemption: there is an ongoing, but as yet incomplete nature to the Spirit's work. Our individual salvation through faith alone in the finished work of Christ alone is only a small part of what God designs in redemption. He purposes to create 'a new heaven and new earth' (Isa. 65:17; 66:22; 2 Pet. 3:13; Rev. 21:1), a process inaugurated by the First Coming of Christ and consummated at his Second Coming. Consequently, believers are even now those 'on

---

[49] J. D. G. Dunn, *Jesus and the Spirit* (London: SCM Press, 1975), 322.

whom the end of the ages has come' (1 Cor. 10:11). God sent his Son 'in the fullness of time' (Gal. 4:4) to fulfill a promise of re-creation. Our present baptism with the Spirit is a testimony to the fact that we already share, through faith-union with Christ, in his resurrection. 'Every spiritual blessing in the heavenly places' is ours (Eph. 1:3), 'sealed' by the giving of the 'promised Holy Spirit' (Eph. 1:13). We have been made 'alive together with Christ – by grace you have been saved – and raised us up with him and seated us with him in the heavenly places in Christ Jesus, so that in the coming ages he might show the immeasurable riches of his grace in kindness toward us in Christ Jesus' (Eph. 2:5-6). The Spirit-presence is a constant reminder that our life in this world is not our final mode of existence. We are set for greater things. Believers are no longer in the flesh but in the Spirit (Rom. 8:9).

It is just here, in the reality of life in the world of tension between the 'now' and the 'not yet', that another aspect of the Spirit's work in relation to Christ is evident. Speaking to the Corinthians of the inability of the letter of the law to fulfill its demands in us, Paul could say of his ministry as an apostle of the new covenant, God 'has made us competent to be ministers of a new covenant, not of the letter but of the Spirit. For the letter kills, but the Spirit gives life' (2 Cor. 3:6). It is precisely here, in a passage demonstrating the need for the law to be written on tablets of the human heart by the Spirit that he makes his claim 'the Lord is the Spirit, and where the Spirit of the Lord is, there is freedom' (2 Cor. 3:17). In the hearts of unbelievers, the law can only bring condemnation and guilt. To a large extent, Paul's point is to demonstrate the ineffectiveness of the entire old covenant. In comparison to the new covenant the entire Mosaic administration is 'no different from [that] of a slave' (Gal. 4:1). Whatever glory it possessed, and the veiling of Moses' face showed that it possessed some form of glory, set over against the surpassing glory of the new covenant it had no glory at all (2 Cor. 3:9-10). Moses and Sinai cannot equate with the ministry of Christ and the subsequent ministry of the Spirit.

The goal of this new covenant ministry of the ascended Christ-Spirit is a restoration to the divine image (Eph. 4:24; Col. 3:10). Nowhere is this more succinctly and apocalyptically put than in Paul's statement to the Corinthians: 'if anyone is in Christ – new creation' (2 Cor. 5:17).[50]

---

[50] English translations fill out the breathless prose of the apostle by adding, '*he is a* new creation.'

The eschatological life has already broken through; the resurrection life has already begun.

The motives for advancing this image-restoration are sharply Christological: sanctification is being restored to the glory-image of God by being conformed to the likeness of Jesus. We are baptized with the Spirit 'into Christ's death and resurrection' (Rom. 6:3-4). And once again, it is the death-and-resurrection of Christ that forms the basis on which the Spirit now implements holiness in the lives of believers. Christ's resurrection by the power of the Spirit was a resurrection into eschatological, pneumatic life. The life he now lives, he lives unto God (Rom. 6:10). If we have been united with him, we have been constituted by the Spirit to live unto God (Rom. 6:4). To continue to live in sin would thereby be a denial of our Spirit baptism, pointing us as it does to a new life in union with Christ.

A tension therefore exists for Christians indwelt by the Spirit and in union with Christ – no more impressively stated than the almost casual way Paul addresses the Corinthians as being 'in Christ' and at the same time 'in Corinth' (1 Cor. 1:2). Sanctification, new life in the Spirit, is lived out in the flesh whose addiction to a past life of sin is difficult to obliterate. However, something definitive has already taken place: a radical break with the dominion of sin:

- 'our old self [Adamic-man] was crucified with him [Christ]' (Rom. 6:6)
- 'those who belong to Christ Jesus have crucified the flesh with its passions and desires' (Gal. 5:24)
- 'In him also you were circumcised with a circumcision made without hands, by putting off the body of the flesh, by the circumcision of Christ' (Col. 2:11)
- 'your old self ... belongs to your former manner of life' (Eph. 4:22)
- 'you have put off the old self ... and have put on the new self' (Col. 3:9-10)
- 'I have been crucified with Christ. It is no longer I who live, but Christ who lives in me' (Gal. 2:20)
- 'You ... are not in the flesh but in the Spirit, if in fact the Spirit of God dwells in you' (Rom. 8:9)

Some of these texts may, in the first place, signify the redemptive-historical tension of the dawning of the new aeon with the old. Herman Ridderbos comments:

We shall have to understand 'old' and 'new man,' not in the first place in the sense of the *ordo salutis*, but in that of the history of redemption; that is to say, it is a matter here not of a change that comes about in the way of faith and conversion in the life of the individual Christian, but of that which once took place in Christ and in which his people had part in him in the corporate sense...[51]

It is, however, too restricting to view these passages (Rom. 6:6, for example) as having nothing to say in an *ordo salutis* sense. Sinclair Ferguson writes with respect to Romans 6:6:

'...the old self/man has been crucified with Christ. While that was true representatively at the cross, this 'with Christ' (*syn Christô*) denotes an existentially-realized, Spirit-wrought, union with him which as we have seen, is multi-dimensional in character. Redemptive-historically this crucifixion took place at Calvary; existentially its significance and implications are realized in us by the Spirit in regeneration, repentance and faith. This latter realization is rooted in the historicity of the former. The believer is no longer identified in terms of the Adamic, but in terms of the Christic. In Paul's terminology, the believer has been 'crucified with Christ'; it is not he, but Christ, who lives; yet he does live – in the life of the new man in Christ – by faith in the Son of God who loved him and gave himself for him (Gal. 2:20).[52]

With Christ's resurrection – a resurrection accomplished by the power of the Holy Spirit (Rom. 1:3-4) – came a new order of existence: a life 'lived to God' (Rom. 6:10). And if we have been united to him by the Spirit, it follows that we, too, live a life 'to God'. How, then, can we continue to sin? (Rom. 6:1). How indeed! It is a revolting concept for the apostle, one from which he recoils in horror. Shall we go on sinning with impunity on the grounds that sin is already forgiven? Is it conceivable that we can sin with no regard for our present nature? 'By no means!' (*me genoito*, Rom. 6:2). More than that, such an attitude flies in the face of what is now true of the Spirit-baptized, Spirit-sealed, Spirit-filled believer: 'one who has died has been set free from sin' (Rom. 6:7). The question then arises: in what sense can it be said that the Spirit's uniting us to Christ has freed us from sin? John Murray limits this statement to the realm of justification:

---

[51] See Herman Ridderbos, *Paul: An Outline of his Theology*, Trans. John Richard de Witt (Grand Rapids, MI: Eerdmans, 1975), 63.
[52] Ferguson, *The Holy Spirit*, 147.

The decisive breach with the reigning power of sin is viewed after the analogy of the kind of dismissal which a judge gives when an arraigned person is justified. Sin has no further claim upon the person who is thus vindicated. ... It shows that the forensic is present not only in justification but also in what lies at the basis of sanctification.[53]

C. E. Cranfield, similarly, views the statement to the effect that 'the man who has died with Christ ... is justified from his sin.'[54] However, this unnecessarily limits Paul's focus. In verse 6, it is not the guilt of sin so much as its power that is in view: 'so that we would no longer be enslaved to sin.' And, as Ferguson points out, in Paul's usage of 'sin' in this and the preceding chapter he almost personifies it as 'The Sin':

> Sin is portrayed as a king who reigns ('sin reigned in death', 5:21; 'do not let sin reign', 6:12); as a general who employs our bodies as weapons in his warfare ('instruments' or 'weapons' [*hopla*] of wickedness, 6:13); as a master who tyrannizes ('sin shall no longer be your master', 6:14, NEB); and as an employer who pays wages ('the wages of sin is death', 6:23).[55]

The eschatological tension of what is true 'now' and what will be true in the 'not yet' marks the believer's relationship to sin as much as it marks his relationship to everything else in this present aeon. This is a perspective that has not been sufficiently noted in the Christian church. Richard Gaffin complains:

> What has sometimes been captured fleetingly, say, in the hymnody of the Church has been too often lacking in its teaching and practical outlook. There has been an undeniable and persistent tendency to isolate the work of the Spirit and eschatological realities from each other. This has happened as part of a larger tendency to divorce the present life of the Church from its future... We have only to ask: How many believers today recognize that the present work of the Spirit within the Church and in their lives is of one piece with God's great work of restoring the entire creation, begun in sending his Son 'in the fullness of times' (Gal. 4:4) and to be consummated at his

---

[53] John Murray, *The Epistle to the Romans*, NICNT, 2 vols published as one (Grand Rapids, MI: Wm. B. Eerdmans, 1968), 1:222.

[54] C. E. B. Cranfield, *Romans*, The International Critical Commentary, Eds. J. A. Emerton & C. E. B. Cranfield 2 vols. (Edinburgh: T. & T. Clark, 1975), 1:311. Cranfield (rightly) makes much of the association of the text with baptism as a 'sign and seal' of justification.

[55] Ferguson, *The Holy Spirit*, 149.

return? How many Christians grasp that in union with Christ, the life-giving Spirit, the Christian life in its entirety is essentially and necessarily resurrection life? How many comprehend that in terms of Paul's fundamental anthropological distinction between 'the inner' and 'outer man' (2 Cor. 4:16), between 'heart' and 'body,' believers at the core of their being will never be any more resurrected than they already are?[56]

What kind of life is the 'resurrection life,' the life lived in union with 'the life-giving Spirit'? What can the believer expect in this aeon? The answer chirped by one TV mega-personality is the 'best life now'. But Paul would see it differently. His great (greatest?) longing expressed in Philippians 3:10-11 puts it succinctly: 'that I may know him and the power of his resurrection, and may share his sufferings, becoming like him in his death, that by any means possible I may attain the resurrection from the dead.' These are not to be viewed as three (definitive) stages in Christian growth but rather as three ways of viewing the same Christian reality. To cite Gaffin again, 'the imprint left in our lives by Christ's resurrection power, in a word, is the cross. This cross conformity, as much as any, is the signature of inaugurated eschatology.'[57] Any view of the Spirit's baptism, filling, sealing, gifting, leading, or witness that does not lead us to fellowship (a sharing) in the cross is an aberration. Before the crown comes the cross, for Christ as well as for those who by the Spirit are in union with him.

Few saw this death-life, *mortification-vivification* duplex more clearly than Calvin:

> How much can it do to soften all the bitterness of the cross, that the more we are afflicted with adversities, the more surely our fellowship with Christ is confirmed! By communion with him the very sufferings themselves not only become blessed to us but also help much in promoting our salvation.[58]

How much indeed!

---

[56] Gaffin, 'Life-Giving Spirit,' 585.
[57] Ibid., 587.
[58] Calvin, *Institutes*, 3:8:1.

10

Re-Visiting The Covenant of Redemption[1]

Iain D. Campbell

Without a doubt, it was the greatest of all privileges to sit as a divinity student in Donald Macleod's Systematic Theology class in the Free Church College in the mid-1980s. He was in his prime, a teacher of theology without peer in the United Kingdom, whose classes often became theatres of worship. I, on the other hand, was a precocious postgraduate, fresh out of a successful University course, who reacted strongly against my new Professor's marking scheme. I well remember my dismay on hearing from him on our first day that he would never, ever give a student more than eighty percent in an essay. Eighty percent?

The reason, as Professor Macleod explained, was that in a theology exam only God himself could get one hundred percent, and eighty out of a hundred was as much as the Professor thought himself capable of. The point was hard to bear, but the rationale was irrefutable. I still have an essay for which Donald awarded me eighty percent. It was the only piece of work for which I gained top marks with a twenty percent deficit. I make no pretence that this chapter will come anywhere close to that, but I offer it as a tribute to my former Systematic Theology Professor, whose insights and formulations shaped my thinking across

[1] I would like to thank Prof Robert Letham of Wales Evangelical School of Theology and Prof R. Scott Clark of Westminster Seminary California for reading this chapter in an early draft and for their valuable comments.

all the theological disciplines. Not least – along with Professor John
L. Mackay in the Old Testament department – Professor Macleod
reinforced my federal theology and taught me that the concept of the
covenant is at the heart of all theology.[2]

The idea that God's eternal plan of salvation is expressed in covenant
relationships has a long pedigree, of course, as has the nuancing of
this to include covenant relationships within the Trinity. The phrase
'covenant of redemption' expresses the idea that the Father and the
Son covenanted together from all eternity, as a consequence of which
the eternal Son was set apart to be the Saviour of sinners, and the
Mediator of a covenant of grace between them and God.

A recent study of this theme defines the covenant of redemption,
also known by the Latin phrase *pactum salutis*, or *covenant of salvation*,
as follows:

> In Reformed theology, the *pactum salutis* has been defined as a
> pretemporal, intratrinitarian agreement between the Father and the Son
> in which the Father promises to redeem an elect people. In turn, the Son
> volunteers to earn the salvation of his people by becoming incarnate
> (the Spirit having prepared a body for him), by acting as the surety
> (*eggus, sponsor, fideiussor* or *extrapromissor*) of the covenant of grace for,
> and as mediator of the covenant of grace to, the elect. In his active
> and passive obedience Christ fulfils the conditions of the *pactum salutis*
> and fulfils his guarantee (*sponsio, vas,* or *fideiussio*), ratifying the Father's
> promise, because of which the Father rewards the Son's obedience with
> the salvation of the elect. And because of this, the Holy Spirit applies the
> Son's work to his people through the means of grace.[3]

This definition contains all the essential elements integral to the
concept of a putative covenant of redemption, although, as the authors
go on to explain, the Son is not a party to the covenant merely as a
volunteer. He is willing, certainly, to be Saviour of his people, but
the voluntary nature of his role will bring stringent demands that
will make the effectiveness of the provision dependent on absolute
obedience. VanDrunen and Clark are certainly accurate in pointing
out that 'when Jesus Christ earned the righteousness to be imputed to

[2] See, for example, Donald Macleod, 'Covenant Theology', in *Dictionary of Scottish Church History and Theology*, Edinburgh, T&T Clark, 1993, 214-18.
[3] D. VanDrunen and R.Scott Clark, 'The Covenant before the Covenants,' in R. Scott Clark (ed), *Covenant, Justification and Pastoral Ministry: Essays by the Faculty of Westminster Seminary California*, Phillipsburg, NJ: P&R, 2007, 168.

his people, he was fulfilling not only the historical covenant of works as the Second Adam … but also the covenant he made with his Father'.[4]

But this concept of a pre-temporal, intra-Trinitarian covenant of redemption – for all its pedigree in the sixteenth century thought of Johannes Oecolampadius[5] – has not been without its critics. O. Palmer Robertson, whose treatment of the historico-redemptive covenant of grace remains unsurpassed in my view, argues that

> to speak concretely of an intertrinitarian [sic] 'covenant' with terms and conditions between Father and Son mutually endorsed before the foundation of the world is to extend the bounds of scriptural evidence beyond propriety.[6]

Andrew McGowan has also argued – explicitly agreeing with Karl Barth on this subject – that

> …there is no inter-trinitarian [sic] covenant. This is a weakness in covenant theology that demonstrates a failure to integrate properly its understanding of covenant with its doctrine of the Trinity … I do believe that there is an encounter between the Father and the Son on the cross, whereby the Son is punished by the Father in our place. I do not believe, however, that this necessitates an inter-trinitarian [sic] covenant.[7]

Professor McGowan is not here aligning himself with Karl Barth's view of the atonement – indeed, he has some significant critiques to make of it – nonetheless his rejection of the classic formulation of the covenant of redemption is noteworthy.

The domestication of Barthianism within Scottish theology, particularly through the writings of T.F. Torrance and J.B. Torrance, has led to a marginalisation of covenant (or federal) theology in contemporary evangelicalism.[8] T.F. Torrance, in particular, accused the

---

[4] 'The Covenant before the Covenants', 169.

[5] See 'The Covenant before the Covenants' (especially169-79) for an overview of literature, ancient and modern, on this topic.

[6] O. Palmer Robertson, *The Christ of the Covenants*, Phillipsburg, NJ:P&R, 1980, 54. A covenant of redemption, properly construed, would have to be described as *intra*-trinitarian (*within* the Trinity), not *inter*-trinitarian (*between* or *among* the Trinity); so also in the following quotation.

[7] A.T.B. McGowan, 'Karl Barth and Covenant Theology', in D. Gibson and D. Strange (eds), *Engaging with Barth: Contemporary evangelical critiques*, Nottingham: Apollos, 2008, p131.

[8] See Ligon Duncan's excellent study (which is not confined to Scotland), 'Recent Objections to Covenant Theology: A Description, Evaluation and Response', in Ligon Duncan (ed), *The Westminster Confession into the 21ˢᵗ Century*, Vol. 3 Mentor (2009), 467-500.

Westminster Confession of Faith of having a sub-Christian view of God, and argued that

> this doctrine of God, not primarily as Father, but primarily as creator, lawgiver and judge, accentuated within the framework of a federalised and logicalised system of Calvinism, was to have problematic and deleterious effects in later Scottish theology.[9]

More seriously, Torrance went on to argue that federalism would hamper evangelism, citing 'the rigidly contractual concept of God' in Scottish theology as being at variance with biblical statements about the free offer of the Gospel to all.[10]

In an incisive critical review of Torrance's analysis, Donald Macleod draws on his vast familiarity with Scottish historical theology to argue that its best representatives – men like Samuel Rutherford, Robert Bruce and Hugh Binning – 'would have taken serious offence at Dr Torrance's constant insinuation that as Federal Calvinists their doctrine of God was defective: particularly at the idea that they portrayed his love as having been bought or purchased by the atonement.'[11] For them, it was not the atonement that secured God's love for us, but God's love that provided the atonement:

> The whole cost of our redemption is borne by the triune God. In that sense, the atonement is a transaction entirely internal to the trinity. But by virtue of the incarnation, it is also external. It takes place not in heaven, but on Calvary; not in eternity, but on Good Friday. The Saviour is Last Adam as well as Son of God.[12]

It is the idea of the atonement arising out of Trinitarian relationships that leads to the classic formulation of the covenant of redemption. Writing explicitly on the theme of covenant theology in the Scottish tradition, Donald Macleod himself defines the concept as

> An eternal covenant between the Father and the Son, according to which the Son became surety for his people, undertook to obey and suffer in their place, and was promised everything that pertains to

---

[9] T.F. Torrance, *Scottish Theology: from John Knox to John McLeod Campbell*, Edinburgh: T&T Clark (1996), 133.

[10] Torrance, *Scottish Theology*, 137.

[11] D. Macleod, 'Dr T.F. Torrance and Scottish Theology: a Review Article', *Evangelical Quarterly* 72:1 (2000), 70.

[12] Macleod, 'Dr T.F. Torrance', 71.

grace and salvation ... its real basis lay in broader biblico-theological considerations. Scripture constantly relates Christ's mission to the will of God the Father. He was sent from God, received his assignment from God and received certain promises from God. Such language, according to covenant theologians, clearly indicates that he did not come on his own initiative alone, but on terms agreed with the Father.[13]

Although he goes on to note the disagreements on the formulations of covenant theology within the Scottish tradition (noting in particular Thomas Boston's subsuming of the covenant of redemption under the one covenant of grace[14]), nonetheless Macleod argues that

The older Scottish theologians believed it would be an impoverishment ... to relinquish the covenant of redemption. It contributes significantly to a clearer and more comprehensive statement of the truth.[15]

Elsewhere Macleod argues that the distinctiveness of the covenant of redemption is essential for two reasons. The first is to understand the relation between Christ and His Father.[16] Why is Jesus in the world at all? The answer of the New Testament is that he came in order to be obedient to death (Phil. 2:8), and the demands of this obedience were nothing other than what was required of Christ in the covenant of redemption. 'These tasks', as Ligon Duncan puts it, 'were not assigned at the incarnation, but were embraced before time in the eternal purposes of God'.[17]

But secondly, Macleod says, 'we need this covenant to understand the relationship between Christ and His people'.[18] It is by virtue of this pre-temporal covenant that Christ is constituted Representative, Vicar and Substitute of his church. Consequently, we can posit that 'what is required in the covenant of grace is provided in the covenant of redemption'.[19] We need a Saviour who will effect mediation between ourselves and God:

---

[13] Macleod, 'Covenant Theology', 215.

[14] In my view, this should not be pressed too far. The covenant of grace is one of the benefits of the covenant of redemption, and highlights the fact that the purpose of salvation became a works covenant for Christ and a grace covenant for us.

[15] Macleod, 'Covenant Theology', 216.

[16] See the discussion of this topic in D. Macleod, *A Faith to Live By: Christian Teaching that Makes a Difference*, Tain: Mentor, 97-99.

[17] J.Ligon Duncan III, 'Recent Objections to Covenant Theology', 486.

[18] Macleod, *A Faith to Live By*, 98.

[19] Macleod, *A Faith to Live By*, 99.

what he mediates are the blessings treasured up in the covenant of grace, and the reason he *is* Mediator is because he is set apart as such in the covenant of redemption: 'God's commitments in the eternal covenant of redemption find space-time realization in the covenant of grace.'[20]

This construction does justice to passages in the Old Testament like Isaiah 53:12, where God says of his messianic Servant:

> Therefore I will divide him a portion with the many,
> and he shall divide the spoil with the strong,
> because he poured out his soul to death
> and was numbered with the transgressors;
> yet he bore the sin of many,
> and makes intercession for the transgressors.

Here, the salvation of men is clearly dependent on the Servant's exaltation; and the exaltation is itself dependent on the Servant's obedience. The first two statements of this verse distinguish the Servant's *reward* for his obedience ('...*because* he poured out his soul...') and his consequent *work* in sharing out the results of his victory ('...he shall divide the spoil...'). As Saviour, the Servant-Jesus is exalted, extolled and made very high (Isa. 52:13) – this in terms of the covenant of redemption; as Mediator, the exalted Servant-Jesus justifies those whose iniquities he bore – this in terms of the covenant of grace.

This construction also does justice to passages in the New Testament like Luke 22:29, where Jesus says that 'I assign to you, as my Father assigned to me, a kingdom'. There is a twofold assignation: a promised kingdom assigned by the Father to the Son, distinct, but not divorced, from the promise of a kingdom by the Son to his disciples. The one plan of redemption finds its implementation in parallel assignations. In commenting on Francis Turretin's exegesis of this passage, James Mark Beach correctly says that

> Just as the elect obtain the kingdom by virtue of some covenantal or testamentary arrangement, likewise Christ – which demonstrates, then, that his work as the incarnate redeemer is part of an intertrinitarian [sic] pact.[21]

This exegesis of these key passages simply follows John Owen's counsel that 'we must distinguish between the covenant that God made with

---

[20] Duncan, 'Recent Objections', 500.
[21] James Mark Beach, *Christ and the Covenant: Francis Turretin's Federal Theology as a Defense of the Doctrine of Grace*, Gottingen: Vandenhoeck & Ruprecht (2007), 169.

178

men concerning Christ, and the covenant that he made with his Son concerning men.'[22] Commenting on Owen's view of the covenant of redemption, Jim Packer argues that it is this Puritan theology that recovers a full-orbed trinitarianism as the foundation for salvation. Packer defines the covenant of redemption in this way:

> The Father appointed the Son to become incarnate and – as prophet, priest and king – to mediate salvation to a great multitude of sinners. He did this through his atoning death in humiliation on the cross, his exaltation from the grave to the glory of the celestial throne, and his joining the Father in sending the Spirit to bring salvation home to blinded and twisted human hearts. Depending upon the covenant of redemption was the covenant of grace, whereby God established a new relationship of pardon, acceptance, adoption and protection, through Christ the mediator, with sinners whom the Spirit had led to faith and repentance. On this similarly nonnegotiable substance of doctrine, communion with God rests, according to Owen.[23]

Two objections

While the concept and formulation may be clear, however, criticisms of the covenant of redemption focus mainly on two issues, one to do with terminology and the other to do with theology. The first question concerns whether we are warranted, in the light of the biblical material, to use the language of 'covenant' to describe the relationship of the Father and the Son in executing the plan of redemption.

The objection to the use of covenant terminology here is twofold. First, there is the general objection that all such language is speculative at best, and unscriptural at worst. So, for example, Robert Culver argues that

> The fully developed covenant (Federal) theology, for many like me who while recognizing certain values in covenant theology do not adhere to it, seems to be speculative, scholastic over-refinement of what is otherwise already plain in the Scriptures. It seems remote from the scriptural simplicity of Calvin's *Institutes of the Christian Religion*.[24]

---

[22] John Owen, 'Federal Transactions between the Father and the Son', Exercitation 28 in *The Works of John Owen*, Vol 19, London: Johnstone and Hunter, 1854, 78.

[23] J.I. Packer, 'A Puritan Perspective: Trinitarian Godliness according to John Owen', in T. George (ed), *God the Holy Trinity: Reflections on Christian Faith and Practice*, Grand Rapids MI: Baker Academic (2006), 101.

[24] Robert D. Culver, *Systematic Theology: Biblical and Historical*, Tain: Mentor (2005), 656. It also seems difficult to justify Culver's earlier statement that federalism was not espoused in the Westminster standards (op.cit. 397-98).

Second, the objection to the terminology is raised because it seems to compromise the essential relationship of equality between God the Father and God the Son. So Bob Letham argues, for example, that the Son who becomes incarnate is the same Son who is the Father's equal in being and in status, and that the incarnation involves no change in the personal identity of the Son, and therefore no change in the personal relation between the Father and the Son. For this reason he wishes to argue that the incarnation is underpinned by the faithfulness of God, and not by any notion of covenant or contractual obligation:

> The faithfulness of God also undercuts the suggestion made by Warfield – only a suggestion, for he does not pursue it – that certain aspects of the relation between the Father and the Son in the history of salvation may have been due to a 'covenant' between the persons of the Trinity by which the Son submitted himself temporarily to the Father, intending to abandon such submission upon the completion of our salvation. If this were so, the Son could not have revealed God to us.[25]

To address this objection – whether the term 'covenant' is the most felicitous and scriptural we could use – we need to reflect on the nature of a covenant in the Bible. There are examples in Scripture of covenants made between people; for example, in Genesis 21, Abraham and Abimelech enter into an agreement over a well, in the context of making specific promises to one another. To ratify the agreement, they made (or literally 'cut') a covenant (Gen. 21:27). Similarly, on the initiative of Laban, Jacob and Laban made a covenant (Gen. 31:44), as did Jonathan and David in 1 Samuel 18:3.

These incidents of covenant-making between individuals show us that the effect of the covenant was not to establish a relationship where none existed before. In each instance, a personal relationship already existed between the individuals concerned; the covenant was the means by which the relationship was formalised.[26] That is to say, a benefit was secured in each case, which could only have arisen out of

---

[25] R. Letham, *The Holy Trinity: in Scripture, History, Theology and Worship*, Phillipsburg NJ: P&R (2004), 401. Although Letham is correct to say that Warfield does not pursue the topic, Warfield is nonetheless comfortable with the Covenant of Redemption terminology (see B.B. Warfield, 'The Biblical Doctrine of the Trinity' in Warfield, *Biblical Doctrines*, Baker Books, Vol 2 (2003), 167).

[26] Cf. Bruce K. Waltke, *Genesis*, Grand Rapids: Zondervan (2001),136: 'A covenant solemnizes and confirms a social relationship already in existence.'

the willingness of the parties, already bound by a personal relationship, to enter into a formal agreement. This officialising of their relationship, moreover, did not detract from the personal nature of it. It added to it, modified it, and redefined it in order that the benefit envisaged could be realised. Thus Jonathan and David, who were already close friends, formalised their friendship in a covenant, which had in view the safety of David, to which Jonathan was pledged. While Saul was growing increasingly jealous of David, and threatening to kill him (1 Sam. 18:11), David's security was guaranteed on the basis of Jonathan's promises and pledges to him.

We rarely cut such covenants in our modern culture, but we do find ourselves formalising relationships in order to secure benefits. The most obvious way in which this is done is when a couple enters into marriage. The covenant relationship is clearly analogous to the marriage relationship. When I officiate at a marriage service and pronounce a man and a woman to be husband and wife, I am not *creating* a brand new relationship between them as if no relationship existed previously. I *am* doing something new, however: I am formalising an existing relationship, in order to create an additional relationship of a different kind, into which two people, already personally connected to one another, are entering freely and willingly. The reason they are doing so is because of an advantage and benefit that marriage will bring into their relationship, through making the commitment formal. Vows and promises are made by one party to the other, in which each undertakes to be exclusively committed to each other until only death parts them. Thus, in addition to the personal relationship that is already in place, there is now a modification of it; the benefits that accrue from that undertaking could not be secured by the personal relationship alone; while the falling in love with each other could not guarantee lifelong fidelity, the marriage vows should.

The analogy between marriage and covenant is used by Paul himself to describe the special relationship between Christ and his church (Eph. 5:32). Indeed, the relationship between these two parties is both a marriage *and* a covenant. It is not that God has no prior relationship to man: God is man's Creator, sustainer and lawgiver – it is in God that man lives, moves and has his existence (Acts 17:28). By nature, however, man is fallen, 'having no hope and without God in the world' (Eph. 2:12). He is a stranger to God, because a covenant-breaker, as Paul goes on to argue, who refuses to relate to the God

who alone can save. The radical nature of fallen man's personal (non-)
relationship with God is expressed in his refusal to obey God. To
enjoy the benefits of salvation – forgiveness, adoption, and glory – the
relationship between God and man must be formalised and renewed.
This is the burden of the covenant of grace, of which God the Son is
Mediator (Heb. 8:6).

The distinction between God and man, emphasised as far back as
Genesis 1, is the ground of any relationship between them. But even
this is not itself sufficient to secure man's eternal happiness. Before
man fell, God had, in fact, modified and adapted his relationship with
Adam in the Garden of Eden, with a view to the eternal happiness of
the entire human race. God allowed Adam the liberty to eat of every
tree of the garden but one, on pain of death (Gen. 2:16-17). It is this
formalisation that transforms the relationship from being merely a
personal one between God and Adam – although it was never less than
that – to being a relationship between God and Adam-as-a-public-
person, a representative man, as Paul argues in Romans 5:12ff.

Was this relationship a covenant? The word itself is not used in
Genesis 1–3, although it is used of Adam in Hosea 6:7, where the
most natural reading of the text is simply that 'like Adam [Israel]
transgressed the covenant.' The absence of covenant terminology in
the opening chapters of Genesis famously led Professor John Murray
to conclude that it would be better not to use the traditional term
'covenant of works' to designate the formal relationship between God
and Adam, and further to argue that 'covenant in Scripture denotes
the oath-bound confirmation of promise and involves a security which
the Adamic economy did not bestow'.[27] Yet, in spite of his disavowal of
the terminology, Murray did express sympathy for the term 'covenant
of life', which appears in the Westminster Catechisms,[28] describing
this designation as 'much more in accord with the grace which
conditions the administration than is the term "covenant of works".'[29]
The debate over the terminology notwithstanding, the elements
of covenant do appear in God's formal relationship with mankind
through Adam, whether designated a covenant of works (highlighting
the conditionality of the covenant in its formal aspect, dependent on

[27] John Murray, 'The Adamic Administration' in *Collected Writings*, Vol 2: Systematic Theology, Edinburgh: Banner of Truth (1977), 49.

[28] Westminster Larger Catechism 20; Shorter Catechism 12.

[29] John Murray, 'Covenant Theology', *Collected Writings*, Vol 4: Studies in Theology, Edinburgh: Banner of Truth (1982), 222.

Adam's obedience), a covenant of life (highlighting the end in view, and the designated benefit that could be enjoyed through obedience), or a covenant of nature (highlighting the context in which the formal relationship was established in the first place).

If such a modification was required before the fall, it was certainly required afterwards. The relationship of fallen man to God could only result in man's eternal misery and ruin. When the children of Israel rebelled against God, God said he would send an angel to accompany them through the wilderness; his presence would only judge and consume them (Exod. 33:3-6). Only by the intercession of Moses does that presence become one of consolation and blessing (Exod. 33:17). Similarly, God's relationship to man can only be one of judgement apart from the intercessory work of Christ our Mediator; it is his intercession that turns the presence of judgement into a presence of grace. Without Christ acting on our behalf, we could only be condemned by our Maker. But on what basis does Christ come into the world to act on behalf of others?

In Romans 5:14 Adam is said to be a 'type' of the one to come, of Jesus Christ. That means that the significance of Adam's position is drawn from the significance of Jesus' position, to which it is analogous and points forward. Adam related to God in a formal, covenant manner as federal head of the race, because the incarnate Jesus, the second Man and the last Adam, would also appear among men as one bound to God in the same formal relationship. Without some such arrangement being in place between the Father and the Son, by which the Son was considered as acting in a public capacity, then God's dealings with him were simply a matter of personal dealings within a personal relationship. On that basis, Jesus would have gone to the cross as a private individual, and the cross would indeed have been no more than a personal encounter between God and Jesus.

Yet the sum and substance of the gospel is that it was not as a private, but as a *representative,* individual that Jesus died, taking the place of those in whose interests he was acting. There was a benefit to be secured through his dying that could be secured in no other way, and certainly could not be secured simply on the basis of the eternal ontological relationship between the Father and the Son. The benefit to sinners of Christ's dying could only be secured through a modification and an adaptation of that timeless, essential and personal bond: in other words, through the formalising of the relationship between the Father and the Son. This detracted in no way from the personal filiation and Sonship, yet at the same time introduced the new element of Servanthood. Being in the form of God (personal relationship), it became necessary, if Christ was going to be a Mediator, that he take the form of a servant (formal relationship).

But is there explicit scriptural warrant to argue that such a formal and official relationship existed in covenantal form between Jesus and His Father? I believe there is, and that it may be found in at least three areas of scriptural testimony.

First, there are those passages in which Jesus uses explicitly subordinationist language in respect of his relationship to the Father. When his Jewish hearers heard Jesus say that 'I and the Father are one' (John 10:30), they immediately concluded that he was making himself equal with God. This could be the only implication of his claim to enjoy such equality: 'It is not for a good work that we are going to stone you,' they said to him, 'but for blasphemy, because you, being a man, make yourself God' (John 10:33).

Yet in addition to the language of equality, Jesus uses the language of subordination. He says that the Father is greater than he is (John 14:28), that the Father has sent him (John 6:57; 8:18), that the Father's will is his meat and drink (John 4:34). He says that he came to earth not to do his own will, but the will of the one who sent him (John 6:38); and he is aware that the Father's will focuses particularly upon the people whom the Father has given him, and whom he, the eternal Son, is now being commissioned to keep, and ultimately to raise up in glory (John 6:39). He is conscious of having been given a commandment respecting his life, in consequence of the fulfilling of which he is assured of the Father's love (John 10:17-18), and he goes to the cross in order to display the love he has for the Father (John 14:31). That Jesus should use the language of a subordinate is not due merely to the fact that he is incarnate, and has become flesh: it is due to the fact that his becoming flesh is a means to another end – that in that flesh he should *obey*. Though he was, and remains, in the form of God, it was in the form of a servant that he was to secure our redemption (Phil. 2:7).

In the same way as Adam was appointed head of the race under the relationship of a covenant, so Christ was set apart as 'a covenant for the people and a light for the Gentiles' (Isa. 42:6). It is in this light that we must interpret the emphasis on the necessity of his sufferings – in the garden, he knows that the cup of suffering and shame is the Father's will for him, and on the road to Emmaus he argues that it was necessary for the Saviour to suffer before entering into his glory (Luke 24:26). Paul explains it thus: 'the head of every man is Christ, the head of woman is man, and the head of Christ is God' (1 Cor 11:3). Just as man and woman have spiritual equality before God, yet have different roles which involve male authority and female submission in marriage, home and church, so the eternal Son and the heavenly Father have equality of status and personal attributes, yet have different roles in the working out of our salvation.

John Owen also suggests that wherever Jesus calls his Father 'God', a covenantal relationship is indicated. This is an important and helpful insight. The Jews recognised that when Jesus called God his *Father*, he was making himself equal with God (John 5:18); we must in turn recognise that when Jesus calls his Father *God*, he is highlighting his official subordination as the servant of Jehovah. One example of this is John 20:17, in the words of Jesus to Mary: 'Touch me not; for I am not yet ascended to my Father: but go to my brethren, and say unto them, I ascend unto my Father, and your Father; and *to my God, and your God.*' Owen says: 'this expression of being a God unto anyone is declarative of a covenant, and is the word whereby God constantly declares his relation unto any in a way of covenant.'[30]

It is in this light too that we must fully exegete the great word of God in Isaiah 42:1 as he says of his Messiah, 'Behold my servant.' Jesus comes into the world, personally and essentially equal to the Father, yet, in addition, officially subordinate to him. The equality does not compromise the subordination, and the subordination is not at the expense of the equality. He remains the eternal Son he has always been, even when he becomes the Servant he has never been before. For that reason, Hebrews 5:8 can and must use the concessive language it does: 'Although he was a son, he learned obedience through what he suffered.' Christ's Sonship included his being in the form of God (Phil. 2:6), and assumes his foreknowledge and absolute sovereignty. What it did not assume, however, was his servanthood. The fact that he has come to obey the Father is an addition to the fact that he is the equal of the Father. It is the covenant idea that safeguards both the personal equality and the official, formal subordination which is grounded in it. It is only of the One of whom he says 'This is my beloved Son' (Matt. 3:17) that God can also say 'Behold my Servant'.

---

[30] Owen, 'Federal Transactions', 84.

Second, there are those passages that explicitly refer to obligations upon Christ, and rewards promised to him. This is particularly evident in the high priestly prayer of John 17, where Jesus grounds all his petitions in the one simple fact of his obedience: 'I glorified you on earth, having accomplished the work that you gave me to do. And now, Father, glorify me in your own presence with the glory that I had with you before the world existed' (John 17:4-5). For the last Adam, as for the first, the benefit in view – the salvation of those whom Jesus represented as Mediator – could only be secured by obedience. It is here that the contrast between them is drawn, for 'as by the one man's disobedience the many were made sinners, so by the one man's obedience the many will be made righteous' (Rom. 5:19). It is true, as Andrew McGowan points out in his study of 'Headship theology', that the Adam-Christ parallel is vital to federal theology.[31] But when he probes this further, he concludes that

> ...the headship of Adam involves the imputation of sin and the headship of Christ involves the imputation of righteousness. It is, however, perfectly possible to maintain this relation of headship without positing covenants as the basis for the relationship.[32]

But is it? Surely this omits a vital element: the element by which Adam and Christ are formally positioned, in parallel with one another, as acting in a public capacity. What is it that confers such headship on them? My headship over my wife may *involve* many things, but it *exists* only by virtue of a formal, marriage commitment. Similarly, neither the position of Adam before God nor that of Christ before God can be regarded as representative or as one of headship unless a formal and official relationship between them and God has actually been established. And it is this which federal theology has helpfully found in the concept of the covenant.

Precisely for this reason, the writer to the Hebrews can say that Jesus endured the cross 'for the joy that was set before him' (Heb. 12:3), and Paul can insert the all-important word 'therefore' into his argument in Philippians 2:

---

[31] A. T. B. McGowan, 'In defence of "Headship Theology",' in J. A. Grant and A.I. Wilson, *The God of Covenant: Biblical, Theological and contemporary perspectives*, Leicester: Apollos (2005), 190.

[32] McGowan, 'In Defence of Headship Theology', 190.

... [Jesus] made himself nothing, taking the form of a servant, being born in the likeness of men. And being found in human form, he humbled himself by becoming obedient to the point of death, even death on a cross. *Therefore* God has highly exalted him and bestowed on him the name that is above every name (Phil. 2:7-9).

The exaltation of Jesus was the consequence of his obedience, just as Isaiah had previously said it would be. Without subordination there could be no obedience, and without obedience there could be no reward. The exaltation was thoroughly conditional. To be our Saviour meant Jesus having to do all that the Father required of him. In other words, the condition of the covenant of grace had to be the fulfilment of the covenant of works. But since the first Adam did not fulfil it, another Adam was required, and was already provided for in the covenant of redemption.

Thirdly, there is the all-important statement of Zechariah 6:13 regarding the counsel of peace. In context, Zechariah hears the word from God declare as follows:

Thus says the Lord of hosts, 'Behold, the man whose name is the Branch: for he shall branch out from his place, and he shall build the temple of the Lord. It is he who shall build the temple of the Lord and shall bear royal honor, and shall sit and rule on his throne. And there shall be a priest on his throne, and the counsel of peace shall be between them both' (Zech. 6:12-13).

The peace spoken of is not, as some commentators have suggested, between the offices of priesthood and kingship, but between the one who is king-priest in this passage, and the Lord of hosts himself. The vision anticipates the exaltation of the Messiah to the throne of God, with divine benediction and favour resting upon him. We know that the One so honoured is the Son of God, the equal of the Father; but it is not as Son merely that the prophet sees him, but as Saviour. In addition to everything that is true of the Son as *autotheos*, God in himself, is everything that is true of him as Messianic office-bearer.

There is every reason, therefore to concur with Hugh Martin when he says that

It is scarcely necessary to refer to the express assertion of the covenant between the Father and the Son in the proposition, 'The counsel of peace shall be between them both' (Zech. 6:13). Our Lord is designated at once the 'Mediator of the covenant' (Heb. 8:6) and the 'Surety of the covenant' (Heb. 7:22) ... The work of Christ is thus in express terms affirmed to be a covenant work – a work having immediate respect to a covenant.[33]

In a sermon on the words of Hebrews 13:8, 'Jesus Christ, the same yesterday, today and forever,' preached in 1738, Jonathan Edwards highlighted that Jesus is unchangeable in two respects: first, in his divine nature, and second, in his office as Mediator. Coming to explain the second of these points, Edwards pointed out that Jesus always acts as Saviour and Mediator in the same way, that is, with respect to the rules that govern his office. Edwards goes on to explain this in the following paragraphs:

The rules that Christ acts by, in the execution of his office, are contained in a twofold covenant:

1. The covenant of redemption, or the eternal covenant that was between the Father and the Son, wherein Christ undertook to stand as Mediator with fallen man, and was appointed thereto of the Father. In that covenant, all things concerning Christ's execution of his mediatorial office were agreed between Christ and his Father, and established by them. And this covenant or eternal agreement is the highest rule that Christ acts by in his office. And it is a rule that he never in the least departs from. He never does anything, more or less, than is contained in that eternal covenant. Christ does the work that God gave him to do in that covenant, and no other. He saves those, and those only, that the Father gave him in that covenant to save. And he brings them to such a degree of happiness as was therein agreed. To this rule, Christ is unchangeable in his regard. It stands good with Christ in every article of it, yesterday, today, and forever.

2. Another covenant that Christ has regard to in the execution of his mediatorial office is that covenant of grace which God established with man. Though indeed this be less properly the rule by which Christ acts as Mediator than the covenant of redemption, yet it may be called a rule ... And the covenant of grace is not essentially different from the covenant of redemption. It is but an expression of it. It is only that covenant of redemption partly revealed to mankind for their

---

[33] Hugh Martin, *The Atonement: in its relations to the Covenant, the Priesthood, the Intercession of our Lord*, Edinburgh: Lyon and Gemmell (1877), 31-32.

encouragement, faith, and comfort. And therefore the fact that Christ never departs from the covenant of redemption, infers that he will never depart from the covenant of grace. For all that was promised to men in the covenant of grace was agreed on between the Father and the Son in the covenant of redemption. However, there is one thing wherein Christ's unchangeableness in his office appears: that he never departs from the promises that he has made to man. There is the same covenant of grace in all ages of the world. The covenant is not essentially different now from what it was under the Old Testament, and even before the flood. And it always will remain the same. It is therefore called an everlasting covenant, Isa. 55:3.[34]

Edwards is surely correct in insisting that the principles which govern Christ's work as Mediator are twofold: one in respect of his official relationship to the Father as his Servant, and one in respect of his official relationship to sinners as their Saviour.

Where is the Holy Spirit?

The second objection to this element of federalism, however, is theological: is such a covenantal scheme, in fact, Trinitarian? Does it safeguard the orthodox doctrine of the Trinity? If the covenant or formal agreement of redemption is between Father and Son, is this not binitarian, rather than Trinitarian? Jonathan Edwards says that

> Some things were done before the world was created, yea from eternity. The persons of the Trinity were, as it were, confederated in a design, and a covenant of redemption. In this covenant the Father had appointed the Son, and the Son had undertaken the work; and all things to be accomplished in the work were stipulated and agreed.[35]

But does this last sentence do justice to the first? How can Edwards posit a confederation of the three Persons, but then explicate it only in terms of the Father and the Son? The difficulty is well articulated by Bob Letham, who suggests that while the intention of the formulation of a covenant of redemption is laudable, the construct itself is not:

> The doctrine of the Trinity should have provided a barrier against the idea of the covenant of redemption. That salvation rests upon

---

[34] Sermon on Hebrews 13:8, Sermon XIV, *Collected Writings of Jonathan Edwards*, Vol 2, Banner of Truth edition, 950.

[35] Jonathan Edwards, 'A History of the Work of Redemption' (*Works*, i.534).

the pretemporal plan or counsel of God is evident from WCF3 [Westminster Confession of Faith, Chapter 3]. This counsel is Trinitarian, as is clear from that chapter and the preceding one on the Trinity. However to describe the relations of the three persons in the Trinity as a covenant, or to affirm that there was a need for them to enter into covenantal – even contractual – arrangements is to open the door to heresy. The will of the Trinity is one; the works of the Trinity are indivisible. For all the good intentions of those who proposed it, the construal of the relations of the three persons of the Trinity in covenantal terms is a departure from classic Trinitarian orthodoxy.[36]

Letham's objection is not to a formulation which grounds salvation in the will of the Triune God, but to one which divides that will in the interests of a theological construct. Undergirding his objection is the evident absence of the Holy Spirit from the scheme. Jon Zens, approaching the question from a different angle to that of Letham, raises a related question:

> The covenant theologians consistently assert that in this covenant the Father and the Son are the parties. On what basis is the Holy Spirit left out? Must not any plan of the Godhead necessarily be Trinitarian?[37]

But is the Holy Spirit omitted? Is it possible to formulate the covenant of redemption in a way that expresses a fully Trinitarian arrangement, and does no violation to Trinitarian orthodoxy? It is, and we must. This compulsion is driven by the Old Testament as much as by the New. We have already noted, for example, the great messianic statement of Isaiah 42:1, where God (the Father) says of the Messiah (God the Son), 'Behold my Servant.' In strictly theological terms, the subordinationist language of the passage requires a modification of the eternal relationship between the first two Persons of the Godhead; and as we have discussed above, this is provided for in the formalised relationship which the covenant introduces.

But the passage does not end there. The speaker continues: 'Behold my servant, whom I uphold, my elect in whom my soul delights: *I have put my Spirit upon him…*'. Here is a new element, as surprising and striking as the subordinationist language which will come to be used of the eternal Son: the third person of the Godhead, the Holy

---

[36] R. Letham, *The Westminster Assembly: Reading its Theology in Historical Context*, P&R (2009), 236.

[37] http://www.searchingtogether.org/articles/zens.covenant.htm, accessed 9 December 2009.

Spirit, is to be given by the first to the second! The three Persons are one, equal in power and glory. One does not need to be given to another, for what Paul calls 'the fullness of deity' (Col. 2:9) belongs to all Three indivisibly. Yet, for the salvation of the people of God, one Person is appointed to a specific role by another, and equipped and anointed for it by the third, who is willing so to be engaged. There is no threatening the indivisibility of the divine will in this formulation; rather, the one indivisible divine will is given full expression in the co-ordinate and co-relative actions of each of the Persons of the Godhead: the Father appoints the Servant and anoints him with the Spirit. The covenant relationship formalises the official role of each Person without compromising the unity and equality of the Three.

In other words, included in the commitments covenanted by the Father to the Son was the promise of Holy Spirit anointing, and consequently the Holy Spirit cannot be excluded from the deliberate counsel of God in the covenant of redemption. This is actualised at the baptism of Jesus, where the Father speaks, the Son is baptised, and the Spirit descends on him. It is further elucidated in Acts 10:38-43, where Peter declares that 'God anointed Jesus of Nazareth with the Holy Ghost and with power', in a context which clearly alludes to the provisions of the covenant of redemption – God raising Jesus, and ordaining him to be supreme Judge of all. Some theologians have spoken of the Holy Spirit *acquiescing* in the arrangement between the Father and the Son, but the biblical material is much more explicit. The Spirit is the Father's gift to the Son for the salvation of sinners.

But there must be more than this. The Spirit is not only the *provision* of the Father for the Son in his humiliation; he is also the *promise* of the Father to the Son following his exaltation. On the day of Pentecost, Peter declares that Christ had poured out the Holy Spirit which had been promised: 'being therefore exalted at the right hand of God, and *having received from the Father the promise of the Holy Spirit*, he has poured out this...' (Acts 2:33). The promise referred to here was not a promise from God to his people, but from God the Father to his exalted Son. Christ would receive the Spirit *in order to* complete the work of atonement on earth, and would receive the Spirit *in consequence of* his perfect obedience in order to pour out the Spirit on the church. John the Baptist, who saw Jesus *anointed* with the Spirit, also predicted that Jesus would *baptise* with the Spirit (John 1:33). This is not a bare prediction, but a promise which hinges upon perfect obedience. At this level, the last Adam is in the same position as the first. But he could never be the last Adam simply on the basis of his eternal equality with the Father. In addition to the equality that Sonship requires there is the subordination that his being the last Adam requires. The promised Spirit is given *to*, then given *by*, the obedient Son.

On any reading of these biblical texts, it is inadequate to formulate the covenant of redemption merely as a contract between the Father and the Son – a committee meeting to which the Spirit gives an apology for absence.[38] The transaction between Father and Son certainly includes stipulations and requirements on the part of the Son to be our Saviour, but the covenant includes his unique anointing and equipping for that task, and the promise of the Father to him that his obedience will result in his being given the Spirit to pour out on his people. Far from being absent, the Spirit is a party as confederate in the covenant as the Father and the Son, and the specific roles which each Person fulfils for our salvation is the outworking of the prior, eternal indivisible counsel which makes the Triune God the Author of our salvation, and each Person, in his own defined way, the executor of that counsel.

How, then, ought we to formulate our theological discourse at this point? What is the covenant of redemption? I suggest that we adopt the following as our definition:

> The covenant of redemption is rooted in the counsel of the Triune God, whose eternal plan to save sinners is the foundation of the gospel. In that covenant, each Person, without compromising his distinctive properties, willingly undertakes an official function: the Father to be the God of the Son, the Son to be the Servant of the Father, and the Holy Spirit to be the gift and the promise of the Father to the Son.
>
> By virtue of this unified plan, grounded in the unity of the divine will, the Son is designated to be our Saviour, given work to do as our Saviour, equipped to be our Saviour, and promised the reward of exaltation and glory on the basis of his perfect obedience. The obligations of the covenant of redemption continue in glory, as the Son, in his exalted state, honours the Father by giving the Spirit to his people.

---

[38] Compare Bob Letham's view that 'If someone can come up with a version that carefully maintains the distinctions of the Father, Son and Holy Spirit within the indivisibility of the trinity, not presenting it like a divine committee meeting, and includes the Holy Spirit they will have done a major service for the church' – Email correspondence between Bob Letham and the author, 9 December 2009.

Thus the covenant of redemption is not to be construed as omitting the Holy Spirit in any sense, or in compromising the essential properties of the Persons of the Godhead. The covenanted relationship is one in which the Father gives, the Son receives, and the Spirit is given. Without such a relationship, formalised by vows and promises, the work of Jesus would benefit no-one but himself. Within it, however, Jesus becomes God's Saviour, in order that he might become our Saviour, and secure for us the blessing of the Holy Spirit.

Conclusion

It is true that a careless formulation of the covenant of redemption will fail to integrate the doctrine of the Trinity and the work of redemption. That work is indivisible, and it is Trinitarian. Its roots are not found in time, but in eternity, and it is nothing but the outworking of a glorious divine plan, in which the Triune God was willing to become our God, our Saviour and our salvation.

No-one has expressed this more felicitously than the great Scottish theologian, Hugh Martin:

> On no scheme whatever that shall be true to the leading contents of Scripture, concerning the work of the incarnate Redeemer, can we possibly avoid coming to the conclusion that He acts according to a covenant with the Father. Whatever Christ did, He designed to do; and whatever He designed to do, He designed because He had been designated to do it. He had been 'sanctified' and 'sealed' and 'sent' into the world. He continually averred, in this view, that He 'did nothing of Himself'. He was acting by commission; and that not merely in general, but by commission reaching to every detail of speech and action alike. He did the 'works of His Father'. He spake his 'Father's words ...'
>
> ... He had been designated therefore by no isolated decree, by no individual or separate oracle, but by regular, full, complete covenant. Under no other category or instrument than that of compact, *foedus*, covenant, is it possible to bring all the fullness, circumstance, detail, history, order, and fruit of His work. We are simply shut up to the theory of an 'everlasting covenant' ... It explains all Christ's history, as the incarnate Son of God; all his interposition as the Saviour of men. It embraces alike the impetration of redemption and the application of it. It expounds Christ's complete offices, and the office and work of the Spirit. It gives doctrinal significance to what were otherwise mere external history; for it places the outward movements of Christ's

career on earth in their true relations with the eternal purpose of the Godhead, and the eternal destinies of men.[39]

The idea of a covenant of redemption is no fallacious, imagined construct: it is the only biblical and theological context in which the cross, which ought never to have been, can be explained as that which alone could secure a place in the fellowship of the Godhead for sinful, fallen men and women.

---

[39] Hugh Martin, *The Atonement*, 35-37.

Theology
and
the Church

11

The Preacher as Prophet: Some Notes on the Nature of Preaching

Carl R. Trueman

There can be little doubt today that good preaching is at something of a premium, even within those churches committed to the Christian faith as articulated in the great confessions of the Protestant Reformation, a movement marked by an emphasis upon the proclamation of the word of God and the centrality of the pulpit.

At first glance, this problem is hard to understand: Reformed and evangelical seminaries probably do as good a job as they have ever done of teaching students exegetical and homiletical skills, the basic building blocks of good preaching. There are probably as many, if not more, fine commentaries available in English today than at any other period of the church's history. Further, there is a wealth of books on preaching and there is podcast access to sermons, the good, the bad, and the downright ugly, which would have been undreamed of even ten years ago. Thus, there can surely be no excuse for not learning from a world of preachers, emulating the strengths of the best and avoiding the mistakes of the worst. Yet still good preaching seems so hard to find.

Part of the reason for this could well be the nature of the wider culture, with its lack of literary ballast, and its bias towards the soundbite and the visual. T. David Gordon has recently argued that these factors are significant in explaining 'why Johnny can't preach.'[1] His arguments, while no doubt overstated at points, certainly have merit and point to wider cultural challenges facing both preachers and teachers. Yet I suspect there is also a theological reason which is a necessary part of the explanation.

Before I address this issue, however, let me give two anecdotes from my own recent experience. In the first, I was at a theological conference where one of the meetings was billed as a worship service. Just before the preacher entered the pulpit, he was introduced by the conference organizer as someone who was about to 'explain the Bible to us'. Notice the language: a text was to be explained; no hint here of proclamation. In the second, I was myself the preacher and I noted, according to the order of service, that I was meant to preach after the pastoral prayer. Thus, as the pastoral prayer ended, I started to rise from my seat, only to hear the following: 'Ok, we'll take a break there; go and fill your coffee cups and we'll reconvene in five minutes for the Bible reading.'

Thankfully, in the first scenario, the preacher did not explain the Bible; he actually preached. He did proclaim God's word. Then, in the second, although my rhythm was somewhat broken, I managed to recover and do what was probably a half-decent job of proclaiming the word. The advantage of having done a fair amount of student work in my time means that there is almost nothing that can shock me in church anymore, and I can put up with almost anything before I preach, providing it is not happening in my own church every Sunday. Yet both incidents underlined for me one of the major problems with contemporary preaching, something which accounts not only for debates about whether preaching is still necessary but also for its often poor quality even in churches which should know better: preaching is not simply explaining the Bible; it is proclaiming the word of God; and the failure to understand what the task is, theologically, will inevitably undermine the way it is practised. If the preacher thinks he is merely explaining the Bible, he will probably be incapable of distinguishing what he does in the pulpit from what he might do in a lecture theatre, where application and exhortation are generally absent; and if he thinks he is merely facilitating a discussion, he will lack the confrontational authority that comes with a 'Thus says the Lord!'. The church, and

---

[1] T. David Gordon, *Why Johnny Can't Preach: The Media Have Shaped the Messenger* (Phillipsburg: Presbyterian and Reformed, 2009).

especially her preachers, need to understand the importance of both the theology of proclamation and of the proclamation of theology.

Preaching was, of course, one of the hallmarks of Reformation Protestantism. This is not to say that preaching was not significant in the Middle Ages; after all, Bernard of Clairvaux preached in such a way as to inspire a crusade.[2] One does not inspire a crusade to the Holy Land by preaching unless one has both remarkable gifts in this area and lives at a time where preachers were significant. To stress the unique importance of preaching in the Reformation is not to deny its significance in earlier times; it is, however, to highlight the fact that preaching came to be a central priority in the Reformation in a way that it had not been during the medieval period. This was because the Reformers, in line with Martin Luther, saw preaching as the principal means by which God made himself present in the church in a manner that made salvation a reality.[3] This is indicated by the Scots Confession, Chapter 18 ('The Notes by which the True Church is Discerned from the False, and Who Shall Be Judge of Doctrine'), where the marks of the church are delineated:

> The notes of the true Kirk, therefore, we believe, confess, and avow to be: first, the true preaching of the word of God, in which God has revealed himself to us, as the writings of the prophets and apostles declare; secondly, the right administration of the sacraments of Christ Jesus, to which must be joined the word and promise of God to seal and confirm them in our hearts; and lastly, ecclesiastical discipline uprightly ministered, as God's word prescribes, whereby vice is repressed and virtue nourished.

Here, preaching is the first mark, and it is clearly the most important as both sacraments and discipline are dependent upon it: the sacrament without the word of promise is but an empty sign; and discipline arises out of the ministry of the word, broadly conceived, as it is used, in public and in private, to press home the demands of God

---

[2] See Hughes Oliphant Old, *The Reading and Preaching of the Scriptures in the Worship of the Christian Church*, volume 3: The Medieval Church (Grand Rapids: Eerdmans, 1999).

[3] See Luther's comment in his *Freedom of the Christian Man*: 'You may ask, "What then is the Word of God, and how shall it be used, since there are so many words of God?" I answer: The Apostle explains this in Romans 1. The Word is the gospel of God concerning his Son, who was made flesh, suffered, rose from the dead, and was glorified through the Spirit who sanctifies. To preach Christ means to feed the soul, make it righteous, set it free, and save it, provided it believes the preaching' (Martin Luther, *Works*, ed. Jaroslav Pelikan, 55 vols [Philadelphia : Fortress Press, 1958-67] 31, 346).

upon individual believers. The clear implication of this is, of course, that preaching is not mere transmission of information: were it so, it could be achieved by reading. No: the communal setting and the proclamation of the word are critical, as these provide the context and the cause for the creation of the church.

Nowhere is this importance made more clear than in the very first chapter of the Second Helvetic Confession, Heinrich Bullinger's doctrinal manifesto for the Reformed churches which looked to Zurich for their leadership. In a remarkable passage, Bullinger makes the following claim:

THE PREACHING OF THE WORD OF GOD IS THE WORD OF GOD. Wherefore when this Word of God is now preached in the church by preachers lawfully called, we believe that the very Word of God is proclaimed, and received by the faithful; and that neither any other Word of God is to be invented nor is to be expected from heaven: and that now the Word itself which is preached is to be regarded, not the minister that preaches; for even if he be evil and a sinner, nevertheless the Word of God remains still true and good.

Given the theological importance of preaching in the Reformation, we might perhaps say that Protestant theology has both a non-negotiable content and a non-negotiable form. The content is the doctrine, the truth about God and his action in Jesus Christ and the church; the form is preaching, which is so central to the life of the church, and through the church to that of the individual believer. Indeed, preaching, as a mark of the church, is God's instrument for the very creation of the church.

It is thus easy to see why a misunderstanding of preaching at this point can ultimately lead to its rejection as a necessary part of the church's life. If preaching is only transmission of information, and if it is thus useful only in so far as it serves that end, then the church had really better find a more effective way of communication, given the fact that we live in an era of soundbites and visual images, not speechmaking and lectures.

This problem of the effectiveness of elaborate oral declamation is not new. In the eighteenth century, Dr. Samuel Johnson, the English wit and prophet of blunt common sense and stating the obvious when others feared so to do, had this to say:

> People nowadays got a strange opinion that everything should be
> taught by lectures. Now I cannot see that lectures can do so much as
> reading from books from which the lectures are taken.[4]

Johnson's point is simple: if information is what is sought, there are
better means than sitting and listening to somebody else. Thus, if
we regard the purpose of the sermon and of preaching as primarily
communicating to the congregation pieces of information about
God and Jesus, we will very soon come to realize that the task can
be performed far more effectively by, say, providing reading lists for
the people or (given that we are often told that people do not read as
much as they did in the past) videos, dramatic presentations, group
discussion etc.

The Reformation insight, however, is that preaching is more than
just transmission of information; it is rather the confrontation of the
people with God as revealed in his word. Luther makes this point
eloquently by stressing that salvation is a word that comes from
outside. It is not some kind of mystical experience which takes place
in an inner private space and is incommunicable to others, but neither
is it simply a case of learning about a state of affairs of the kind we see
in the statements 'Two plus two equals four,' or 'Napoleon died on
St. Helena.' Such statements involve little or no existential relation
to the individual who hears them; to hear the death and resurrection
of Christ proclaimed, however, transforms the individual in terms
of their own understanding of themselves and their relationship to
God and the world. In other words, preaching is confrontational and
transformative; its end cannot be achieved as well by, say, reading
a mere book of theology or sermons, or even, one might add more
provocatively, the Bible itself. The word proclaimed has profound
significance beyond the word merely read or remembered.

The reasons for this are numerous and we need to understand
them in order to understand what we are doing when we stand up
and preach. First and foremost, there is the biblical teaching that God
is the one who is present in and through his word. We see this right
at the very start of biblical history, when God speaks creation into
being. His creative activity is described by Moses in Genesis 1 as that
of speaking: there was nothing other than God; God spoke; then there

---

[4] James Boswell, *Boswell's Life of Johnson*, abridged by Charles Grosvenor Osgood (New York:
Scribner's, 1917), 139.

was something else, the created realm. Further, just as God's speech inaugurated the first creation, so it is fundamental to the second, new creation. In Genesis 12, for example, God calls Abraham by addressing him in speech: Abraham is constituted as the recipient of the covenant, the father of the faithful, and the one through whose seed the great Seed and heir of the promise will come. There are covenant ceremonies that surround this call, of course; but the speech of God is central in establishing the covenant, just as the words 'I do' are crucial in the ceremony of marriage, whatever other ceremonies might be involved.

This kind of emphasis continues throughout scripture. While it is, of course, true to say that God is always present everywhere, there is a presence of God which is, we might say, merely ontological in supporting creation, and a presence which is special, powerfully connected to his mighty acts of judgment and salvation. This latter presence is not ubiquitous as is demonstrated by the fact that scripture can actually talk of its absence. Thus, Amos 8:11-12 points to the absence of God as a sign of judgment against his people and articulates this in terms of a famine, not of bread or water, but of the word of God. We might also point to other passages which hint at this same divine speech-divine presence connection. For example, the desperate journey of the Shunammite to Elisha in 2 Kings 4 is surely connected to the fact that it is the prophet who brings the word of the Lord and who therefore embodies God's saving presence at that time in Israel's history. Thus, she must go to him and, indeed, must fetch him back to touch her son; his staff in the hands of his servant will simply not suffice because the salvation of God comes by his word, and, at this moment in history, the word of God, God's saving presence, comes only through the mouth of the prophet not his assistant carrying some mute stick of wood.

This theme continues in the New Testament. In Mark 1:10 we are told that when Jesus was baptized, the heavens were torn open (Gk. *schizein*). Though sometimes translated simply as opened, this is not a good rendering: the only other time Mark uses the word is in Mark 15:38 with reference to the Temple curtain. To translate this latter passage as 'the curtain opened' would be a wholly inadequate and inaccurate description of the event. Yet there are more than just linguistic arguments internal to Mark's Gospel to lead us to favour the translation 'torn open.' It was apparently a commonplace of Second Temple Judaism that with the cessation of Old Testament prophecy, the Holy Spirit had stopped speaking directly to the people of God; and specific traditions relating to Isaiah 64:1 saw the tearing open of the heavens as the moment when the Spirit would descend upon the Messiah.[5] Thus, when Mark describes Jesus' baptism in such terms, he is highlighting the fact that God is once again speaking to his people or, we might say, God is once again *present* with his people, in the person of Jesus Christ, in accordance with his great covenantal promises; and, of course, the dramatic movement of the narrative at this point makes this clear, since the tearing open of the skies is immediately followed by God the Father's verbal declaration and public commissioning of his Son.

The second point, in addition to speech being God's mode of presence, is the fact that God's word has been inscripturated. This is arguably a necessary part of the covenantal nature of God's plan of salvation.[6] Covenants require words, and this goes a long way to explaining the continual emphasis on the writing down of words throughout the Old Testament. Thus, Isaiah 30:8, Jeremiah 30:1-2, Daniel 9:1-2, and Habakkuk 2:2-3 all refer either to the writing down of God's words, to a divine instruction to write God's words, or to the reading of God's word which had already been written down. The inscripturated word is thus a normal and normative thing within the Old Testament. It defines God's relationship to his people and, when read aloud, can involve the re-establishment of the same (2 Kings 23:1-3; Neh. 8:1-3).

This continues in the New Testament, where the phrase 'It is written…' is frequently used, not least by the Devil and Christ as they trade blows in the wilderness. Indeed, it is surely very significant that the battle between Christ and the Devil in the desert is fought over the meaning of God's words, the assumption on both sides being that these are normative and binding. Further, the command to write down the words of God is found throughout the book of Revelation (1:11, 19; 2:1, 8, 12, 18; 3:1, 7, 12, 14; 10:4; 14:13; 19:9; 21:5). God's presence, God's speech, and God's word written are all intimately connected.

---

[5] James R. Edwards, *The Gospel According To Mark* (Leicester: Apollos, 2002), 35.

[6] This point has been helpfully made by scholars Meredith Kline, *The Structure of Biblical Authority* (Grand Rapids: Eerdmans, 1975) and Michael Horton, *Covenant and Eschatology: The Divine Drama* (Westminster John Knox Press: Louisville, 2002). See also the comment of Edmund Clowney: 'The inscripturation of the word of God occurs at Sinai with the establishment of God's covenant with his people. While God's calling of the fathers had a covenant form, the redemption of the assembly of God's people, the congregation of Israel, calls for a formal covenant ratification with a precise and objective covenant instrument in writing' (*Preaching and Biblical Theology*, Grand Rapids: Eerdmans, [1961], 39).

The third point, in addition to God's word being spoken and written, is that God's word has also always been preached. The greatest example of this in the Old Testament is Moses, the paradigmatic prophet of ancient Israel. Like many subsequent preachers, Moses is acutely aware of his inadequacy for his task. When commissioned in Exodus 4, his lack of confidence leads the Lord to assure him that, though it is he, Moses who physically speaks, it will be the Lord God who speaks through him (Exod. 4:11-12). Later, his preaching forms part of his intermediary function between God and the people when the latter are so terrified at Sinai that they beg Moses to speak to them on God's behalf (Exod. 20:18-19). What Moses is not doing at any point is merely communicating information from God to the people; his speeches are definitive of the relationship that exists between God and his people; and, indeed, are constitutive of that relationship too.

These points hold true throughout the Old Testament, with the prophets being the other obvious examples. Their words do not simply explain the present or predict the future; they also confront the Israelites with the identity of God as he has revealed himself to be in his dealings with the people, the people's own identity in relationship to him, and the moral demands these place upon the people. The unnamed prophet in Judges 6:8-10 is a good example of this: he comes to remind an apostate people of who God is (the one who brought them out of bondage in Egypt, put their enemies to flight, and gave them the promised land) and thus of who they are and what they are obliged to do (not fear the pagan gods of the land). In context, his word is not simply informational; it stands as a sentence of condemnation against the nation. It is also rooted in the word of God as it has been written in the Torah, where the exodus, and indeed the consequences of syncretism, were laid out in great detail. The prophet brings a word from the Lord here which, in a sense, merely applies what has already been written to the current circumstances.

The emphasis on preaching continues in the New Testament whose key figures – John the Baptist, Stephen, Peter, and Paul, to name just a few, along with Jesus Christ himself – are marked by their proclamation of the word. Stephen's sermon is particularly instructive, focusing on the identity of God as he had revealed himself in his great acts of salvation in the Old Testament, and culminating in the work of Jesus Christ, a history which places such acute accusations and demands at the feet of the Jews that they stone him on the spot. Further, in

1 Corinthians, Paul rejects the ancient (and modern) obsession with aesthetics and emphasises that it is not the style of preaching but what is preached (Christ crucified) that is vital. Of course, the King James Version famously misleads the reader by translating 1 Corinthians 1:21, 'it pleased God by the foolishness of preaching to save them that believe.' The text is better rendered by the English Standard Version, 'it pleased God through the folly of what we preach to save those who believe.' In other words, it is the content, not the method of delivery, which is Paul's concern here.

Nevertheless, it does not seem to cross Paul's mind at this point that the content would not be preached, and this is entirely consistent with the emphasis upon verbal proclamation which goes right back through the Old Testament. Indeed, the nature of the message (the proclamation of the cross) and the nature of the delivery (preaching) both seem to be closely connected to each other. There is, it seems, a fit between New Testament (and Old Testament) practice and the message which was to be communicated. Indeed, it is hard to see how the identity of God and his action in Christ and in the church could be more adequately expressed than by the use of words. In fact, the sermons in Acts and in the epistles indicate that the prophetic model of Moses (exposition, application, exhortation rooted in God's revelation) is the standard; and as this action is clearly connected to a theology of God as a speaking God, the preacher simply cannot see his task as mere communication of information.

Again, Paul's comments in 1 Corinthians are apposite here, where he is keen to emphasise that the power of what he has preached is rooted, not in his eloquence or impressive presence (both of which he denies) but rather in the demonstration of the Spirit and of power. From a post-Nicene perspective, with Trinitarian language at our disposal, we might say that what Paul is describing is a dynamic rooted in the nature of God: preaching brings men and women to God the Father via the actions of his Son, crucified, resurrected, and ascended, by the power of his Holy Spirit through the medium of the message of the history of God and its significance being verbally communicated by preachers. The information communicated is merely instrumental to the realization of fellowship and communion with God which are the real end of preaching; and that remains the task of the preacher today just as it was for Paul.

In sum, there is a close connection between God, the Bible, and the act of preaching: God's (re)creative action is intimately connected to his speech; the Bible is his speech in written form; and preaching is both central to God's action within the pages of scripture itself and to the pattern of church life as established in the New Testament. The Bible as God's speech is a prophetic book; and the church, as united to Christ, is a prophetic institution.[7]

This then brings us to the question of how one reflects this in one's preaching, in other words, how one preaches prophetically. The first thing necessary is surely a solid understanding of the task in terms of its broad theological contours and purpose as laid out above. The preacher must first understand what exactly he is doing in order to understand its basis, purpose, and limits, for only then can he be prophetic in terms of the confidence with which he speaks. If he thinks he is merely communicating information, he will be incapable of distinguishing the act of giving a lecture from the act of preaching; and he will also become absorbed primarily with issues of technique, perhaps even abandoning the medium as less effective than some others. Yet, if he thinks it is mere exhortation to practical action, then he will be incapable of distinguishing the teaching of moral principles from preaching the word, and may well, if he is honest, not really understand why the Bible is the best book for the task and not, say, one of Aesop's Fables or even the latest storyline from a television soap opera.

If what I have said above is correct, then basic to good, prophetic preaching will be the understanding that God is a speaking God; that he has spoken definitively in scripture; and that he continues to speak through the faithful exposition of that scripture today. If the preacher holds to these three principles, he will have the confidence to do what he does every Sunday with authority, safe in the knowledge that the growth of the kingdom does not depend upon his eloquence but rather upon the action of the Spirit using the words which the preacher himself has carefully prepared under the authority of the inscripturated word.[8]

Further, and by inference if I am right, the current malaise in preaching must be seen as a crisis not simply in the kind of cultural

---

[7] On the Bible and preaching, John Stott quotes James Packer as follows: 'Having studied the doctrine of Scripture for a generation, the most satisfactory model is to describe it thus: "The Bible is God preaching."' J. I. Packer, quoted by John Stott, *Between Two Worlds: the Challenge of Preaching Today* (Grand Rapids: Eerdmans, 1994), 103.

[8] Karl Barth perhaps captures the point nicely: [In preaching] I have not to talk about scripture but from it. I have not to say something, but merely to repeat something.' Barth, *Homiletics*, trans. Geoffrey W. Bromiley and Donald E. Daniels (Louisville: Westminster John Knox, 1991), 49.

changes forged by the arrival of television, information technology, and pragmatic educational methods so ably analysed by Gordon, but it would also seem to be a crisis in the doctrines of God and of scripture, two elements of Christian theology which are obviously intimately related. If God has not spoken in the past, then there is no basis upon which to believe that he continues to speak today. For this reason, it is crucial that theological education retains a central place for systematic theology. Far from being a speculative appendage to the task of ministry, systematic theology provides the basic definitions of God and his revelation that undergird the understanding of scripture and provide the foundation – the theological foundation – for understanding the task of the preacher. It is surely no coincidence that the current so-called hermeneutical crisis, indicated by the lack of confidence either in texts having meaning, or in the ability of the human knower to discern such meaning, has coincided with a shift in many churches away from preaching-centred ministries to one-to-one counselling, small group discussion, and an accent upon conversational language. The cultural moment is not conducive to preaching; but then the cultural moment is not to determine what is and is not true. The Reformation did not place the reading and preaching of scripture at the centre because of the cultural momentum of the time; it did so because the God described in scripture is a speaking God.

If the act of preaching is driven by theological conviction rather than cultural preference and plausibility, prophetic preaching can only be done effectively in the power of, and confidence in, the Spirit. Paul's anti-aesthetic tirade in his letters to the Corinthians should not be read as a blanket attack on good presentation, clear argument and fine public speaking skills, all of which are helpful to the preacher and things greatly to be desired. Paul's point is rather that the Corinthians' mindset is so preoccupied with these things that they have lost sight of where the real power of God is to be found. To return to the statement of the Second Helvetic Confession: the Word truly and legitimately preached is the Word of God. We might hesitate to use quite such unequivocal language today, but the underlying point is sound: preaching carries a power which is ultimately divine in origin; it does not inhere in the words themselves but as those words are seized by God's Spirit and driven home into the hearts and minds of the hearers; that is what gives the preacher ultimate confidence in what he does; and, that is what demands that the congregation sit and listen, testing all by scripture, of course, but doing so with an attitude of humility and of those being addressed by one who speaks for God himself. *The Westminster Larger Catechism*, Question 155, expresses it this way:

> *How is the Word made effectual in salvation?* The Spirit of God maketh the reading, but especially the preaching of the Word, an effectual means of enlightening, convincing, and humbling sinners; of driving them out of themselves, and drawing them unto Christ; of conforming them to his image, and subduing them to his will; of strengthening them against temptations and corruptions; of building them up in grace, and establishing their hearts in holiness and comfort through faith unto salvation.

This understanding of preaching is most significant: it relativises all questions of method and contextualization, not rendering them irrelevant but rather of secondary importance; and it gives the preacher confidence to do what he does, for ultimately the effectiveness of his ministry is not dependent upon his personal competence, inner moral qualities or even, in certain American contexts, his British accent.

Second, if the post-apostolic preacher stands in a line which goes back through the New Testament to the prophets of the Old, then preaching should be prophetic in content. What I mean by this should be obvious by now: it should involve confronting the world in which the preacher finds himself with the word of God as inscripturated in the Bible. This imposes various demands upon the preacher. First, for preaching to be prophetic, God's word should have priority in defining exactly what is and is not relevant. Of course, preaching should address needs; but those needs themselves must first be defined by the word of God. In God's act of creation, his word was the creative force and thus had priority: creation was what God said it was to be. So in recreation, the speaking of God comes first, defining the problem and then providing an answer. That is the case in the Gospels; it continues to be so today.

This is what Luther expressed in his notion of the law and the gospel: the law comes first, convicting of sin;[9] then the gospel comes and brings Christ to the broken sinner. Not only his preaching, but also his catechisms embody this structure, placing it at the heart of

---

[9] E.g., *The Preface to Romans*: 'It is right for a preacher of the gospel in the first place by revelation of the law and of sin to rebuke and to constitute as sin everything that is not the living fruit of the Spirit and of faith in Christ, in order that men should be led to know themselves and their own wretchedness, and to become humble and ask for help.' *Works* 35, 372.

Christian pedagogy.[10] Now, Lutheran and Reformed theologians disagree on some of the details of connecting law to gospel, but the principle of allowing God's holiness as expressed in the law to define the human predicament is basic to both traditions, as is evident in the tripartite structure of the Heidelberg Catechism, which moves from the misery of sin, to the grace of God, to the believer's response of gratitude.

By definition, therefore, prophetic preaching cannot be preaching that merely takes up the priorities and emphases of the world around and seeks to find some means of applying God's word to such. This is not to deny the need for contextualization, though it is to argue that contextualization can be a much over-used and over-hyped term. At one level, it merely states the obvious: for example, preaching should be done in a way that takes account of the context; thus, one does not preach in Urdu to a congregation made up of those who only speak English; and it is well worth avoiding the kind of gaffe described by Luther in the following quotation from his *Tabletalk*:

> One should preach about things that are suited to a given place and given persons. A preacher once preached that it's wicked for a woman to have a wet nurse for her child, and he devoted his whole sermon to a treatment of this matter although he had nothing but poor spinning women in his parish to whom such an admonition didn't apply. Similar was the preacher who gave an exhortation in praise of marriage when he preached to some aged women in an infirmary.[11]

Such is clearly a case where a little bit of contextualization might well have been of considerable benefit. Yet recent decades, with their preoccupation with hermeneutics, diversity, difference, and the various movements characterized as 'postmodern,' have seen a veritable explosion in the contextualization industry. Thus, at another level, the over-complication of matters of contextualising can actually end up

---

[10] 'In chapter 8 he comforts these fighters, telling them that this flesh does not condemn them. He shows further what the nature of flesh and spirit is, and how the Spirit comes from Christ. Christ has given us his Holy Spirit; he makes us spiritual and subdues the flesh, and assures us that we are still God's children, however hard sin may be raging within us, so long as we follow the Spirit and resist sin to slay it. Since, however, nothing else is so good for the mortifying of the flesh as the cross and suffering, he comforts us in suffering with the support of the Spirit of love, and of the whole creation, namely, that the Spirit sighs within us and the creation longs with us that we may be rid of the flesh and of sin. So we see that these three chapters (6–8) drive home the one task of faith, which is to slay the old Adam and subdue the flesh' (*Ibid.*, 277).

[11] Luther, *Works* 54, 138.

inverting the proper order of Christian thinking by placing the making
the diversity of human context the grid through which the word of
God is to be interpreted, rather than vice versa. The preacher must
remember that the ultimate context of the world, of God's creation,
is the word of God, and that the problems of humanity as defined by
that word – alienation from God, rebellion against his rule – are the
same all over the world, regardless of the way in which these might
find specific manifestation in any given situation. One would presume
that Luther would have regarded his anonymous preacher as just as
incompetent if all he had done was describe the life of a poor spinning
woman to his audience of poor spinning women.

Given the contemporary world's obsessions, of course, we are
unlikely to be dealing with spinning women or wet nurses on a regular
basis; but we have our own set of cultural fetishes. The words of R.
Albert Mohler, Jnr., are apposite on this point:

> The rise of therapeutic concerns within the culture means that many
> pastors, and many of their church members, believe that the pastoral
> calling is best understood as a "helping profession." As such, the
> pastor is seen as someone who functions in a therapeutic role in which
> theology is often seen as more of a problem than a solution.[12]

The shift in the understanding of the pastor's role to which Mohler
refers is a part of the general shift from allowing the word to set the
agenda rather than the world. Doctrine can only become part of the
problem when the world becomes the context for understanding
the word, when our questions and problems become the dominant
theme of our thinking, and when we thus judge relevance by our own
autonomous psychological or sociological criteria.

On this definition, prophetic preaching is always likely to be
irrelevant preaching as far as the world is concerned simply because
it demands that the world listen before it speaks, and sees itself as
God's word sees it, not as it understands itself. The prophets of the Old
Testament both defined the real problems in Israel by digging under
the surface of political and economic conditions to the underlying
spiritual state of the nation, and then pointed the minds of the people
to the way things really ought to be; their agenda was driven by God's

[12] R. Albert Mohler, Jnr., *He Is Not Silent: Preaching in a Postmodern World* (Chicago: Moody
Press, 2008), 108.

210

word which came from outside, from God himself, and did not rise up merely as Israelite self-reflection. They were no doubt irrelevant: they gave answers to problems which the Israelites did not even know they had, and about which they certainly did not want to hear. So it is with the modern preacher: he is to interpret the world via the word, diagnose the problem, and point to the future kingdom, all on the basis of God's own speech as laid down in scripture.[13]

If the first mark of the content of prophetic preaching is the priority it gives to the word over the world, a second mark is surely the fact that preaching seeks to communicate the whole counsel of God. This is important because it is the whole counsel of God which provides the whole context for understanding the world in which we live. Now, this notion has a twofold implication. The first is very simple and practical: while it is clearly impossible for the preacher to preach the whole counsel of God in any single sermon, it does require that, over a period of time, all of the basic elements of God's word need to be covered. Practically, I believe that this requires a good, solid grounding in theological education for those who are going to occupy pulpits and pastorates. The depth and scope of the whole counsel of God is difficult to grasp on a part-time basis; a theological education for full-time pastors is still important. It also requires considerable thought and planning on the part of the preacher and elders in a church and, quite probably, a combination of expository and catechetical preaching.

A diet of simple exposition has the advantage of preventing the preacher from focusing just on those themes which are dear to his own heart or which are simply the flavour of the month in the wider culture; it also demonstrates to the congregation how the word of God should be approached, explained, and applied; but it also limits the speed at which all the key theological bases can be covered. Catechetical preaching, of the kind which was once strong in the Dutch Reformed tradition, can then supplement (not replace) expository preaching as a means of covering all the major themes in a set period of time. The Heidelberg Catechism is famously divided into fifty-two Lord's Days in order to facilitate annual sermon cycles; this may be an ambitious timetable today, but it can be modified; and, in a world where church

---

[13] William Willimon, commenting on Barth's preaching, makes the following statement: 'How do we make the Bible relevant to people in their various situations? Barth's simple answer is that we don't. It is the resurrected, speaking Christ who makes the story relevant to all people everywhere by fundamentally altering who they are and what their situation is' (Willimon, *Conversations with Barth on Preaching* [Nashville: Abingdon, 2006], 30).

congregations are increasingly fluid because of the nature of modern life and employment, it is surely good to know that, if someone is in your congregation for, say, two years, you will have given them opportunity to hear all of the great creedal truths of Christianity proclaimed from the pulpit. This is not, of course, the *whole* counsel of God; but it does represent the essential building blocks of such; and the preacher who follows its pattern will find that nothing of vital significance is omitted. This is also, of course, a good reason why the provision of two Sunday services is important: first, it precludes having to choose between exposition and catechesis; second, it reverses the strange tendency in modern churches of lamenting the growth of biblical illiteracy while, at the same time, cutting down the amount of biblical teaching.

Second, if the preacher is to proclaim the whole counsel of God, then his preaching is never to be less than *doctrinal* in content. Again, catechetical preaching is one possible help here. The basic distinctions necessary for understanding the world from a biblical perspective – that between creator and creature, between fall and redemption, between sin and obedience, between Adam and Christ – are all in essence doctrinal and need to be preached as such. Various preaching styles may be used, expository, topical or narrative, but all should at some point come to grips with the fact that doctrine is important to making sense of what the Bible teaches. Fundamental to confronting the church and the world with God is the proclamation of his identity: this has been revealed in his actions and speeches in history, all of which point back to who he is in eternity and who we are in relation to him; and, at bottom, that must be expressed not simply as a story but as doctrine. Of course, biblical genres must be respected as part of the exegetical process underlying good exposition and proclamation; but undergirding all proclamation must be a basic commitment to doctrine. This is another point in favour of at least reflecting on catechetical categories in sermon preparation and delivery.

The third aspect of the whole counsel of God is the existential connection that the preacher needs to draw between God's truth and the individuals being addressed. Calvin's opening statement in the *Institutes*, that almost all knowledge we have is either of God or ourselves, and the two are intimately connected, makes this clear. Good preaching demands the self-involvement of the congregation in what is being said. This is not something analogous to a weather forecast or a news report on some event thousands of miles away; the biblical, doctrinal categories used by the preacher in his exposition of the word have immediate implications for the self-understanding of the members of the congregation. As with Nathan's sermon before David in 2 Samuel 12, with its famous trap/twist – 'You are the man!' – good preaching will draw the congregation into the biblical story and thereby force them to confront their own standing before God. As Paul says in 1 Corinthians 1, the cross is *foolishness* to those who are *perishing* but to those who are *being saved* it is the *power of God*. These are existential terms that speak of more than just intellectual assent or the incremental increase of knowledge; they speak of a confrontation which affects the whole man.

Preaching, as said above, is therefore not simply an explanation of the Bible; nor is it, as is sometimes the case even in conservative Reformed circles, the demonstration that Jesus is in a text or a passage where the congregation have never seen him before. As one former student told me, 'I am tired of waiting for the "aha" moment every Sunday; "I bet you never saw Jesus in this passage before" is not an application!' The temptation always with doctrinal preaching is just to state the facts, so to speak; and the dual fear of legalism and of an over-specificity can both serve to undermine the confrontational and applicatory aspects. Again, the Heidelberg Catechism provides a good model here, with its consistent use of the first person in its answers, and its inexorable movement towards the response of gratitude in the lives of believers. It does not leave the response blank, as if it will flow automatically or mystically from the simple realization that we are sinners but Christ is the mediator and the church our mother; it gives more guidance than that.

We do not, of course, need to rely on man-made documents like the Heidelberg Catechism for the insight that the preaching needs to terminate in exhortation and application: a study of Moses' sermon in Deuteronomy, or the proclamations of the prophets, indicates that the counsel of God must not simply be proclaimed as an objective state of affairs; it must be used to confront the audience, to change their understanding of God and of themselves in relationship to him, and to change their way of life accordingly, often in ways which are clearly specified by said prophets. It may be hard to express in general, abstract terms exactly what this looks like; but every preacher should ask himself what the difference would be if he were merely lecturing on his chosen text. If he cannot tell the difference, then he is likely not preaching the text.

Next, a further mark of prophetic preaching is that it should not be boring: the truths of God's holiness, humanity's sin, and the cross of Christ might be good news to some or horribly offensive to others, but they should never be boring. That so many sermons inspire little but tedium in congregations is highly suggestive that their content might not be all that it should be. Barth puts this rather nicely:

> Preachers must not be boring. To a large extent the pastor and boredom are synonymous concepts. Listeners often think that they have heard already what is being said in the pulpit. They have long since known it themselves. The fault does not lie with them alone. Against boredom the only defense is again being biblical. If a sermon is biblical, it will not be boring. Holy scripture is in fact so interesting, and has so much that is new and exciting to tell us that listeners cannot even think about dropping off to sleep.[14]

Note what Barth does not say: he does not say that the answer to the boredom of a congregation is to make the presentation more interesting by telling jokes, anecdotes, or exciting stories. No. The way to make the sermon more interesting is to be biblical. I am no fan of Barth's theology; but I wonder who, on this point, is more faithful to the biblical notion of preaching: the confessional Protestant who spends the first ten minutes of every sermon entertaining his flock, or the man who says that interest is generated by being more, not less, biblical.

Finally, to be prophetic, preachers need to communicate to their people that preaching is not simply communication of information or exhortation to action, but involves the very presence of God in and through his word. This is expressed beautifully by the Dutch theologians, J. van Genderen and H.J. Velema:

> Why would I go to church? One of the answers to this question given by Van Ruler – although in his view it is not the most important one – is that we go there to receive salvation in all of its forms and variations. The mediation of salvation in Christ is the work of the Holy Spirit in us. But the Spirit engages helpers. In a sermon, God in Christ comes up to us with his grace. When I have to some extent discovered myself

---

[14] *Homiletics*, 80.

to be a sinner, as being lost and in the wrong, it is hard to believe that there is mercy for me. Preaching continually opens up new vistas. The spirit is enriched, and the heart is filled. Those who have once truly tasted something of the mystery of redemption seek to hear the gospel over and over again.[15]

Those who come to church with the thought that they are to meet God there, in the reading and preaching of his word, will have a very different attitude to those who come seeking a theological lecture or a moral exhortation; they will come to listen, to worship, and to respond; they will come to church in order to be the church, the body of Christ and the temple of the Holy Spirit.

It is perhaps fitting to end an essay written to honour one great Scottish theologian by quoting from another. In what is probably the finest book ever written on preaching, Peter Taylor Forsyth begins with the following: 'It is, perhaps, an overbold beginning, but I will venture to say that with its preaching Christianity stands or falls.'[16] Given all that I have said above: that preaching is prophetic, that it connects to the doctrine of God and the doctrine of scripture, that it is God's means of action and presence in the church, that it is not explaining the Bible or simply encouraging people to behave better, I think it is not an overbold ending to say that, unless individual churches and denominations address both their understanding of preaching and its content, they cannot stand but will most certainly fall. Let us focus once again on the education and training not of therapists, life coaches and general managers, but of preachers, those tasked with bringing us the very Word of God.

---

[15] J. van Genderen and H.J. Velema, *Concise Reformed Dogmatics* (Phillipsburg: Presbyterian and Reformed, 2008), 761.
[16] P. T. Forsyth, *Positive Preaching and the Modern Mind* (London: Hodder and Stoughton, 1907), 1.

12

David and Derrida:
The Psalms and Postmodernism

Fergus Macdonald

All who hear Donald Macleod preach or lecture are impressed by the degree to which his theology echoes the lyrical and experiential nature of the Psalms, and reflects their power to inspire listeners to worship. The organising confession of the Psalter – 'the LORD reigns' – is both the bedrock and the summit of Macleod theology. Like the psalmists, Donald does not hesitate to agonise with issues of the day that challenge the rule of God over his creation. He boldly carries Christian theology out of church and academy, letting it loose in the public sphere to challenge the myriad of siren voices making themselves heard in today's postmodern culture. For all these reasons it is surely entirely appropriate that one of the tributes to Donald Macleod in this volume should focus on the Book of Psalms and its contemporary relevance.

North-African born, French philosopher Jacques Derrida (1930–2004) has been chosen for inclusion in the title of this chapter as one of the leading exponents of the postmodern movement that has swept through the Western world (and, indeed, farther afield) since the 1970s. The choice of 'David,' the psalmist *par excellence*, is even more obvious. Seventy-three of the one hundred and fifty psalms bear his name, making it virtually synonymous with the Psalter from very early times (Heb. 4:7).[1]

---

[1] David is regarded as the patron of Israel's liturgical music. He is described as 'the sweet psalmist of Israel' (2 Sam. 23:1, RSV).

Although the terms 'modern' and 'postmodern' are probably overused, they remain of value as shorthand for the two main paradigms currently driving Western culture. In popular understanding modernity describes the worldview emerging from the Enlightenment of the eighteenth century which built on the ideas of rationality, individual autonomy and progress. It assumes the existence of universal truth, discoverable and verifiable by science rather than revealed by religion. It regards universal principles and procedures as objective, while preferences are subjective. Socially it expresses itself in terms of industrialisation, bureaucratisation and secularisation.

Postmodernity, on the other hand, is less easy to define because of its focus on difference. But popularly understood, it regards the universal perspective of modernity as an illusion and considers the world to be a construct of culture and language, regarding the latter as the 'creator' rather than the mirror of reality. Postmodernity is viewed as being suspicious of truth claims, whether these are made by science, philosophy or religion. Those who assign a chronology to modernity and postmodernity, asserting, for example, that modernity began with the fall of the Bastille in 1789 and ended with the destruction of the Berlin wall in 1989, are almost certainly oversimplifying matters. Modernity is still very much with us, while postmodernity is perhaps most usefully regarded as the condition of the history in which late twentieth century and early twenty-first century westerners find their lot cast. Today our society is both modern and postmodern and we live, as Kevin Vanhoozer says, 'in parenthesis' between these competing worldviews, often finding ourselves jostled as they compete for dominance.[2]

The question this chapter attempts to address is: Do the Psalms have anything relevant to say to people striving in this parenthesis to find meaning and purpose for their lives? At first sight, postmodernist acolytes, fascinated by semiotics and simulacra, and Iron Age psalmists appear to live in different universes. It does not take long to hear distinct dissonances ringing in our ears as we attempt to reconcile the thought and ethos of the psalms with postmodernist theories and lifestyles, and there can be little doubt that this discord presents a formidable obstacle to postmodernists engaging with these ancient poetic texts.

---

[2] Kevin Vanhoozer (2003), *The Cambridge Companion to Postmodern Theology*, Cambridge, 9.

Dissonance

I will illustrate this dissonance by exploring one specific psalm that exhibits a range of the features which postmodernists find problematic. To fulfil this purpose I have chosen Psalm 78 for a variety of reasons. First of all, it is an historical psalm.

History

Psalm 78 is one of the four 'historical psalms' in the Psalter. (The others are 105, 106 and 136). Denoting these four psalms as 'historical' does not imply that others are non-historical. Many psalms contain textual allusions to historic events, some identified (e.g. the Babylonian destruction of the Jerusalem temple in Psalm 74), and many unidentified (e.g. the urban violence of Psalm 55). While some 'wisdom' psalms tend to be mainly conceptual (e.g. Psalm 119), many of the others have an historical ambience in that they allude to human experience, both personal and corporate, in unidentified given situations. All of this creates a problem because one of the principal features of the postmodern movement is its historical scepticism. The French postmodern historian Michel Foucault rejects as a failed modernist enterprise the premise that history moves in accordance with a unified linear logic, and considers that there is no 'one true story' of the past. According to postmodern historian, Hayden White, all historical narratives are suspect, little more than 'verbal fictions.' White, who has been described as 'the most magisterial spokesman' for relativistic postmodernist historiography, defends the idea that 'the techniques or strategies that [historians and imaginative writers] use in the composition of their discourses can be shown to be substantially the same, however different they may appear on a purely surface, or dictional, level.'[3]

Such postmodernist qualms about the credibility of historians has contributed to the fractured nature of popular historical knowledge today. The tendency of the media to zap out the past reinforces this state of affairs, leaving the impression that the present is 'a mega clearance sale of the past'.[4] Marshal McLuhan, the Canadian Catholic media professor of the mid-twentieth century, claimed 'The media have substituted themselves for the older world. Even if we should wish to recover that older world we can do it only by an intensive study

---

[3] *Tropics of Discourse* (1978), cited in *Postmodernism: A Very Short Introduction*, by Christopher Butler, 2002:33.

[4] R. Appignanesi and C. Garrett (1995), *Introducing Postmodernism*, Cambridge, 152.

of the way the media have swallowed it'.[5] British Marxist historian Eric Hobsbawm, writing in the early 1990s, alleges that 'most young men and women at the century's end grow up in a sort of permanent present lacking any organic relation to the public past of the times they live in'.[6] In such a cultural atmosphere it is hardly surprising that many are reluctant to engage an ancient poem that acclaims distant events such as the plagues of Egypt, the exodus, the wilderness pilgrimage, the conquest of Canaan, the fall of Shiloh and the rise of Jerusalem. The prevailing suspicion is that Psalm 78 and others like it are highly fictionalised accounts. However, this is but the first difficulty such psalms present to a postmodern mindset.

Grand narratives
Not only is Psalm 78 historical; it is also gives a poetic resumé of Israel's 'foundational narrative',[7] and as such, touches a sensitive postmodern nerve. Master narratives are regarded as oppressive. 'Simplifying to the extreme,' wrote Jean-Francois Lyotard, the French philosopher and literary theorist, 'I define *postmodern* as incredulity towards meta narratives.'[8] Master stories are no more than 'mere narratives' of purely local, and certainly not of universal significance. Thus any formative historical tradition of a community becomes suspect as the instrument, if not the invention, of powerful élites, designed to entrench their position in society. Metanarratives are regarded as authoritarian attempts to universalise the values of one culture over all others, and are rejected as projects of power and domination. Postmoderns are explicitly suspicious of the grand narratives of western modernity, like the rationalism of the eighteenth century Enlightenment and the economic globalisation of today, which they regard as ideological tools of western domination of the world. The Bible, despite belonging to a totally different category from economics and militarism, is accorded similar scepticism because of its claiming a universal authority. Its genre as a master story creates a strong disincentive to investigating individual biblical texts, such as the Psalms. But that is not all. A further disincentive for postmodernists is the inductive method of argumentation evident in Psalm 78.

---

[5] In Appignanesi and Garrett, 151.
[6] Eric Hobsbawm (1994), *Age of Extremes: The Short Twentieth Century 1914–1991*, London.
[7] J.L. Mays (1994), *Psalms*, Louisville, 254
[8] Jean-Francois Lyotard (1984), *The Postmodern Condition: A Report on Knowledge*, Minneapolis, xxiv

Reason

The psalmist seeks to promote the generational renewal of what schol-ars describe as Israel's 'core memory' of the exodus and conquest. The psalmist utilises his panoramic sweep of history from the exodus through the wilderness wanderings to the conquest and the establish-ment of the Davidic monarchy by interpreting it as a series of 'para-bles' (v. 2). The basic meaning of the Hebrew word *mashal*, parable, is comparison. The psalmist's desire is that readers and hearers might compare themselves to their ancestors, and in consequence draw infer-ences that might enable them avoid making the same mistakes (v. 8).[9] Today this methodology creates problems because the Enlightenment's privileging of reason prompts postmodernists to be wary of logic and rational deduction. They prefer punning word-play to plodding logic, and deny the notion of universal rationality.[10] For this reason they tend to approach lessons drawn from all grand narratives with a hermeneu-tic of scepticism. They point out that repeatedly in history, grand nar-ratives have been employed by the strong to manipulate and oppress the weak. They would probably detect in Psalm 78 an attempt to shore up support for the religious and political 'powers that be' alluded to in references to Asaph[11] in the superscription and, toward the end of the psalm, to Zion and David in verses 68-72. This despair about reason, together with historical scepticism and suspicion of master stories, has persuaded postmodernist philosophers to undertake a fundamental re-evaluation of all texts in an exercise they call 'deconstruction'.

Deconstruction

The rationale of deconstruction is 'intertextuality' – that is, an assumption that every text relates itself implicitly to other texts through the author either assuming these other texts or suppressing them. Thus there are underlying meanings 'in' a text that the author has either assumed or suppressed in giving his or her text its actual form. Deconstruction seeks to combat this exclusion of the meaning of 'the other' by rescuing the text from the author's intention, thus liberating it from any fixed meaning or context.[12] Deconstruction is a process of peeling away the layers of constructed meaning like the skins

---

[9] J.C. McCann, 'The Book of Psalms' in *New Interpreter's Bible*, IV, L.E. Keck (ed.) (1996), Nashville, 990. In 1 Corinthians 10:1-11, Paul adopts a similar pedagogical method.

[10] Butler, 9.

[11] The Asaphites were a guild of temple musicians (2 Chr. 20:19; 1 Chr. 16:7).

[12] J.D. Caputo (ed.) (1997), *Deconstruction in a Nutshell: A Conversation with Jacques Derrida*, New York, 59, 109.

of an onion.[13] Thus no text – including Psalm 78 – is self-contained; its meaning can only be provisional and relative, and dependent at least as much on the reader as on the author.

Jacques Derrida is popularly regarded as the father of deconstruction. To be fair, he contends that deconstructing a text is not a cavalier assault on it. He claims that 'respect for the great texts, for the texts of the Greeks and of others too, is the condition of our work'.[14] In fact, deconstruction, he claims, 'is an analysis which tries to find out how their [the authors'] thinking works or does not work, to find the tensions, the contradictions, the heterogeneity within their own corpus.' In Derrida's view deconstruction is not negative for it is already happening inside a text. The task of literary criticism in detecting this 'auto-deconstruction' of a text is, in fact, a work of love and a search for truth, stability and meaning. The challenge for someone engaging with a psalm (or any text) is that Derrida considers this search to be never-ending. And if the reader is to rescue the psalm from the intention of its author, one wonders how likely it is that a sense of rapport will develop between them. Further, if deconstruction is an attempt to trace the complexity and paradoxes that characterise all human attempts to express or define truth it means that truth is elusive. This claim that truth is virtually indefinable creates a fifth obstacle.

Truth

One reason why postmodernism's account of truth is difficult to grasp is its fundamental assumption that all language systems are intrinsically unreliable cultural constructs. This means that one of the main principles of deconstruction, in the words of Christopher Butler, 'is to deny that final or true definitions are possible, because even the most plausible candidates will always invite a further defining move, or "play", with language'. Butler defines relativism as 'the view that truth itself is always relative to the differing standpoints and predisposing intellectual frameworks of the judging subject.'[15] Thus it is possible for Michel Foucault to argue that all discourses on truth are disguised expressions of the will to power by vested interests. Steven Shakespeare points out that, while Derrida maintains that his writings

---

[13] Appignanesi and Garrett, 79.
[14] In Caputo (1997), 9.
[15] Butler, 16-17.

have an intended meaning, it is not clear what this is because he is 'both questioning our preconceived ideas about meaning and evoking a radical and paradoxical structuring and de-structuring of truth that can never be directly stated, grasped or defined.'[16]

This dependence of deconstruction on relativism has been strongly challenged by theologians who adopt a realist epistemology. Kevin Vanhoozer, for example, raises the question 'whether certain forms of postmodernity act as corrosives to the conditions for the possibility of commitment, poisoning the will by depriving it of anything in which to believe ultimately'.[17] In Vanhoozer's view, the besetting sin of postmodernity is sloth. He cites Dorothy Sayers' definition of sloth as the sin 'that believes in nothing, enjoys nothing, hates nothing, finds purpose in nothing, lives for nothing, and remains alive because there is nothing for which it will die.'

If such severe sloth is indeed the ultimate plight of postmodernists, thankfully empirical knowledge suggests many of them stop well short of falling to the bottom of this pit, for they give evidence of an active quest for meaning and purpose in life. Nevertheless, there can be little doubt that the assumption that any firm faith will remain beyond our grasp is yet another postmodern inhibitor to meaningful engagement with the Psalms. This leads us to consider the impact this unattainability of faith makes on the postmodernist concept of God.

God

From beginning to end Psalm 78 is an appeal to trust God (see especially v. 8). Like all psalms it illustrates what James W. Fowler terms 'radical monotheism'. This type of monotheism is 'a type of faith-identity relation in which a person or group focuses its supreme trust and loyalty in a transcendent center of value and power, that is neither a conscious or unconscious extension of personal or group ego nor a finite cause or institution.'[18] The psalmist urges hearers to believe that 'the recollection of a history of failure [can] lead to a future

---

[16] Steven Shakespeare (2009), *Derrida and Theology*, London, 6.

[17] Kevin Vanhoozer (2003), 'Theology and the condition of postmodernity: a report on knowledge (of God)' in *Cambridge Companion to Postmodern Theology*, K.J. Vanhoozer (ed.), Cambridge, 23-24.

[18] James W. Fowler (1981), *Stages of Faith: The Psychology of Human Development and the Quest for Meaning*, San Francisco. While Fowler explores religious faith in its broadest sense, Chicago practical theologian, Don Browning, reckons that Fowler's *Stages of Faith* has 'enormous relevance to practical theology and through it to the entire body of theological reflection' (*Anglican Theological Review*, LXV, [1983] 124).

of hope'.[19] He urges them to commit themselves to 'the Most High' (vv. 17, 35, 56). This divine title, along with the others in the psalm – 'Rock', 'Redeemer' and 'Holy One of Israel' (vv. 35, 41) – point to a transcendent Deity as the source of significance and authority.

Despite its endemic scepticism, postmodernism does not lack theologians. But they tend to take as their compass Derrida's famous rubric 'There is nothing outside the text.' For example, Don Cupitt declares that 'however far we go in chasing after some extra-terrestrial reality which can function as an objective criterion for checking the text, we will still be operating with the realm of text.' All attempts to describe 'reality' are, as is all human thought, language-shaped and subject to textual logic.[20] It is not surprising that those inspired by the Death-of-God theology of the 1960s have welcomed Derrida as a luminary. According to Carl Raschke, deconstruction 'is in the final analysis the death of God put into writing'.[21] Similarly Mark C Taylor declares that 'deconstruction is the hermeneutic of the death of God'.[22] Both writers welcome deconstruction because they think it liberates them from any idea of God as a stable presence or absolute truth.

Others seek such liberation not so much in deconstruction as in introspection. They abandon sacred texts as a sphere for exploring spirituality and seek spiritual power, not from on high, but from within.[23] This dismissal of any concept of sacred scripture in favour of sacralising the self into an inner source of existential significance constitutes yet another deterrent to psalm engagement.

Identity

Postmodern fascination with the self deserves a closer look. It is a feature of the miscellany of spiritualities that compose the New Age movement, which Paul Heelas categorises as 'self-religions'. It is fortified by major theories of psychology that assume 'reward for the self (i.e. egoism) is the only functional ethical principle'.[24] Commercial consumerism aids and abets selfism, even in the church. Eugene Peterson laments that the self has replaced the soul in many of today's

---

[19] McCann, 992

[20] Don Cupitt (1987), *Long-Legged Fly*, London, 193.

[21] Carl Raschke in *Deconstruction and Theology*, Thomas Altizer et al, (eds), (1982), New York, 3 [176].

[22] Mark C Taylor (1984), *Erring: A Postmodern A/Theology*, Chicago, 6.

[23] P. Heelas and L. Woodhead (2005), *The Spiritual Revolution: Why religion is giving way to spirituality*, Oxford, 6.

[24] P.C. Vitz (1994), *Psychology as Religion: The Cult of Self-Worship*, Grand Rapids.

evangelical expressions of Christianity, and recommends entering the 'school of the Psalms' as an antidote.[25] There can be little doubt that another major contributor to 'selfism' is the concept of the self in postmodernist philosophies which Christopher Butler highlights:

> The preferred term to apply to individuals is not so much 'self' as 'subject', because the latter term draws attention to the 'subject-ed' condition of persons who are, whether they know it or not, 'controlled' (if you are on the left) or 'constituted' (if you are in the middle) by the ideologically motivated discourses of power which predominate in the society they inhabit.[26]

Butler cites cultural critic Catherine Belsey's terse critique: 'A human being, on this view, is not a unity, not autonomous, but a process, perpetually in construction, perpetually contradictory, perpetually open to change.' He then goes on to point out that the subject 'cannot ever "stand aside" from actual social conditions and judge them from a rational, autonomous point of view'.[27] Others contend that this disabling view of the self encourages people to see themselves as victims, and is contributing to the development of a 'blame and claim' society. In the context of the theme of this chapter there can be little doubt that those who tend to absolve themselves from responsibility for their own identity are unlikely to appreciate the psalmists' initiative in repeatedly and boldly petitioning God to intervene in human affairs.

Having undertaken a short and somewhat cursory review of some aspects of the postmodern condition, it is difficult to avoid concluding that many of our twenty-first century contemporaries seeking to engage with the Psalms will repeatedly hear the psalmists striking discordant notes. But happily that is not the whole story.

Resonance
Paradoxically, between psalms and postmodernism there is resonance as well as dissonance. This is specially the case in the voluminous writings of Jacques Derrida, who as a Jew of Spanish descent brought up in North Africa, developed a deep love for language and images drawn from the Hebrew Scriptures and the writings of Augustine, whom he regards as his 'compatriot'. While reluctant to be considered

---

[25] Eugene Peterson (2005), *Christ Plays in Ten Thousand Places*, Colorado Springs.
[26] Butler, 50.
[27] Butler, 51.

a theologian, Derrida in his later years participated in a series of 'Religion and Postmodernism' conferences at Villanova University in the United States. Those with whom he conversed acknowledged the difficulties of 'confining the energy of deconstructive analysis within the limits of a determinate faith.' However, they reckon that Derrida's indebtedness to the Judeo-Christian tradition makes facing this challenge not only inevitable, but worthwhile:

> For what else can one do with a philosopher who writes about the gift and forgiveness, hospitality and friendship, justice and the messianic, with someone who has radicalised these notions in such a way that anyone with an ear for these matters, with half an ear, can hear the biblical resonance, even if that is not something that Derrida himself is conscious of or consciously monitors?[28]

In this section I argue that such biblical undertones in Derrida's thinking provide points of contact between the Psalms and postmodernity and create an incentive to postmodernists to explore the Psalms. They encourage us to foster the hope that engaging with these ancient texts might diminish, and even remove, prevailing suspicions of the Bible. For postmodernists there is a natural attraction in the Psalms, as they love poetry. The Psalms are perhaps especially attractive in that they abound in the kind of vivid metaphors that postmoderns find fascinating. In addition, postmoderns express considerable interest in spirituality. True, much of this interest is self-focused and tainted with New Age thinking. But experience suggests that some who are engaged in a search for meaning and purpose find the robust, outspoken spirituality of the psalmists attractive, and conducive to exploring their poems reflexively. Such appealing features of the Psalter together with Derrida's borrowing from the lexis of the Hebrew Bible, create links between the ancient and postmodern worlds. Such points of contact can be developed by exploring some implications of four Derridean religious themes. The first of these is justice.

Justice

Derrida distinguishes justice from the law. The law requires to be continually deconstructed in order that it might advance. On the other hand, 'Justice,' he declares, 'is what gives us the impulse, the drive, or

---

[28] John Caputo, Mark Dooley and Michael Scanlon (2001), *Questioning God*, Bloomington IN, 2.

the movement to improve the law, that is, to deconstruct the law.'[29] Justice is thus 'beyond' deconstruction. 'Every deconstructive analysis is undertaken *in the name of something*, something affirmatively *un*-deconstructible.[30] In fact Derrida goes on to say that 'Deconstruction is justice'.[31] One deconstructs the law (the regulations of a judicial system) in the name of a justice to come, a justice beyond our present reach.

Justice is a major theme in the Psalms. The LORD is Judge. He 'has established his throne for judgment. He will judge the world in righteousness; he will govern the people with justice' (9:7). Psalms 9-10 are 'a virtual anthology on the LORD's judgment of nations and individuals'.[32] 'His judgments are in all the earth' (105:7). He is the judge of the gods (82:1), of all peoples and nations (96:3) as well as individuals (94:2). When injustice festers, the psalmists boldly confront God, demanding he intervene. If he fails to act immediately the psalmists wrestle with the problem of theodicy (the justice of God) as, for example, in Psalm 74. In doing so, they often adopt an eschatological perspective, prompting biblical scholars to recognise that 'the time of the psalms is interim'.[33] Psalmists continue to declare that 'The LORD reigns,' despite the fact that circumstances seem to deny and belie this. They are confident that God is reigning in heaven now and that ultimately his justice will be demonstrably effected in human life and experience. Derrida's concept of justice as being out of our reach, beyond the conditions of finitude could be interpreted as an echo of the eschatological justice the psalmists longed for. The second Derridean theme I want to highlight is the 'other.'

The 'other'

Derrida's desire for justice is occasioned by the plight of the 'other', a category used to denote ideas and people who do not fit the prevailing conceptual systems and lifestyles. In developing this theme, Derrida frequently acknowledges his indebtedness to Jewish philosopher Emmanuel Levinas (1906–95) whose philosophy is based on the ethics of the Other. Derrida's concept of the 'other' inspires many postmodernists to genuine concern about the widening gap between rich

---

[29] in Caputo, 16.
[30] Caputo (1997), 128.
[31] in Caputo (1997), 131.
[32] Mays, 32.
[33] Mays, 31.

and poor and the related growth of endemic injustice and corruption in our global economic system. There is also a challenge to understand the others living in our midst who have come from ethnic and religious traditions different from our own. Here is another creative point of contact with the Psalms, for the Derridean notion of the 'other' harmonises to a remarkable extent with the Old Testament welcome to the 'stranger' or 'alien' (Heb. *ger*) and its preoccupation for the predicament of the poor (*'ani*). Sympathy for the 'stranger', nurtured by the memory of Egyptian bondage and the experience of Babylonian exile, finds expression in numerous psalms. Above all, it is born and sustained out of a sense of God's providential care for his people during traumatic episodes in their history. The psalmist can testify: 'The LORD watches over the foreigner and sustains the fatherless and the widow' (Ps. 146:9). Furthermore, psalmists are aware that sin has rendered them spiritual 'strangers' in the holy presence of the LORD. 'I dwell with you as a foreigner, a stranger, as all my ancestors were' (Ps. 39:12, TNIV; cf Ps. 119:19). The verbal root to which *ger* is related occurs in the Psalms carrying the sense of living in God's presence and finding refuge there: 'I long to *dwell* in your tent forever and take refuge in the shelter of your wings' (Ps. 61:4). Alongside God's care for the 'stranger' is his consideration of the poor which is particularly prominent in Book 1 (Pss. 1–41) of the Psalter.[34] In the words of one contemporary commentator, 'The weak are the needy, poor, lowly, humble, afflicted (all variant translations and synonyms of *'ani*), who know they cannot save themselves and depend on the LORD for help against the forces with which they cannot cope.'[35] The prominence of God's compassion for the oppressed prompts another to observe: 'The way one treats the poor follows from the way one relates to God.'[36] The two great commandments (Mark 12:29-31, and parallels) may not be cited as such in the Psalter, but their import is amply demonstrated by the psalmists' passion to honour God and by their concern for the poor from within and the stranger from without. This strong focus on the underprivileged provides an opportunity to invite postmoderns to interact with the Psalms by comparing the many emotive psalmic expressions of the second great commandment with Derrida's concern for the other. The next theme taken from Derrida is the gift.

[34] See Psalms 9:9, 18; 10:17-18; 12:5; 14:6; 22:24; 34:19; 37:1.1; 40:17.
[35] Mays, 35.
[36] McCann, 847.

The gift

The Derridean concept of the gift brings together the notions of justice and the other. Caputo describes this triad as follows: 'Justice is the welcome *given* to the other in which I do not, so far as I know, have anything up my sleeve; it is the hospitality that I extend to the other, the expenditure without return, given without a desire for reappropriation…'[37] However, as justice is impossible, so also is the gift because neither is subject to calculation and measure. 'As soon as I say "thank you" for the gift, I start cancelling the gift.' Derrida tells us: 'As soon as I know that I give something, if I say "I am giving you something," I just cancelled the gift.'[38] This is why, according to Derrida, 'the gift is another name for the impossible.' And precisely because it is impossible, the gift creates passion. Derrida and those who follow him are exhilarated by the call of the gift to make on behalf of the other an expenditure without reserve or desire for payback. This animation inspired by the impossibility of the gift is captured by Caputo: 'That is why we love it so much, like mad. It is the one thing that is above all *desirable*. What we truly desire above all, wildly, in a desire beyond desire, is this impossible thing that can never be experienced, never be met with in the sphere of phenomenal presence.'[39]

In this case the correspondence between Derrida and David may not be quite so marked as in the case of justice and the other. Nevertheless Derrida's fascination with disinterested giving to the other resonates to an extent with characteristics of the LORD's grace (*hen* from the Hebrew root *hnn*) and steadfast love (*hesed*) given to the people of God and which are so eloquently extolled in the Psalms. Verbal forms of *hnn* are found 50 times in the Old Testament including 30 in the Psalms. The term *hesed* occurs 246 times with just over half of these in the Psalms. The adjective *hanun* (gracious) and the noun *hesed* (love) combine in what is perhaps the most basic creed in the Old Testament: 'You, O LORD, are a compassionate and gracious God, slow to anger, abounding in love and truthfulness' (Ps. 86:15; cf. Exod. 34:6-7). A slightly different form of words – with 'good' (*tob*) replacing 'gracious' (*hanun*) – is found in a similar confession of faith quoted and explored in Psalms 118 and 136: 'The LORD is good, his love (*hesed*) endures for ever.' These creedal testimonies resonate

---

[37] Caputo (1997), 149.
[38] in Caputo (1997), 19.
[39] Caputo (1997), 144.

with Derrida's gift in that they highlight the benefits which the LORD freely gifts to his people. This giving and receiving, which is expressed so freely by psalmists, is set within a covenant relationship which is alluded to no fewer than twenty times in the Psalter and is based on God's undeserved gift of election.[40] On the other hand, unlike Derrida's gift, the LORD 's benefit is undeserved and, originating beyond the sphere of 'phenomenal presence', can be experienced by recipients in space and time. Nevertheless, the tension between Derrida's gift and the covenant's benefits is an attractive theme for postmoderns to explore further in the Psalms. Some of the psalmic references to covenant focus on the people's representatives: Moses (103:7), Abraham (105:9) and David (89:3, 20, 35, 49). The concentration in Psalm 89 on the permanence of the covenant with David creates a logical bridge to the fourth Derridean theme – the messianic.

The messianic

Alongside the conviction about the impossibility of realising both justice and the gift 'in the sphere of phenomenal presence,' Derrida expresses, in his later works, an expectation for the future which he calls 'the messianic structure'.[41] Here Derrida is clearly borrowing from the expectation of his Jewish tradition that a messiah, a king like David, will come. But he is careful to distinguish this messianic structure from the concept of 'messianism' which in his understanding focuses on a determinate Messiah. Derrida neither envisages nor expects a personal messiah to come. But he appears to expect something. Deconstruction's messianic tone turns toward the future – not the future of future's thinking, but the absolute future that lies beyond the horizon of phenomenology. It does so, Derrida maintains, in expectation of 'the other to come.' Caputo explains:

> The messianic future of which deconstruction dreams, its desire and passion, is the unforeseeable future to come, absolutely to come, the justice, the democracy, the gift, the hospitality to come. Like Elijah knocking on the door! The first and last, the constant word in deconstruction is come, *viens*.[42]

---

[40] See Psalms 25:10, 14; 44:17; 50:5, 16; 74:20; 78:10, 37; 89:3, 28, 34, 39; 103:18; 105:8, 9, 10; 106:45; 111:5, 9; 132:12.
[41] In Caputo (1997), 23.
[42] Caputo (1997), 156.

Caputo argues that Derrida's 'messianic affirmation of the coming of the impossible' is a sign of faith rather than an expression of nihilistic despair.[43] It expresses a longing for something or someone unavailable in our present world order. A postmodern person enthused by the messianic idea, who wishes to explore the wellspring out of which Derrida drew this evocative notion, could find no better place to begin than the Psalms. For it is in these poems that both the term 'messiah' (anointed one) and the concept of the Messiah have their origin.[44] Derrideans do not believe that a personal Messiah has come or will come. Yet they live in expectation of 'the other to come' in an absolute future. Perhaps, were the psalmists able to return and meet Derridean readers of their songs, they would follow Paul's lead in the Areopagus and say: 'The other you expect to come in an absolute future we proclaim to you.'

There is little doubt that these four themes from Derrida – justice, the gift, the other, and the messianic – provide openings in the postmodern cultural medley of today through which the cries and hopes of ancient Psalms can address the ambiguities of the postmodern condition. Might, therefore, these four themes, together with their echoes in the Psalms, provide pillars for a 'Derridean-Davidian' bridge that might span the gap many postmoderns perceive to exist between them and the Bible? A fascinating thought! But any bridge will be traversed only if suspicions of the Bible as a master narrative can be laid to rest. For this reason in the next section I describe two ways which might be used to disarm the metanarrative bogey.

Relevance

Hans-Georg Gadamer spoke of texts becoming *actualised* when a reader or reading community enter the 'world' of the text and discovers that it is shaping their judgments in a meaningful way. The resonances noted above can create real sympathy among postmoderns for the psalms, but the dissonances remain as formidable barriers seriously hindering the actualisation of psalmic texts in the lived experience of postmoderns. If they decide to ignore these dissonances, setting them aside, they may discover that their sympathy for the psalmists will

---

[43]J. D. Caputo and M. J. Scanlon (2000), *God, the Gift, and Postmodernism: Indiana Series in the Philosophy of Religion*, 197.

[44] I.H. Marshall, 'Some Thoughts on Hermeneutics Arising from the Psalms', *Scottish Bulletin of Evangelical Theology*, Vol. 26, No. 2, Autumn 2008.

be short-lived, because sooner or later unresolved philosophical and religious conflicts will return to haunt them. Rather than trying to find a way *around* the difficulties, it is surely better for postmoderns to discover a way *through* them. In this section I look at some ways they might do this with regard to the suspicion of metanarratives.

The Bible is a 'non-modern metanarrative'

Richard Bauckham gives us a helpful lead. He acknowledges that there are sound reasons for suspecting some contemporary metanarratives, not least that of economic globalization. He defines a metanarrative as 'an attempt to tell a single story about the whole of human history in order to attribute a single and integrated meaning to the whole'.[45] Bauckham observes that any metanarrative will inevitably find itself in conflict with postmodernity's espousal of diversity and heterogeneity.[46] He points out that Lyotard's critique of metanarratives was not directed specifically at the Christian story, but at projects of modern reason that aspire to 'a comprehensive explanation of reality, including the human condition, and seeks thereby rationally based universal criteria by which to order society and to liberate humanity through technology.' Nevertheless, many have used Lyotard to attack the Bible. This is why Bauckham argues that the biblical narrative is essentially distinguishable from the dubious totalisation of modern metanarratives. He claims that the biblical story is a 'non-modern metanarrative'. Although the Bible tells

> an overall story that encompasses all its other contents, … this story is not a sort of straitjacket that reduces all else to a narrowly defined uniformity. It is a story that is hospitable to considerable diversity and to tensions, challenges and even seeming contradictions of its own claims.[47]

The lament psalms are an example of such tensions, challenges and seeming contradictions. Apart from the Book of Job and Ecclesiastes, these 'songs of complaint' have no rivals in demonstrating that the Bible is, indeed, a non-totalising grand narrative. Having expressed the needs of their original composers, laments became for later worshippers,

---

[45] Richard Bauckham (2003), *Bible in Mission: Christian Witness in a Postmodern World*, Carlisle, 87.
[46] Ibid. 88-94.
[47] Ibid. 93-94.

suffering various forms of injustice, a medium for articulating to God grievances, personal and communal. The superscriptions of certain laments point to their composition during the ten-year period David spent as a fugitive from Saul when his life was often in grave danger. Some laments enabled him and others, harried by ruthless enemies, to vent the frustration and anger they felt at the injustice of their predicament. By handing over their raw emotions to God the ultimate Judge they were released from the power of deep desires to inflict personal revenge. Lament psalms undoubtedly constitute a literature of protest, not one of oppression, and provide evidence in support of Bauckham's contention that the Bible is a metanarrative with a difference. I now turn to a second approach to clearing the charge that the Psalms are authoritarian.

The Psalter as a 'classic text'

This approach is to present the Psalms as 'classic' texts. David Tracy borrows the concept of the religious classic from Hans-Georg Gadamer and utilises it as a potential bridge to span the gap between orthodox Christianity and the 'postmodernities' of today. Many postmoderns are sympathetic to Gadamer's concept. The advantage of classic texts is that they are regarded as self-authenticating. They 'so disclose a compelling truth about our lives that we cannot deny them some normative status' says Tracy.[48] He further contends that classic texts stimulate a two-way questioning process that makes possible a 'critical correlation' between text and audience. He explicates this correlation as a conversation or dialogue taking place between 'the implicit questions and explicit answers' of the classic text and 'the explicit questions and implicit answers' of contemporary experiences and practices.

Postmoderns, while suspicious of modern grand narratives, may be more kindly disposed to exploring the Psalms as poetic classic texts set within the non-modern narrative of the canonical Scriptures. Presenting the Psalms as such would help to make viable the metaphor mooted earlier of a 'Derridean-Davidian' bridge. But how can we make this bridge a reality? In the final section I suggest this might be done by setting up small groups where postmoderns are invited to experience specific psalms by performing them.

---

[48] David Tracy (1981), *The Analogical Imagination: Christian Theology and the Culture of Pluralism*, New York, 108.

Performance

I am not using the term 'performance' in the sophisticated modern sense it has in the entertainment industry. Rather, in this section it carries the more basic meaning attributed to it in the emerging discipline in biblical studies of performance criticism which seeks to analyse performance as the site of interpretation for those biblical documents originally composed for oral presentation. The basic principle of performance criticism is that texts intended to be heard can be adequately interpreted only by hearing them. This principle is particularly relevant to the Psalms which were originally read, recited and sung in order to be heard. Ernst Wendland describes the aural-oral culture of the Bible as high-context, face-to-face, socially oriented, participatory and relational.[49] Internal textual evidence suggests that psalms were performed creatively in temple worship. However, it is unlikely that all psalms were originally composed for use in a formal liturgy.[50] Individual laments probably began as personal prayers of individuals, only later becoming congregational through incorporation into the Psalter.

If the best way to interpret texts intended to be heard is by hearing them, perhaps a key strategy in enabling postmodern users of the psalms to discover the power of these ancient hymns and laments to effect worldview formation amidst the ambiguities of human existence, is to encourage these users to speak and hear them. How might we do this? An appropriate social context is the small group for the following reasons. First, most postmoderns have a preference for discovery learning and wish to be actively involved in the learning process. Second, many in this audience are allergic to church. Third, the participatory nature of small groups helps to counter suspicions of any manipulation by the facilitator. In advocating small groups here I am not disparaging formal teaching or preaching which, of course, have a vitally important role in the life of any Christian community. I am simply saying the small group is a good place to begin in attempting to reach a postmodern audience. In addition, it should be pointed out that whoever facilitates such small groups interacting with the text of a psalm, will get opportunities to exercise an informal teaching role as members of the group raise questions. Such groups create an

---

[49] Ernst Wendland, 'Performance Criticism: Assumptions, Applications, and Assessment' in *T·I·C Talk: Newsletter of the United Bible Societies Translation Information Clearinghouse*, Number 65, 2008. Cf. 'Performance Criticism: An Emerging Methodology in Biblical Studies, by David Roads, in *SBL Forum*, 2005.

[50] R. Alter (2007), *The Book of Psalms: A Translation and Commentary*, New York, xvi.

initial pre-evangelism opportunity and ultimately a stepping stone to the church. Here I suggest three possible lines of simple oral-aural performance of psalms that might be encouraged in small groups. The first is recitation.

Recitation

Reciting a psalm from either text or memory replicates the way it was originally used, for in the ancient world all reading, even private reading, was vocal. It also reflects the original purpose in producing the Book of Psalms. Very few ancient Israelites would have read the psalms, first, because many of them probably were illiterate, and, second, because the copies of Scripture scrolls were relatively few. So few, that were careless priests to mislay only one, the whole nation would live in ignorance of its contents (2 Kings 22). Some psalms have been identified as lending themselves for antiphonal recital (Pss. 24; 102; 107; 115; 121; 118; 136), a practice alluded to in Ezra 3:11.[51] In addition to different 'voices', sometimes there is a change of addressees (often God, sometimes the congregation, less frequently the king). Psalm 118 suggests that three distinct groups – 'Israel,' 'the house of Aaron,' and 'those who fear the Lord' – were called on to say 'His love endures for ever' (vv. 2-4). While living as we do under the new covenant, it is not appropriate to reproduce temple liturgy, nevertheless, it is open to us to communicate the psalms in ways that reflect the different movements within the text.[52] Many postmoderns wish to be active in any learning process and are likely to be more drawn to participatory readings than to a monologue. In the context of small informal groups participatory reading enables members to obtain a greater sense of a psalm's original context than is likely from a solo reading. Those who employ dramatised Scripture reading affirm that it makes the content of the passage more memorable to readers as well as having a positive effect on the attention given it by hearers.

Paradoxically in our hi-tech age people are discovering that lo-tech personal reading aloud helps them to relate to the text. This phenomenon became evident in the Psalm Journey research project

---

[51] 'And they sang responsively' (Ezra 3:11, ESV), lit. 'and they answered', the same word is rendered 'responded' by the NIV in Ezra 10:12 and Nehemiah 8:6.

[52] Examples of how this might be done are found in *The Comprehensive Dramatised Bible* (London, 1989). This compendium includes ninety-seven of the one hundred and fifty psalms, offering a series of readings taken directly from the text, with sections of each psalm allocated to various voices.

undertaken among Edinburgh University students in 2003–2004, when several respondents chose on their own initiative to read the psalms aloud to themselves as they privately reflected on the text. This may be because reciting poetry draws attention to the 'how' of its message as well as to the 'what'.[53]

The value of C. S. Lewis' remark that 'the Psalms are poems, and poems intended to be sung, not doctrinal treatises, nor even sermons'[54] was demonstrated by Psalm Journey respondents finding it helpful to sing as well as to recite, the psalms. The more musical among the respondents sang *a capella* a metrical version of the psalms being used in the research programme. They reported that this exercise reinforced their meditation by alerting them to shifts in tone as they followed the different foci within the psalm's theme. The act of performing the psalm enhanced their capacity to appreciate its message. So perhaps it is not surprising that in the USA one of the denominations which reportedly is successful in attracting new adherents from a postmodern milieu is the Antiochian Orthodox Church which recites psalms in its daily and weekly liturgy, covering the whole Psalter many times in a year.

The Reformed tradition has also placed great focus on the liturgical use of psalms, making the Psalter the main, in some cases, the exclusive manual of praise. However, the disadvantage of Reformed practice – over against, the Orthodox, Anglican and Catholic – is that we mutilate many psalms by singing only a fraction of them, thus in effect depriving worshippers of the opportunity to appreciate the flow of the whole psalm with its changing moods and nuances as a narrative of encounter with God.[55] The insistence on rhyme in composing our metrical versions unnecessarily lengthens and intrudes the text, making the longer psalms virtually impossible to sing as a single item of praise. New ways of rendering the psalms may be required if Reformed churches are to take advantage of their key resource in reaching the postmodern world. The resonance already noted between the Psalms and elements of postmodernity suggest that churches which make psalms central in their worship may well be more likely to become 'cities

---

[53] Adele Berlin observes that the special structuring of language in Hebrew poetry reinforces this effect ('Introduction to Hebrew Poetry' in *New Interpreter's Bible*, Vol. IV, Nashville, 1996).
[54] C. S. Lewis (1958), *Reflections on the Psalms*, 2.
[55] Calvin in his *Commentary on The Book of Psalms* (1845) constantly underlines the importance of discovering the 'scope' or purpose of each psalm viewed as a unit.

of refuge' when the strains and stresses of the postmodern condition increase to intolerable levels. However, this high view of the renewed potential of the Psalter today must be qualified by an awareness that reciting and singing psalms perfunctorily can all too easily become a formal routine devoid of spiritual activity. The need for reflection on what is read, recited or sung, highlights the importance of meditating.

Meditation

Michael LeFevre points out that singing psalms is closely associated in the Psalter with meditating. Writing on 'Torah-Meditation and the Psalms', he explains that the Hebrew verb most commonly translated 'meditate' (*hagah*), which occurs in ten psalms, communicates a vocal, rather than a silent, activity.[56]

One form of vocal meditation that is renewing its appeal today is the ancient practice of *Lectio Divina*. *Lectio divina*, or 'spiritual (lit. divine) reading,' has from the early centuries of the church been practised by small groups and involves four steps in engaging with a biblical passage as it is read through audibly several times. First, participants listen for a word or phrase that demands their attention. Second, they reflect on that word or phrase in relation to their memories, hopes and desires. Third, they respond to what they believe they have heard by offering silent prayers of confession, thanksgiving, petition or commitment. Fourth, they linger in the presence of God rejoicing in his attributes and promises. These steps can be adapted to include opportunities to reflect on how group members understand the Word to be impacting their everyday living: How does it change the way contemporary world events are viewed? What new actions does it demand?

One great advantage of this and other forms of meditating is that they take us beyond analysis into a holistic appreciation of the biblical text. Modern psychology distinguishes the functions of the left hemisphere of our brain from those of the right. The left brain undertakes analytical and logical tasks while the right brain activates our imagination and intuition. *Lectio divina* engages both brains and enhances our appreciation of the psalmists whose meditation on the *torah* (teaching) of Scripture evoked powerful metaphors and colourful images. *Lectio divina* creates space and time for the biblical text to

---

[56] Michael LeFevre, 'Torah-Meditation and the Psalms,' in *Interpreting the Psalms: Issues and approaches*, P.S. Johnston and D.G. Firth (eds.) (2005), Leicester, 217-20. The ten instances of *hagah* in the Psalter are 1:2; 2:1; 35:28; 37:30; 38:12; 63:6; 71:24; 77:12; 115:7; 143:5.

catch our imagination, enabling us 'to *hear* and *feel* the text as well as see it'.[57] The abundance of metaphors in the psalms kindles the left brain to force the right brain to draw conclusions. Psalmic metaphors 'encourage listeners (or readers) to mentally conceive and emotionally experience for themselves a particular situation or event by supplying them with a vivid picture or even an entire scene into which they can enter by way of their imagination'.[58] *Lectio divina* is not without its risks; the most obvious being its subjectivity. Practising this form of meditation it is easy to succumb to self-deception or advance self-interest on the misunderstanding that Scripture is guiding us. But steps can be taken to minimise such risks by regularly reminding readers that Scripture is the best interpreter of Scripture and encouraging them to evaluate their readings in this light. Those of us who assist such groups are to trust God's Word to do its own work through the power of the Holy Spirit.

A further advantage of *lectio divina* as an initiation into Scripture engagement for postmoderns is that is creates space for a scriptural text to authenticate itself. David Tracy has already reminded us that self-authentication is a feature of all 'classic' texts, and, indeed, the Westminister Confession of Faith (I.v) highlights the authentication by the Holy Spirit as the ultimate attestation of the authority of Holy Scripture. For this reason we can have confidence in Scripture as it interprets itself to communicate its message independently of any magisterium, whether of papacy or of presbytery. It is important to reaffirm this confidence in commending Scripture to a generation that is fearful of being manipulated by authority figures. Because the Book of Psalms contains extraordinarily colourful poetic imagery and gives vent to a vast range of human emotions, it has a unique capacity to engage with this generation. Antony Thiselton points out that the practice of *lectio divina* has distinct advantages in helping postmoderns to engage with Scripture in that it 'allows gentle contemplation to move amidst a kaleidoscope of ever-changing biblical imagery in a way which almost anticipates the post-modernist notion of textual play.'[59] In addition to demonstrating the value of meditative reading

---

[57] Ernst Wendland (2002), *Analyzing the Psalms*, Dallas, 205.

[58] Ernst Wendland (2003), 'A Literary Approach to Biblical Text Analysis' in *Bible Translation: Frames of Reference*, T. Wilt (ed.), Manchester.

[59] Antony Thiselton (1992), *New Horizons in Hermeneutics: The Theory and Practice of Transforming Biblical Reading*, Grand Rapids, 142.

as a means of accessing biblical texts, the Psalm Journey research also reveals that psalm meditation stimulates new ways of viewing the world.

Contextualisation

Psalms have been given to be a lamp to our feet and a light to our path (Ps. 119:105). Calvin uses the metaphor of spectacles to underline the role of Scripture in enabling us to see life within a God-given perspective.[60] Regular engagement with psalms can become a critical component in developing a biblical worldview and lifestyle. The Psalter fulfilled a vitally practical role in the life of our Lord. In the words of my first teacher of biblical Hebrew: 'It was the prayer-book which He would use in the synagogue service, and His hymn-book in the Temple festival. He used it in His teaching, met temptation with it, sang the Hallel from it after the Last Supper, quoted it from the cross, and died with it on His lips.'[61]

The majority of respondents in the Psalm Journey project of 2004, already alluded to, were non-church attending and some, indeed, belonged to other faiths. They were selected because all expressed a strong interest in contemporary spirituality. All willingly underwent a month-long course involving daily meditation on a psalm, and a weekly group *lectio divina* meeting on the psalm of the previous week. Both in their daily journals and during the weekly meeting, respondents shared how their reflection on the psalm affected the way they followed the daily news. What they wrote and said indicated that they had little difficulty in using the psalms as a lens through which to interpret news topics like the invasion of Iraq, tensions in Zimbabwe, immigration policy, or economic exploitation of the poor. A specific example is the lament of Psalm 74 concerning the destruction and desecration of the Jerusalem temple. It prompted respondents to reflect on the Palestinian-Israeli conflict and an arson attack on a Canadian synagogue. Discussion over coffee after the weekly meeting often focused on specific actions respondents felt the psalm was asking them to take in real life. Thus, viewing some of the public issues of the day through the lens of psalm meditation helped to develop a perspective that lifted the psalm out of the private sphere and brought it into the public square.

---

[60] John Calvin (1979), *Commentaries on the First Book of Moses called Genesis*, J. King (tr.), Grand Rapids, 62.

[61] J.G.S.S. Thomson (1962), 'Psalms, Book of', in *The New Bible Dictionary*, London, 1059.

Effecting worldview transformation in face of the powerful pressures of dominant cultures is a formidable challenge facing the church in every generation. Formidable, but not impossible. From the earliest days as Christianity advanced, it turned the world upside down (Acts 17.6). This dramatic inversion of values is not to be equated with the total rejection of cultures. The apostolic missionaries sensitively related the gospel to the cultural values of their audience, whether Jewish (as in Pisidian Antioch, Acts 13:47) or Gentile (as in Lystra, Acts 14.8-20). Today we are called to follow their example and find a biblical balance in presenting the gospel as *pro* culture and as *counter* culture. My contention is that the evidence reviewed in this chapter points to the Psalms offering us a unique means of communicating in this way the Word of God to our postmodern culture. The Psalms' resonance with certain features of postmodernity reveals that they are sympathetically *pro* culture. And the dissonance we have noted indicates that they are also decisively *counter* culture. In other words, the Psalms seem to be uniquely suited to penetrate and influence the inner world of postmodern culture. If through personal and small group reciting and hearing, reading and meditating, contextualising and practising psalms, seeds are sown in the hearts of those seeking meaning and purpose amidst the ambiguities and uncertainties of early twenty-first century life, surely those seeds will grow like the mustard tree of the parable and perhaps turn the postmodern world upside down!

Conclusion

In this chapter we have, in effect, attempted to answer the question, 'What has David to do with Derrida?' Can ancient Psalms from Israel's iron age speak in any meaningful way to the kaleidoscopic world of postmodernity? We began by acknowledging the width of the gap between these two worlds that has been created by following some key lines of postmodern thought: history at a discount, master stories under suspicion, reason in the dock, deconstruction rampant, truth privatised, God declared redundant, and human identity rendered unstable. However, in the subsequent section this negative appraisal of the Psalms' chances in today's culture was qualified by the discovery that four of Jacques Derrida's key themes – justice, the 'other', the gift and the messianic – resonate with the heartbeat of the Psalms to the extent that it is possible to envisage a 'Davidian-Derridean bridge' spanning the gap and providing a means by which postmoderns can explore not only the Psalms, but the Bible. The third section of the chapter is a plea to postmoderns to recognise that both the Bible as a whole and the Book of Psalms as a unit belong to a different genre of grand narrative from that of the Enlightenment project or economic globalisation. The fourth and final section explores ways in which postmoderns might be encouraged to cross the Davidian-Derridean bridge into the world of the Psalter and the story of the Bible. It highlights three ways of performing the Psalms – recitation, meditation, and contextualisation – that have the potential to change seekers into finders.

Facilitating postmodern exploration of the Psalms may become a key strategy in reaching today's generation with the Good News of Jesus Christ. Our Lord's message to his generation and to ours is that in him the Kingdom (or Kingship) of God has come near (Mark 1.15). For millions of postmoderns, the Psalms as 'the poetry of the reign of God'[62] could be the antechamber leading to that Kingdom.

13

Layered Reading:
The Preacher as Reader of Scripture

Alasdair I Macleod

When Donald Macleod was appointed to the chair of systematic theology by our General Assembly in May, 1978, I was in the class which had come to the end of their first session at the Free Church College. We were thrilled at the appointment, especially as we were soon to be the new professor's first students. Systematic theology was taken in the second and third years of the course and we were to be taught by Donald (while the final year continued their studies with the retiring professor). And so, on the first morning of classes in October, we sat in the little classroom and awaited the lecturer's arrival, hotfoot from Waverley and the Glasgow train. Having prayed briefly and then warned us not to interrupt him, he launched into the doctrine of general revelation. I remember thinking at the end of that hour, as I did consistently after his classes, that it was worth coming in for that one period alone. I learned more from Donald's lectures than I did from any other teacher, anywhere, ever.

I do not keep much from the past but I have kept these lecture notes. They were constant companions in the early years of ministry and it would seem almost sacrilegious to throw them out now. They are open beside me, at the point where Donald was rounding off his discussion of the Lord's Day before moving on to a block of teaching on the sacraments. I will never forget how he pleaded for the kind of preaching that makes Sunday 'a high day' for our hearers.[1] That has always been an inspirational, if ever elusive, goal.

I returned to teach at the College this past session, 2009-10, in a part-time visiting role for three years. Much to my surprise, the first module Donald wanted me to prepare was a brand new one in hermeneutics and preaching. This was for practical theology students in their final year and I was asked to wrestle with some of what is being written today in the field, from the perspective of a pastor rather than a scholar. Hermeneutics is important for any preacher, as every one of us is called to try to model good reading of the Bible week by week and to be a reliable guide to others.

Having agreed in a moment of weakness to write something for once, I thought I might reflect on the preacher as a reader of Scripture. I do not wish to imply that the ten perspectives which follow are of equal significance, or that they form a checklist through which we should move religiously as we prepare every sermon. Nor do they offer more than what some restaurants describe as a 'taster menu', a lot of little dishes to sample the range rather than a hearty helping of any.

It would be good to illustrate each of these perspectives applied to biblical texts (as we do in a weekly seminar, with a version of the following main headings as a template[2]), but space does not permit that here and anyway I would never put my exegetical fumblings into print. I wish specifically to distinguish my layered reading from attempts to find levels of meaning, whether that be the mediaeval *quadriga* (literal, allegorical/doctrinal, tropological/ethical, and anagogical/eschatological senses), or the more recent *sensus plenior*.[3] But that would be another long story.

1. Humble Reading
The first mark of the regenerate reader of Scripture is humility. And this is humility before the triune God whose Word it is. Our Christian

---

[1] This autograph is dated 1st February, 1980.

[2] In the actual template, the second heading here ('Personal') is the opening one, and the exegetical steps hinted at under the third one here ('Faithful') are divided between numbers 2 and 3. Then 4 to 10 are as you have them. For the purposes of this essay I have brought in material from an introductory lecture to be the first topic and I have jettisoned discussion of the exegetical steps as unmanageable within the limits available.

[3] The simple image of 'layered reading' was inspired by a book on the tabernacle, containing a section of clear plastic overlays, each with an illustration of part of the furniture or structure. Any layer could be viewed separately, and then as each one was laid on another the whole picture was successively built up. Contemporary analogies would be welcome!

doctrine of Scripture should celebrate the triune agency of God, both in the giving of the Word and in the giving of understanding. Each of these is the gift of the God who is Father, Son and Holy Spirit.

In recent evangelical writing on hermeneutics, the work of Kevin Vanhoozer has been especially influential. He has used speech act theory as what he calls a 'handmaiden' to a Trinitarian theology of communication. The technical vocabulary will now be familiar to many. Thus for Vanhoozer, the Father is the 'locutor', the speaker; the Son is his great 'illocution', his Word; and the Spirit is the 'perlocutor', the one who ensures that God's words do not return empty. 'The triune God is therefore the epitome of communicative agency: the speech agent who utters, embodies, and keeps his Word.'[4]

One of Vanhoozer's doctoral students from his New College, Edinburgh, days has recently produced a superb book on the doctrine of Scripture. Timothy Ward's *Words of Life* has a back-cover commendation from Donald Macleod: 'Textbook and treat in a single volume!' Here is Ward concluding his discussion of the Trinity and Scripture:

> The Father presents himself to us as a God who makes and keeps his covenant promises. The Son comes to us as the Word of God, knowable to us through his words. The Spirit ministers these words to us, illuminating our minds and hearts, so that in receiving, understanding and trusting them, we receive, know and trust God himself.[5]

We are to be properly humble before this God, first, in our acceptance of *divine inspiration*. The breathed-out book is unique. While we do not deny the humanity of Scripture, we affirm that it is absolutely, qualitatively and authoritatively different from any other book. I wish to stress that the Bible is the product of the three creative persons and is the speech of the three, though I do not have space to explore that here. It is vital to remember that we are always privileged readers, and we should never open the book in class or study without bringing to mind its divine and triune provenance.

We also need to be humble, secondly, in our prayerful dependence on *divine illumination*. Some writing on hermeneutics seems almost

---

[4] Kevin Vanhoozer (1998), *Is There a Meaning in This Text?*, Apollos, 457.
[5] Timothy Ward (2009), *Words of Life: Scripture as the living and active word of God*, Inter-Varsity Press, 97.

deistic, as if God gave the book and then left us to fend for ourselves.[6] I want to suggest that triune agency is vital here too, and that the doctrine of illumination might be developed to take account of the broader testimony of Scripture. Each of the persons is hermeneutically engaged.

To illustrate this point, it is the Father who delights to reveal truth to children (Matt. 11:25-26) and it is specifically the Father who is to be asked for the Spirit of wisdom and revelation (Eph. 1:17). Perhaps the image of a father reading to a child, patiently helping the child understand, is a helpful one for our hermeneutics? Further, it is the Son who is the great interpreter throughout his earthly ministry, re-reading the Hebrew Scriptures and continually bringing out new things. He is the one who opens up the Scriptures and who opens his disciples' minds after the resurrection (Luke 24:27, 45), and he continues this in his exalted prophetic ministry. And the Spirit is the interpretative Counsellor promised in John 14–16. On the Day of Pentecost he is the one who gives new depth to Peter's reading of Scripture, and in the theology of Paul it is the Spirit who gives spiritual discernment for us to understand his words (1 Cor. 2:10-16).

Who is equal to the task of reading Scripture properly? Only the triune God is sufficient for these things. We will return to this theme of dependent reading in the conclusion, where we give prayer the last word.

2. Personal Reading

The preacher's reading must be personal and not just professional. I need to read any preaching passage for myself before I ever read it for others. I should encounter the text, not simply in a circle in which I stay as I am but in a spiral through which I move to a new level, changed by what I have read. Let me select three of the things that are important here.

First, there is *penitence*. To read Scripture properly is to be read by Scripture. I must read as someone who is open to the critique of this particular text on my life, and ready to receive the cleansing and healing I need in whatever area is being addressed. God blesses the contrite, those who tremble at his word (Isa. 66:2b). John Webster has appealed for our reading of Scripture to be set in a theological

---

[6] See the useful discussion of various typologies in Mark Alan Bowald (2007), *Rendering the Word in Theological Hermeneutics: Mapping Divine and Human Agency*, Ashgate.

framework and to be understood as taking place in the economy of grace. Such reading means facing our ongoing ignorance and idolatry, and overcoming them through the work of Christ and the Spirit. We are sinful readers who need the purging and quickening power of the Spirit of the crucified and risen Christ. And so he insists, 'Reading Scripture is thus best understood as an aspect of mortification and vivification: to read Scripture is to be slain and made alive.'[7]

Secondly, there is *hunger*. We read for nourishment. Eugene Peterson invites us to eat the book, as his preferred image of what he calls 'spiritual reading'. He is commending the kind of engaged reading which does not simply want to be informed about God but to be transformed by him. He reminds us of the incident when John, like Jeremiah and Ezekiel before him, is invited to eat a scroll (Rev. 10:9-10).

> Eating the book is in contrast with how most of us are trained to read books – develop a cool objectivity ... But the reading that John is experiencing is not of the kind that equips us to pass an examination. Eating a book takes it all in, assimilating it into the tissues of our lives. Readers become what they read.[8]

It is such a basic and biblical image. The preacher is not just to feed others with milk, or meat, or bread, or wine, or honey, but to feed his own soul on Scripture, internalising the Word and being nurtured by it. Why starve, if you're a chef in heaven's kitchen?

Thirdly, there is *obedience*. Insofar as it is possible, I read as someone who applies any particular Scripture to my own life before I dare apply it to a congregation. I need to be open to what it is saying to me and to be willing to put it into practice, today. As John Owen said, 'A man preacheth that sermon only well unto others, which preacheth itself in his own soul.'[9] We all know sometimes what it is to feel freedom in preaching, aware we are speaking with reality and integrity because the text has begun to be lived out in our own lives. The ideal is summed up neatly in the dictum of Johann Bengel: 'Te totum applica ad textum, rem totam applica ad te.' It can be translated as, 'Apply your whole self to the text; apply the whole matter to yourself.'

---

[7] John Webster (2003), *Holy Scripture: A Dogmatic Sketch*, Cambridge University Press, 88.

[8] Eugene H Peterson (2006), *Eat This Book: The Art of Spiritual Reading*, Hodder and Stoughton, 20.

[9] John Owen (1968 reprint), *The Works of John Owen*, Volume XVI, Banner of Truth, 76.

There are all sorts of links between our personal spiritual walk and our hermeneutics. Is it not obvious that walking in the light will mean we are able to see more clearly? And did Jesus not promise to show himself to the obedient (John 14:21)?

3. Faithful Reading

Reading must be faithful to the text. I understand that to mean reading which is faithful to the intention of God as we see that expressed through the words of a human author. God spoke and still speaks through real human words.

The way in which, over the last couple of centuries, the focus has moved from the author to the text to the reader is well known. As some might put it, we have seen a shift from attention to the world behind the text, to the world of the text, to the world in front of the text. These options are illustrated in an oft-used analogy: the first approach sees the text as a window onto the world of the author; the second views it as a picture to be studied in its own right; the third holds it as a mirror in which the interpreter sees herself.

My own preference is to speak of 'authored text' and not to put asunder those whom God has joined together. Texts are not free-floating, with a life of their own, but they are given in a context with meaning embodied in them. Furthermore, I assume that this is always 'Authored text', from one divine mind. It is important to affirm today that there is meaning in the text before the act of reading. This needs to be said in a world where the reader often usurps the place of the author. But meaning is not controlled by the reader and, however unfashionable it may be to say it, the most dearly held interpretations can be quite wrong.

Our responsibility, then, is to seek to read texts with respect and integrity. That means hard digging, but it is the painstaking labour to which every expository preacher has been called. The treasure is so often in the detail. And we have such a wealth of tools, resources and methods at our disposal today. I cannot here work through the various steps (as we do in hermeneutics class[10]). I will just state the obvious, in two general points.

---

[10] I came up with a composite method of my own, perhaps a curious amalgam of different elements. I cannot now recall all the sources which fed into it. I was certainly helped in different ways by: Jeannine K Brown (2007), *Scripture as Communication: Introducing Biblical Hermeneutics*, Baker Academic (her method is summarised in Appendix A, 275-80); and by Sidney Greidanus (1999), *Preaching Christ from the Old Testament: A Contemporary Hermeneutical Method*, Eerdmans, especially 279-318.

First, we learn to read as we should by being exposed to *good practice*. Some future preachers imbibe this long before their formal education in exegesis, and they are fortunate indeed. They grow up in the faith under a ministry where the pastor reads the text with awareness of its authorship and its backgrounds, and with sensitivity to its literary genre, carefully setting it in its immediate and wider contexts, following the contours of the passage, explaining the meaning and relationships of words, illuminating figures and symbols, and so on, but all packaged in a sermon rather than a lecture. May we all aspire to be such mentors! Others will only learn these lessons at seminary, studying the biblical languages and embarking on serious and close reading. Then throughout our ministries, all of us need to be involved in ongoing education in this area, honing our interpretative skills as we read, and listen to, expert practitioners. It is never too late to learn from workmen who correctly handle the word of truth.

But secondly, we also learn from *bad practice*, as long as we have the personal nous or the expert help to see it for what it is. Sometimes these lessons are the memorable ones, and occasionally in class they are the amusing ones, especially when the practice being illustrated comes uncomfortably close to home. They might be mistakes at a technical level, as so helpfully discussed in Don Carson's book, *Exegetical Fallacies*.[11] Or the error could be at a more basic level, in a whole approach to text which is misguided. So we might do some historical work and study the allegories perpetrated by the Alexandrians of long ago; or we might find more recent examples of the same kind of thing. As long as we do this to learn and not to mock, remembering that we may have a plank in our own interpretative eye.

Through study of the text the meaning should become plain. And the plain meaning is always the best. Here is John Stott on expository preaching:

> To expound Scripture is to bring out of the text what is there and expose it to view. The expositor prizes open what appears to be closed, makes plain what is obscure, unravels what is knotted and unfolds what is tightly packed .... Whether [the text] is long or short, our responsibility as expositors is to open it up in such a way that it speaks its message clearly, plainly, accurately, relevantly, without addition, subtraction or falsification.[12]

---

[11] D A Carson (1996, 2nd edition), *Exegetical Fallacies*, Baker.
[12] John Stott (1982), *I Believe in Preaching*, Hodder and Stoughton, 125-6.

I have never heard anyone who does that more skilfully than Stott himself. To borrow a football analogy, the simple game is the beautiful game.

4. Canonical Reading

Good reading will be canonical. We believe both Old and New Testaments form one Christian canon, one organic whole, and that assumption cannot but inform our reading of any particular text. So reading must not be atomistic but inter-textual. Canon is always the context, though the sermon must focus on the one passage in front of me.

This means, first, a respect for the *biblical story*. I think I learned to read canonically at Westminster Theological Seminary (the Philadelphia one). Redemptive-historical reading pervaded most classes and it simply became the way one read Scripture. Geerhardus Vos and Herman Ridderbos seemed to stalk the corridors. 'Honk if you love Vos' was a bumper sticker and 'already but not yet' a t-shirt slogan.

The Bible itself bears clear internal witness to its telling of a unified story. Richard Bauckham has illustrated some of the ways in which both testaments do this. For one thing, the Old Testament contains various summaries of the ongoing history of Israel (e.g. Pss. 78, 105, 106). When we come to the New Testament Gospels, they recount the life and ministry of Jesus in continuity with Israel's story and also within an even larger narrative. The Gospel of Matthew opens with a genealogy which recapitulates Old Testament history (1:1-17) and closes with a reference to 'the end of the age' (28:20). John begins his Gospel with an echo of the opening words of Genesis and then at the close of the Gospel the last recorded words of Jesus are a promise of his return (21:22).[13]

So the Bible has no incredulity towards one particular meta-narrative. Indeed the Story makes sense of all the stories of Scripture and it judges every alternative one. N. T. Wright has encouraged us to see the divine drama of Scripture as a 'worldview story', a comprehensive and controlling narrative through which we are to view everything else.[14] We read each part of Scripture within the flow of the plot line, and we

---

[13] Richard Bauckham (2003), 'Reading Scripture as a Coherent Story', in *The Art of Reading Scripture* (ed. Ellen F Davis and Richard B Hays), Eerdmans, especially 40-42.

[14] For helpful discussion of Wright and much else, see Craig Bartholomew and Michael Goheen (2004), 'Story and Biblical Theology', in *Out of Egypt: Biblical Theology and Biblical Interpretation* (ed. Craig Bartholomew et al), Paternoster, 144-71.

interpret the world and its competing stories in light of the true one.

Secondly, canonical reading will mean a respect for the *biblical books*. Each individual book of the Bible has been given to us in a final canonical form, and its unity and shape and inner-connections are all to be honoured. Various influences have brought many biblical scholars to be more interested in the literary unity of books than in their hypothetical sources, and this is all wonderfully fertile ground for exegetes and expositors.[15]

Thirdly, we will have a respect for *biblical variety*. The Bible is a book rich with diversity, in its writers and literatures and characters and subjects. In our preaching programme, perhaps a series on how the different voices and genres of Scripture handle a particular topic would help shape thinking on that issue without flattening the perspectives. Paul and James should not sound as if they had got together to make sure their stories tally.

But fourthly, canonical reading will mean a respect for *biblical harmony*. God is consistent and his book is coherent. We read about creation, covenant, election, holiness, kingdom, temple, and so on and on, a host of unifying canonical themes. The different voices may have their own parts to sing, but Paul and James harmonise in the same choir. Polyphonous reading is what some call it, though it is hard to think of a less musical expression.

It may surprise you that it is better to be thick than to be thin. At least it seems to be when offering descriptions at various levels of complexity. According to Kevin Vanhoozer, thick description is Scripture interpreting Scripture, in the context of a canon which has one overarching purpose, to make us wise unto salvation:

> One can speak of neural firings, of the movement of an index finger, of pulling the trigger, of assassinating a President – all might be descriptions of the same act, though they work on different explanatory levels. However, the first description is 'thin' when compared to the last. Thin descriptions are the result of using too narrow a context to interpret an intended action.... Thin descriptions of the text suffer from a poverty of meaning.... The canon is a great hall of witnesses in which different voices all testify to the Lord Jesus Christ.[16]

---

[15] See Sidney Greidanus (1993), 'The Value of a Literary Approach for Preaching', in *A Complete Literary Guide to the Bible* (ed. Leland Ryken and Tremper Longman III), Zondervan, 509-19.

[16] Kevin J Vanhoozer (2000), 'Exegesis and Hermeneutics', in *New Dictionary of Biblical Theology* (ed. T D Alexander and Brian S Rosner), Inter-Varsity Press, 61-62.

In terms of preaching Christ from the Old Testament, I was helped a few years ago through reading a nicely balanced piece by Sinclair Ferguson. He offered four principles: first, there is the relationship between promise and fulfilment; secondly, between type and antitype; thirdly, between the covenant and Christ; and fourthly, between proleptic (anticipatory) participation and post-Pentecost experience. Most helpfully of all, he set all of these in the context of simply wanting to develop an instinct to preach Christ:

> We never 'arrive' or 'have it cracked' when it comes to preaching Christ. But as we come to know the Scriptures more intimately, as we see these patterns deeply embedded in the Bible, and – just as crucially – as we come to know Christ himself more intimately and to love him better, we shall surely develop the instinct to reason, explain and prove from all the Scriptures the riches of grace which are proclaimed in Jesus, the Christ, the Saviour of the world.[17]

We will return to the theme of Christ and his gospel, a little later.

5. Theological Reading

Theology and Bible reading should belong together. But the theological reading of Scripture is the Cinderella of the evangelical expository world today. Reflection informed by systematic and confessional theology is seldom asked to the ball. We need this to change. To ignore theological reading is simply wrong.

First, this attitude makes us guilty of sinning *against the past*. We should be profoundly thankful for our rich theological heritage. The ecumenical creeds enshrine the great affirmations of faith, shared with the saints of the ages, and our historic confessions express the truths which we hold dear with our fellow reformed. In addition we have the classics, the great Christian books which have stood the test of time. But there is a greater debt than just the one we owe to these framers and authors. It is the Triune God himself who has been at work throughout this history, guiding his church and enriching her with insight into his truth. So to ignore the theological past is to dishonour God. I need to repent of this sin. Donald Macleod used to tell us to read the great works, and I ignored his advice in favour of a

---

[17] Sinclair B Ferguson (2003 edition only), 'Preaching Christ from the Old Testament', in *When God's Voice is Heard* (ed. Christopher Green and David Jackman), Inter-Varsity Press, 89-90.

myopic devotion to new commentaries. Too late, I realise I was wrong. Hermeneutically, it is important to move in the right spirals.

Secondly, this attitude makes us guilty of sinning *against the present*. We short-change ourselves and others, and we deny to our listeners many good things which they deserve to enjoy. Theological shallowness in our reading is bound to impoverish our hearers. The great theologians and expositors of the past read the Scriptures for their own day, but informed by their theological inheritance. For example, the Fathers welcomed the guidance of the *regula fidei* or the 'Rule of Faith', an understanding of essential belief which offered a road map for hermeneutics.[18] And John Calvin saw his *Institutes* in this same light, and made that point in each edition from the second one onward:

> Moreover, it has been my purpose in this labor to prepare and instruct candidates in sacred theology for the reading of the divine Word ... the godly reader will be spared great annoyance and boredom, provided he approach Scripture armed with a knowledge of the present work, as a necessary tool.[19]

Calvin was a theological reader of Scripture and therefore a more trustworthy exemplar of consecutive exposition.

Donald Macleod himself has shown us, especially in *The Person of Christ*, what richly theological exegesis looks like. And he had earlier written an important essay on preaching and systematic theology, arguing that theology was essential to preaching.[20] He illustrated there how the system of truth can elucidate and guide exegesis, but warned against letting the system suppress or even silence the message of a particular text. He discussed how systematic theology might shape an individual sermon and also how it might shape the content and balance of our preaching over the course of a year. Attention was given to theological preaching in relation to evangelism and pastoral care, and there was discussion of the use of creeds and catechisms.

I want at this point to note something else which I think significant. This is the movement within contemporary biblical scholarship

---

[18] See Paul Hartog (2007), 'The "Rule of Faith" and Patristic Biblical Exegesis', in *Trinity Journal*, 28NS:1, 65-86.

[19] John Calvin (1960, ed. McNeill, trans. Battles), *Institutes of the Christian Religion*, Westminster, Volume I, 4.

[20] Donald Macleod (1986), 'Preaching and Systematic Theology', in *The Preacher and Preaching: Reviving the Art in the Twentieth Century* (ed. Samuel T Logan Jr.), Presbyterian and Reformed, 246-72.

which has become known as 'Theological Interpretation'. It now has its dictionary,[21] two commentary series,[22] a journal,[23] various monographs, international conferences (including the St Andrews Conferences on Scripture and Theology), and degree programmes. An excellent introduction to what is going on is provided in a recent book by Daniel Treier.[24]

Their concern to read the whole Bible as Christian Scripture and to do that theologically is hugely promising. I want to welcome this, while I express the following concerns. First, there is a theological pluralism, with texts being read from very different perspectives. So how does one judge a theologically worthy interpretation? Secondly, some can sit loose to history, as the text is what matters to them, not the events which may or may not lie behind it. Thirdly, I am amazed at the respect accorded to some early readings. They remind me of the fanciful allegorising and spiritualising which I heard in my Highland youth. And fourthly, whole swathes of theological interpretation are ignored by many. To take an example, there seems little engagement with the wealth of Puritan exegesis. Perhaps we could also have The Reformed Theological Commentary Series, edited by Campbell and Trueman, responding to these four concerns by being confessional, historical, sober and catholic?

Of course, not everyone needs to be told to read Scripture theologically. If the Christians of Donald's beloved Isle of Lewis were introduced to the notion of a theological interpretation of Scripture, they would probably feel like the character in Molière who is surprised to discover he has been speaking prose for over forty years without realising it.

6. Contemporary Reading

Some might have placed this topic earlier. However, I want to read the world through the text rather than read the text through the world. Others might place this topic later. But having wrestled with the meaning of the text, we need to begin as quickly as possible to

---

[21] Kevin J Vanhoozer, general editor (2005), *Dictionary for Theological Interpretation of the Bible*, Baker Academic.

[22] Brazos Theological Commentary on the Bible (2005–), Brazos Press; The Two Horizons New Testament Commentary (2005–), Eerdmans, now with Old Testament volumes being added.

[23] *Journal of Theological Interpretation* (2007–), ed. Joel B Green, Eisenbrauns.

[24] Daniel J Treier (2008), *Introducing Theological Interpretation of Scripture: Recovering a Christian Practice*, Apollos.

unpack its significance for today. So I wish now to heed John Stott's oft-repeated plea for 'double listening', both to the Word and to the world, faithful to the former and sensitive to the latter.[25]

First, I want to read *with cultural eyes*. I must be able to read the Scriptures as someone who knows my hearers' worlds. There is an obvious gap between the cultures of the biblical world and our contemporary cultures (we will come back to that later). The preacher longs to build bridges between both worlds, to mesh the two horizons in some way. But he always needs to sound as if he truly belonged to this one, here, at this moment. Some preach as if they actually lived in biblical times, or perhaps in a beloved era somewhere between then and now![26]

It is not easy to keep up to speed. We have the twin problems of the sheer diversity of modern cultures and the bewildering speed of change. But we need to make the effort, motivated by the love of Jesus:

> Some of us, quite frankly, are short of compassion, of Christ-like love.... Where such love is operative, it will find a way to understand the culture ... this means time and energy devoted to an empathetic understanding of the people to whom the Lord has sent us.[27]

For some, this may mean new disciplines of reading, listening and viewing. We will meet people and ideas who have been outside our purview and who may sometimes be outside our comfort zone. Others will operate at a more sophisticated level of analysis, perhaps with the help of Vanhoozer's method for cultural hermeneutics, applied by his students in a fascinating collection of essays to things like 'The Gospel according to Safeway', 'A Theological Account of Eminem', the 'Blogosphere', and 'Designer Funerals'.[28] Some may find local study groups helpful, perhaps for reading and for watching plays and movies, like those from which John Stott benefitted at All Souls.[29] There are also organisations which equip Christians to engage

---

[25] For example, in John R W Stott (1992), *The Contemporary Christian*, Inter-Varsity Press, 24-29, 110-13.

[26] For the best example of culturally relevant preaching in Scotland today, check out David Meredith of Smithton-Culloden Free Church, Inverness. You can watch and listen at www.smithtonchurch.com.

[27] D A Carson (1995), 'Preaching that Understands the World', in *When God's Voice is Heard: Essays on preaching presented to Dick Lucas* (ed. Christopher Green and David Jackman), Inter-Varsity Press, 155.

[28] Kevin J Vanhoozer, Charles A Anderson and Michael J Sleasman, eds. (2007), *Everyday Theology: How to Read Cultural Texts and Interpret Trends*, Baker Academic.

with the culture, of which the best example in the UK is the superb work of The London Institute for Contemporary Christianity.[30] We must work out our own salvation.

Secondly, I want to read *with imaginative eyes*. I envy those who seem able to enter the biblical world, to see it, hear it, smell it, and then translate that into an imaginative connection with this world. How do they do it? All I can say is that I know it when I hear it. These preachers offer us new readings of texts, fresh analogies for biblical teaching, creative and contemporary retellings of stories, and modern illustrations that help listeners touch and taste the truth. As Donald Macleod has said of theology and preaching: 'He who finds a serviceable new image puts the whole world in his debt.'[31]

We certainly need to do all that we can to feed our imaginations in helpful ways. C.S. Lewis was such a model of this:

> We want to be more than ourselves.... We want to see with other eyes, to imagine with other imaginations, to feel with other hearts, as well as with our own.... My own eyes are not enough for me, I will see through those of others ... in reading great literature I become a thousand men and yet remain myself.[32]

As one example of an imaginative connection sparked with today, take this modern analogy to the experience of Psalm 22:

> My God, you have abandoned me. And you won't tell me why. I am at the stake. Baited by my enemies. They stand round me in a circle. I am here – at bay. The child taunted by bullies.... The one who is jostled and mocked and cannot break out of the ring. They encircle me and taunt, jeer and deride. Their faces distort, become animal like, bestial, demonic, the face of the bull and the lion and the dog and the wild ox.[33]

What a difference such a reading might make to a bullied adolescent. It is hard to read it without tears. She couldn't help but know, 'Jesus understands me!'

[29] John R W Stott (1982), *I Believe in Preaching*, Hodder and Stoughton, 194-201.
[30] www.licc.org.uk.
[31] Donald Macleod (1998), *The Person of Christ*, Inter-Varsity Press, 264.
[32] C S Lewis (1961), *An Experiment in Criticism*, Cambridge University Press, 139-41.
[33] David Day (1998), *A Preaching Workbook*, Lynx: SPCK, 85.

7. Gospel Reading[34]

The evangelical is, by definition, called to read with good news in mind. There should be no contradiction between being true to any text and true also to the evangel.[35]

Gospel reading means, first and primarily, always reading *with Christ in mind*. As the whole Bible centres on Christ, so our interpretation of the Scriptures needs to have him as the one around whom everything coheres. Our canonical reading and our theological reading will already have fed reflection on Christ. He is the hero of Scripture's story and the heart of Scripture's message. As Ed Clowney used to say to us, in many different ways: 'Let others develop the pulpit fads of the passing seasons. Specialize in preaching Jesus!'[36]

Why would any preacher want to argue with that? Especially as we ourselves, and the Christians whom we address, need the gospel as much as anyone. So we deliberately read with gospel eyes and we ask continually, 'How does Christ walk from this passage into today's world?'

Gospel reading means, secondly, reading *with grace in mind*. We serve the God of all grace and we preach grace from all the Scriptures. This is the undeserved and amazing grace of forgiveness for the guilty, covering for the naked, adoption for the orphan, freedom for the captive, friendship for the lonely, food for the hungry, drink for the thirsty, rest for the restless, a home for the traveller, and more. The Scriptures are full of stories and themes and symbols and pictures of the spiritual needs of men and women, and all of these wants are met by grace alone through faith alone in Christ alone. So we need to read with eyes that seek pointers to grace in every passage. If we don't look for grace, we may not see it. If we learn to look, then we will always have good news.

And it means, thirdly, reading *with hearers in mind*. We study as those who hope to preach from this particular Scripture to some who do not yet know Christ. So gospel reading will reflect on how I may

---

[34] For a whole-Bible, missional hermeneutic, with a properly broad understanding of mission, see Christopher J H Wright (2006), *The Mission of God: Unlocking the Bible's Grand Narrative*, Apollos.

[35] For a detailed attempt to think through the principles behind gospel-centred interpretation, see Graeme Goldsworthy (2006), *Gospel-centred Hermeneutics: Biblical-theological foundations and principles*, Apollos.

[36] Edmund P Clowney (1986), 'Preaching Christ From All the Scriptures', in *The Preacher and Preaching: Reviving the Art in the Twentieth Century*, (ed. Samuel T Logan, Jr.), 191.

bring the gospel to them, from this passage. And there is not just one kind of unbeliever. They have their different needs or questions or misunderstandings or objections. So, for example, we may read with a burden for the person we are counselling who believes this news is good, but too good to be true for her. Or someone may have said they are bringing along a friend who is intellectually suspicious of the faith. Or we may know there will be a person there who assumes the only argument required for heaven is their moral life-style and their good deeds. In the serendipity of the Spirit of Acts this may be the appointed moment for any, and we can begin 'with that very passage of Scripture' to tell them the good news about Jesus (Acts 8:35).

Not every sermon is evangelistic, in the sense that its whole design and purpose is to bring people to faith. But no sermon should be gospel-less. Perhaps we should always speak so that a one-off visitor would hear there was good news for them. And that kind of preaching will take a certain kind of reading.

8. Pastoral Reading

Scripture is formative as well as normative. So reading needs to be pastoral and ethical. This heading and the next one focus on the issue of application, in complementary ways. We read as those who are charged to bring the Word to bear on people's lives, for their spiritual formation. Pastoral reading engages the text with human hurt in mind.

Pastoral reading is marked, first, by *knowledge of people*. Readers of texts have to become readers of people as well! Any preacher should be involved in a network of pastoral relationships, and we find through experience that there is an intimate connection between daily care of people and weekly exposition of Scripture. In some ways, therefore, when we study for preaching we are to be vicarious readers. We ask God for empathy, so that we might hear how Scripture speaks to the needs of those in front of us.

One of the things we do in class is brainstorm about the kinds of people and the sorts of problems which might be represented on a Sunday morning. Some students may have thought about congregations in very general terms, as rather amorphous blobs to which a message will be tossed. But this simple exercise makes a class realise how they can come up with a host of situations and needs, in less than sixty seconds. So hearers may be spiritually dry, or backslidden, or guilty about a specific sin, or struggling with temptation, or having doubts about their faith, or resentful and angry, or depressed, or having problems in their marriage, or worried about their teenage children, or struggling with singleness, or anxious about their health, or facing the problems of old age, or bereaved and alone, or exhausted in caring for others, or struggling financially, or experiencing tensions at work, or looking for work, and so on. And this is without beginning to consider those who might be doing well, and who need help too!

Without getting into the specifics of any of these problems, I simply wish to remind myself that I should read with an awareness of people's real needs. It means especially that I should hear their cries as I read, and be ready to bring counsel, wisdom, comfort, encouragement and strength from God's Word, into a variety of different situations.

Pastoral reading is marked, secondly, by *love for people*, without which all the knowledge in the world is useless: '...and can fathom all mysteries and all knowledge ... but have not love, I am nothing' (1 Cor. 13:2). Paul's own ministry demonstrated his loving commitment to those under his care. Perhaps most vividly, when talking about his time among the Thessalonians, he compared himself to a nursing mother caring for her little children (1 Thess. 2:7). This pastoral apostle loved them, he felt bereaved when he was torn away from them, and he continued to pray for them.

One of the most important ways of loving people is to pray for them. There is a wonderful link between pastoral prayer and our reading of Scripture. Again and again pastors will find that moving from study of a passage to a time of prayer for specific people, and perhaps back to the passage and then back to prayer, sparks off all kinds of new connections between the passage we are thinking about and the people we are praying for. The textbooks on hermeneutics do not mention it. We only need to try it, to see the miracle happen.

9. Ethical Reading

We continue the theme of application, but with the focus now more on the challenges of the Word.

We need a hermeneutic to know how to live. This is nowhere better illustrated than in *The Year of Living Biblically*, where A. J. Jacobs tries to follow the Bible's commands as literally as he can for one whole year.[37] I am not recommending you buy the book. It is often ridiculous

---

[37] A J Jacobs (2009), *The Year of Living Biblically*, Arrow Books.

and sometimes irreverent. But it does demonstrate that Scripture cannot be lived out without an appropriate hermeneutic. Just to put random commands into practice leads to goofiness, not to godliness.

Ethical reading means, first, that we *translate biblical principles*.[38] The gap between the first and twenty-first centuries is a wide one. Whenever I travel to London (usually just to attend the Proclamation Trust's excellent conferences[39]) and I ride the Underground, I remember to 'Mind the gap!' And so we should in our reading, remembering we are embedded in one world as we try to hear a word from another. There are lots of possible issues here but let me just touch on one obvious area. We have New Testament commands which we cannot apply directly today because the situation no longer exists for us, on issues like eating meat offered to idols or ordering slaves to be obedient to their masters. But we are often able to make progress through the time-honoured route of determining the original meaning and application, discovering the theological truths or principles being taught, and then finding appropriate applications for that cross-cultural principle in today's world. As Duvall and Hays put it, simply and neatly, we have to 'Grasp the text in their town' and then 'Grasp the text in our town.'[40] We translate the principle and see it moving into our neighbourhood.

Secondly, ethical reading will mean that we *follow biblical examples*. Earlier I affirmed the importance of preaching Christ from all the Scriptures, but I have never been comfortable with the way that advocates of this approach often seem to regard 'exemplary preaching' as a betrayal. A better way has recently been advocated by Jason Hood who wants us to be Christ-centred in our interpretation and also to follow Scripture's own lead in honouring moral examples.[41] It is simply being true to Scripture's self-interpretation to do both things. I also want to honour the tradition of ethical reading in the history of the best Christian preaching, in men like John Chrysostom and John Calvin, to name but two giants. Today the approach of narrative ethics

---

[38] On the general topic of the translation of Christianity into different cultures in history, see Andrew F Walls (1996), *The Missionary Movement in Christian History: Studies in the Transmission of Faith*, T&T Clark.

[39] www.proctrust.org.uk.

[40] J Scott Duvall and J Daniel Hays (2001), *Grasping God's Word: A Hands-On Approach to Reading, Interpreting, and Applying the Bible*, Zondervan, 204.

[41] Jason Hood (2009), 'Christ-Centred Interpretation Only?: Moral Instruction from Scripture's Self-Interpretation as Caveat and Guide', in *Scottish Bulletin of Evangelical Theology*, 27:1, 50-69.

is also bearing fruit in the academy. The supreme narrative ethic, of course, is the example and imitation of Christ.

Thirdly, it means that we *confront biblical surprises*. There are so many different readings in hermeneutics today, from feminist (with all its schools) to post-colonial, and from readings of colour to those of ecology. I am critical of the hegemony of the reader in many of these, and I am also concerned that many scholars approach the text with a hermeneutic of suspicion rather than one of trust. They stand over the Word, which is by definition not the way to under-stand. But I do not wish to deny that they may sometimes challenge us where our pre-understandings make us prejudiced, especially when they come from the wider global church and from cultures very different from our own. So we need to be open to learn from readings that might give us new ways of seeing what the Bible is saying. At its most obvious, no-one will deny that women see things that men don't see, and the poor see things that the rich don't see.[42]

And fourthly, it means that we *encourage biblical performance*. Various scholars writing about hermeneutics in recent years have advocated a performance model.[43] In this, the Scriptures are held to be like musical scores or dramatic scripts. These are adequately interpreted only in actually being performed, and they can also be truly interpreted in rather different performances. Now I recognise the dangers of the analogy, but the responsibility to interpret and play the part for myself is surely right. We encourage interpretation which is practical and personal.

10. Liturgical Reading

All of our reading should move towards worship. This is consonant with the whole movement of Scripture's story, enriching the worship of God's people and then bringing them at last to worship in the presence of God forever. While I do not endorse his personal theological journey, Scott Hahn is right to conclude: 'Our liturgical reading of the canonical text reveals a clear liturgical *trajectory* and *teleology*.'[44] I want to note two things which link the themes of reading and worship.

---

[42] For an example nearer home of how an evangelical scholar finds new things in texts when asking them fresh questions, see Richard Bauckham (1989), *The Bible in Politics: How to Read the Bible Politically*, SPCK.

[43] Significant in this, but with a very different doctrine of Scripture from mine: Frances Young (1990), *The Art of Performance: Towards a Theology of Holy Scripture*, Darton, Longman & Todd.

[44] Scott W Hahn (2006), 'Canon, Cult and Covenant: The Promise of Liturgical Hermeneutics', in *Canon and Biblical Interpretation* (ed. Craig Bartholomew et al), Paternoster, 225.

First, we read *for worship*. In all of our reading of Scripture in preparation for preaching, we remember that we are preparing for a liturgy, where a community will engage in the worship of God. Our preaching will be a key component of that. Thus we must think both about how the message will feed people's worship, and also about how the rest of the liturgy will support and forward the message.

For preachers in the reformed tradition, the sermon is at the heart of worship. This has seldom been expressed more strongly than by Hughes Oliphant Old:

> The preaching and the hearing of the Word of God is in the last analysis worship, worship in its most profound sense. Preaching is not an auxiliary activity to worship, nor is it some kind of preparation for worship which one hopes will follow ... the proclaiming of the Word of God, simply in itself, is high service to God. The solemn reading and preaching of Scripture in the midst of the congregation is a cultic act.... The reading and preaching of Scripture is worship of an even greater intensity, an even greater depth, and an even greater magnificence than were ever the sacrifices of the Temple.[45]

We read so that we might preach, and we preach so that people might worship.[46] The coming worship service should always give a trajectory to our reading.

Secondly, we read *as worship*. It is not just that we study the Scriptures with a view to a worship event on the Lord's Day, but also that we see our own exegetical labour as an act of personal worship. We read and we prepare as those who want to give their best, and who eventually lay this prepared message on the altar as an offering to God. And we preach it in the same attitude of worship, asking the Lord to receive it and to use it for his own glory. But even our very best is spoiled by our sin and far short of what he deserves. Therefore we rejoice in the wonderful comfort that we have a great high priest. He alone can take what we offer and make it acceptable before the throne of God.

May our priest grant us mercy and grace to help us every time we read, and as he gives us good things may we not forget to

---

[45] Hughes Oliphant Old (1998), *The Reading and Preaching of the Scriptures in the Worship of the Christian Church, Volume 1: The Biblical Period*, Eerdmans, 189.

[46] On 'worshipful' preaching see John Piper (1995), 'Preaching as Worship: Meditations on Expository Exultation', in *Trinity Journal*, 16NS:1, 29-45.

share these with others, 'for with such sacrifices God is pleased' (Heb. 4:14-16;13:15-16).

In Conclusion

I hope that these ten perspectives on reading may help to remind us of some of the key moves we need to make. Some will already do all of these things and more, and will perhaps read at several of these levels simultaneously. If so, I am jealous of you (it is a righteous kind of jealousy).

The antitheses of the ten certainly help us see what is to be avoided: namely, being a reader who does not approach the sacred text with humility, who does not apply the passage to himself, who does not try to exegete it faithfully, who does not see what other biblical passages have to say, who does not reflect on what theology has to say, who does not think or speak as if he lived in this century, who does not include any gospel, who does not offer pastoral comfort, who does not offer ethical challenge, and who takes no account of the sermon's context in worship. May these ten words drive us to our knees!

Our interpretation must be done in an attitude of prayer. We might even reinforce this by sometimes reading and rereading the passage for study in an actual posture of prayer (arthritic joints allowing). Early in his Christian life, George Whitefield wrote in his journal:

> I began to read the Holy Scriptures upon my knees, laying aside all other books, and praying over, if possible, every line and word. This proved meat indeed and drink indeed to my soul. I daily received fresh life, light and power from above.[47]

The relationship between prayer and hermeneutics is an interesting topic, and in some respects one that has not been sufficiently explored. But it is not difficult to find theologians bearing testimony to the essential link between the two. Take John Owen for one. For Owen, personal piety is crucial in the task of interpretation, and the primary spiritual discipline is that of prayer, specifically '*fervent and earnest prayer* for the assistance of the Spirit of God revealing the mind of God.'[48] Or take Karl Barth as another witness. Recently Mark

---

[47] Quoted in John Stott (1984, revised edition), *Understanding the Bible*, Scripture Union, 168.
[48] Carl Trueman (1997), 'Faith Seeking Understanding: Some Neglected Aspects of John Owen's Understanding of Scriptural Interpretation', in *Interpreting the Bible* (ed. A N S Lane), Apollos, 153.

Gignilliat has argued that for Barth the hermeneutical posture for a theological exegete of Scripture is one of prayer. When Barth says that the theological task is *Ora et Labora*, he is not saying that prayer is the first in a series of steps, as either a preliminary to work or as itself the first work. According to Gignilliat, Barth sees all the *Laborare* as *Orare*, so that the whole task is one of prayer and all exegesis is to be done *coram Deo*.[49]

So may God grant each of us the spirit and practice of prayer, to ask for and to receive the wisdom we need in each interpretative task. 'If any of you lacks wisdom, he should ask God, who gives generously to all without finding fault, and it will be given to him' (James 1:5). That is such a reassuring promise, not least for the preacher as reader of Scripture.

---

[49] Mark Gignilliat (2009), '*Ora et Labora*: Barth's Forgotten Hermeneutical Principle', *The Expository Times* 120:6, 277-281.

14

Leadership in the Church

Donald M MacDonald

Leadership is a subject which has attracted a great deal of attention in recent years, both in secular circles and in the church. Indeed there has been a cross-fertilisation between the two realms. While secular writers on leadership have begun to use religious concepts such as spirituality, pastoral care and servant leadership, Christians have looked to the world of business management and human resources for insights into leadership. This may lead to the church operating like a business corporation, the minister like a Chief Executive Officer and the elders or deacons like a Board of Management.

Banks and Ledbetter credit Robert Greenleaf, the American expert on leadership in business who was of Quaker background, with introducing the concept of servant leadership into the world of business.[1] He was the founder of the Greenleaf Center for Servant Leadership in Indiana, USA, and he published a seminal essay on 'The Servant as Leader' in 1970. Leadership should not be confused with management. Whereas management is concerned with the efficient running of a complex organisation and is largely responsive, leadership is concerned with overall vision and is largely proactive.[2] Of course both

---

[1] Banks, Robert and Ledbetter, Bernice M. (2004), *Reviewing Leadership: A Christian Evaluation of Current Approaches*, Grand Rapids: Baker Academic, 34, 108.

[2] Ibid., 17-20.

are necessary and it would be foolish to polarise priorities between the two. We need efficient management, but most of all we need visionary, spiritual and theologically informed leadership.

Leadership may be defined in various ways. At its simplest it is a relationship of influence, in which one person influences another person or a group to bring about change towards the achievement of certain agreed aims.[3] This may be done formally, as when someone is appointed as leader of a group, or informally, as people exert influence on others in their daily lives.

Leadership in the church is primarily spiritual and theological in the sense that it is modelled on the pattern of leadership laid down in Scripture by the Head of the church, the Lord Jesus Christ. While we may learn much about the practicalities of leadership from studying great leaders in history and from modern research, the nature of leadership, its spirit and the character of those who would be leaders in the church are of first importance and for these we must turn to the Bible.

In the past Reformed writers on church government have concentrated on church power and the officers of the church who are to exercise this power as leaders in the church (see, for example, John Calvin[4], John Owen[5] and James Bannerman[6]). The discussion has usually been about what offices are laid down in Scripture for the church, what qualifications are needed for officers, how they are ordained to office and what duties they are to perform. It was taken for granted that the church required leaders who would fill certain offices prescribed in the Bible.

More recently the whole concept of office and ordination has been questioned as being foreign to the New Testament.[7] The concern seems to be to guard against the abuse of these concepts, as happened in the past, leading to an unscriptural elevation of the 'clergy' as an order above the 'laity' and an unhelpful portrayal of ordination as a sacrament which confers grace through the church. However, if

---

[3] Wright, Walter, C., Jr. (2002), *Relational Leadership*, Carlisle: Paternoster Press, 2.

[4] Calvin, John (1960), *Institutes of the Christian Religion*, Philadelphia: The Westminster Press, Battles Edition, IV, iii-iv.

[5] Owen, John (rpt. 1968), *The Works of John Owen, Vol. 16, The Church and the Bible*, Edinburgh: The Banner of Truth Trust, 42-151.

[6] Bannerman, James (1868), *The Church of Christ*, Vol. 2, Edinburgh: T. & T. Clark, 201-95.

[7] Tidball, Derek (2008), *Ministry by the Book: New Testament Patterns for Pastoral Leadership*, Nottingham: IVP Apollos, 94, 98, 143, 153-54.

office is understood as a duty of service and ordination as the official recognition of the grace and gifts of God by the church, conferring the authority and concomitant accountability of leadership in the name of Christ and under the authority of the Scriptures, I fail to see why they are not in accord with the New Testament.

Rather than deal with the question of the organisational structure of the church, I will look at the concept of leadership as it is found in the New Testament and then draw some lessons for today. While leadership may be exercised at many different levels and in various activities and situations, I am particularly concerned with the leadership exercised by ministers and elders.

The language of leadership

The first thing to notice is that the language used to describe leaders of the church in the New Testament differs in some significant ways from that used in the Greek and Roman world of the time. For instance, Greek words beginning with *arch* (indicating rule) are not used to describe Christian leaders, except for Paul's figurative use of the term master builder (*architechtōn*) to describe how he laid the foundation of sound doctrine for the church in 1 Corinthians 3:10.[8] It would be wrong, however, to conclude that the New Testament is not interested in leadership and that the church is envisaged as an entirely egalitarian body directly dependent on the Holy Spirit for leadership. Despite the absence of a hierarchy, there is much evidence to show that leadership is prescribed and regulated in the New Testament.

For example, Paul urges the Thessalonians to 'respect those who work hard among you, who are over (*proistamenous*) you in the Lord and who admonish you' (1 Thess. 5:12). He uses a word widely used in secular Greek for leadership in the army, the state and in society with the connotation of up-front leadership which is also responsible for individual protection and care.[9] The writer to the Hebrews uses the word *hēgoumenoi* (a general word for leaders in the secular world of the day) to refer to teachers in the church and exhorts believers to obey them, imitate them and submit to their authority (Heb. 13:7, 17, 24).[10] The New Testament uses many of the words for leaders in

---

[8] Bennett, David W. (1993), *Biblical Images for Leaders and Followers,* Oxford: Regnum Lynx, 145.

[9] Ibid., 151.

[10] Ibid., 147.

common use at the time, but in each case the context shows how different they were to be from current patterns of leadership. It is not, of course, the words in themselves, their etymology or secular usage, that determine the nature of leadership, but their usage in a particular context seen in the total context of Biblical teaching on the subject.

Both in the Gospels and in the Epistles the emphasis is on calling, character and service rather than on status and power, and leaders in the church are contrasted with those of the world. For instance, Jesus said to the disciples, who were arguing about which of them was the greatest, 'The kings of the Gentiles lord it over them;… but you are not to be like that. Instead the greatest among you should be like the youngest, and the one who rules (*hēgoumenos*) like the one who serves' (Luke 22:25-26). Peter's words to the elders echo this: 'Be shepherds of God's flock that is under your care, serving as overseers, … eager to serve; not lording it over those entrusted to you, but being examples to the flock' (1 Pet. 5:2-3).

It is clear from these verses that Jesus intended that there should be those who had the responsibility to lead and rule in the church, but he stressed that their rule was to be of a different character from that of the world. It is this peculiar character of Christian leadership that I would like to explore.

Leadership in the Gospels

The four canonical Gospels have much to teach us about leadership, both from their accounts of the way Jesus led the disciples and from their record of his teaching. Jesus has fascinated many people over the ages. In a recent book John Adair, who served as a professional soldier and then as the world's first Professor of Leadership Studies at Surrey University, provides an interesting study of Jesus as a leader.[11] While some of his views are far from orthodox theologically (for example he doubts the authenticity of some of the accounts in the canonical Gospels and draws on the apocryphal gospels), he finds Jesus to be an exemplary leader. In particular he stresses the vision of Jesus (the kingdom of God) and his ability to communicate that vision in order to set the task for his followers, his team-building skills and his attention to individuals – the three important strands in effective leadership of a group.[12]

---

[11] Adair, John (2001), *The Leadership of Jesus and its Legacy Today*, Canterbury Press.
[12] Ibid., 119.

The figure of Jesus dominates the four Gospels. While the Evangelists present Jesus and his mission each in his own individual way, we can see certain themes in common. Jesus was determined to complete the work given to him by the Father, to do his Father's will. His vision never faltered as he progressed through his ministry, his betrayal, his trial, his sufferings and his death. He came proclaiming the kingdom or rule of God and he lived out the reality of that kingdom in his authoritative teaching, his miraculous acts of power and tender compassion, and his firm and unrelenting resistance to the powers of evil. His calling, training and commissioning of his disciples form a large part of the narrative and in these he demonstrates his skill in knowing human nature and dealing with them both as individuals and as a group. Above all it is his loving, self-denying service at great personal cost which sets the gold standard for leadership.

Jesus had the Holy Spirit 'without limit' (John 3:34). He delighted to do the Father's will and was constantly in conscious communion with the Father, except for that period of dereliction on the cross as he was made sin for us. This alerts us to the Trinitarian dimension of Christian leadership. Christian leaders must have a deepening relationship with God the Father through Jesus Christ the Son and rely on the indwelling Holy Spirit to empower and enable them for the heavy responsibility of leadership.

The first leaders of the church were the twelve disciples, also designated apostles (Luke 6:13). They were chosen by Jesus, deliberately and after prayer, to be with him and learn from him and then be sent out in his name to continue his work. They were, as Acts 4:13 tells us, 'unschooled, ordinary men', but 'they had been with Jesus' for about three and a half years and that made all the difference, especially after Pentecost when the Holy Spirit was poured out. The emphasis throughout the Gospels is not on the Twelve as leaders, but as followers. They had to be taught before they became teachers, to become disciples before they made disciples of others, to follow before they became leaders. That is still the first requirement for Christian leaders and it is a life-long process. During their training they were sent out 'to preach the kingdom of God and heal the sick' (Luke 9:1-2) – a pattern of word and action which Paul followed (Rom. 15:18) and which is still essential to the church's witness. Later Jesus sent out the seventy-two (Luke 10:1), showing that the work of witness and service in his kingdom was not to be confined to its leaders.

Disciples

Disciple (*mathētēs*) is one of the most characteristic designations for the followers of Jesus in the New Testament. In the Gospels it is often paired with teacher (*didaskalos*).[13] Jesus was the Teacher and, unlike the rabbis of his day, chose his disciples so that they might literally follow him, be with him, learn of him and become like him. Although his call to 'follow me' went out to many, not all were ready to respond. While the Twelve left everything and followed him, others, such as the Rich Young Ruler, were unwilling to give up what was most precious to them. John 6:66 records that, on hearing Jesus' puzzling teaching about his giving his flesh and blood as food and drink, 'many of his disciples turned back and no longer followed him.' Jesus then challenged the Twelve as to whether they too would go away and this elicited from Peter that great declaration of faith recorded in John 6:68-69. Jesus immediately told them that even among the chosen Twelve there was 'a devil'. This, of course, was Judas Iscariot, who later betrayed him.

This highlights the fact that the disciples were not conscripts who unwillingly followed a mesmerising, manipulative, tyrannical leader, but those who willingly followed a leader who had the spiritual power to attract and to change them without violating their wills or personalities. This is an important model for Christian leaders to follow. They are not to rely on force of personality, psychological technique or pulling of rank but rather to point people to the Lord Jesus by their teaching and example in reliance on the Holy Spirit. As well as the Twelve, there was an outer circle of disciples, both men and women, who followed him, perhaps on a more 'part-time' basis, so that on the Day of Pentecost there were 120 men and women gathered in the upper room, all of whom partook of the outpouring of the Holy Spirit.

Servants

Another term that Jesus often uses for his disciples is servant. The two main Greek words here are *doulos*, which literally means slave, and *diakonos,* a word originally denoting table-service. The former, along with its cognate, *douleuein* (to serve), emphasises the complete obedience and allegiance due to God as Master and Lord, while the latter and its cognates, *diakonein* (to serve) and *diakonia* (service or ministry) emphasise the humble, self-denying service due to others.[14]

---

[13] Bennett, *Biblical Images*, 37.

In many of the parables of the kingdom, the disciples are likened to servants who are accountable to a king or master and the utmost loyalty and hard work are expected of them, with the promise of a reward for faithful service.

The use of the word *ergatēs,* worker, stresses the task to be done at the command of the master, as in Matthew 9:37-38, where Jesus instructs the disciples to pray that the Lord would send out workers into the ripe harvest field.[15] The same word is used for the workers in the parable of the vineyard in Matthew 20:1-16, where the emphasis is on the sovereign generosity of the master and the duty and responsibility of the workers to heed the call to labour and to give their utmost effort. In John 18:36 Jesus tells Pilate that his kingdom is not of this world, otherwise his servants would fight to defend him. The word he uses, *huperētēs,* is generally used in the New Testament for officers who carried out the orders of superiors.[16] This shows how different is his kingdom and the behaviour of his servants from the kingdoms of the world and their officials.

Jesus set the pattern for service. Again and again he had to rebuke the disciples for arguing about status and he held out his own example as one who came 'not to be served, but to serve, and to give his life as a ransom for many' (Mark 10:45). Here we have the true spirit of servanthood allied to the inevitability of suffering. The servant is not greater than his master, and thus faithful service of Christ would involve suffering and persecution (Matt. 10:24-25, John 15:20). However, in the same way that Jesus' humiliation and death resulted in resurrection, ascension and glory, the loving, faithful service of the disciples will be honoured by the Father (John 12:26). This is a great encouragement for those who take up the costly burden of leadership.

Friends and family members
The designation of the disciples as servants is supplemented by other, more relational, terms. In Luke 12:4 he addresses the Twelve as his friends and in John 15:14-15 he tells them that he will no longer call them servants but friends (*philoi*). This denotes the intimate, trusting relationship they had developed. It did not do away with the authority of Jesus as Lord: 'You are my friends if you do what I command.' His

---

[14] Ibid., 25.
[15] Ibid., 30.
[16] Ibid., 36.

command was that they should love one another as he loved them – the supreme standard for love – and their love was to be shown in their obedience. This transformed the master-servant relationship into something unique, as well as emphasising the loving attitude that should characterise fellow workers and leaders in God's kingdom.

Jesus uses many other terms for the disciples indicating close relationship, even family ties. For instance, they were to be brothers, pointing to the equality that existed between them, despite the obvious prominence that some enjoyed, such as Peter, James and John. In Matthew 23:8 Jesus says, 'You are not to be called "Rabbi", for you have only one Master and you are all brothers.' He often uses the term *brother* when he is dealing with interpersonal tensions[17] and the need for forgiveness and reconciliation, while at the same time stressing the need for discipline of an unrepentant brother (Matt.18:15-17). To show that the bond between his disciples and himself transcended even the close ties of kinship he said, 'Whoever does the will of my Father in heaven is my brother and sister and mother' (Matt. 12:50). Jesus also calls them sons of God (Matt. 5:45), refers to them as little children (Luke 10:21) and commends a child-like attitude of trust and humility (Luke 18:17). The emphasis on brotherly love is continued in the epistles and stresses for us the importance of Christian leaders maintaining the family relationship of brothers and sisters among themselves as well as with those whom they lead.

Jesus specifically forbids his disciples to 'call anyone on earth "father", for you have one Father and he is in heaven' (Matt 23:9). How then can the apostle Paul appeal to the Corinthian church to heed his authority because '… in Christ Jesus I became your father through the gospel' (1 Cor. 4:15)? It is clear that he is alluding to his role in bringing them the gospel as a means of their conversion. The emphasis is on Christ and the gospel and Paul did not expect the Corinthians to go on being dependent on him as a father figure. Indeed he specifically repudiates the party spirit which claimed human leaders as the focus of allegiance and addresses them as brothers (1 Cor. 1:11-17). The role of the father is to prepare children for maturity, not to perpetuate an immature dependency on himself. Paul also uses the figure of the nursing mother to describe his relationship with the Thessalonian church (1 Thess. 2:7) and this reminds us of Jesus' longing to gather the people of Jerusalem as a mother hen gathers her chicks under her wings.

<hr>

[17] Ibid., 17.

The parental imagery certainly implies authority, but the main emphasis is on the tender, compassionate, self-sacrificing care which protects, instructs (by precept and example) and prepares for maturity. There is no place for paternalism, the unhealthy prolonging of dependence on a domineering, though supposedly benevolent, father figure.

Shepherds and sheep

A figure which stresses the vulnerability and defencelessness of the disciples is that of sheep (*probaton*). Jesus sent the Twelve out 'like sheep among wolves' (Matt. 10:16). This is complemented by the figure of Jesus as the Good Shepherd (*poimēn*). The disciples are referred to as sheep much more often than as shepherds in the Gospels, but Jesus does instruct Peter, as a representative of the others, to 'feed my lambs, … feed my sheep' (John 21:15-17), using terms related to the work of a shepherd in caring for and pasturing sheep. It is important to notice that the sheep are Christ's, not Peter's, indicating that pastors do not have ownership of the flock, the Lord Jesus does, and they are accountable to him, the Chief Shepherd. In Matthew 10:6 Jesus sends out the Twelve to 'the lost sheep of the house of Israel'. Although they are not specifically called shepherds here, this echoes his saying that he had come to seek and to save the lost and also his parable of the lost sheep. This designation of shepherd or pastor was taken up later by the church for its leaders (Eph. 4:11).

The example of the Good Shepherd (John 10:1-21) is therefore highly relevant for the work of church leaders.[18] Jesus draws on the rich shepherd imagery of the Old Testament. As Tidball comments, Ezekiel 34:15-16 summarises the work of the Divine Shepherd, fulfilled in the ministry of the Lord Jesus and to be imitated by his followers:

> Not only is he to feed, guide and protect the flock but also to understand that there are individual sheep to which he must give special attention. The lost must be found, the wandering restored, the injured tended, the weak strengthened and the strong disciplined.[19]

The costliness and dangers of the life of the shepherd are also highlighted. Leadership in the church is to be pastoral, and this includes evangelism and discipline as well as what we usually regard

---

[18] Tidball, *Ministry by the Book*, 80-84.
[19] Ibid., 81.

as pastoral work in caring for the weak, the immature, the suffering and the wayward. In Ezekiel 34 God passes judgement on his people as well as on their leaders, their shepherds. There was injustice, cruelty and lack of care among the sheep as well as the shepherds (vv. 17-21)! This shows that the pastoral attitude was not to be confined to the leaders, but were expected of all God's people in their dealings with one another.

Scribes

Derek Tidball notes that a somewhat neglected model for the disciples is found in Matthew's Gospel – the scribe (*grammateus,* teacher).[20] He points out that this term usually has negative associations in the synoptic Gospels. The scribes, or 'teachers of the law', of Jesus' day were influential in society as custodians and interpreters of the Law of Moses. They arose as a class in the time of the monarchy as secretaries and recorders of history (1 Kings 4:3). Baruch, the scribe, wrote down the words of Jeremiah the prophet (Jer. 36:4). During the exile, the scribes became important as guardians of the Law. Ezra the scribe 'devoted himself to the study and observance of the Law of the Lord, and to teaching its decrees and laws to Israel' (Ezra 7:10).

In the Gospels they are usually mentioned along with the Pharisees, sometimes with the priests and sometimes by themselves. By this time they were far more than secretaries, recorders or copyists. They were experts in the interpretation of the law and the traditions and had high social status. However the synoptic Gospels present them in a negative light and Jesus' words about them are scathing. For instance, in Matthew 23 he condemns them, along with the Pharisees, as hypocrites and legalists who neither understood nor obeyed the Law and who were therefore 'blind guides'. He pronounces a series of 'woes' on them. In verse 34 he goes on to tell them, 'Therefore I am sending you prophets and wise men (*sophous*) and teachers (*grammateis*).'

Earlier, after asking the disciples if they have understood the parables of the Kingdom he had just told, Jesus said, 'Therefore every teacher of the law (*grammateus*) who has been instructed about the kingdom of heaven is like the owner of a house who brings out of his storeroom new treasures as well as old' (Matt. 13:52). Jesus was thus indicating that his disciples, having been instructed in the mysteries of the kingdom of God, were to be the equivalent of the prophets, wise

[20] Ibid., 25.

men and scribes for the new covenant gospel era. They would have a true spiritual understanding of the Scriptures and be recipients of fresh revelation which they would apply to life.

Tidball summarises the characteristics of true scribes: they are people of understanding and they are people of authority.[21] The understanding of the true scribe is a spiritual insight, divinely given, so that they can appreciate and then pass on the true meaning and application of the teaching of Jesus such as his exposition of the Law in the Sermon on the Mount. Their authority rests not on the tradition of the fathers but on their allegiance and conformity to the Holy Scriptures.

Thus church leaders should be earnest and expert students of the Bible, applying it in their own lives as well as teaching it authoritatively and pastorally to God's people. Tidball lists the temptations that the scribes of Jesus' day succumbed to and which church leaders must guard against today: ostentation, authoritarianism, fanaticism, casuistry, legalism, hypocrisy, professionalism and inconsistency.[22] Jesus condemns all of these in Matthew 23.

Witnesses

Towards the end of his earthly ministry Jesus informed the disciples that they were to be his witnesses (Luke 24:48; Acts 1:8). David Bennett summarises the significance of this term on its various appearances in the Gospels: 'The image of the "witness" [martus] is associated by Jesus with first hand experience, public proclamation, worldwide ministry, and the suffering of persecution.'[23] Indeed so common was the death of faithful witnesses to become that we get our English word martyr from the Greek martus. This is a powerful reminder to Christian leaders that faithful witnessing to personal experience of the truth of the gospel is demanding and costly.

Stewards

A figure which Jesus uses only once in direct relation to the disciples is that of the manager or steward (oikonomos). In Luke 12:42, addressing the disciples on the need to be ready for his coming, he says, 'Who then is the faithful and wise manager, whom the master puts in charge of his servants to give them their food allowance at the proper time?' The

---

[21] Ibid., 26-28.
[22] Ibid., 36.
[23] Bennett, Biblical Images, 41.

manager or steward was an important servant, often a slave, in a large household or estate. He had authority over others, but was himself under authority and was held accountable to the master or owner for fulfilling his responsibilities. This is taken up by both Paul and Peter. Paul refers to himself as a 'steward of the mysteries of God' (1 Cor.4:1-2, KJV) and calls on overseers to be 'blameless, as stewards of God' (Titus 1:7, KJV). Peter calls on all believers to use the gifts they have received to minister to one another, 'as good stewards of the manifold grace of God' (1 Peter 4:10, KJV). We are all called to serve, we are all stewards. The particular form our service takes will depend on the gifts and calling of God. The leaders of the church have a responsibility to encourage all members to exercise their gifts, to provide opportunities for them to do so and to recognise and appreciate their contribution. Not that official sanction is necessary, but often people tend to be passive and prefer to be ministered to rather than engage in service themselves.

In summary we may say that the Gospels present various themes that illuminate the subject of leadership in the church.[24] Church leaders are called to be followers, to be identified with Christ and his mission, to serve him wholeheartedly, whatever the cost in personal suffering. They are called to love and serve one another and the church, the flock, which Christ has redeemed at such a great cost. Their leadership is to be modelled on the leadership of Christ. They exercise authority only because they derive their authority from him. His word, illuminated by the Holy Spirit, is their guide. They are all equals, though there are differences of gifts and therefore of responsibilities. They are responsible to maintain relationships within the family of God, while at the same time carrying out the task of making disciples of all nations.

As Bennett points out, maintaining the balance between attention to relationships with people and carrying out a task is often a point of tension for leaders. If leaders are too focused on the task of the mission of the church, they may neglect attention to individuals and to group relationships. Conversely, the people-focused leader may find it difficult to maintain momentum towards accomplishing the task. Leaders are accountable to one another, but ultimately to God who will test each one's character and faithfulness and will allot appropriate rewards.

---

[24] Ibid., 61-64.

Leadership in the early church

With the word 'church' (*ekklēsia*) appearing twice on the lips of Jesus in the Gospels (Matt. 16:18, 18:17), it is the most common designation used for Christ's followers in the rest of the New Testament. As Bennett points out,[25] the word had long been used for the gathering of the citizens of the Greek city (*polis*) and was used in the Septuagint to translate *qahal,* the assembly of God's covenant people. Its usage for the believing community in the New Testament emphasises the fact that it is not a voluntary grouping of people, but one summoned by the call of God. It usually refers to particular assemblies of believers in a specific place or area, but is also used in a broader sense, as in 1 Corinthians 15:9 and Galatians 1:13, where Paul writes, 'I persecuted the church of God.' Paul also uses it in this wider sense when he speaks of Christ as the head of his body, the church (Eph 1:22; Col. 1:18) and of the church as the bride of Christ (Eph 5:23-32). Thus 'church' can apply to groups of believer in a local, regional or world-wide setting and also to the whole number of believers in time and eternity (Heb. 12:23). This unifying aspect of the church is stressed in the New Testament by the 'Council of Jerusalem' (Acts 15), the frequent travel and communication between churches and the material aid sent to the church in Jerusalem.

Several important aspects of the nature of the church impinge on the pattern of leadership appropriate for it. It is the church of God, not any human constituency, and the church is constituted by his call. Christ is the only head of the church, which is his body. All leadership is under his authority. Every member of his body has a function, though some are more prominent, more gifted, than others. The Holy Spirit distributes these gifts in a sovereign way and calls and equips for service. The church has to recognise and confirm the calling of its leaders. Church leaders have the responsibility of enabling the church to carry out its calling as God's worshiping, serving and witnessing people. This will involve maintaining regular corporate worship, including the preaching of the Word and administering the sacraments; discipleship and discipline; fellowship and mutual service; and bringing the gospel to unbelievers by word and action in order to make disciples of all nations. This latter aspect, the missionary or missional responsibility, is integral to the church's nature and not an add-on extra. Church leaders also have the

---

[25] Ibid., 101.

responsibility of encouraging and enabling all members of the church to grow to maturity and to use their gifts in the service of Christ.

Apostles

The Twelve were also called apostles or messengers (from *apostellō*, to send) and they were the foundational leaders of the Christian church. On the Day of Pentecost it was Peter who took the lead and he who was chosen by God to bring the gospel to Cornelius, the Roman centurion, to illustrate that the Gentiles were to be received on the same basis as Jews. The work of spreading the gospel, however, was not left to them alone. Philip and Stephen, members of the Seven, were powerful preachers and evangelists and the gospel was brought to the Gentile people of Antioch first by ordinary, unnamed believers.

As well as being normally used in the restricted sense of the Twelve plus Paul, who received a special call from the risen Christ on the Damascus Road, the term *apostle* was also applied to some of those associated with them: for example, Barnabas (Acts 14:4, 14) and Silas and Timothy (1 Thess. 1:1; 2:6-7). The function of the apostles in the strict sense was to bear witness to the risen Lord and maintain and pass on the doctrine of Christ. Jesus Christ was the foundation of the church and the apostles were the guardians of the foundational doctrine which they then passed on to those who came after them (Eph. 2:20). There is no hint that they were to be followed by a new generation of apostles in the strict sense of the term. The apostles' doctrine was their legacy. They were marked out by having seen the risen Lord (Acts 1:22, 1 Cor. 9:1), by planting new churches (1 Cor. 9:2), by suffering for Christ (1 Cor. 4:9-14) and by the performance of 'signs, wonders and miracles' (*dunamesin,* works of power) (2 Cor. 12:12).

While we do not have apostles in the church today, we may learn lessons about leadership from their example. Paul, about whom we know more than the other apostles, sets the pattern of Christ-centred, humble, courageous, resilient, self-denying, disciplined, theologically directed leadership. He was not afraid to stand alone, yet he delighted in working with others and rejoiced in their fellowship and help. He was not a loner, self-sufficient and aloof. He claimed apostolic authority, but also pled with people to heed his word rather than threaten or brow-beat them. His all-consuming passion was to make Christ known and to bring people to faith and then build them up in their faith and witness. As an apostle and church-planter, he had a deep commitment to the church, its growth, its unity, its purity and its perseverance. He used all the rich resources he possessed, both of his Jewish and Greek-speaking background, for this purpose. Leaders *today*, especially ministers of the word, should be familiar with the particular forms and expressions of unbelief that hold people captive today, so that they can communicate the gospel effectively and build up God's people for the glory of God.

Elders

When we look at the pattern of leadership which emerges from Acts and the Epistles, we see that the early leadership of the Twelve (in which Judas is replaced by Matthias) is very soon supplemented by the addition of the apostle Paul and James, the brother of the Lord. Indeed when the leaders meet in the 'Council of Jerusalem', they consist of 'the apostles and elders' (Acts 15:6) and James plays a leading part. The elders (*presbuteroi*) in the Jerusalem church had already been mentioned in Acts 11:30 as receiving the gifts from the church in Antioch. They are introduced without any explanation. Bennett suggests that this was because the church naturally followed the pattern familiar in the Jewish community, which was governed by elders – wise, mature, respected heads of households – reflecting Old Testament patterns. Members of the Sanhedrin were also called elders, 'though later a distinction was made between lay and priestly members.'[26] As the church grew and spread beyond the confines of Judea, elders were appointed in the new churches, for example by Paul and Barnabas (Acts 14:23). Paul summoned the elders of the church in Ephesus to give them his parting instructions (Acts 20:13-38) and he instructed Titus to appoint elders in Crete (Titus 1:5).

Overseers

The term 'overseer' (*episkopos*) is also used of church leaders and indeed is used interchangeably with 'elder' (Titus 1:5, 7). It was widely used in secular Greek to describe a deity watching over a city, the office of men who carried responsibility in the state, and in some religious communities.[27] In Paul's address to the Ephesian elders he charges them to 'keep watch over the flock over which the Holy Spirit has made you overseers (*episkopoi*)' and to 'be shepherds (*poimenein*) of

---

[26] Ibid., 149.
[27] Ibid., 147.

279

the church of God' (Acts 20:28).[28] As Bennett points out, these three terms, elders, overseers and pastors, refer to the same group of people in the New Testament church. The terms elders and overseers usually occur in the plural, indicating a plurality of equals in the leadership of the local church. The term overseer is used in the singular in 1 Timothy 3:2 and Titus 1:7 and this has led some to see the overseers as having a supervisory capacity over the other elders in a particular vicinity. However, the use of the singular may be merely stylistic, or to particularise the reference to personal qualities.[29]

In 1 Timothy 5:17 Paul instructs Timothy that the elders who rule (*proestōtes*, from *proistēmi*, a general word for to rule or to lead) well should be given double honour, especially those whose work is preaching (literally, the word) and teaching. This shows that, while all elders are to be 'able to teach' (1 Tim. 3:2), some of them have the special responsibility of preaching and teaching the Word of God. Verse 18 clarifies that the honour refers to payment for work done, indicating that some elders gave themselves full-time to serve the church, especially as preachers and teachers, and thus had the right to financial support from the church.

Peter, addressing the elders in 1 Peter 5:1-4, appeals to them as a fellow elder (*sumpresbuteros*) to shepherd (*poimanete*) God's flock, acting as overseers (*episkopountes*) willingly, not out of greed for money. Here again the three terms, elders, overseers and shepherds, are applied to the same men and a solemn warning is given about one of their serious temptations. The apostle speaks as a brother and fellow-elder, thus exemplifying the style of leadership commended by Christ.

The apostle John in his second and third epistles introduces himself as 'the elder'. This is noteworthy as the only use of the word in the singular. Several explanations have been offered,[30] the simplest and most likely being that John was writing to people who knew him as an elder in their church and who would recognise his individual style of writing.

Pastors and teachers
In Ephesians 4:11, Paul writes that the ascended Christ 'gave some to be apostles, some to be prophets, some to be evangelists, and some to

---

[28] Ibid., 147.
[29] See Tidball, *Ministry by the Book,* 155 and the commentaries for a fuller discussion.
[30] Ibid., 198.

be pastors and teachers (*didaskaloi*)...' for preparing God's people for service and for the unity, growth to maturity and stability of all believers, both individually and corporately. It may well be that pastors and teachers refer to the same people because both words have the same article. Pastoral care and teaching ministry are closely related. Pastoral care is to be carried out under the guidance of God's Word, while teaching is to be informed by pastoral care, applying God's word to the varying needs and situations of God's people. Although they are not called elders here, Paul's address to the elders in Acts 20 makes the connection clear.

Teachers and preachers

Paul twice refers to himself as a preacher or herald (*kērux*) of the gospel (1 Tim. 2:7; 2 Tim. 1:11). The herald delivers an important, authoritative message in public. The related word *kērugma* is often used for the message preached and the verb *kērussō* for the activity of preaching. Paul claimed that God had sent him to preach the gospel (*euangelizesthai*) (1 Cor. 1:17) and this he did constantly in public and in private, by proclamation and by more interactive means, as he did in Ephesus, debating in the hall of Tyrannus (Acts 19:9) and by teaching from house to house (Acts 20:20). It would be wrong to draw a firm distinction between preaching and teaching or between the message taught (*didachē*) and the message preached (*kērugma*). Paul travelled widely as he pursued his calling of making Christ known to people not yet reached, although he spent more time in such places as Corinth and Ephesus. These places then became centres from which the gospel was relayed by others to the surrounding areas, as happened in Thessalonica (1 Thess. 1:8).

The qualifications for overseers/elders are set forth in 1 Timothy 2:1-7 and Titus 1:5-9. They stress the need for godly character, conduct and reputation as well as knowledge of the truth. The method of appointment of elders is not spelled out in the New Testament, but it appears from the little data we do have that the initiative was taken by those who were already leaders, such as the apostles and their representatives, and the local believers would have been consulted as to reputation and character and their approval and agreement sought.

Not much is said about their preparation or training. However, from the example of Jesus' training of the Twelve and Paul's time of preparation in the Arabian desert unlearning his Pharisaism and learning from the risen Christ, we may infer that preparation and training were required. Indeed Paul instructs Timothy to pass on what he has learned from Paul to faithful men who will then be able to teach others (2 Tim. 2:2). He exhorts Timothy to 'devote yourself to public reading of the Scripture, to preaching and to teaching ...' (1 Tim. 4:13), to be a 'workman ... who correctly handles the word of truth' (2 Tim. 2:15) and to 'preach the Word; be prepared in season and out of season; correct, rebuke and encourage...' (2 Tim. 4:2). This highlights the priority of the study and faithful proclamation of God's Word for those who would be leaders. Paul also uses the figures of the soldier, the athlete and the farmer to illustrate the training, discipline, courage, rigour, commitment and rewards associated with Christian service (2 Tim. 2:3-6). Taking 1 Timothy 4:14 along with 2 Timothy 1:6, we may say that the preparation, training and commissioning of Timothy for the particular work of the gospel for which he was gifted and sent involved not only the apostle, but the body of elders in a particular church.

Prophets and evangelists
During the apostolic period there were prophets in the church who received revelations from God in a similar way to the Old Testament prophets; but once the full revelation of Scripture had been given there was no longer any need for such revelation. What is now needed is faithful interpretation and application of the Scriptures by preaching and teaching. Evangelists were literally those who told good news – the gospel of Jesus – to others. Although the verb *euanngelizō* occurs very often in the New Testament, the noun *euangelistes* is used only three times: in Acts 21:8 to describe Philip; in Ephesians 4:11 in the list of Christ's gifts to the church; and in 2 Timothy 4:5 where Paul instructs Timothy to 'do the work of an evangelist'. While all believers are expected to tell the good news to others, church leaders are responsible for ensuring that this is done, and some will be specially gifted as evangelists.

Servants
In Acts 6 the Twelve dealt with the controversy over the neglect of the Greek-speaking widows in the daily distribution of food by arranging for the appointment of the Seven. Although they are not specifically called deacons, the word group is used by the Twelve when they said

that it was not fitting for them to neglect the Word in order to wait on (*diakonein*) tables (Acts 6:2). It is probable that this is the origin of the office of deacon (see below). However, most uses of this word group are in the general sense of service and they are applied to a wide range of service or ministry: the ministry of the Twelve (Acts 1:25); Paul's apostolic calling and ministry (Acts 20:24; 1 Tim. 1:12; 2 Cor. 4:1); the collection for the poor saints in Jerusalem (2 Cor. 8:4; 9:1, 12-13); and the ministry of the whole church (Eph. 4:12).[31] All Christians are called to be servants, including the leaders of the church.

Paul used the even more emphatic word for servant, *doulos*, for Timothy and himself in Philippians 1:1. Servant was one of Paul's favourite designations for himself and his co-workers: he was a servant of Christ (2 Cor. 11:23), of the gospel (Col. 1:23) and of the church (Col. 1:25). He often refers to co-workers as *sundouloi* (fellow servants). This shows how deeply the teaching and example of Jesus had been learned and applied by the leadership of the New Testament church. The apostles did not consider themselves the apex of a hierarchy but as fellow workers with other believers in the Lord, whom they regarded as brothers and sisters.

Paul also uses another word to denote the service he gave to God in Romans 1:9 and 2 Timothy 1:3. The verb *latreuō* (to serve) refers to 'serving in the context of worshipping'.[32] Paul also uses the related noun in Romans 12:1 when he calls on Christians, in response to the mercies of God, to present their bodies as living sacrifices, their *logikēn latreian* – 'reasonable service' (KJV) or 'spiritual act of worship' (NIV). This shows that the service we give to God is part of our worship and this raises the level of such service beyond the mundane and the ordinary. Indeed the saints in glory will continue to 'serve (*latreuousin*) him day and night' before the throne of God (Rev. 7:15).

A related word, from which we derive our term liturgy, *leitourgeō* (to serve), along with its cognate *leitourgos* (servant), is used in the Septuagint exclusively for the service of priests, but in classical Greek it is used for the public service of a benefactor.[33] Paul uses this term in Romans 13:6 for the officials of Roman government as 'God's servants'. In Philippians 2:25, 30 he uses it for the service Epaphroditus rendered him on behalf of the Philippians. Bennett maintains that in these

---

[31] Bennett, *Biblical Images*, 124.
[32] Ibid., 127.
[33] Ibid., 127.

two instances there is no religious connotation, but it appears to me that in the case of Epaphroditus his service was indeed offered in the name of Christ. Paul uses this word in a specifically religious sense in Romans 15:16, where he speaks of the grace given him by God 'to be a minister (*leitourgon*) of Jesus Christ to the Gentiles'. He goes on to use priestly language to describe his duty of preaching the gospel so that the Gentiles might be presented as an offering acceptable to God. He is not saying that he is a priest in the literal sense, but using the figure of a priest as an illustration of the fruits of his service being offered to God.

Nowhere in the New Testament are the leaders of the church called priests, but in 1 Peter 2:5, 9 all believers are said to constitute a 'holy priesthood' and a 'royal priesthood'. As Tidball says:

> Both collectively and individually, believers are priests called to offer not the animal sacrifices of the old covenant but the spiritual sacrifices of thankful worship (Heb. 13:15), of humble service (Phil. 4:18), of intercessory prayer (1 Tim. 2:1) and of declaring the gospel (1 Pet. 2:9; 3:15).[34]

There is no separate class of priest, but surely the leaders of the church should lead God's people by teaching and example in this as in all aspects of the Christian life.

Deacons

The appointment of the Seven in Acts 6 may well be the beginning of the appointment of servants of the church with a specific responsibility for ministry of mercy. Deacons are mentioned as a specific group along with overseers in Philippians 1:1 and Paul sets forth the qualifications for deacons in 1 Timothy 3:8-13. The requirements for character and theological knowledge are as stringent as those for overseers, but there is no mention of teaching ability. This would support the conclusion that deacons were in charge of the practical administration of the affairs of the local church, especially the ministry of mercy. However, Paul the apostle was involved in organising and transporting the collection for the poor saints in Jerusalem and the elders in Jerusalem received the gift, so this type of service was not confined to deacons.

The mention of women or wives (*gunaikas*) in verse 11 would seem to refer to deacons' wives rather than female deacons, given the

---

[34] Tidball, *Ministry by the Book*, 191.

context, but this is disputed. It could well refer to women who carried out a ministry of mercy, for example as is detailed in 1 Timothy 5:10 with regard to widows. Phoebe, a valued helper of Paul, is called a *diakonos* of the church in Cenchreae (Rom. 16:1-2), but the word could be used there in a general sense rather than indicating an official position in the church. However, given that teaching and ruling is not mentioned as a responsibility of the deacons, the appointment of female deacons or deaconesses would not contravene Paul's prohibition on women teaching or having authority over men in the church (1 Tim. 2:12).

Leadership in the church today

As we have seen, a main stress of the New Testament is that church leaders are servants – of God, of the church and of the gospel. Thus leadership is theological, ecclesial and evangelical. Desire for the glory of God, the welfare of the church and the advance of the gospel must shape the form of leadership in congregations and denominations. Church leaders must be godly in character and conduct and well taught in doctrine; they must have a thorough understanding of the church and a pastor's heart; and they must love the gospel of Christ and long to see others come to know him. Furthermore, leadership is never to be vested in a single individual. Plurality is mandatory, although one person ought to preside or moderate in the group.

Among the many qualities necessary for church leaders I would highlight just a few: the capacity for hard work and the ability to inspire others to join in; humility when God is blessing one's ministry; a willingness to take up new challenges rather than becoming complacent; the capacity to continue to love others even when under criticism rather than becoming embittered; and the ability to persevere under pressure and disappointment.

While there are many terms used in Scripture to describe those who lead and serve in the church and many gifts of the Spirit mentioned in the various lists in the Epistles, the essential ministries may be summarised in the words of Donald Macleod: 'a ministry of tables, a ministry of oversight and a ministry of preaching.'[35] These are not watertight compartments. Those with a diaconal ministry of mercy and administration of the temporal affairs of the church should be

---

[35] Macleod, Donald (2003), *Priorities for the Church*, Fearn: Christian Focus Publications, 56.

well-grounded in the faith and thus effective witnesses; those with the ministry of pastoral oversight and rule should be able to teach; and preachers of the word must be fully involved in the pastoral care and supervision of the life of the church. Indeed full-time ministers of the word should be the main leaders in the leadership team, providing theological input and vision and enabling the other members of the team to contribute their gifts fully.

I believe that presbyterian church government has scriptural warrant and best fits the requirements for such ministries. One of the dangers of any form of church government is to allow traditions and structures so to dominate our exercise of leadership that we fail to respond to new challenges with the flexibility shown in the New Testament and at crucial times in church history. To go to the opposite extreme, however, and attempt to recover an imagined 'simple' New Testament church without structures is also doomed to failure.

According to Donald Macleod, leadership in the church context involves three things: vision, expectations and enabling.[36] The vision must be Bible-based, theologically informed, gospel-centred and applicable to congregations and denominations, with adaptations to individual situations. This will include emphasis on the core activities of the church: worship, ministry of the word, fellowship, service and witness, and fostering unity in Christ across all human barriers, including denominational ones. The vision has to be communicated by preaching, consultation, discussion and example, and fostered by individual and corporate prayer. It will include local, national and international ecumenism and cooperation in the work of the gospel. Strategic planning and efficient organisation will be necessary to implement the strategy and to mobilise all the resources, human and material, that God has provided.

Having expectations means believing in the promises of God, that he will not allow his word to return to him without accomplishing his purpose, that the weeping sower will return bearing a harvest, always conscious that one may plant, another may water, but God alone gives the increase. We should expect and aim for growth both spiritually and numerically. This requires patience, perseverance and mutual encouragement rather than back-biting, criticism and defeatism. It also means having high expectations of people and encouraging them to

[36] Ibid., 21.

fulfil those expectations in holy living, loving service, cheerful giving and vibrant witness.

Enabling the whole church to take part in the work and witness of the church rather than rely on the minister and a few others to do everything is surely a priority for any church leadership. This will involve encouraging all Christians to use their gifts, providing training at the local level and giving opportunity to exercise those gifts.

The situation facing the church in Scotland today is alarming. Less than 10% of the population attend any church regularly. The Protestant church is splintered into many, often competing, denominations. Denominational loyalty has diminished and many Christians shop around for the style of worship and the level of required commitment that suit them. Many Christians are affected by the materialism, self-centredness and relativistic morality of the age and this is reflected by, for example, the increasing incidence of marital breakdown among Christians. Despite the prevailing secularism and an aggressive 'New Atheism' there is a resurgence of interest in various 'spiritualities', such as Eastern religions, paganism and New Age. This interest may provide a point of contact for the gospel.

Shortage of ministers means that many congregations cannot have a settled ministry and some rural areas have no resident minister of any denomination. We face a situation demanding fresh missionary initiatives. Various measures are appropriate: training of gifted 'laypeople' both for preaching and more informal teaching roles and evangelism; electronic relaying of preaching and worship services to scattered small congregations; a more mobile ministry, remembering the Scriptural practice of sending out workers 'two by two'. Team ministry is Scriptural. Those with special evangelistic gifts can complement the ministry of those more gifted in teaching and pastoral work. If there are insufficient people in a situation to help a minister and prevent him burning out by attempting to do everything by himself, help should be provided by the denomination at large. This is especially the case in a church planting or redevelopment situation.

Some ministers are discouraged and are either leaving the ministry or seeking other forms of service. There is a shortage of young men offering themselves for the full time ministry of the word. Is this because they fear the burden of unmet expectations with consequent disillusionment and failure? Much has been written about stress and burn-out in the ministry and this is undoubtedly a problem. Lack of space prevents me dealing adequately with this here, but I have written in more detail elsewhere.[37] Suffice it to say that Christian leaders are engaged in spiritual warfare and cannot expect life to be easy. They do have the promise of God's presence and enabling and should also have the loyal support of God's people.

Can these dry bones live? Yes they can – but only as we faithfully proclaim God's word and pray for the reviving power of the Holy Spirit (Ezek. 37:4, 9). Let us humble ourselves, confess our ineffectiveness and plead with God to raise up godly and effective leadership at every level in the church.

[37] http://freescotcoll.wordpress.com/2009/04/06/resilience-in-the-ministry/

15

Systematic Theology and the Church

Rowland S. Ward

As a sound Biblical theologian Donald Macleod once answered the question 'Is there such a thing as an atheist?' with a resounding 'No' based on Biblical passages such as Romans 1:18-32.[1] God has revealed something of his invisible perfections to every human so that they are clearly seen and understood, hence each individual's religious behaviour, or lack of it, is inexcusable. A further implication of this general revelation everyone has is that in a sense everyone is a theologian, everyone has thoughts about God. The real question is whether our thinking about God is controlled by God's revelation of himself or by ideas from other sources. Given our sin, general revelation is both distorted by us – to false religion and even to the point of professed atheism – and inadequate. God's special revelation in Holy Scripture is therefore absolutely necessary.

Theology is literally the science concerning God. It presupposes the existence of God, and that he has revealed himself so as to be known to the extent of that revelation. The Bible contains theology that is normative, but theology as a discipline of the church is essentially our response to God's self-revelation, and as such it necessarily involves dealing with absolute truth in a systematic way. Our theology to

---

[1] Donald Macleod, *Behold Your God* (Fearn: Christian Focus, 2005), 9-15.

be adequate must be a believing response, but it is always a human response and thus does not possess the inerrant character that belongs to God's words. It is always subject to review and correction in the light of better understanding of what God has said. It is not bare rationalism although it involves the reason. B.B. Warfield well expressed it when he said

> that the truths concerning divine things may be so comprehended that they may unite with a true system of divine truth, they must be: first, revealed in an authoritative word; second, experienced in a holy heart; and third, formulated by a sanctified intellect. Only as these three unite, then, can we have a true theology.[2]

Back in 1623 'the learned doctor', William Ames of Franeker, spoke in similar vein when he wrote, 'Theology is the doctrine or teaching of living to God.' As far as students for the ministry were concerned it was the task of the university to 'call theology away from questions and controversies, obscure, confused, and not very essential, and introduce it to life and practice so that students would begin to think seriously of conscience and its concerns.'[3] The same was the aim of the ministry itself. To fulfil it the ministry had to be godly, the sense of call to a spiritual work of the highest importance deep, and the approach one in which doctrine, method and practice were all appropriately present.

Some history

Systematic theology does not really exist in a recognisable form in the early centuries. Augustine's *Enchiridion* (c. 421) provides a reflection on the Christian Faith under the headings of Faith, Hope and Love. Isidore of Seville (c.560–636) wrote his *Three Books of Sentences* (opinions) drawing particularly from Augustine and Gregory the Great. John of Damascus (676–749) wrote his *Exposition of the Orthodox Faith* in the eighth century. With the extension of universities in Europe, the twelfth century saw the *Sentences* of Peter Lombard. This was written about 1150 as a compilation of propositions from earlier sources, and soon attained normative status, so that any aspiring master wrote a commentary on it. The *Summa* of Thomas Aquinas (1225–74) was

---

[2] John E. Meeter (ed.), *Selected Short Writings of Benjamin B. Warfield – II* (Nutley, New Jersey: Presbyterian and Reformed Publishing Co., 1973) 671.

[3] William Ames, *An Exhortation to the Students of Theology* (trans. Douglas Horton & privately printed 1958) 1.

more elaborate. It survived the condemnations of the thought of Aristotle in 1277, but, except among the Dominicans who continued to study his commentary on Lombard, was usurped by Duns Scotus and his school. Cardinal Cajetan (1469–1534) started the trend of writing commentaries on the *Summa* itself (1507/22).[4] Thomas was made a Doctor of the Church in 1567. The *Summa* subsequently was influential in Roman Catholic thought, experiencing a resurgence in the twentieth century.

However, the Reformers did not seek to overthrow all past Christian thought, but to reform and recast it in those areas they regarded as having moved from Scripture lines. Philip Melanchthon wrote his influential *Loci Communes* (Common Places/Topics) in 1521 drawn chiefly from the Epistle to the Romans: it was the first systematic treatment of the Protestant faith but limited largely to the issues of salvation then disputed.

In the medieval church instruction in the faith had been largely in terms of memorisation of the Creed, the Lord's Prayer and the Ten Commandments. Small manuals of instruction, many in explicit question and answer form, appeared among the Reformers. They often utilised these elements but provided detailed explanation as well. Notable are Luther's *Small Catechism* (1529), Calvin's *Catechism of the Church at Geneva* (1545), and the *Heidelberg Catechism* (1563), all of which used the question and answer format. Larger Confessions of Faith also appeared. The Roman church countered with similar productions, particularly the Jesuit Peter Canisius' *Summa doctrinae* (1556), a catechism which was widely translated and used for the next two hundred years. The *Catechism of the Council of Trent* (1566) was a reference text for use by priests, and that Council also defined the doctrine of the Roman church on disputed matters.

Volumes on common topics were soon superseded by larger more fully developed systematic treatments of the faith. Calvin produced the first edition of his *Institutes of the Christian Religion* in 1536, the title implying instruction or education in Christianity was the aim. It was significant in stabilising the Reformation movement but numerous others works were produced by Reformed scholars over the next 150 years. Andreas Hyperius (1511–64), professor of theology

---

[4] I acknowledge my debt to Martin Foord, Senior Lecturer in Systematic Theology and Church History at Trinity Theological College, Perth, WA for the detail in the previous two sentences.

at Marburg from 1542, made significant contribution to Protestant theological method, as did Franciscus Junius (1545–1602) of Leiden a generation later.[5]

Rationalism and anti-supernaturalism made inroads into Christian thought in the eighteenth century, and accelerated in the nineteenth century aided by scientific advances. This was not because the sciences as such are hostile to Christianity, but because frequently they were wrapped in a naturalistic philosophy that was essentially atheistic.

Systematic theology

If theology is the response we formulate to God's Word, that is, our endeavour to understand what God has revealed and what he requires of us, systematic theology in its broadest meaning could be described simply as the appropriate organising of the truths revealed in God's Word.

This statement could be misconceived if we thought it was merely necessary to collate a few proof texts. If taken in this narrow sense systematic theology might refer simply to mere abstract propositions, and thus tend to intellectualism, a merely cerebral approach that fits the stereotype of Reformed people. But proper attention must be given to 'appropriate' in the phrase 'appropriate organising of the truths revealed in God's Word'. For among other things (1) we need a recognition of the intent of Scripture and what it aims to teach us: this will keep us from literalistic thinking on some matters and/or treating the Bible as a textbook of the sciences; (2) we need to recognise the historical character of God's revelation, its unfolding to the fullness of revelation in the person and work of Christ: this will mean that themes of kingdom and covenant, or perhaps creation – fall – redemption, will be the context in which we develop our interpretations; and (3) we will recognise that all truth is important but some truths are more important than others: this will keep us from the cultic mentality. Each of these areas will be considered in turn with more particular attention to the first, given current misunderstandings.

The Bible and science

Although faults occur on both sides from time to time, the clash between Christianity and science has been greatly exaggerated over the last

---

[5] Richard A, Muller, *Post Reformation Reformed Dogmatics* (Grand Rapids: Baker, 2003) 1:107-108, 113ff.

century, and the conflict thesis of men like J.W. Draper (1874) and A.D. White (1896) has fallen into disfavour.[6] The conflict has been fuelled by two extremes. On the one hand, there are those in the scientific community who insist that some kind of naturalistic philosophy necessarily accompanies the scientific method. To them evolution is not even a possible method of the Divine procedure, but an unsupervised, impersonal, predictable and natural process, originated by chance; in short, evolution is inherently atheistic. This is to move beyond empirical science to an unverifiable religious belief that is all the more pernicious because this atheism is advanced under the guise of an objective, rational science. Andrew Dickson White, Carl Sagan, Richard Dawkins and a host of others over the years are guilty of promoting this fundamentalist religion, often grossly distorting the facts and proving an embarrassment to the large body of scientists who are also believers.

If the naturalistic scientist dispenses with God's special revelation in Scripture and in effect worships the creature rather than the Creator, the conservative Christian does not always give sufficient weight to God's general revelation in creation. It is true that sin has darkened our minds and blighted our understanding so that the natural man does not understand spiritual things, but it does not follow that nature teaches us nothing. Hence we are happy to go to a well-qualified doctor who is not a Christian rather than to an untrained doctor who is. Still, it is also true that only the regenerate person truly appreciates the nature of reality as he/she understands that 'this is my Father's world.'

Consistent Calvinism did not accept the autonomy of human thought (Aristotle) nor a nature-grace dualism (Aquinas). Rather, its aim was to integrate all knowledge for the glory of God. If God has revealed himself in creation *and also* in Scripture then both must be considered for an adequate understanding of reality. There can be no ultimate conflict between theology and the other sciences, and our obligation to heed God's Word, and to glorify him in his world by seeking to understand and apply it, is paramount. If conflict arises, then something is wrong with our approach in one or the other, or both. Apparent conflicts, gaps in our knowledge, mistakes, loose ends – certainly, but ultimately there can be no real conflict. 'Christ is the truth of creation as surely as he is the truth of redemption.'[7]

---

[6] For example see works by Ronald L. Numbers such as *When Science and Christianity Meet* (Chicago: University of Chicago Press, 2003) ed. with David C. Lindberg.

[7] Donald Macleod, *A Faith to Live By* (Fearn: Mentor, 2002), 93.

The text of Scripture needs to be approached with reverence and in dependence on God's Spirit, and with the awareness that no one comes to Scripture without thoughts already in his mind which may distort the true meaning. If good scientists recognise the provisional nature of their work, Biblical theologians know their limitations too, but they cannot help but affirm that God has spoken. God has given an intelligible revelation of himself. While we do not have answers to everything, and not all that is revealed is equally clear, there is much we can affirm dogmatically but also with humility, since we have not attained true knowledge by our cleverness but by God's good grace.

Literal interpretation

It is a commonplace in all ages of the church to speak of taking the Bible literally. This term is a bit confusing to modern ears. If we mean by it that we give Scripture the meaning intended in the context there can be no objection. However, often it is used as if equivalent to the surface meaning of words. An example of this is the expression 'this is my body' used by Jesus at the Last Supper. The intent of the phrase in its context does not allow the surface meaning of the phrase to be the one actually meant.

> Jesus is in their immediate presence physically as he distributes the bread; it would have occurred to none of them that he was, or was going to eventually be, somehow physically present in the bread…. He is providing them a covenantal theology of the atonement, not a sacramental theology of elemental corporeal presence.[8]

A less recognised example is the assertion that Israel in Scripture always refers to ethnic and literal Israel, a position even advocated by some Reformed writers.[9] It is more typical of dispensational thinking

---

[8] J.Ligon Duncan III in J.Ligon Duncan III (ed.), *The Westminster Confession into the 21ˢᵗ Century* Vol. 3 (Fearn: Mentor, 2009), 461.

[9] Stephen Voorwinde's article, 'How Jewish is Israel in the New Testament?' in *Reformed Theological Review*, 67.2 (August 2008), 61-90, is somewhat disappointing. Voorwinde rightly rejects a bald 'replacement' theology in favour of an 'engrafting' theology, but he does not draw out the implications of the teaching of both Old and New Testaments that 'they are not all Israel who are of Israel', that they are true Jews who worship Jesus as Lord (Phil 3:3; Rev 2:9), and that the family of God is one across the testaments. He insists 'Israel' is always used of the nation, but how he can deal consistently with Old Testament prophecies concerning Israel which the New Testament shows as fulfilled in the church is not clear. To my mind Scripture teaches that to the spiritual Israel of Jewish Christian beginnings are engrafted believing Gentiles who together form the expanded Israel of God, the rebuilt tent of David now welcoming the Gentiles (Acts 15:16-17) and having accessions from ethnic Israel too, for God's ancient people are not utterly cut off (Rom. 11).

where the literal principle runs riot, although of course even here it is impossible to carry it out consistently. Thus no dispensationalist thinks the curse on the snake is exhausted in the surface meaning of the words. If Luther spoke of the snake as originally the most beautiful of God's creatures walking with its head erect and losing its reptilian legs at the fall,[10] Calvin avoids such language, and confines himself to seeing the snake's travels in the dust as an illustration of the humiliation to which the evil one, who used the serpent, will come. He has a more sensitive nose for the text's concerns than Luther, who remained in many ways a medieval man.

Early earth history is a particular area of conflict related to literalism since the early 1960s. It was not always so pronounced. In 1667, seven years after the founding of the Royal Society, Thomas Sprat wrote:

> ...the Church of England *will not only be safe amidst the consequences of a* Rational Age, *but amidst all the improvements of* Knowledge, *and the subversion of old Opinions about* Nature, *and introduction of new ways of Reasoning thereon. This will be evident, when we behold the agreement that is between the present design of the Royal Society, and that of our Church in its beginning. They both may lay equal claim to the word* Reformation, *the one having compassed it in* Religion, *the other having purposed it in* Philosophy. *They both have taken a like course to bring this about; each of them passing by the* corrupt Copies, *and referring themselves to the* perfect Originals *for their instruction; the one to the* Scripture, *the other to the large volume of the Creatures.*[11]

In fact life has not been as easy as Sprat might have led people to expect. Quite apart from the problem of the pre-suppositional framework of those involved, which, as we have seen, can be atheistic, there was the practical problem of agreement between Scripture and the observations of nature.

Of course, a measure of accommodation of Scripture language to human capacity was always recognised by the best interpreters from Augustine through Aquinas to Calvin. The Reformation emphasis on Scripture as being for the common person reinforced this belief. Still, in the sixteenth and seventeenth centuries the tendency was to regard the surface meaning of Scripture references to the world of nature as

---

[10] Martin Luther, *The Creation: A Commentary on the First Five Chapters of the Book of Genesis* translated by Henry Cole (Edinburgh: T & T Clark, 1858), 249.

[11] Thomas Sprat, *History of the Royal Society of London for the Improving of Natural Knowledge* (London: J. Martyn, 1667), 370-71.

the intended meaning. In short, observational descriptions of nature in what we would call a pre-scientific context were generally taken as strict descriptions of reality. But what about those points, other than the supernatural, at which Scripture seemed to contradict the book of nature? When a friendly Cardinal Baronius (1538–1607) stated to Galileo that the Bible was intended 'to teach us how to go to heaven, not how the heavens go', he spoke truth. Still, the Church, both Roman and Protestant, took a long time to accept that the earth moved around the sun, perhaps an indication that theology was being considered too much in isolation from other disciplines, and that many thinkers viewed the Bible according to the Aristotelian-Ptolemaic presuppositions. The prejudice that still is raised against Christianity from this reading of Scripture should be a salutary warning against tying Scripture too closely to prevailing assumptions of science.

Flood geology
Certain it is that the church has not always had an easy time in other areas of natural science. Take the Flood. Different opinions on its extent existed from early times among the Jews. However, the mainstream opinion among Christians into the eighteenth century seems to have been that it was geographically universal. The role of fossils in the discussion was not central since not everyone regarded them as the remains of once-living things. Of course, the discovery of the New World raised questions about the Flood's extent. Thomas Burnet (1635–1715) issued a book in 1681 with the modest title, *The Theory of the Earth Containing an Account of the Original of the Earth, and all the General Changes Which it Hath Already Undergone, or Is to Undergo Till the Consummation of All Things*. It propounded a theory of 'flood geology' that stimulated debate and on-site research that ultimately undermined Burnet's speculative theorising.

How then did this conclusion relate to Scripture? Only if the days of Genesis were taken as ordinary days in which creation was accomplished was there any conflict, was the response. The Flood itself may have been total as regards humans. It may have been extensive but local to provide an illustration of sin's ultimate judgment, and of God's salvation through a righteous man, Noah. Even if we do not share all their suggested solutions, Presbyterians of the nineteenth century saw no great problem of adjustment. The Scottish Free Church and the theologians of old Princeton were not advocates of flood geology, anymore than is Donald Macleod, who notes that it is a scientific construct which lacks adequate Biblical support.[12]

Of recent years flood geology is associated with 'scientific creationists' who rightly reject the naturalism held by some scientists but also reject the careful conclusions of many scientific disciplines that attest to the great age of the earth/universe far beyond the six to ten thousand years these creationists allow.[13] Their critique of biological evolution is not so much to weaknesses in the hypothesis, especially as regards humanity, but to the whole notion of the introduction of different creatures over an extended time frame, and to animal death before human sin. Unjustified discredit is brought upon the more general Christian position by these claims, particularly in cases where they are agitated with as much passionate dogmatism as the militant atheists on the other side. It is sometimes hard to get a hearing for the real message of Scripture for, as the Shorter Catechism reminds us, 'the Scriptures principally teach what man is to believe concerning God and what duty God requires of man'.

Bible science?

If in 'scientific creationism' we have a genuine concern to safeguard the dogma of creation but an over-reaction against secularism that makes a doubtful/wrong interpretation part of the dogma, we certainly have a misplaced use of Scripture in arguments to prove the divinity of the Bible from some alleged revealing of a truth before it was discovered by scientific method. Thus the statement of Isaiah 40:22 – 'It is he that sits upon the circle of the earth' – is regularly cited to prove Isaiah was aware of the global nature of the earth before such was generally known. Of course, it does nothing of the kind but is simply an observational way of describing the horizon. Similarly, the ancients thought of the world as like a disc supported by pillars and floating on the sea (Ps. 24:2; cf. Ps. 75:3, Job 9:6). But Scripture is not teaching us physics or geology, and the statements above are perfectly fine so long

---

[12] *A Faith to Live By*, 89-90. The best historical treatment is Davis A. Young, *The Biblical Flood: A Case Study of the Church's Response to Extrabiblical Evidence* (Grand Rapids: Eerdmans, 1995). Apart from Thomas Chalmers himself, Rev Dr John Fleming (1785-1857), who taught natural science at the New College, Edinburgh from 1845, and Hugh Miller (1802-56), the great apologist for the Free Church of Scotland and an able self-taught geologist, are examples of orthodox evangelical Calvinists in Scotland opposing 'flood geology'. For Princeton, see David B. Calhoun, *Princeton Seminary: The Majestic Testimony 1869–1929* (Edinburgh: Banner of Truth, 1996) 10-20, 79ff.

[13] Cf. Donald Macleod, *A Faith to Live By*, 86.

as we do not make them teach the sciences but recognise them as non-scientific, naïve descriptions in the same category as contemporary forms of human speech, such as references to the sun 'rising'.

Interestingly enough, this misguided approach to proving the Scriptures to be of divine origin is paralleled in some Islamic and Hindu writers in regard to their sacred texts.[14] Such arguments are not necessary for the Christian believer since if a text is divine revelation it cannot be disproved, nor should we flirt with rationalism as if external proofs can give us the full persuasion of the truth of Scripture as the Word of God (cf. WCF 1:5).

Our theology needs to be based on careful explanation not only of words in their immediate context, but whole passages in their overall context in the particular book and in the totality of redemptive history (see below). The intent of Scripture needs to be recognised, and the relevance of the other sciences in illuminating the text appreciated. The early part of the Bible is a kind of prologue to the covenant at Sinai in Exodus 19ff. It addresses issues that are relevant to the slaves who had been freed from Egypt twelve or fourteen centuries before Christ came, and not necessarily the issues that preoccupy post-Enlightenment man in the twenty-first century after Christ's coming. If there are things intentionally taught in religious texts that are contrary to right reason, the status of the text as from God has to be questioned, for God is no liar. Christians are quite happy to show that their belief in the plenary inspiration of Scripture is not irrational if only fair interpretative principles are followed.

General revelation sometimes will lead us to reconsider our interpretation of special revelation. Thus, Psalm 96:10 – 'the earth is fixed, it cannot be moved' – was understood, even into the eighteenth century, to teach that the earth did not rotate. The challenge from investigation of the natural world led to a better understanding. The text is actually teaching that the Lord perfectly governs his creation so that it does not know the constant change found in human kingdoms.

Doubtless, the relationship between general and special revelation is not always easy to set, yet the level of possible adjustment is relatively slight

---

[14] Maurice Bucaille, the French physician to the Saudi royal family, wrote *The Bible, the Qur'an and Science* in 1975 along these lines, and it has been widely influential. William F. Campbell, the physician to the Tunisian royal family, wrote a very interesting and thorough response entitled *The Qur'an and the Bible in the light of History & Science* (Middle East Resources, 1992) also available on the web at http://answeringislam.org.uk/Campbell/contents. Note also Nem Kumar Jain, *Science and Scientists in India*, (Delhi: Indian Book Gallery, 1985); cf. Pakistani physicist Perved Hoodbhoy's *Islam and Science* (Zed Books, 1991) for a general critique.

given Scripture is not an encyclopaedia but is given to teach 'what man is to believe concerning God and what duty God requires of man.' Still, the issue is important since we must insist that theology is an objective science. Following Reformed theologian Herman Bavinck (1854–1921), we should recognise the Bible as a book *for* science rather than a book *of* science.[15] Creation reflects God's wisdom, power, order and imagination. We may study it and develop our sciences because creation is coherent, ordered, meaningful. Christian theology offers the possibility of the integration of knowledge, and of understanding the reason for things, and it provides an ethical framework for science. But with Hodge and Warfield we hold that 'although truly established scientific fact may illuminate the meaning of Scripture, science must not determine the content of faith.'[16]

A redemptive-historical approach

If good theology must be based on careful exegesis it is also important to recognise, as noted above, that the Scripture is the progressive unfolding of God's purposes for humanity from creation to new creation. In various ways this has always been recognised in Christian theology; yet the insights of covenant theology at the end of the sixteenth century from within the Reformed camp aided a better argumentation, and the Westminster Standards exhibit some of these traits.[17] Jonathan Edwards' *A History of the Work of Redemption* (preached 1739, published 1774) was another effort. Like the movement of a flower from bud to full bloom, this unfolding in history is organic, each stage having within itself the seed of the next until the fullest disclosure is made in Christ. Geerhardus Vos (1862–1947) is generally recognised as the pioneer practitioner of modern biblical theology in the Reformed tradition.

> The Gospel of Paradise is such a germ in which the Gospel of Paul is potentially present; and the Gospel of Abraham, of Moses, of David, of Isaiah and Jeremiah are all expansions of this original message of salvation, each pointing forward to the next stage of growth, and bringing the Gospel idea one step nearer to its full realisation.[18]

---

[15] H. Bavinck, *Reformed Dogmatics* (Grand Rapids: Baker, 2003), I: 445-446.

[16] David B. Calhoun, *Princeton Seminary: The Majestic Testimony 1869–1929* (Edinburgh: Banner of Truth, 1996), 259.

[17] Robert J. Cara, 'Redemptive Historical Themes in the Westminster Larger Catechism' in J. Ligon Duncan III (ed), *The Westminster Confession into the 21ˢᵗ Century* Vol. 3 (Fearn: Mentor, 2009) 55-76.

[18] Geerhardus Vos, *Redemptive History and Biblical Revelation* (Phillipsburg: P & R, 1980) 11.

This organic unity eliminates the possibility of revelation that is not part of this unfolding history, whether Islam or Mormonism or anything else, and provides an important interpretative principle. While later revelation can elaborate and bring to fulfilment previous revelation, it cannot contradict it.

Moreover, the history of revelation provides the proper structure, the Bible's own structure, to help us ask the right questions and reach the right interpretative conclusions. If someone can't see the timber plantation for the trees, he'll likely get lost or somewhat confused as he seeks to find his way. If one wishes to reach his destination a clear view of the whole landscape is desirable. Thus there is no conflict in the redemptive/historical and systematic approaches properly practised: precision in both should be aimed at and the speculative avoided, the redemptive/historical seen as a handmaid to good systematics. Certainly we must not so emphasise the redemptive/historical that the systematic is neglected. Indeed, so far from 'system' being a pejorative term, it refers to a comprehensive and regularly arranged treatment of some subject. That's hardly something we should be embarrassed about – unless we think there is no unity in Scripture and thus no coherent theology!

By the same token, properly constructed systematic theology assists in exegesis as a guide and test of it. Thus Hebrews 6:4ff. is pointing in the direction of temporary faith and not that the true believer can commit apostasy.[19]

The Church and a form of sound words
The church as 'the pillar and ground of the truth' (1 Tim. 3:15) needs to be very clear on Scripture as God's infallible Word: any departure from this risks at best erecting a good superstructure on a faulty foundation, and at worst an abandonment of Christianity altogether. But it is easy enough to affirm the Bible's verbal inspiration but to neglect its content.

While all Scripture is God-breathed and all it truly intends to teach is true, not all truths are of equal importance and, as a corollary, not all truth is equally clear. Accordingly, Paul writes to remind the Corinthians of the matters 'of first importance'[20] which he had delivered

---

[19] J. I. Packer, *Collected Shorter Writings*, Vol. 3 (Carlisle: Paternoster, 1999), 313, citing Donald Macleod, 'Preaching and Systematic Theology' in Samuel T. Logan (ed.), *The Preacher and Preaching* (Phillipsburg: P & R, 1986), 250.

[20] *en prōtois* (1 Cor 15:3, NIV). A translation such as Moffatt's 'first and foremost' brings out the double meaning of *en prōtois*.

to them in his ministry – Christ's death for our sins according to the Scriptures, his burial, his resurrection the third day according to the Scriptures,[21] and his appearings after his resurrection.

Yet we should not conclude from this that it is sufficient to list a few key doctrines from Scripture as a brief statement of faith to which the church adheres and leaving other areas ignored, a matter of liberty or relegated to insignificance. Of course it may well be appropriate to avoid over-specifying doctrines in a Confession of Faith, but one is not to treat Scripture as if some of it does not matter.

Then again, the plea is sometimes made for 'the Bible only', in line with William Chillingworth's cry: 'The Bible, I say, the Bible only is the religion of Protestants.'[22] This sounds pious but is misleading and false. Every group (Protestant or otherwise) claiming 'the Bible only' has its interpretation of the Bible, and a creed is simply the expression of these beliefs, either verbally or in writing. Christians should not quibble over mere words but they do wish to adhere to the true meaning of Scripture, and words are needed to do so. Hence the necessity and honesty of declaring our understanding of controverted teachings of Scripture in a public confession of faith. As Dutch theologian Herman Bavinck put it: 'For the Holy Scripture was not given to the church by God to be thoughtlessly repeated but to be understood in all its fulness and richness....'[23]

The church is bound to be a confessing church, bound to subscribe a statement of what she believes Scripture teaches. Latitudinarians like William Chillingworth in the seventeenth century, and radical liberals like Bishop Spong in the twenty-first century, attack orthodox theology since they do not want to be bound to orthodoxy. Others are influenced by a biblicist approach, perhaps contributed to by a misuse of creeds as the instrument of a narrow sectarianism. In their rejection of theological statements in favour of 'the Bible only', they seem oblivious to the fact that their distinctive interpretation is a creed and functions as such, as one will soon find if one advances a different viewpoint!

---

[21] On this phrase note Michael Russell, 'On the Third Day, According to the Scriptures' in *The Reformed Theological Review* 67.1 (April 2008) 1-17. He argues that the OT pattern in references to 'third day' and 'three days' indicates it carries the meanings of sufficient time for certainty (ie Jesus was certainly dead) and a climatic reversal from death to life.

[22] William Chillingworth (1602-44), Anglican latitudinarian scholar, was the popularizer of the phrase in his *The Religion of Protestants a Sure Way to Salvation* (London: n.p., 1638) pt. i, ch. vi., sec. 56.

[23] H. Bavinck, *Our Reasonable Faith* (Grand Rapids: Eerdmans, 1956) 157.

For the church a statement of faith such as the Westminster Confession is a virtual necessity for the maintenance of a full-orbed Biblical testimony. Still, the danger of elevating such a Confession to a sacrosanct position, as if beyond improvement, must be recognised. The Westminster Confession is not the rule of faith but a help to faith (cf. WCF 31.4). Greater insight into the formulation of Scripture's teaching must not be precluded. The Westminster Confession's Catholic (Trinitarian), Protestant and Calvinistic character is not subject to change for Scripture is clear on these issues, but the possibility of rearrangement/restatement to better reflect the balance of Scripture, address contemporary errors and maintain current language must be kept in view.[24]

A Confession of Faith should make sure that Scripture is the primary standard and rule of faith. A public Confession reflects the fact that it is within the community of faith that we learn and confess together as Christians, and thus provides a check against individualistic interpretation as well as a helpful means of instruction. It provides a bond of fellowship and co-operation for the office-bearers of the church to whom is committed the care of Christ's flock.

Systematic theology and the preacher

In our current circumstances we cannot assume even a basic knowledge of the contents of the Scripture. This serves to emphasise even more the importance of a ministry that addresses this. The *lectio continua* method (going through book after book) is recommended in the Directory for Public Worship of the Westminster Assembly (1644):

All the canonical books of the Old and New Testament (but none of those which are commonly called Apocrypha) shall be publicly read in the common language, out of the best allowed translation, distinctly, that all may hear and understand.

How large a portion shall be read at once, is left to the wisdom of the minister. It is appropriate that ordinarily one chapter of each Testament is read at every meeting, and sometimes more, where the chapters are short or the coherence of matter [the content] requires it.

It is necessary that all the canonical books be read over in order, so that the people may be better acquainted with the whole body of

---

[24] For a survey of the relationship of Scripture's primacy to creeds and creedal subscription to them see Rowland S. Ward, 'Subscription to the Confession' in J. Ligon Duncan, *The Westminster Confession into the 21st Century* Vol. 3 (Fearn: Mentor, 2009) 77-138.

the scriptures. Normally, where the reading in either Testament ends on one Lord's Day, it is to begin the next. We commend also the more frequent reading of such scriptures as he that reads shall think best for edification of his hearers, such as the Book of Psalms and such like.[25]

The preacher will do well to apply this principle in a manner appropriate to his situation, particularly if his congregation is biblically illiterate. Continuous reading of a section or chapter at a time week by week, perhaps with a very brief introduction to orientate the hearers, exposes them to the content of Scripture, the norm and source of the church's teaching.

As regards preaching itself, the *lectio continua* or expository method in preaching through successive books has been a mark of the Reformed church in her best years. It forces preachers to deal with the whole range of biblical material, avoid hobby-horses or one-sidedness, and helps gives each subject its relative importance. The danger can be to model oneself on a man like Dr Martyn Lloyd Jones, or some of the Puritan preachers, who spent an inordinate amount of time on one verse or section. Joseph Caryl (1602–73), the eminent Puritan, preached an average of ten sermons on each chapter of the Book of Job. They are full of insight, nevertheless the hearers deserved greater exposure to the range of Biblical material. On the other hand, C. H. Spurgeon (1834–92), the great Baptist preacher, was in general not an expositor but moved from one place to another like a butterfly. He always derived the gospel from the chosen passage yet one fears that he did not give enough attention to the overall structure of Scripture. But unique men are not the model to follow. The great thing is to be yourself, and to have regard to the specific needs of your hearers.

The sermon needs to be more than a running comment on the passage. It needs to explain the passage in its immediate and larger context, but it also needs to gather specific doctrines evident from the passage and apply them to the mind, heart and conscience of the hearers. Expository and topical preaching with application should be aimed at, always recognising that the work is rendered effective only through the Holy Spirit. Modern preachers are not always good at application, nevertheless it is essential. A good grasp of systematic

---

[25] Text in Richard A. Muller & Rowland S. Ward, *Scripture and Worship* (Phillipsburg: P & R, 2007) 146.

theology will assist here because it provides the substructure and framework in which to explain and apply the Scriptures correctly.

The use of the catechism should be encouraged. A brief explanation of the Shorter Catechism and its repetition by the whole congregation may be appropriate instead of the usual children's talk which can easily degenerate into moralistic stories. The Larger Catechism with its thorough section on Christian conduct will also be found valuable in a study class as a help to systematic coverage of Christian doctrine and practice, and the Confession likewise, especially for office-bearers. The Heidelberg Catechism had been arranged into 52 sections in 1566, so that one section could be taken at the second Lord's Day service throughout a year. This 'catechism preaching' was mandated by the Synod of The Hague in 1586.[26] The general British opinion appears to have been that a text of Scripture should always be the basis of preaching on the Lord's Day. This accepted, it is still possible in pulpit ministry to cover the main topics of Christian theology using the Catechism as a help rather than as the text itself, and doubtless many on the continent do just this.

It remains that we evangelise by teaching (Matt. 28:19-20), and superficial ministry with little doctrinal content is not what is wanted. It is striking to note that some of the most profoundly theological passages of Scripture arise out of practical issues and are regarded as vital to their solution – Philippians 2 for example.[27] Preaching must be rooted in balanced biblical theology, right practice springing from right doctrine. It is a mistake to treat your hearers as simpletons or to trivialise theology. And it is a mistake for a minister to neglect constant reading of good theology, and subscription to two or three helpful theological journals helps alert him to current issues and recent literature. The minister needs to grow if he is to remain fresh. A minister must indeed strive to speak with clarity using contemporary illustrations where appropriate, and must not feel it is obligatory for a truly Reformed minister to preach for 45 minutes. One must seek to know one's hearers and break the bread of life as they are able to hear it. Good preaching is logic and truth on fire with relevant application, all in dependence on the Spirit.

---

[26] Daniel R. Hyde, 'The Principle and Practice of Preaching in the Heidelberg Catechism' in *Puritan Reformed Journal* 1 (2009), 115.

[27] Note Donald Macleod's fine exposition of this passage in his *The Person of Christ* (Downers Grove: Intervarsity Press), 212-20.

Systematic theology and the pew

There are good books on preparing and delivering sermons but not so many on listening to them. Hearers can place too much confidence in their minister but also too little. His authority as a servant of God and the mouthpiece of God's Word needs to be kept in mind lest our attitude be one which slights God's provision. Perhaps the sage comment of the Larger Catechism 160 escapes us: *What is required of those who hear the word preached?*[28]

'It is required of those who hear the word preached that they attend on it with diligence,[1] preparation[2] and prayer;[3] examine by the Scriptures what they hear;[4] receive the truth with faith,[5] love,[6] meekness[7] and readiness of mind[8] as the word of God;[9] meditate on[10] and discuss it;[11] hide it in their hearts,[12] and bring forth its fruit in their lives[13] ([1]Prov. 8:34. [2]1 Peter 2:1-2, Luke 8:18. [3]Ps. 119:18, Eph. 6:18-19. [4]Acts 17:11. [5]Heb. 4:2. [6]2 Thess. 2:10. [7]James 1:21. [8]Acts 17:11. [9]1 Thess. 2:13. [10]Luke 9:44, Heb. 2:1. [11]Luke 24:14, Deut. 6:6-7. [12]Prov. 2:1, Ps. 119:11. [13]Luke 8:15, James 1:25).'

It can help to focus concentration to take notes, even if these notes are not referred to again. Taking notes can also encourage the preacher and stimulate his presentation of the material in logical form.

Sometimes we hear that congregations do not want serious preaching and reverent worship. In some cases the blame may lie on boring preaching and mere formality, but it may well be due to the itching ears syndrome, and the desire to have man-centred therapeutic preaching of one kind or another. Part of the answer lies with thoughtful but passionate preaching by those who have themselves felt the truth of what they preach and have seen something of the glory of Christ. And another part lies in prayer for the blessing of God to be upon the preacher in his preparation and presentation.

Conclusion

In this essay I have not addressed the approach of those who operate in a Kantian framework which views Scripture as an interpretation of a particular experience and the task of theology to reinterpret that experience to the present. Rather, accepting the Scriptures as the inspired Word of God and revealing the truths of God, I have stressed that our attitude must be one by which we listen to God's

---

[28] R.S. Ward (ed.), *The Westminster Confession & Catechisms in Modern English* (Wantirna: New Melbourne Press, 1996, [4]2007) 109.

Word and seek the Holy Spirit's illumination of it to our hearts and minds.

Recognising the Bible is not an encyclopaedia or textbook for the natural sciences, we are to appreciate its organic unity and build our theology from careful exegesis in the immediate context and in the context of Scripture as a whole. Preaching needs to be more than running commentary: a pointed application of the great truths established by exegesis is required. Theology in which we are much in the main things, is certainly a great current need, and signs of an increased interest in the great confessional history of the church are encouraging. But the right balance must always be maintained. Describing Donald Macleod's little book on Christology – *From Glory to Golgotha* – John Nicholls of London City Mission wrote: 'This is the very heart of Christianity. Here is a "generous orthodoxy", lucidly expounded, honestly defended, and passionately enforced.' These are characteristics every preacher should aim at, and every occupant of the pew pray might be in the minister.

Appreciations

From Changwon Shu, minister of Samyang Presbyterian Church in Korea

It was in 1985 that I became one of the first three Korean students in the Free Church of Scotland College in Edinburgh. For me Scotland was a completely unknown nation apart from John Knox, the Reformer. The time was not that of the Internet but of the typewriter. I did not have much information of the College, though I did have her prospectus.

Before I got permission to study there, I had an interview with several of the College professors, as all the other new students had to do as well. To me it was exciting to meet good teachers but I was fearful because of the language barrier. I do not remember what I was asked to answer, but I remember one question I asked them after they had completed questioning me. It was: 'How many foreign students do you have?' In response Prof. Macleod said, 'Well' (in his unique form of pronouncement), 'we have a few; one from Ireland, one from England, one from Germany, and so on.'

I was very surprised to hear other UK citizens described as foreigners! That was the Scottish spirit I found after I studied the history of Scotland. Then he added, 'My English is my second language, my native language is Gaelic.' I thought, 'This is how you want to encourage me to learn the English language.' But it was news for me to know that there is another Scottish language. Later I discovered that singing psalms in the Gaelic language is so beautiful, very like Korean traditional tunes.

During the three years of courses I was so much blessed in learning the essential teachings of the Reformed Theology of the Presbyterian Church. In the Systematic Theology Classroom Prof. Macleod emphasised the importance of such theology by saying, 'Unless the theology is being preached in the pulpit it is no longer theology at all.'

This emphasis made a big impact on my ministry. Until then I thought theology was only for professors in Seminaries. But his teaching changed my opinion and I began to study theology as much as possible. Now the pastoral activities of my ministry are based on sound doctrines. I truly thank Prof. Macleod for that. Though I often disturbed his lectures as I had to record them (I have the tapes still – ninety of them), he never complained. I listened each day to my recording, sometimes until 2.00 AM in order to write it all in my note book. The note book was used in exam preparation, not only by Korean students but also by some of the Scottish students.

After I heard Prof. Macleod's preaching on the loveliness of Christ, I always tried to be faithful in my preaching, both to the doctrines and the Bible. He preached for seventy minutes with a little memo, but his sermon was logically well constituted and spiritually on fire. It was the first time I was moved to tears in an English sermon. Since I returned to Korea in 1990 one of the things I have missed most is his preaching. Because of that I always wanted to invite him to Korea but so far without success..

Now as I hear of his resignation from the College, I truly give thanks to God for him. And it is my prayer that the Lord may say to him at last, 'Well done, my dear faithful servant, enter into the joy of your Master!' Dear Prof. Macleod, I really thank you with all my heart for what you have done in the College. My memory of you will go with me to the end. Many thanks for your faithful labouring. Once again I say, please come to Korea and enjoy the natural creation before your eternal enjoyment in seeing the far better creation in the Lord Jesus Christ!

From Mary Ferguson

There is an idea abroad that theology is only for 'clever' people (and certainly not for women). It's probably part of the anti-intellectualism and general dumbing-down of modern evangelicalism. Donald Macleod taught me that I am as much a theologian as he is. I may know only a fraction of what he knows; nevertheless we are on the same journey of knowing God and knowing ourselves. As Rabbi Duncan put it, 'The direction we are taking is of greater consequence than the point we have reached; for our journey is an endless one.'

Donald often quotes Isaac Newton's assessment of himself and his achievements: that he was like a small boy 'playing on the seashore … whilst the great ocean of truth lay all undiscovered before me.' It is the testimony of great scientists and great theologians: the more they learn, the more there is to know. So they spend their lives learning not only for the sake of becoming more knowledgeable but driven by the desire to impart to others what they have discovered in the study of God's truth. My dictionary defines an idealist as 'a person who cherishes or pursues high or noble principles, purposes and goals; a person who represents things as they might or should be rather than as they are.' It aptly describes Donald. He longs for the Church to be holy like her Lord; while recognising the impossibility of it in this world. Nevertheless, convinced that only the Truth can set us free, he keeps on speaking and keeps on writing, believing that God will bless his word, if not now, to another generation.

And Donald does it with clarity and winsomeness and conviction. Every thought is carefully worded, every sentence and paragraph beautifully crafted. The result is – whether in sermon or lecture or writings – the hearer or reader is enlightened, informed and challenged. (He is not good at speeches though; probably too frivolous an activity!) His book *A Faith to Live By* is a gem of succinct biblical teaching which should be presented to every new communicant; or at least commended to them. He is especially illuminating on Christology and it is a particular joy to be led by him into the mysteries of the Person and work of the Saviour.

In the dark days of the 1990s some of us formed a group with the slightly pretentious name of the *Lewis Evangelical Lecture Fellowship*. Donald's voice was not being heard much in those days and we wanted to give him (and others) a platform. The teaching had a stabilising effect on many in the Christian community and helped to focus minds on the things that are from above. In a natural progression from there, in 2000 the Free Church College, in an attempt to give the Church access to in-depth theological teaching, began offering a part-time course in theology and biblical studies. Now in its eleventh year it has proved a rewarding and fruitful venture and the credit for its continued usefulness is in large measure due to Donald's organisation and commitment. It would be good to think it could be continued beyond his retirement; but if not, the internet can be a wonderful pulpit. Falkirk Free Church, where Donald has delivered *Lectures in the faith* every winter since 1992, have done a brilliant job of making them available online. He is far too self-effacing to promote himself; in a day when self-publicity is the norm, it would not occur to him to even have a blog.

Being a librarian, I am quite a useful person to know and I've been glad to be able to help the Honorary Librarian of the Free Church College with various projects over the years. He's very good at most things himself (although Gaelic grammar is not one of his strong points); but it has been a privilege to relieve a little of the burden occasionally. And he carries many burdens, not least the running of the College and the care of its occupants. I hope and pray that retirement will mean fruitful labour for him and many more years of spiritual vitality.

Finally, I cannot but mention his weekly column in the *West Highland Free Press*. It must be unique in modern Britain for a Calvinist theologian to be given free rein in a secular newspaper; and it is to the paper's great credit that they recognise the value of his particular worldview even though it often contradicts their own. His articles are worth organising into a durable format; they may yet prove to be one of the most influential aspects of his life's work.

From David George

I had recently come to faith when I first heard Professor Macleod preach, and had started on a journey which would eventually bring me to the pastorate of the church[1] where I sat that day utterly overwhelmed and astonished by the experience.

---

[1] Mount Pleasant Baptist Church, Maesycwmmer. It would have been infinitely more fitting had this tribute been written by my esteemed predecessor, Rev Malcolm S. Jones, a long-standing friend of Professor Macleod. At the time of writing, ill-health prevented this. Malcolm Jones passed away in June 2010.

The description 'shock and awe' is now familiarly used to describe the military doctrine of rapid dominance through the use of overwhelming power; and something akin to this happened on that occasion. There was a rapid dominance of hearts and minds by the overwhelming power of the Spirit at work in and through the word.

The text was, *Christ hath redeemed us from the curse of the law, being made a curse for us* (Gal. 3:13) and the sermon concerned the sheer depth and awesomeness of Christ's sufferings. The mysterious paradox of the cross – its glory and its curse – were introduced to us; and speaking in terms that utterly captivated the congregation Professor Macleod developed the theme by drawing our attention to Christ's sufferings in terms of his physical pain, his emotional pain, his social pain and his spiritual pain – before our very eyes Jesus Christ was clearly portrayed as crucified.

In quite shocking terms he let various texts speak their own truth, until finally we were brought to the reason for his being made a curse: it was *for us*. Christ falls under the anathema because he is my Substitute. And the glorious consequences of that were detailed: no condemnation; a cleansed conscience; redemption from the law; liberty in Christ; and the promise of the Spirit.

Such a bald description of a sermon cannot begin to convey its power. Nothing motivates and moves the believer more than the preaching of the cross and a proper appreciation of its significance. It is the animating principle of the Christian gospel; its soul and life-blood. Here was the most tangible example of the truth that *Christian experience is the influence of doctrinal truth upon the affections.*[2] The entire sermon was unashamedly theological, and yet dealt with profundities in such a manner that appealed to the simplest soul. Minds were gripped, hearts deeply moved, and wills energized by truth so vivid and powerful that no one was left in any doubt.

Dr. Lloyd Jones once said that preaching 'addresses us in such a manner as to bring us under judgment; and it deals with us in such a way that we feel our whole life is involved, and we go out saying, "I can never go back and live just as I did before. This has done something to me; it has made a difference to me. I am a different person as the result of listening to this."'[3]

I can say that I am a different person as a result of what I heard that day. We know that, because of the weakness of the flesh, so striking an

---

[2]Charles Bridges, *The Christian Ministry*, Edinburgh, Banner of Truth, 1961, p.259.
[3]D. Martyn Lloyd-Jones, *Preaching and Preachers*, Grand Rapids, Zondervan, 1972, p.56.

apprehension of Christ crucified cannot be constantly maintained, yet it is true that the impression made upon me that day has never been entirely extinguished. Both during and following the preaching I was compelled to worship so wonderful a Saviour and Lord.

I left the chapel that day thinking that if ever I should preach, I want to preach like that; in a manner full of power and pathos. If only it were so!

From Donna Macleod

Donald Macleod and I shared the same class in the Nicolson Institute from 1953 to 1956. Prior to commencing fourth year I moved sideways but Donald moved onwards and upwards and through the years to higher and greater things.

If my memory serves me well, my next recollection of seeing him was at the induction of the Rev Donald Macdonald in Carloway around 1962/63; and it was much later, possibly in the very early 70s, before I became aware of him as an outstanding preacher when visiting Lewis at communion times.

I vividly remember a Monday morning service in the Crossbost church during the time of the late Rev. Donald Gillies when Donald preached from the Book of the Revelation – passages from chapters 4 and 5. He had no particular text but spoke on the Throne in Heaven and the One who sat on it, the rainbow surrounding it and what looked like a sea of glass before the Throne, and the scroll in the hand of the One who sat on it. The memory of that day still lingers on in my memory; as I leaned forward with my hands on the back of the seat in front I could truly say in the words of the unknown poet, 'I leaned my arms awhile upon the windowsill of Heaven and gazed upon my God, I then went with that vision in my heart and turned strong to meet the day.'

This was not to be an isolated instance because, throughout the years until the present, Donald's preaching has been of immense blessing to my soul when I have been fed, strengthened, encouraged, uplifted and comforted under his preaching. In the words of Paul to Timothy regarding Onesiphorous, 'for he often refreshed me.'

If I ever had any criticism to make it would be on occasions when he warmed to his particular theme I felt like shouting, 'Please say that again and say it slowly this time,' but then he seldom did! This problem was solved for me when his books came on stream – especially *A Faith to Live By* and *Behold your God*. I could then linger, read and absorb these great themes he so obviously loved to preach on and move from mere understanding to actually experiencing and enjoying God in the exposition of his Word. As the sub-title of *Behold Your God* says in quoting Stephen Charnock – 'It is impossible to honour God as we ought, unless we know Him as He is.'

I well remember listening to Donald as he preached and expounded on the theme of God's divine love and his frequent use of the word 'extravagant' which at that time was a word I had not been used to hearing regarding God's love. This again is beautifully expanded and highlighted in the last paragraph of the chapter called 'Love Divine, All Loves Excelling' in *Behold Your God*. The greatest compliment I could pay Donald is to quote from it: 'Electing, redemptive love is utterly realistic. God knows those he loves. Indeed, in many passages of Scripture to know is virtually synonymous with to love. God's love is totally perceptive; it is also extravagant, bestowing its blessings with infinite largesse. He gives every spiritual blessing (Ephesians 1:3); he ordains that all things are ours. He works all things together for our good and he bestows his Spirit without measure. As the incident of the anointing at Bethany shows, it is of the very essence of love to be careless of cost. Mary's affection can find expression only in a deed which, to the onlooker, is utterly wasteful. God's giving his Son for the world is surely in the same category. The elder brother is introduced into the parable of the Prodigal precisely to highlight the fact that love goes beyond the bounds of reason when it makes so splendid a provision for such a wastrel. God's love will not rest until it has placed his people in the very glory which Christ had with the Father before the world was.'

As Donald approaches this special milestone I pray that the Lord will continue to uphold him and give him the necessary health and strength to enable him to continue with his own brand of expositional preaching from the Word of God. Over many years, this has been so blessed and so edifying to God's people. We look forward to more of his writings so that the Church of Christ will continue to be fed and encouraged in the life of faith.

From David Meredith

I remember in some detail the very first conversation I had with Donald Macleod. I was eighteen years of age and had started as an undergraduate at the University of Strathclyde in Glasgow. It was during our first week of lectures and we had discussed the contrasting features of a matriarchal society as opposed to a patriarchal. I was telling Donald about this and he immediately extended the discussion and gave me a few more ideas to think about. This pattern of encouraging and teaching me to think was to be a feature of my relationship with Donald over the next few years.

My previous exposure to Macleod had been through the tape ministry of Partick Highland Free Church. My teenage years must have appeared somewhat bizarre as I awaited the latest tape sent from an address in Cardross with the same excitement that my friends had when they bought their *New Musical Express* or *Melody Maker*. I cannot forget dashing to my bedroom to listen to these strange nasal tones articulating in such a fresh way my new found faith in Christ. The fact that he was viewed with suspicion for his writings and preaching simply added to my admiration and appreciation. It was said that his views on 'the old man and the new man' were suspect; I thought that they were just clearly part of the Bible. They said that he said God suffered and that was wrong. I thought it was wrong to speak of a God who didn't suffer or who couldn't feel.

It has been my privilege to experience Donald Macleod at two crucial periods of my life. As a student I attended Partick Highland with so many other young people. It is hard to describe the sense of God which fell on the services during these days. Donald was always at his best when speaking explicitly about the person and work of Christ. During so many of these sermons there was a palpable sense of the presence of God. I can honestly say that I have very rarely experienced such power since which may have more to say about me than about that particular time. It was preaching which broke so many of the rules: it was long, delivered with a strong and unusual provincial accent, the body language can only be described as being contorted and it was not always consecutive exposition. Yet it was always fresh and relevant to my world, and such preaching I had never experienced before. I remember many of the sermons to this day. I received my call to the ministry during a sermon on 2

Timothy 1:6, 7: 'fan into flame the gift of God which is in you ....'
He preached a sermon on alcoholism which was the first sermon I
had ever heard explicitly on that subject. At that time in my life I was
interacting with the great names like Dostoevsky, Camus and Sartre;
my mind was full of questions but they were being consistently
answered at Partick Highland.

I had been baptized and raised within the Free Church and so I
was never a self-conscious Calvinist, it's just what we were, we never
thought about it. There was never a time when I asked Calvin into my
heart. I think that one of the greatest debts I owe to Donald is that
he made me love and understand the whole Reformed tradition. He
showed me that great theology did not just belong at conferences to
be discussed by the good and the great but it had to be applied in our
broken communities. There were a number of us who attended Partick
Highland who are now in ministry all over the world and who were
moulded during these formative years.

On graduation I enrolled in the Free Church College where
happily Donald Macleod had just been installed as Professor of
Systematic Theology. There is no doubt in my mind that he is one
of the greatest theologians of our generation. The course was very
much in the Scottish tradition of being an ongoing commentary on
the Westminster Confession of Faith. In those days the College was
very much old school, the Professors wore gowns, each desk had its
own ink well and until we came there was still a strict dress code. In
the systematic class we did not merely learn, we worshipped. The same
sense of the presence of God was there and Donald excited us about
the work of the ministry. He walked us through the greats of the past
and recommended some of the sages of the present.

There are various specific features of the College which I especially
appreciated. Donald spoke to us about the need to aim at high
standards and to make your people long for Sundays – he would
say 'make it a high day for your people.' He taught us to think and
challenged our ideas constantly, not to destroy us or even to demean
us but to make us stronger. Although he was a charismatic figure and
had many admirers and even perhaps some imitators he never sought
to develop a grouping within the church or develop a personality cult.
He has always been a great Free Churchman, even if that has meant
spending a lifetime challenging and critiquing its rather quant ways
– he seemed to believe that a good church was always strong enough

to be challenged. He was a man who took risks with his students, the greatest being that he taught them the methodology to disagree with him!

I thank God for my contact with Donald Macleod and I join with many others at home and abroad and I'm sure in the church militant and triumphant who were given a more focused view of the glory of our Saviour through Donald's preaching and teaching.

A Faith to Live By

Understanding Christian Doctrine

Donald Macleod

This is a comprehensive examination of Christian doctrine, practically explained – The Inspiration of Scripture, the Trinity, sin, the Incarnation, the Atonement, Justification, Christian Liberty, Baptism, the Church, the Lord's Supper, the Second Coming, the Resurrection, Hell and Heaven. It equips the reader to present their faith intelligently to others.

" . . . a master of making difficult things seem simple, without compromising their profundity . . . Macleod is simultaneously an able apologist and a world class exegete . . . Learn from Macleod. Argue with Macleod. And then bow the knee to your Saviour, the Lord Jesus Christ, and worship."

Ligon Duncan
Senior Minister, First Presbyterian Church, Jackson, Mississippi

"A person who does not have a formal Bible or theological education can read and enjoy Macleod."

Eric Redmond
Senior Pastor of Reformation Alive Baptist Church, a 2009 church plant in the suburbs of Washington, DC

"Here is excellent theology made both relevant and exciting. I can think of no better book for equipping Christians to present their faith intelligently and attractively to real people.

John Nicholls
Chief Executive, London City Mission

ISBN 9781845505851

The Reformed Faith

An Exposition of the Westminster Confession of Faith

Robert Shaw

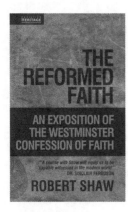

The Westminster Confession is the most accurate and comprhrehensive creed so far produced by the church. Many of its statements are short explanations of a profound doctrine that needs to be unpacked. The classic explanation of the confession provides a thorough theological grounding.

This book is completely re-typeset for this 5th reprint by Christian Focus Publications.

"If personal testimony is any encouragement, perhaps I may be allowed to place my own on record. I recall, with great gratitude,a period in my later teens when I first became acquainted with the Westminster Confession, and began to study it with the aid of a commentary. Looking back, I think of that as one of the most valuable investments of time and thought I ever made. It took me a stage further in understanding the greatness of God, the glory of Christ, the ministry of the Spirit, the nature of the Christian life, the church and the world to come. I sometimes compare that time of study to the activity of a squirrel gathering nuts which will see him through the winter! So it has proved to be. Let Robert Shaw be your guide, reading him with careful and prayerful thought, discernment and appreciation, and you will know what I mean."

Sinclair B. Ferguson
Senior Minister, First Presbyterian Church, Columbia, South Carolina

ISBN 9781845502539

Christian Focus Publications
publishes books for all ages

Our mission statement –
STAYING FAITHFUL
In dependence upon God we seek to impact the world through literature faithful to His infallible Word, the Bible. Our aim is to ensure that the Lord Jesus Christ is presented as the only hope to obtain forgiveness of sin, live a useful life and look forward to heaven with Him.

REACHING OUT
Christ's last command requires us to reach out to our world with His gospel. We seek to help fulfil that by publishing books that point people towards Jesus and help them develop a Christ-like maturity. We aim to equip all levels of readers for life, work, ministry and mission.

Books in our adult range are published in three imprints.

Christian Focus contains popular works including biographies, commentaries, basic doctrine and Christian living. Our children's books are also published in this imprint.

Mentor focuses on books written at a level suitable for Bible College and seminary students, pastors, and other serious readers. The imprint includes commentaries, doctrinal studies, examination of current issues and church history.

Christian Heritage contains classic writings from the past.

Christian Focus Publications, Ltd
Geanies House, Fearn, Ross-shire
IV20 1TW, Scotland, United Kingdom
www.christianfocus.com